An Illustrated Guide to

Minton Printed Pottery 1796–1836

Geoffrey H Priestman

Endcliffe Press, 2001

An Illustrated Guide to Minton Printed Pottery 1796–1836
by Geoffrey H. Priestman

First published in Great Britain in 2001 by Endcliffe Press

Copyright © Geoffrey H. Priestman 2001

The right of Geoffrey H. Priestman to be identified as the author of this work has been asserted by him in accordance with the Copyright, Designs and Patents Act 1988.

All rights reserved. No part of this publication may be reproduced, stored in a retrieval system, or transmitted in any form or by any means, electronic, mechanical, photocopying, recording or otherwise, without the prior permission of both the copyright owner and the above publisher of this book.

Copyright for all material reproduced from the Minton archives is held by Royal Doulton Ltd and may not be reproduced, stored in a retrieval system or transmitted in any form without the prior permission of that company.

A CIP catalogue record for this book is available from the British Library.

ISBN 0-9541234-0-9

Typeset by BBR Solutions Ltd, Chesterfield
Printed in the UK by SRP Ltd, Exeter.

Endcliffe Press
PO Box 2001
Sheffield
S11 8ZN

www.endcliffepress.com

Contents

v	Foreword *by Joan Jones, Royal Doulton Museums Curator*
vi	Author's Preface
viii	Acknowledgements
1	*Chapter One* Thomas Minton: Engraver, Manufacturer and Gentleman
11	*Chapter Two* Early Minton Earthenwares: The Archive Evidence
25	*Chapter Three* Pattern Reference Guide
49	*Chapter Four* Catalogue of Patterns 1. Early Landscapes
87	*Chapter Five* Catalogue of Patterns 2. Early Floral Designs
111	*Chapter Six* Catalogue of Patterns 3. Early European Influence
153	*Chapter Seven* Catalogue of Patterns 4. The Semi-China Period
195	*Chapter Eight* Catalogue of Patterns 5. Opaque China, Stone China and Improved Stone China
249	Colour Plates
257	*Chapter Nine* Catalogue of Printed Wares
331	*Chapter Ten* Early Minton Factory Marks
337	*Chapter Eleven* Black Printed Wares and Bat Prints
357	*Appendix* Dinnerware Designs from an early Minton Factory Shape Book
367	General Index
371	Index to Patterns

Dedicated to:

*Moira,
Michael and Helen*

Foreword

From the foundation of the Minton factory in 1793 the Minton name has, over 200 years, become synonymous with high quality and innovative design. Minton's extensive output included bone china and earthenware tablewares, tiles, Parian statuary, pâté-sur-pâté ornamental wares and Majolica glazed tours de force, such as life-sized animals, figures and a forty foot high fountain! Minton examples of these wares were normally well marked and many records have been preserved in the Minton Archives. The more humble blue printed Minton earthenwares, however, have remained largely anonymous, despite their undoubted importance in underpinning success and prosperity at the factory. Indeed, the factory was established by Thomas Minton with the specific aim of exploiting his expertise as an engraver and the ready market for blue printed pottery at the end of the eighteenth century. This book is therefore long overdue as it represents the first serious attempt to research and identify these early printed wares, specifically those produced by Thomas Minton from the origin of the factory to his death in 1836.

The output of blue printed pottery from Staffordshire during the early decades of the nineteenth century was enormous, with most factories competing with the same basic shapes and patterns. Thus the products of an individual manufacturer are only easily identifiable if regular and clear factory marks were employed. Such was the case with Thomas Minton's near neighbour Josiah Spode II, whose use of unambiguous impressed and printed marks have enabled the fine quality early Spode blue and white wares to be collected for over a century and catalogued in several specialist books. Minton, however, used no factory name mark during this period. Thus the identity of these early Minton products, described by Simeon Shaw in 1826 as at the 'summit of the scale of excellence', has, until now, remained elusive.

On his long journey to unravel this mystery, Geoffrey Priestman began by examining almost 30,000 copper plates stored at the Minton factory, in search of the earliest engravings. The vast store of material in the archive room was diligently examined for information relating to the early printed products. Although Minton have preserved several pattern books illustrating the early bone china on-glaze decoration, no underglaze printed pattern books survive from this early period. The work has therefore relied upon the gradual and informed extraction of relevant records and illustrations, accompanied, over the last 10 years, by the assembly of a representative reference collection of Minton products. Despite the somewhat iterative nature of the process, it has culminated in a major advance in our understanding of the early printed wares, with close to 100 patterns now being attributable to Minton.

The evidence for each attribution is clearly presented and illustrated, as is the lengthy chapter cataloguing the wide and varied range of printed wares produced. The consistently fine quality of the products identified, together with the evidence of innovation in the designs produced, confirms Shaw's claim that Minton was indeed producing blue printed wares of the highest quality and with much elegance of pattern, and which rank alongside the wide range of other fine quality wares produced by the factory throughout the nineteenth century.

Joan Jones, Royal Doulton Museums Curator

Author's Preface

My interest in Minton began, indirectly, over 10 years ago with the purchase at a local auction of a fine pearlware teapot, illustrated here in Plate 5.10. Classified as 'Staffordshire, maker unknown' its quality suggested that it had originated from a major factory. Some of its potting characteristics suggested Minton, but it was soon apparent that trying to verify this was not straightforward. The only published works of significance relating to the early Minton wares were the pioneering book by Geoffrey Godden and the more recent analysis of factory inventories by Terence Lockett, neither of which had been able to identify with any certainty details of the early Minton earthenware patterns. Whilst discussing this problem at a Northern Ceramic Society meeting, Robert Copeland pointed out to me that there remained a large stock of copper plates at the Minton factory, and that there was a chance that some of these may be engraved with early patterns. I therefore contacted Joan Jones, Curator at the Minton Museum, who very kindly allowed me access to the copper plate room in an attempt to locate and identify any early coppers. Although this did not reveal any evidence linking my teapot to Minton, it did mark the beginning of my researches into the early Minton printed wares. Thus started a series of visits to the copper plate room soon to be followed by numerous sessions delving into the many boxes of early documents held in the Minton archives, access to which was greatly facilitated by the comprehensive Catalogue of the Minton manuscripts prepared by Alyn Giles Jones.

Fortunately the copper plate room did reveal significant evidence relating to the early patterns although, given the vast number of plates in storage, the number of very early coppers was disappointingly small. Thus it was possible to start identifying early Minton blue and white wares with some certainty, and as the number and variety of pieces grew, characteristic shapes, potting characteristics and workman's marks started to become apparent. These led to the identification of further patterns, which could often be related to various documentary evidence found in the archives, including original source material used as a basis for the engravings. It is through this process of careful research and identification that the number and range of patterns has grown to the relatively large number presented here. Note that most of the pieces illustrated are from the author's reference collection. Experience has confirmed that when trying to distinguish between the almost identical shapes and patterns of several factories, it is invaluable to be able to readily compare the pieces directly.

The book starts by examining the early life of Thomas Minton and the establishment of the factory. Previously unpublished contemporary accounts by factory workers help to illustrate how Thomas Minton and his immediate family were intimately involved in all aspects of the business, with Thomas remaining a leading and well-respected figure throughout his life. The second chapter clearly sets out the available archive evidence, as used in the first instance to determine a number of key Minton patterns, from which the further designs could be attributed. The various patterns identified as Minton are then presented, followed by a first attempt to catalogue the various shapes used for the early printed wares.

The majority of the patterns presented in the book were previously unattributed to Minton, especially those produced during the first 30 years up to c.1825. The earliest patterns are seen to be typical Chinoiserie landscape and floral designs, based directly on patterns found hand painted on imported Chinese porcelain. These are followed by patterns with a more European influence, including rural views, animals and flowers. Finally, by the 1830s, the designs are seen to exhibit a more romanticised treatment. Although this evolution of design was typical for the period, it is seen that Minton was at the forefront of these changes, with many of his most popular designs being copied by other potters.

Throughout the book care is taken to clearly present the evidence for each attribution and to highlight any similar patterns produced by other factories. Where there remains some doubt about the certainty of attribution, this is also highlighted. There are, no doubt, further patterns and shapes waiting to be identified, and hopefully this work will aid and encourage such discoveries.

In addition to the wares printed underglaze in blue, some consideration is also given to black and on-glaze bat printed wares. This preliminary treatment will hopefully enable further wares in this category to be identified, especially given the illustrations of early prints reproduced from a surviving factory Bat Print book. The wide range of early Minton shapes illustrated throughout the book may also provide a starting point for identifying the various other Minton earthenware products which are listed in such large number in the factory inventories, including the currently unidentified but no doubt fine quality early Minton painted pearlwares and creamwares.

Geoffrey H. Priestman
June 2001

A Note on Dimensions

Dimensions of the pieces illustrated are recorded in millimetres (1 inch = 25.4 mm). The majority of wares are shown in plan view and the dimension given then normally relates to the horizontal distance across the piece as illustrated. This is recorded either as a diameter for round items such as circular plates, or as a width for non-circular items such as octagonal plates and oval dishes. For hollow ware items shown from the side, such as teapots, mugs and bowls, the dimension recorded is either the length, measured horizontally, or the height, measured vertically, or for circular items a diameter.

Acknowledgements

First I wish to thank Joan Jones for her strong support, encouragement and assistance throughout my research, without which the work would not have been possible. I also thank Royal Doulton for allowing access to the Minton copper plate room and archives, and for granting permission to reproduce the archive material which is used and referred to so extensively throughout the book.

The research reported in this book has relied heavily upon information offered through discussion and correspondence with many fellow collectors and the uncanny ability of dealers to produce an interesting pot from behind their stall. In this respect I would like to thank the following: Brian Allaker; Renard Broughton; A. Bunce; Tim Carr; Harry and Rosie Cooke; Robert Copeland; Alwyn and Angela Cox; Robert Cumming; Jean Duke; Roger Edmundson; Trevor Evans; Tony Fields; Laurie Fuller; Geoffrey Godden; John and Dorothy Griffin; Jeremy Holmes; Leonard Holmes; Ann Hughes; Peter Hyland; Margaret Ironside; Peter Jones; Trevor Kentish; Anthony Knight; Duncan Langford; Gerard Ledger; Ken Linacre; Trevor Markin; Phillip Miller; Steve Millington; Eleanor Mulvey; Howard Mumford; Patricia Parkes; Ray Parkin; Roger Pomfret; John Shepherd; Arleen and Grahame Tanner; Peter Tomkins; Jill Turnbull; Sue Wagstaff and Ian Webber.

A further key component of the work has been the accumulation of a structured reference collection of Minton wares. This has been greatly aided by the expertise offered by several specialist dealers. The following are thanked specifically: Peter Scott of Bartlett Street Antiques, Bath; Sue Norman at Antiquarius, King's Road; Anna Wolsey at Libra Antiques off Kensington Church Street; and Gillian Neale.

Further specific thanks and acknowledgement are given to the following for either sending me photographs which have been used in the book or for allowing me to photograph items in their collections: Brian Allaker (Plate 4.39); Leonard Holmes (Plate 4.46); Philip Miller (Plate 4.73); Howard Mumford (Marks M31 and U8); Arleen and Grahame Tanner (Plates 3.46, 4.56, 5.12b, 6.64, 6.69, 6.76, 9.110, 9.132, 9.139, 9.140, 9.141 and 9.143); Sue Wagstaff (Plates 3.55 and 7.50); The Castle Museum, Norwich (Plate 6.71).

The remaining wares illustrated are from the author's reference collection.

Chapter One

Thomas Minton: Engraver, Manufacturer and Gentleman

Production at the famous Minton factory started in 1796 with, according to Simeon Shaw, 'the manufacture of blue printed pottery, of much elegance of quality, and with additional elegance of patterns, which speedily secured considerable celebrity.' Shaw goes on to say that Minton's 'blue printed pottery was, in 1826, so much improved in its various properties, as to place it at the summit of the scale of excellence, and to secure for it an unprecedented share of patronage.'[1] Shaw, who was writing in 1829, also credits Minton as having 'been closely connected with most of the improvements of the last forty years' and to be of 'excellent character as a parent and a gentleman'. Despite being a leading manufacturer of his day producing large quantities of top quality earthenwares, only with the gradual introduction of identifiable printed factory marks during the 1820s did his wares start to become attributable with any certainty, the earlier earthenwares remaining largely anonymous. The main purpose of this book is to present evidence for the identification of the celebrated Minton blue and white printed wares, from the earliest years of production up to the death of Thomas Minton in 1836, and hopefully to establish them alongside the fine quality products of his near neighbour Josiah Spode II.

A first step is to examine the early life of Thomas Minton and the establishment of his factory. Shaw gives details of early blue printing at the porcelain manufactory of Thomas Turner at Caughley:

> In 1780, he [Thomas Turner] completed the first blue printed dinner service made in England, for Whitmore, Esq. father of the present Member for Bridgnorth. The pattern was called Nankin; and had much similarity to the Broseley Tea pattern, which in 1782, was copied from a Nankin [Chinese export porcelain] pattern, and by Mr Turner adapted to Tea Services. Thos. Minton, Esq. of Stoke, assisted in the completion of the Table service, and named the other Broseley, by way of compliment to the adjacent town.[2]

Shaw's account is given extra credence in that, in his Preface, he acknowledges help from Thomas Minton in finalising the manuscript. More detail of the early life of Thomas Minton is given by Llewellynn Jewitt, writing in 1883 about the Minton works:

> Mr Thomas Minton, the founder of these works, was born in Wyle cop, Shrewsbury, in 1765, and received his education at the Shrewsbury Grammar School. He had an only brother, Arthur Minton, and a sister, Elizabeth. On leaving school, Thomas Minton was apprenticed to an engraver (probably Hancock) at the Caughley China Works, at Broseley, one of his fellow-apprentices (also a Salopian) being Richard Hicks, who became a founder of the firm of Hicks, Meigh, and Johnson. On the expiration of his apprenticeship, Thomas Minton continued to be employed for a time at the Caughley China Works under Mr Turner, and then removed to London, where he engraved some patterns for Josiah Spode. From London, having married, he removed to Staffordshire, in 1788 or 1789, where the rapidly increasing demand for blue printed earthenware

gave promise of a good opening for so skilful a draughtsman and engraver as he had become. On removing into Staffordshire, he set up as a master engraver at Stoke-upon-Trent, his residence and engraving shop being one of a block of buildings then called Bridge Houses, erected by Thomas Whieldon, the first partner of Josiah Wedgwood. Here he became very successful, one of his chief employers being Josiah Spode, for whom he engraved a tea-ware pattern called the Buffalo, which continued in demand for many years; the Broseley, so called from being first produced at the Caughley works, the Willow Pattern, and many others. In the latter he was assisted by Henry Doncaster of Penkhull. The original plate from which this pattern was thus engraved passed from Mr Doncaster into the hands of Mr Wildblood, engraver, of Burslem, and from him into the possession of Minton & Co., where it appropriately remains, as do also some drawings and other interesting relics. Mr Minton had two apprentices, one of whom, Greatbach (father of the eminent artist William Greatbach, engraver of the Waterloo Banquet), became chief engraver and manager of that department at Spode and Copeland's.[3]

Jewitt was writing some hundred years after Minton started his career so, unlike Shaw, was unable to check his facts first hand. Thus, although his basic account of events is probably reliable, errors in detail are possible, as have become apparent in other aspects of his work. For example Jewitt states that Minton was born in 1765, but given that he was not baptised until 30 January 1767[4] it seems probable that he was born towards the end of 1766 or even early in 1767. Jewitt and Shaw both place Minton at Caughley, and an arrival by 1780, as indicated by Shaw, would correspond to him being 13 or 14 years old. This was the age at which, according to Jewitt, Minton's son Herbert also left grammar school, joining the Minton works. The reported move to London after his time at Caughley, sometime in the mid 1780s, places Thomas with his brother, Arthur Minton, who had become established in the pottery retail trade in London. This is supported by Godden,[5] who refers to the dissolution of a partnership between Thomas and Arthur, a successful 'chinaman' selling pottery and porcelain in Swallow Street, Hanover Square, as recorded in the *London Gazette* of 15 December 1792, with Arthur continuing on his own account from 29 October 1792. Godden quite rightly points out that this report raises doubts as to whether Thomas had been actively engaged as an engraver in London or was purely a partner in the retail business, and also the date of his return to Stoke. It is possible that Thomas moved to London to join his brother, both to gain experience in retailing and also to continue his trade of engraving, with Spode one of his clients.

At this time blue printing on earthenwares was still in its infancy. According to Shaw, Josiah Spode I was amongst the first potters to produce blue printed earthenwares, in about 1784, having employed an engraver, Thomas Lucas, and a printer, James Richards, both from Caughley. Thomas Minton was therefore well positioned to engrave designs for Spode. Not only was he one of the few trained engravers at that time, but he had previously worked with Spode's engraver Lucas at Caughley. Minton was quite likely also acquainted with Spode's son, Josiah Spode II, who was at this time also in the pottery retail trade in London. An additional advantage of being based in London would have been that Minton had easy access to the latest and most popular Chinese porcelain designs on which to base his engravings. With respect to the details surrounding Minton's return to Stoke, although we can question Jewitt's reported date, it is difficult to discount the rest of his account. He not only reports a return to Stoke as a master engraver, but also gives his work address, names one of his apprentices and a fellow worker and gives details of some of his patterns engraved. It is possible that Thomas had already become established at Stoke at the time of the dissolution of his partnership with Herbert late in 1792, and that the formal ending of his London connection was linked to his impending plans to establish a pottery.

Plate 1.1. *Earthenware dinner plate, probably of Staffordshire origin, c.1785. This design is traditionally identified as the Full Nankin pattern, as used on porcelain at Caughley on the first blue printed table service in c.1780, reportedly with the assistance of Minton. Note the coarse engraving and angular shape of these very early wares. Width 225 mm.*

Plate 1.2. *Porcelain saucer made at Caughley c.1785, decorated with the famous Broseley pattern. The design was reportedly named after the adjacent town by Minton in 1782. Diameter 125 mm.*

It is worth examining the designs associated with Minton during the early development of blue printing, as these may give some insight into his early products. Shaw links Minton with two specific Caughley printed patterns, Nankin and Broseley, though he was no doubt involved in the engraving of a range of designs. Plate 1.1 shows an example of the basic pattern identified by Godden[6] as 'Full Nankeen' from contemporary Caughley records of table and dessert porcelain wares. The pattern became popular with several earthenware manufacturers and the illustration shows the use of the pattern on an earthenware plate, which is probably of Staffordshire origin. Both the coarse engraving technique and the pronounced angular octagonal shape are characteristic of this early period. The Caughley Broseley pattern, as christened by Minton, is shown in Plate 1.2. As with Full Nankin, the pattern is a close copy of a Chinese export porcelain design. Broseley became arguably the most popular printed teaware pattern ever introduced, remaining in production into the twentieth century.

The early engraved patterns tended to be referred to under the generic term of 'willow', which can lead to confusion with the specific and famous 'Standard Willow Pattern'. For example Jewitt mentions that:

> In 1780 Mr Turner introduced the making of the Willow Pattern – the first made in England – at Caughley, and about the same time the Broseley Blue Dragon pattern. The Willow is still commonly known in the trade as Broseley pattern.[7]

Clearly the willow pattern referred to here is the famous Broseley teaware pattern shown in Plate 1.2. Shaw refers to Spode's earliest patterns as, for tea wares, Broseley and for tablewares, Old Willow with a border of a willow and a dagger, both engraved by Lucas. Robert Copeland[8] gives a comprehensive review of early Spode patterns, but the Old Willow referred to by Shaw is not clearly identified. Perhaps the earliest identified Spode tableware pattern is that referred to by Copeland as Two Figures, illustrated in Plate 1.3. Popular with several Staffordshire potters, the pattern was a faithful copy of an original Chinese design and shows some similarity to Full Nankin. According to Jewitt, Minton engraved Buffalo, Broseley, Willow and many other patterns, all for Spode, whilst he was working as a freelance engraver in Stoke in the early 1790s. Buffalo was another pattern that had originated on Chinese export porcelain, and became popular with many Staffordshire potters in the 1790s and

Plate 1.3. *Two Figures pattern pearlware plate made by Spode, c.1790. This is perhaps the earliest of the printed tableware patterns so far attributed to Spode. Early Spode examples used a slightly less refined central engraving and three different border variations are known. The same basic design was used by several factories, including Joshua Heath and probably Swansea. Diameter 253 mm, no foot ring. Impressed mark 'SPODE' (9 mm long).*

early 1800s on both tea wares and tablewares. The Willow pattern mentioned by Jewitt could refer to several possible early Spode patterns, such as the popular teaware pattern Mandarin, illustrated in Plate 1.4, again a faithful copy of a Chinese design as shown in Plate 1.5. Mandarin may well have been combined with another Chinese design to form the famous Standard Willow Pattern, which was introduced on tablewares in the 1790s. Copeland makes a case for its introduction first at the Spode factory in about 1790.[9] This may well be correct, in which case Thomas Minton could have been involved in its original design and engraving. Plate 1.6 shows details of an early example of the Spode Standard Willow pattern.

The patterns illustrated so far give a good indication of the range of designs with which Thomas Minton was probably associated during his engraving career in the years leading up to the establishment of the Minton factory. Both Godden[10] and Cumming[11] have examined the foundation of the factory: Cumming gives valuable detail about land purchased by Minton in 1793, when Stoke and its surrounding area was being rapidly developed. In April Minton bought land close to Penkhull from Ephraim, Hugh and Jos. Booth, then in September a further – probably adjoining – plot from John Ward Hassels. In 1794 Minton first made land tax payments, interestingly as owner/occupier. A Court Rolls Sketch from April 1794 identifies Mr Minton's plot as bounded on the east side by the New Turnpike Road, on the west by a new street, on the north by a new street dividing it from Mr Kenright's [sic] plot, and on the south by Mr Ephraim Booth's field. For details of the early history of the factory we are indebted to Mr Joseph Stringer, a clerk and cashier to the firm, who gave an account of the early progress of the works to

Plate 1.4. Pearlware cup and saucer printed with the Mandarin pattern plus gilding. The pattern was first engraved at Caughley and then at Spode, before becoming popular at many factories. This example was probably made by Spode c.1795. Cup with two-line printer's mark. Saucer diameter 132 mm.

Plate 1.5. Chinese porcelain saucer c.1780 painted with the design on which the Mandarin pattern was based. This design is thought to have been combined with another Chinese pattern to give the basis of the Standard Willow pattern. Diameter 128 mm.

Jewitt.[12] This clearly describes the growth of the factory from modest beginnings to an established works:

> To start with, there was one Bisque and one Glost oven, with slip house, for preparing the clay, and only such other buildings and appliances as were necessary to make good working commencement. Mr Minton formed an engagement with the brothers Poulson, who owned the works opposite to the land he had purchased, known as the Stone Works, and who were potters on a small scale, and, as was then the practice, had houses on the works, now converted into potters' workshops. They belonged to an ancient family which had been located at Boothen for several centuries. Mr Joseph Poulson was the practical potter, and his brother Samuel was modeller, mould-maker, and useful man-of-all-work. It was not until May 1796 that Mr Minton's works were in operation. The next year's transactions showed a satisfactory advance in every respect, as did every subsequent year; and amongst the circumstances favouring Mr Minton's prosperity may be named – first, that aided by Mr Poulson's experience as a potter, and his own good taste as an engraver and designer, he produced a quality and style of ware that commanded a ready market; and in his brother, Mr Arthur Minton, who had established himself in the trade in the metropolis, a ready and devoted agent to extend the trade; so much so that the business done by him in 1800 amounted to nearly £2,000. He was also fortunate in having the acquaintance of Mr Pownall, a merchant from Liverpool, who aided him with capital to extend his operations, and who was, for a few years, a sleeping partner in the business. Mr Joseph Poulson was in a short time admitted as partner, and the firm traded as Minton and Poulson for a short time, and then the style was altered to Minton, Poulson and Pownall. Mr Poulson remained a partner until his death in 1808; and it would seem up to this period china or soft porcelain was made at the stone-works, but was abandoned as unprofitable until Mr Herbert Minton's experiments in after years were fully successful.

The details of this account have, in the main, been substantiated by subsequent studies, with the only real doubt being the precise date at which the manufacture of china was ended at the Stone Works.

Although Minton and Poulson traded as partners up to Poulson's death, the Stone Works, which produced the china, was owned and built by Poulson on land he had purchased in 1792, and the Pot Works, which produced the earthenwares, was owned and built by Minton on his land. Further expansion and acquisitions made after 1796, funded in part by Pownall, were probably done jointly under the partnership. Details of the extent of the factory, some 10 years after building commenced, are contained in the Fire Insurance Policy taken out by the partnership in January 1803:

Plate 1.6. Pearlware Spode wicker basket decorated with an early line engraved version of the Standard Willow Pattern c.1795. This famous tableware pattern may have been originally designed and engraved by Minton for Spode. Width 226 mm. Impressed 'SPODE' (9 mm long).

> Messieurs Thomas Minton and James Poulson of Stoke upon Trent. Mr Thomas Minton's Dwelling House in Stoke £400; His warehouse adjoining £200; Stable adjoining £30; His household Furniture in the aforesaid house £200; Mr James Poulson's Household Furniture in his now dwelling house opposite the Market Hall in Stoke £100; Their China Manufactory situate on the East side of the Canal in Stoke £500; China Ware therein £200; Their Earthenware Manufactory situate on the West Side of the Canal £1,000; China and Earthenware therein £600; Fixtures and Utensils therein £400. Total £3,630.[13]

(The mistake in Poulson's Christian name was eventually corrected in later policies.) Thomas Minton is seen now to own a significant house in Stoke and Poulson has likewise moved to Stoke. The canal referred to was the Newcastle-under-Lyme branch from the Trent and Mersey canal, which had been built in 1795–96, conveniently passing between the Stone Works and the Turnpike Road.

After the death of Poulson, the practical pottery side of the business was taken over by John Turner who, according to Jewitt, joined the company shortly after the failure, in about 1803, of the pottery at Lane End that John operated with his brother William. According to Shaw, the Turners had produced excellent pottery and been responsible for technical advances. This supports Jewitt's claim that John Turner 'effected great improvements in the bodies and glazes, and in the general character of the productions of the [Minton] works'. The partnership between Minton and Poulson was formally ended on 31 December 1808 with Thomas carrying on under his name only, as reported in the *London Gazette* in March 1810. In January 1810 another insurance policy shows how the company had continued to expand:

> Thomas Minton of Stoke upon Trent. His dwelling house and warehouse adjoining each other, in his own occupation £1,000; His household furniture therein £500; His Earthenware Manufactory at Stoke £2,000; His stock of Earthenware and China therein £1,500; His Utensils consisting of Copper Plates, Lathes, Moulds, Wheels, Benches, Sagers and Tables £800; His stock of Earthenware in the earthenware manufactory which he occupies from the Executors of the late Mr James Poulson £500; His Utensils therein £200; His small dwelling house at Shelton, in the occupation of — Simpson £100. Total £6,600.[13]

Noting that the policy no longer covered the Stone Works buildings, which Minton was now renting, we see that the value had approximately doubled since 1803.

It is interesting that in January 1810 the Stone Works is referred to as an earthenware manufactory, seemingly indicating the discontinuation of china production shortly after Poulson's death. It is normally accepted that china production was continued for a few years after 1810, based both on the shapes of the later china wares and the maximum pattern number reached of 948 (by 1810 the pattern numbers had only reached about 560).[14] It is possible that the policy mistakenly used earthenware instead of china in describing the Stone Works.

The French and American wars contributed to a poor economic climate in the years following 1810, and subsequent insurance policies clearly indicate that the growth of the Minton factory was curtailed during this period. In the policy of January 1812 the total sum covered had fallen to £6,000, despite an increase of £400 in the stocks of china and earthenware. A very similar policy, again for £6,000, was taken out in May 1815. Payments to Poulson's executors for the Stone Works ended during 1816,[11] probably denoting the end of the first period of china production. In January 1817 Thomas Minton formed a partnership with his sons Thomas Webb and Herbert, who had by then been involved in the business for many years, Herbert joining directly from school. Thomas still owned the factory buildings, but the business was now operated as Thomas Minton and Sons. This is reflected in the two policies taken out in January 1819:

> Thomas Minton of Stoke upon Trent Esquire. His now dwelling house situate as above, in his own occupation £500; His household furniture therein £400; His earthenware manufactory in Stoke, together with the Slip Houses, Stables, Straw House, Lead House thereto belonging £2,000. Total £2,900.

> Messrs. Thomas Minton and Sons of Stoke upon Trent. Their stock of earthenware and China in their manufactory [at Stoke] £2,500; Their utensils in the manufactory foresaid consisting of Copper Plates, Wheels, Lathes, Moulds, Blocks, Benches, Tools, Warehouse pens and moveable boards £800; Their stock of straw and hay in their stable and store house thereto belonging £100. Total £3,400.[13]

As expected there is no mention of the Stone Works. The combined value of the policies at £6,300 is very similar to that in 1810. In 1821, according to Jewitt, 'the elder brother, Thomas Webb Minton, quitted the works, for the purpose of studying for the Church, and was ordained in 1825'. On 1 January 1823 the Minton partnership was dissolved, but Herbert was still fully committed to the business. The second period of china production was heralded by an additional insurance policy taken out in November 1823: 'Thomas Minton of Stoke upon Trent Esquire. A China Manufactory consisting of rooms for manufacturing the same and Slip Kiln, at Stoke £400.'

A period of recovery in the factory had clearly begun, as is confirmed by the value of the policy taken out in December 1825, which covered the entire works and Minton's residence, and had a value of £8,110. Thomas remained owner of the works until his death in 1836, when Herbert took complete control of the business. Later that year Herbert took as a partner John Boyle, the son of Zachariah Boyle, an experienced potter. The partnership operated as Minton and Boyle but was short-lived, being dissolved in November 1841. The following year Michael Hollins was taken into partnership, the company trading as Herbert Minton & Co. or simply Minton & Co.. Herbert Minton died in 1858, since when no Minton has been connected with the firm. The company traded as Mintons from 1873 to 1884, after which it became know as Mintons Ltd.

The formation and successful growth of the Minton factory was founded upon the individual efforts of Thomas Minton and his family. According to Jewitt:

> Mr Minton married, on January 1st 1789, Miss Sarah Webb, of Bruton Street, London, and by her had a family of four sons, two of whom were the Rev Thomas Webb Minton and Herbert Minton, and six daughters. After his marriage, his mother-in-law, Mrs Webb, resided with them, and was a valuable acquisition to him in his business, keeping his books and accounts, and being, in fact, the financial manager of the concern. She received and paid all money, and superintended the entire office arrangements, thus leaving Mr Minton at liberty to devote his entire time to the manufactory and to the engraving. Mrs Minton, also, so far as the cares of her home and family would permit, took her share in the business.[15]

It is possible that, as with the early factory history, this information was given to Jewitt by Joseph Stringer. During 1873 Stringer interviewed several long-standing factory employees and neighbours, and these are recorded in a book at the factory referred to as Minton's Notebook.[16] Many of the characters interviewed had been at the factory for over 50 years and they paint a vivid picture of early life at the works. Miss Elizabeth Poulson spoke of the Minton household:

> There are four houses still standing which used to be called the Bridge Houses (built by Wheildon the potter). In the first house next to the Trent lived my grandmother Wayte, her husband was in the carrying trade, Mr Minton occupied the next, they were very friendly neighbours and assisted each other in every way as they only kept one servant each. Mrs Minton always remained a greatfully [sic] attached friend and was free to acknowledge her obligations when a young wife and mother. Herbert Minton was born in this house (Feb. 3 1793). Old Mrs Minton had three children before she was twenty one. I have heard her say 'The cock never crows before I'm up in the morning'. Her husband always used to call her second child 'Mrs Minton's son', and she would say, 'Well Herbert is like me'. My Grandmother Mrs Wayte took my sister Harriet by request of Mrs Minton to see Old Mr Minton when in his coffin. It was not uncommon in these days for friends to pay such visits after death. The coffin was placed downstairs in the butlers pantry and the picture of his snow white hair and pink complexion is still vividly recollected by her.
> Old Mrs Webb was very fond of whist and played a game in the evening before she died. She usually walked with a stick which was not uncommon with ladies in those days.
> Mr Joseph Poulson a relative of my family, was a practical potter as you will see by the inscription on his gravestone.

There is no mention of Elizabeth or Harriet Poulson in Cumming's study of the Poulsons,[11] so their exact relationship is unknown. However, it is possible that Minton's neighbour in Bridge Houses, Mrs Wayte, may have been related to his soon-to-be partner Poulson. It may also be possible that some of the funds for the new venture were provided by Mrs Webb, who perhaps moved from London to Bridge Houses in Stoke at the same time as Thomas and his wife. Jewitt claims that Minton and his family moved from Bridge Houses to a house erected in the works, and from there to a house on Talbot Bank. John Ward, writing about the Borough of Stoke-on-Trent in 1843, gives more information on Minton's house in Stoke.[17] He confirms that Minton died in the house in 1836, having purchased it from a Mr Samual Parkes, for whom it had originally been built. Parkes was described as a Grocer, Soap Boiler and Tallow Chandler, who had moved to Stoke in 1793, but then left for London within about 10 years. Ward mentions that the house had recently been converted into Board Rooms and Offices for Parish Business. Minton had clearly moved to Stoke before 1803 when the house is included in his insurance. According to Shaw the house was 'a modest edifice in a retiring situation on the road through Town', where 'in a circle of numerous and intelligent family, he enjoys the well-earned reward of his ingenuity and perserverance'.[18] Another interesting account was given to Stringer by Thomas Smith who had joined the works just before the Peace Rejoicing of 1814:

> Old Mr Minton gave a treat to all the work people on the day of the Peace Rejoicing. All the work people had dinner at the Public House, and all the women had tea in the grounds of Mr Minton's House, which is now the Parish Office. Boys of ten or twelve or under (there was no factory act in those days) were served by Old Mrs Minton with a large three cornered piece of plum cake, it was a piece about two inches thick, and each boy had half a pint of ale.
>
> There was a grand procession of the work people of Spode's, Wolfe's, Booth's and Minton's. A large loaf was carried on a pole from our works by a man named Walton who lived in Hanford and was a packer, and a big man named Wakefield carried a large banner, he was a thrower. It was a jolly day. I remember that the boys had paper rosettes in their overcoats, but Wolfe's lads had ribbon, they taunted us about the paper and thought themselves much bigger folks than us. When the procession returned to the works, Mr Minton stood at the top of the steps, and led the cheers, reminding the people that they would have two Wakes that year.[16]

Further insight into the Minton family, including mention of the youngest son Arthur, born in 1803, is given by William Walker, a mould maker who had joined the factory in August 1817:

> My father worked at Booth's 10 or 12 years and began to work for Mr Minton soon after he started. The firm was then Minton & Poulson, but Mr Minton was considered the master.
>
> Mr Minton was very fond of horses, and at one time he had eight fine animals all grays. There were no boundary walls to the works in those days the hovals were open to the street. The Stone Works stood empty after the first trial of China.
>
> When I first came here, there was only a small part of the present Earthenware works erected. The making of china first began at the Stone Works, but after a time it was given up. Some 45 or 50 years, I can't exactly recollect, they began again. Mr Herbert was the head master and persevered in it. Where the China Works are now built, Mr Minton had a stable with a loft over it and there were stocks of straw and part of the land was garden. I was grown up a young man when the building was commenced. It may be added from another source that Mr Minton was his own architect and drew the plans having no other aid than that of a practical but uneducated builder named Samual Steel. The central part certainly does credit to an amateur
>
> When I first came young Mr Thomas [Webb] Minton was at the works attending chiefly to orders. Mr Herbert was everything, he got on very fast. The Old Gentleman [Thomas Minton] did not do so much as formerly. He was a fine and fresh old gentleman as you would see in a days march. I mean a blooming fresh old gentleman. He used to scold us sometimes, but if he was cross with you one minute, he would soon forgive you. Mr Arthur began business soon after me, and if living would be about my age, I was 66 last Valentines day. He was a nice feeling gentleman, kind and very good to all the people about. I have heard him blame my father for working such long hours, but he would do it. Mr Arthur was often ill. On his birthday, being 21, he was riding from Newcastle to Trent Vale and fell off his horse and injured himself very much. He afterwards had fits. He built a little church and schools at Oak Hill in the grounds near his house. His brother Thomas was very kind and charitable. He used often to take bottles of wine and other things as well as money to my Father to take to different sick people, but always told him that he was never to let people know it came from him.

The same impression of Herbert being very much in charge of the works, but Thomas still actively involved, is given by Mary Cartlidge, a transferrer who had joined the works in June 1824:

> Mr Herbert Minton lived in Hartshill, I met him there early in the morning. He would be round the shops before seven and scold the late comers or those not well at their

work. Old Mr Minton was often in the Bat printing shop. Old Thomas Carter was the printer, he was the father of John who has been here fifty six years. Mr Minton was very familiar with the old people and liked to have a gossip with them. One day he was in Mr Hollinshead's shop, who interrupted the talk by saying, 'I want to do a trial for Mr Herbert or I shall have a noise'. Then said Mr Minton, 'He finds fault with you does he? Well he does the same by me sometimes. Does it do you any good'. 'Well perhaps it does'.

Mr Minton was a nicer looking man than any of his sons, he was usually dressed in black and wore gaters and low shoes.

The information reviewed in this chapter charts the rise of Thomas Minton from an apprentice engraver in Shropshire to the owner and founder of one of the leading pottery manufactories of his time. Initially his engraving skill, combined with an intimate knowledge of the latest Chinese porcelain designs being imported into his brother's London warehouse, helped him to become established as a leading engraver. Having moved to Stoke around 1790 he was very soon able to take advantage of the growing market demand for printed pottery by forming a partnership with a local potter Poulson and founding the famous Minton works, with financial support from the Liverpool merchant Pownall. That Thomas Minton had achieved all this before his thirtieth birthday is strong testament not only to his skills as a designer and engraver but also to his personal qualities. The early accounts of the Minton works clearly demonstrate how Thomas, together with his wife and her mother, were central to both the development and the day-to-day running of the works. The family involvement is seen to strengthen with his sons joining the company, Herbert eventually taking the leading role, although even in his later years Thomas clearly remained involved in activities at the factory. The recollections of the factory workers from this early period also demonstrate how both Thomas and his family were held in high esteem by a loyal workforce, not only in their position as managers, but also by many as both friend and colleague.

References

1. S. Shaw, *History of the Staffordshire Potteries* (published privately, 1829), p. 225.
2. Shaw, *Staffordshire Potteries*, p. 212.
3. L. Jewitt, *The Ceramic Art of Great Britain*, 2nd ed. (1883; repr. Collector's Edition, 1985), p. 383.
4. P. Atterbury and M. Batkin, *The Dictionary of Minton* (Antique Collector's Club, 1990), p. 10.
5. G.A. Godden, *Encyclopaedia of British Porcelain Manufacturers* (Barrie & Jenkins, 1988), p. 540.
6. G.A. Godden, *Caughley & Worcester Porcelains 1775–1800* (Antique Collector's Club, 1981), p. 20.
7. Jewitt, *Ceramic Art of Great Britain*, p. 160.
8. R. Copeland, *Spode's Willow Pattern and other Designs after the Chinese*, 3rd ed. (Studio Vista, 1999).
9. Copeland, *Spode's Willow Pattern*, p. 33.
10. G.A. Godden, *Minton Pottery & Porcelain of the First Period* (Barrie & Jenkins, 1968).
11. R. Cumming, 'Joseph Poulson Bone China Pioneer, 1749–1808, Minton & Poulson 1796–1808', *Journal of the Northern Ceramic Society*, Vol. 12, 1995, pp. 59–91.
12. Jewitt, *Ceramic Art of Great Britain*, p. 396.
13. R. Edmundson, 'Staffordshire Potters Insured at the Salop Fire Office 1780–1825', *Journal of the Northern Ceramic Society*, Vol. 6, 1987, pp. 81–94.
14. Minton MS 1228, Inventory and Valuations for Minton Factory 1810–13 (Minton Archives).
15. Jewitt, *Ceramic Art of Great Britain*, p. 397.
16. Minton MS 277, Minton's Notebook (Minton Archives).
17. J. Ward, *The Borough of Stoke-on-Trent in the Reign of Queen Victoria* (1843), p. 503.
18. Shaw, *Staffordshire Potteries*, p. 61.

Chapter Two

Early Minton Earthenwares: The Archive Evidence

The difficulty in identifying the celebrated blue printed earthenwares, produced at the Minton manufactory from 1796, is due largely to the lack of any known formal factory mark during the first 30 years and the absence of an extant early printed pattern book. Fortunately the success of the Minton works has meant its continued operation to the present day, and preserved within the factory is a wealth of archive material. Some of this dates back to the earliest years of production and includes factory inventories, a number of source prints used for patterns and some original copper plates. Some customer's records of early retail trade have also been preserved. This early material provides a fascinating insight into the extensive range of printed earthenwares being produced in the early 1800s. It also gives details of numerous early pattern names and of some of the early shapes produced at the Minton factory.

Early Sales Accounts

Valuable information is contained in three sets of accounts discovered and reported in detail by Geoffrey Godden.[1] The earliest accounts record sales of Minton earthenwares in January 1798 to Richard Egan, who had a china warehouse in Bath. Full dinner services printed with Nankeen, Dagger Border and Willow patterns are included. Predictably these earliest patterns would seem to be imitating Chinese export porcelain designs, as were the patterns produced by Minton whilst engraving for Caughley and Spode. The second and more extensive set of accounts was found in the Wedgwood archives, and details wares supplied to Messrs Wedgwoods between June 1801 and February 1806. Specific patterns mentioned are, on tablewares, Nankeen Temple (1801) and Lily, Tulip, Image and Hermit (1804), and on tea wares, India, Willow, Pine and Image (1806). In addition, an interesting note in 1804 states 'Have no patterns of printed ware consisting of border alone'. The third set of accounts was in the books of Messrs Chamberlain, the Worcester Porcelain Manufacturers, whose retail shop sold Staffordshire earthenware. They cover the period 1804 to 1811 and include tablewares and toilet wares printed with only one design, the Hermit pattern. The many shapes mentioned in the three sets of accounts confirm that, within a few years of starting production, Minton was producing an extensive range of wares. Full dinner services listed in 1804 comprised 199 pieces and were priced at £14 1s. 8d. or £26 17s. 0d. with gilding (£1 = 20s. = 240d.). Additional dessert services were available in several designs. Tea wares included five teapot shapes (round cap^t., oval, upright, parapet and egg-shaped), vase-shaped coffee pots and fluted and plain cups with square, bell or round handles.

Further details of Minton sales are contained within the business records of a London Staffordshire warehouse run by Thomas Wyllie between 1794 and 1825. The records have been analysed by Eatwell and Warner[2] and show trade with over

40 Staffordshire potters. In 1796 Wyllie began to buy earthenware from Minton, Poulson and Co. on a regular basis. By 1798 annual sales were around £250, a level which was largely maintained until 1808, after which sales fluctuated but were typically of the order of £50 p.a.. For the period 1809 to 1825 the records give some descriptions of the wares, including pattern names. The following Minton patterns are mentioned: India (first listed in 1809), Chinese (1809), Cottage (1810), Broseley (1811), Farm (1813), Grotto (1813), Image (1814), Apple Tree (1816), Rose Bud (1819), Abbey (1820), Flower (1820), Bridge (1820) and Castle (1820). In line with other manufacturers, the designs are seen to be evolving away from the early chinoiserie influence towards the rural British scenes, which were more typical of the 1820s. The transactions with Wyllie are confirmed in surviving early Minton sales books,[3] although these only record the total value and type of transaction, with no details of individual items. These factory accounts record the first receipt from sales on 23 May 1796, and regular sales are booked to Arthur Minton's London sale rooms. Also recorded in 1796 is regular sundry cash income from Pownall, confirming his role as a financier to the business. Later accounts show the money being repaid to Pownall.

Factory Inventories

Some details of the shapes and patterns of early Minton wares are included in two sets of factory inventories in the Minton Archives,[4,5] covering the periods 1810 to 1813 and 1817 to 1826 respectively. These inventories list and value all the stock, fittings, utensils etc. at the factory, although the detail given each year varies significantly. The 1810 inventory is particularly detailed and was examined, together with other archive material, by Lockett to give a snapshot of the factory at that time.[6]

The overall valuations in the inventories are summarised in Table 2.1. It is interesting to note that both the stock and total valuations are significantly higher than the sums insured in the Salop Fire Office Policies discussed in Chapter One.

Table 2.1. Inventory Valuations 1810 to 1826

Year ending	Stock of china & earthenwares Discounted at 20%	Buildings, moulds, fittings, materials, biscuit ware, etc.	Total valuation
Dec 1810	£4,048	£5,695	£9,743
Dec 1811	£4,310	£6,037	£10,347
Dec 1812	£3,684	£5,916	£9,600
Dec 1813	£4,296	£7,458	£11,754
	Discounted at 25%		
Jan 1817	£2,121	£4,839	£6,960
Jan 1818	£2,869	£4,785	£7,654
Jan 1819	£2,070	£5,135	£7,205
Jan 1820	£1,406	£4,442	£5,848
Jan 1821	£1,448	£4,442	£5,890
Jan 1822	£1,780	£4,294	£6,074
Jan 1823	£2,083	£5,028	£7,111
Jan 1824	£2,765	£5,064	£7,829
Jan 1825	£4,033	£5,512	£9,545
Jan 1826	£3,447	£6,260	£9,707

For example, the total inventory valuation in December 1811 of £10,347 is almost twice the sum insured in the policy of January 1812 of £5,400 plus £600 for Minton's dwelling house, which is not in the inventory. The stock insured is only £2,400, again much lower than the inventory amount. The inventories between 1810 and 1813 include an entry of £1,500 for land and buildings, with the 1813 valuation having an additional 'new building' at £750. The 1817 to 1826 inventories do not include an entry for buildings and land, which is reflected in the lower valuations shown in Table 2.1. On formation of the partnership with his sons in 1817, Minton retained ownership of the main buildings and land, as confirmed by the separate insurance policies taken out in 1819. The inventory of 1817 was clearly used as a valuation of the newly formed Thomas Minton and Sons, as next to the final total of £6,960 a note states 'Enter'd Private ledger A fo[r] 1– purchased from Thomas Minton'. Subsequent inventories merely note entry into ledger A.

By 1817 the stock valuation is seen to have fallen to about half that in 1813, levels remaining relatively low until about 1823, after which there are seen to be signs of growth. A significant factor in this is the production of china wares. The inventories include china wares between 1810 and 1813, with a valuation in 1813, before discount, of £1,038 4s. 9d.. No china is listed in January 1817, confirming that Minton and Sons initially only produced earthenwares. The next mention of china wares is in the inventory of 1822 which contains chinaware valued at £91 10s. 2d.. In 1823 there is an entry of sundry china and earthenware at £19 3s. 4d., but at the beginning of 1824 there is no obvious entry for china. By January 1825 the china stocks are valued at £398 15s. 9d., which had increased by the beginning of 1826 to £1,043 6s. 5d.. These entries seem to indicate some development work on china starting in 1821, with significant production from 1824. This is largely consistent with the insurance policy taken out by Thomas Minton in November 1823 for a new china kiln. A good indication of the changing level of factory production up to 1836 is given by the total income recorded in the early factory accounts.[3] A total annual income of £11,434 had been established by the end of 1798. By the end of 1802 this had almost doubled to £21,228 and by the end of 1814 a further increase to £35,461 had been achieved. Total sales recorded for 1823 had dropped to £22,213 but, with the reintroduction of china production, income during 1825 had risen to £30,405. Further steady growth is seen to be maintained over the next 10 years, with a total sales income in 1835 recorded as £45,091.

The 1810 inventory starts with a listing of 'Lily Tableware best', which continues for nearly three pages, ending with single entries for lots of 'Tulip Ware', 'Trophy and Brick', 'Cream Colour' and 'Printed'. The next sections are headed 'Printed Ware Best', 'Printed Ware Seconds', then 'Printed Tea Ware Best'. It has been suggested that 'Lily' refers to plain white-bodied wares. This cannot be the case as the Lily prices are slightly higher than in the following 'printed ware' section, whereas in a surviving early factory price list (see Chapter Nine) the plain or painted wares were much cheaper than printed ones. Clearly Lily ware refers to stock printed with the popular Lily pattern. The 1817 inventory has separate listings for 'Printed Ware Best' and 'Lily Ware', now both valued the same and corresponding exactly to the price list entries for 'Printed Ware other patterns', followed by an entry for cheaper 'Willow Ware Best' again corresponding exactly to the price list. The individual earthenware values were lower in 1817 than in 1810, a reflection of the difficult economic climate during that period.

Details of the main earthenware stock valuations (in pounds sterling before discount) are given in Table 2.2. As noted above, the categories used each year are not consistent. In certain years Willow, Lily and Printed Teawares are listed separately, whilst in other years they are included within the main 'Printed Wares Best' listing. The large majority of earthenwares in stock are seen to be blue printed wares, especially up to 1813, but after 1817 other types of ware are seen to become increasingly significant. Given that a full printed dinner service cost about £15, the stock of such wares throughout the 1810 to 1813 period is seen to be equivalent to approximately 100 services. This is confirmed by the 'Printed Ware Best' listing in 1811 having over 200 of each of the larger flat oval meat dish sizes, each dinner service containing two. The listing also includes over 350 wicker baskets, 36 dozen teapots and 105 dozen ewers and bowls. The entries for blue topped were exclusively tea wares, black printed included tea wares, jugs and mugs, whilst the Japan and Embossed entries included tea, table and toilet wares. Several entries in these sections are worthy of note. Those for black printed wares included Embossed muffin plates in six-, five- and four-inch sizes, which presumably had moulding embossed on the surface. The 1826 entry for Embossed wares is headed 'Dresden and other patterns', indicating that Dresden was a pattern, not a shape. The section of Japan wares in 1824, 1825 and 1826 refers to both Old Japan and Japan Rose tea and toilet. Also included in 1826 is an entry for Ironstone No. 53, valued at £83.00. The relatively small separate entry for 'Lily and other Patterns' in 1826 is interesting in that the dinner plates are priced at 7s. per dozen, compared to only 4s. for Printed Best and 3s. 6d. for Willow pattern; the extra cost could be associated with additional painted decoration on these wares. The Japan plates, which would have had several colours painted over an original printed outline, were priced at 9s. per dozen.

Most of the inventories list the stock in terms of the number, size, basic type and value, as shown in the extract from 1817 given in Plate 2.1. The majority of entries correspond to the basic descriptions used in the factory price list, but there are numerous wares and sizes not included in the list, and some entries give important clarification of shape or design. The 1817 inventory has a full listing of 'Block Moulds' (see Table 9.2) which gives generic information on the shapes of the moulded wares being produced.

Table 2.2. Inventory Stock Valuations of Various Earthenwares and Copper Plates

	1810	1811	1812	1813	1817	1818	1819	1820	1821	1822	1823	1824	1825	1826
Printed ware best	2075	2601	1507	1594	985	1579	1205	811	658	919	1400	1798	2111	1274
Willow					176	647	273	174	196	275	318	495	421	445
Lily	150	121			43									50
Printed tea wares	469		543	572	516									
Printed ware seconds	391	242	140	255	117	74	59	40	67	39	74	86	200	84
Blue top't	57	17		21										
Black printed						4	2		50	28	30	40	45	
Embossed Dresden													327	298
Japan			146	218	102	12	19	9		11		10	21	18
Painted	8	8	5	33	146	233	260	99	182	108	190	291	120	90
Cream colour	73	179	170	204	381	805	611	445	588	727	585	747	1031	786
Blue edge	50	43	44	85	119	221	130	109	192	141	138	149	178	91
Brown line	8					132	53	43	44	28	43	38	75	66
Copper plates	770	915	915	960	392	442	450	450	450	450	450	450	450	450

Plate 2.1. *Extract from the Minton Factory inventory of January 1817 detailing the printed tea wares held in stock. Of the three sizes of teacup the London size is clearly the most popular and there were many more 'common' round teapots than oval ones. A substantial stock of toy tea wares is apparent, with plain (not handled) cups being most common.*

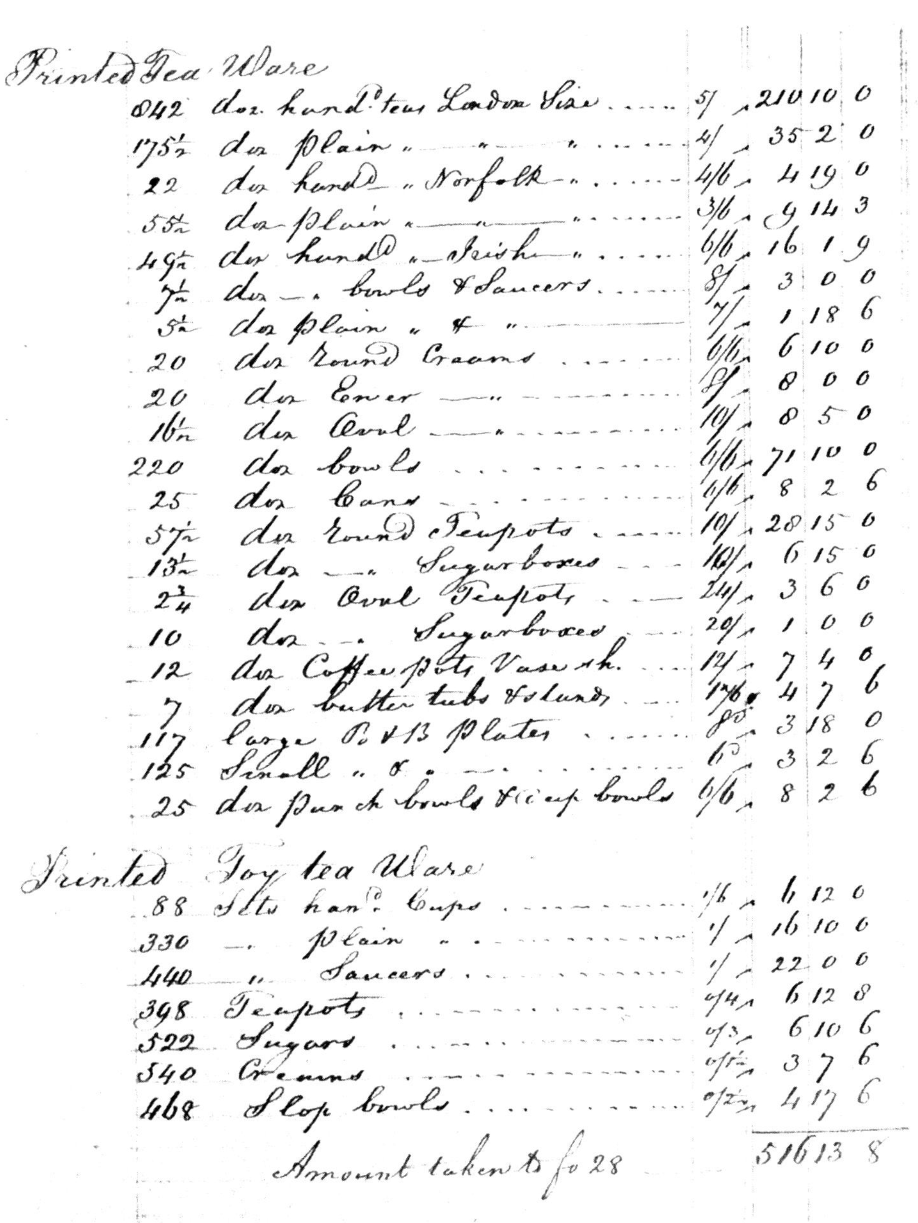

Printed Tea Ware

842	doz. hand^d teas London Size	5/	210 10 0
175½	doz plain " " "	4/	35 2 0
22	doz hand^d " Norfolk "	4/6	4 19 0
55½	doz plain " " "	3/6	9 14 3
49½	doz hand^d " Irish "	6/6	16 1 9
7½	doz " bowls & Saucers	8/	3 0 0
5½	doz plain " & "	7/	1 18 6
20	doz Round Creams	6/6	6 10 0
20	doz Ewer "	8/	8 0 0
16½	doz Oval "	10/	8 5 0
220	doz bowls	6/6	71 10 0
25	doz Cans	6/6	8 2 6
57½	doz Round Teapots	10/	28 15 0
13½	doz " Sugarboxes	10/	6 15 0
2¾	doz Oval Teapots	24/	3 6 0
10	doz " Sugarboxes	20/	1 0 0
12	doz Coffeepots Vase sh.	12/	7 4 0
7	doz butter tubs & stands	17/6	4 7 6
117	large P & B Plates	8d	3 18 0
125	Small " "	6d	3 2 6
25	doz punch bowls & cap bowls	6/6	8 2 6

Printed Toy tea Ware

88	Sets hand^d Cups	1/6	6 12 0
330	" plain "	1/	16 10 0
440	" Saucers	1/	22 0 0
398	Teapots	0/4	6 12 8
522	Sugars	0/3	6 10 6
540	Creams	0/1½	3 7 6
468	Slop bowls	0/2½	4 17 6
	Amount taken to fo 28		516 13 8

Copper Plates and Contemporary Pattern Names

Although the type and basic shape can provide a useful guide to the early printed wares produced by Minton, specific detail of the patterns used is required in order to distinguish them from the very similar products of other potters. Both the 1810 and 1817 inventories give full listings of copper plates, which are reproduced here in Plates 2.2. and 2.3 respectively. In the 1810 list values are assigned to individual patterns or groups of patterns. The basic copper value of the plates is listed separately: 173 pounds of old copper valued at 1s. (or 5p) per pound with the 2,005 pounds of engraved coppers listed at 1s. 6d. per pound. Typically each plate weighed between two-and-a-half and three pounds. The quoted value of each set of coppers thus referred to the value of the engraving work alone, a low value presumably indicating a very simple or badly worn engraving or perhaps an obsolete shape. Some of the 1810 tea plates would appear to be badly worn at this time, in particular the group of five patterns – Nanking, Pagoda, Willow, Red House and Trophy – and to a lesser extent the three patterns: Jasmine, Pine and Image. Included in these are the patterns mentioned in the earliest sales records.

Plate 2.2. Listing of copper plates from the 1810 inventory. For each pattern details are given of the number of plates, their total weight and cost, as well as the type of ware on which it was used.

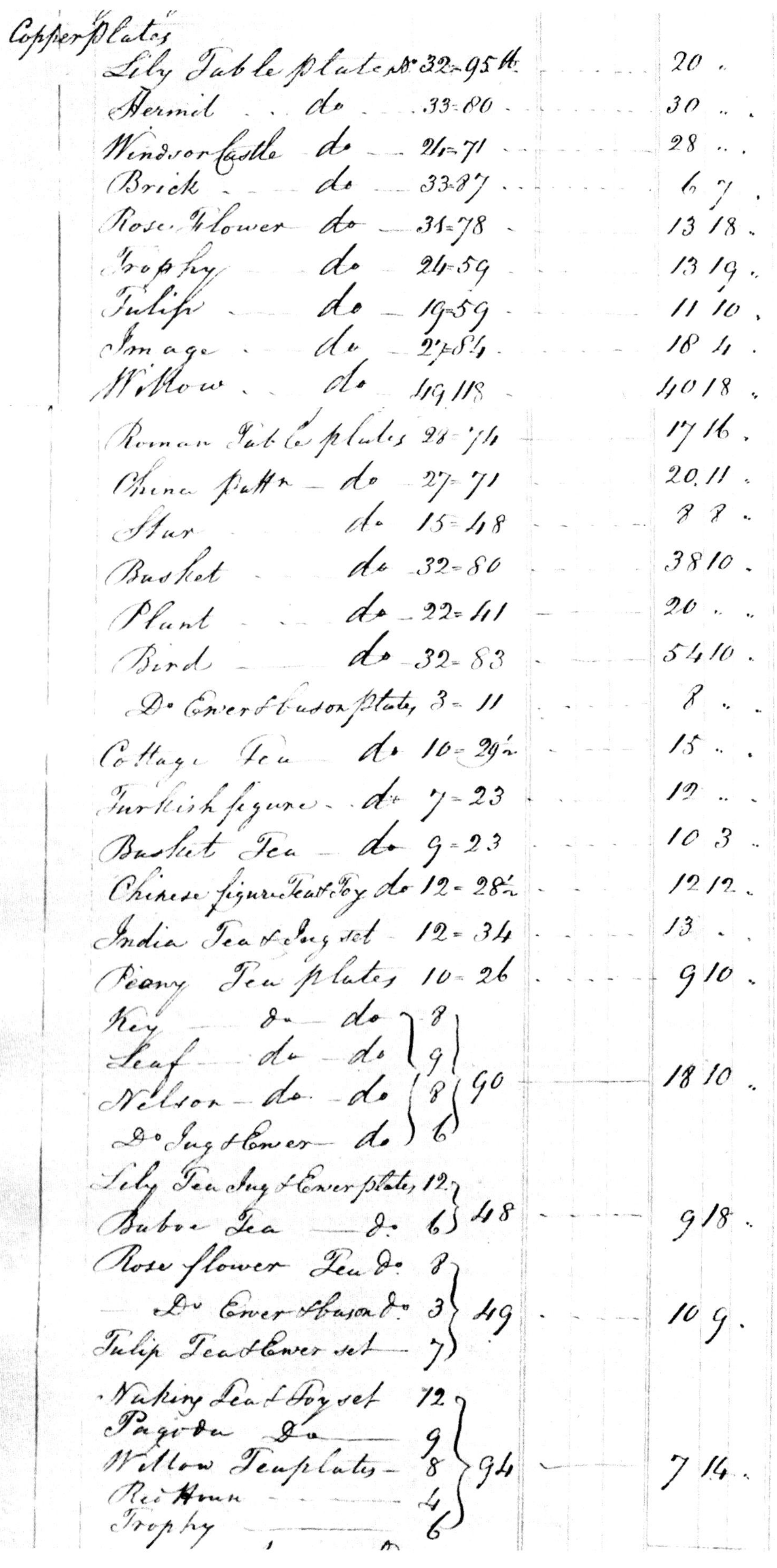

Copper Plates

Lily Table plates N°	32-95 lb		20 ..
Hermit do	33-80		30 ..
Windsor Castle do	24-71		28 ..
Brick do	33-87		6 7
Rose Flower do	31-78		13 18
Trophy do	24-59		13 19
Tulip do	19-59		11 10
Image do	27-84		18 4
Willow do	49-118		40 18
Roman Table plates	28-74		17 16
China Pattn do	27-71		20.11
Star do	15-48		8 8
Basket do	32-80		38 10
Plant do	22-41		20 ..
Bird do	32-83		54 10
Do Ewer & buson plates	3-11		8 ..
Cottage Tea do	10-29½		15 ..
Turkish figure do	7-23		12 ..
Basket Tea do	9-23		10 3
Chinese figure Tea & Toy do	12-28½		12 12
India Tea & Jug set	12-34		13 ..
Peony Tea plates	10-26		9 10
Key do do	8		
Leaf do do	9	90	18 10
Nelson do do	8		
Do Jug & Ewer do	6		
Lily Tea Jug & Ewer plates	12	48	9 18
Bubro Tea do	6		
Rose flower Tea do	8		
Do Ewer & buson do	3	49	10 9
Tulip Tea & Ewer set	7		
Nuking Tea & Toy set	12		
Pagoda do	9		
Willow Tea plates	8	94	7 14
Red House	4		
Trophy	6		

16

Old Patt.n Ewer & bowl Jug & Chamber pots plates & Mourning	13-38	12 .. .
Jessamine Teaplates — 11 Pine do 9 Image do 9	77	10 7 .
Shepherd do 8 Steed do 10 Sprig do 5	59	11 10 ..
Chinese Temple do 9-21		4 4 .
Broseley do 8-25½		12 ..
China patt.n do 5-11½		6 ..
Copper that hath work on of Various patterns	60	12 10 .
Plates for black printing & printing on the Glaze	33-41	15 13 .
Part of Table Service	6-26	27 4 4
New Copper & work done the Broseley Pattern & New Jug Ewer & Bason set in part	56	30 ..
Old Copper @ 1/ ℔	173	8 13 ..
	723 = 2005℔ @ 1/6	150 7 6

Plate 2.3. Listing of copper plates from the 1817 inventory.

Copper plates

			lbs			
32	Plates	Cottage table Ware	134	116	3	4
22	do	Landscape do	85	30	0	0
28	do	Dove do	97	32	0	0
33	do	Lily Table Ewer & Jug	97	15	0	0
52	do	Willow Table	145	35	0	0
33	do	Hermit do	78	20	0	0
33	do	Basket do	84	25	0	0
9	do	Dragon Teas	24	7	0	0
9	do	Appletree do	32	11	12	0
12	do	Farm Yard do	41	13	0	0
11	do	Image landscape	31	11	0	0
11	do	Broseley do	33	9	0	0
12	do	Cottage do	33	11	0	0
12	do	Village Ewer basins & Chambers	59	20	0	0
8	do	Castle do do do	40	10	0	0
6	do	Grotto Jugs	29	9	0	0
5	do	Maypole do		12	15	0
3	do	Toy tea pattern	10	2	10	0
	New Copper		25	2	2	0
		Amount taken to fo 56		392	2	4

The most valuable tea plates in 1810 are seen to be Cottage, Turkish Figure, Basket, China Pattern and Broseley.

Of the tableware coppers listed in 1810 the most valuable are seen to be Bird and Plant, followed by Basket, Windsor Castle, Hermit and Willow. An interesting entry is the 'part table service', presumably under preparation. These relatively heavy coppers are seen to be more than twice the value of any other current pattern, presumably indicating particularly elaborate engraving. They may correspond to the Cottage tableware plates listed in 1817, which were significantly heavier and more valuable than the other plates; Cottage as a teaware pattern was already in use in 1810. The only other new tableware patterns in 1817 were Landscape and Dove, and only one set of plates for toy tea wares is listed, but the other sets of teaware plates may have included such coppers. It is of note that the old favourites Lily, Willow and Hermit were still in use in 1817, as were the Broseley teaware plates, presumably now on an earthenware body.

Compared to 1810 the number of patterns listed in 1817 is surprisingly small and the entry is less detailed, with no corresponding listing for Old Copper, plates for bat printing or partly engraved patterns. It is also surprising that only 11 new patterns are mentioned given that there appeared to be at least four or five new patterns under preparation eight years earlier in January 1810. It seems likely that the 1817 listing of patterns concentrated on those in regular production at that time, with other 'non-production' coppers omitted. Although a detailed

Table 2.3. Recorded Early Factory Pattern Names

Pattern	Date	Wares	Pattern	Date	Wares
Dagger Border	1798	Table	Bamboo	1810	Tea
Nankeen Temple	1798, 1810	Table, Tea, Jugs, Toy	Pagoda	1810	Tea
Willow	1798, 1810, 1817	Table, Tea	Red House	1810	Tea
Lily	1804, 1810, 1817	Table, Tea, Jugs, Toilet	Jesamine	1810	Tea
Tulip	1804, 1810	Table, Tea, Toilet	Shepherd	1810	Tea
Image	1804, 1810, 1814	Table, Tea	Steed	1810	Tea
Hermit	1804, 1810, 1817	Table, Toilet	Sprig	1810	Tea
Pine	1806, 1810	Tea	Chinese Temple	1810	Tea
India	1806, 1809, 1810	Tea, Jug	Nelson	1810	Tea, Jug, Toilet
Windsor Castle	1810	Table	Old Patt'n	1810	Jug, Toilet
Brick(house?)	1810	Table	Broseley	1810, 1811, 1817	Tea, Jug, Toilet
Rose Flower	1810	Table, Tea, Toilet	Farmyard	1813, 1817	Tea
Trophy	1810	Table, Tea	Grotto	1813, 1817	Jug
Roman	1810	Table	Apple tree	1816, 1817	Tea
China Pattn	1810	Table, Tea	Landscape	1817	Table
Star	1810	Table	Dove	1817	Table
Plant	1810	Table	Dragon	1817	Tea
Bird	1810	Table, Toilet	Image Landscape	1817	Tea
Basket	1810, 1817	Table, Tea	Maypole	1817	Jug
Cottage	1810, 1817	Table, Tea	Village	1817	Toilet
Turkish Figure	1810	Tea	Castle	1817, 1820	Toilet
Chinese Figure	1810	Tea, Toy	Rose Bud	1819	
Peony	1810	Tea	Abbey	1820	
Key	1810	Tea	Flower	1820	
Leaf	1810	Tea	Bridge	1820, 1822	

listing of coppers is only given for two years, all of the inventories have a total valuation, as shown in Table 2.2. The 1811 inventory includes the 1810 valuation, followed by 'copper plates additional £145'. This is equivalent to six or seven new tea and tableware patterns, in addition to the work on new patterns already accounted for in 1810. Alternatively much of the increase could be associated with the introduction of a single highly valued set of coppers such as the Cottage tableware pattern listed in 1817. A further indication of the rate at which new patterns were introduced can be obtained from the amounts of new copper purchased. Between 1823 and 1828 accounts[3] indicate that about £25 per year was being spent on copper. Based on the 1817 inventory valuation for new copper, this is equivalent to about 300 pounds of copper. Typically a tableware pattern required 100 pounds of copper plates, a tea pattern 33 pounds and a toiletware pattern about 50 pounds. This indicates that new patterns were probably being introduced at about four or five per year during this period. The constant inventory valuation for copper plates of £450 during this period is either an indication that old patterns were being continually discarded or, more likely, that the entries represented only a nominal valuation. This practise of simply copying the valuation from the previous year was also evident with several other entries, where an accurate audit would have been very time-consuming. Expenditure on copper increased significantly in 1829 to £85, a level approximately maintained until 1835. This would indicate introduction of at least 12 new patterns per year, unless copper had become more expensive or the plates significantly thicker.

The patterns listed in the 1810 and 1817 inventories have been combined with those mentioned in early sales accounts to produce the list of early patterns in Table 2.3. This gives the factory pattern name, the years in which it was mentioned and the type of ware on which the pattern was used. Note that copper plates used for jugs and mugs are distinguished from those for toilet wares including ewers, chambers and bowls. The Table clearly indicates the wide range of blue printed wares produced by Minton during this early period, with over 50 different patterns. More were probably used but are not named in the archive material available. In attributing the wares it may be useful to note that a number of patterns were used on both table and tea wares.

Several of the factory employees interviewed by Mr Stringer in 1873[7] mention early patterns used at the factory, including some in production in the early 1820s when the pearlwares were probably being superseded by the new Semi-China body. Thomas Smith recalls:

> When I came to the works (1814) young Mr Minton looked after the orders and Herbert took an active part in the potting. Samuel Keeling was over the Printers. I recollect a pattern called 'Old English Scenery' of which Mr Minton was very proud, a portion of the engraving was done by himself. This might have been ten years after I came, but I cannot tell precisely. The body of the ware on which this pattern was first printed was of Mr Minton's composition, he said to Hammersely, the Dipper, 'This is my body, and not my body, how do you make that out Dick?' This pattern proved a great success and was only withdrawn altogether but a few years ago.

Further details including an insight into the naming of patterns is found in the recollections of Joseph Day, a printer working at the factory from the early 1820s, who recalled that:

> I have been at the works about 50 years, I can't tell to a year or two, it may be longer. I have been 48 years at printing and recollect that some of the patterns I first worked at were called 'New Flowers', 'Old Corinthian', and old English Scenery. When I came there were a number of old copper plates which had been engraved by Old Mr Minton.

Plate 2.4. Copper plate engraving, c.1810, held at the Minton factory. This was one of the few early engravings found amongst the thousands of plates in the copper plate room. Width 250 mm. See also Plate 4.3.

Plate 2.5. Selection of Willow pattern prints included in the factory pattern book of 1886 (MS 2576). Production of this famous pattern continued into the twentieth century, but some of these engravings probably date from c.1820. See also Plate 4.25.

There was one called the 'Old Brickhouse', another the 'Farmyard' and another 'The Lily'. We printers used to give funny names to the patterns, I remember Arthur Minton coming into the shop and seeing a great lot of ware about of an outline pattern, he enquired what the name of it was, and was told Joe & Charlotte, so called because I Joseph Day printed it and a paintress named Charlotte filled it in. There was another which is still going which always went by the name of Jim in Brown or Jim in Blue, and so named because it was always done by the same printer whose name was James. We generally had the christening of a new pattern – the master engraver Mr Joseph Ford at that time used to give us a present and then we added a little each and sometimes had tea together, and sometimes ale. The engravers I first remember were Saml Buxton, Foreman Jon Hassels and Jesse Shaw who had been apprentice under him, and there was Geo. Hemmings and also Geo. Buxton a son of Saml, the head man. Old Thomas Minton always took much notice of the engraving department, Mr Herbert was very strict with the lads, & he used to be round the works looking after everything by seven in the morning or soon after.

Naming of the patterns by the printers probably meant that it was their general appearance or a distinguishing feature which was more important than, say, the origins of source prints. This approach seems to be confirmed by the rather generic names used in the copper plate lists.

Mary Cartlidge, a transferrer working with Joseph Day and interviewed in March 1873, mentioned further patterns. Note that some of the details are unclear, as denoted by the question marks included in the original text, perhaps due to uncertainty in preparing the transcript from handwritten notes.

> I have worked with Joseph Day 37 years, I was a cutter at first, it will be 49 years next June when I began work. At that time we printed much of the pattern called 'Bridge' and another called 'Basket' done on concave ware, others were named 'Old Hegaist?', 'Old Joe', and 'Kings Lily'. This last continues to sell to this day in tea ware. The copper plates were very thin of the old patterns to what they are now. There was also 'Old Groups', 'Old English Scenery', Gadrae Moisse ?? the subjects in the centre all being different. The last was designed by Mr Baerne.

20

One of the last entries in the notebook comes from Mr J. Hassels, presumably the foreman mentioned by Joseph Day. He gives valuable detail of, presumably, the Roman pattern listed in 1810, and also indicates that the earliest china produced included blue printed wares:

> I forgot to mention a pattern that was done in the Old Gentleman's days, it consisted of a variety of Roman & Grecian figures with a dark ground and was thought very good. I send you two dirty impressions of patterns, the one with the fruit was done I understand in Mr Minton's days of engraving. I send you a china saucer. It was the first china printed pattern they ever had and I believe it came out of the first oven of china made at this works. I send it that you may see the great change that has taken place since those days.

Surviving copper plates have been examined to obtain more definitive information of the early Minton patterns. The copper plate room at the Minton factory contains many thousands of plates tightly racked in pens. Though well designed for plate storage, the dimly-lit room does not lend itself to the location and study of any surviving early plates but fortunately, as indicated above by Mary Cartlidge, early coppers are significantly thinner than later ones, enabling fairly rapid screening of racked plates. The vast majority of the pens contain the later, thicker plates, sorted in patterns. An old index board lists many of these later patterns by name, referring to the location of the plates by pen number. Most of the copper plates had impressed numbers on them, a pen number common to a given pattern, in larger figures, and an individual plate number in smaller figures.

The number of very early plates found was disappointingly small. There were sets of Lily, Willow and Basket plates, mainly in sorted pens, though additional plates were found in odd pens around the room. Also found was a pen containing mainly Broseley pattern plates, together with three other interesting early engravings, one of which is shown in Plate 2.4.

Pattern Books and Source Prints

Although pattern books have been preserved from the first period of bone china production, the earliest blue printed pattern book[8] in the Minton archives is much later, probably dating from around 1870. It contains mainly floral patterns, including pulls from the early Lily pattern. A later book[9] from 1886 contains a number of patterns introduced prior to 1836, including Lily, Willow, Broseley and Old Basket, indicating continued use of these popular patterns throughout the nineteenth century. A typical page from the print book is illustrated in Plate 2.5, showing how only parts of engravings were printed into the book. Another record of some early patterns is provided by a small book simply titled 'Bat Prints',[10] which is undated but probably originated at the end of the nineteenth century as some of the prints are quite late and one includes the date 1882. The prints are roughly grouped into similar subjects and seem to be mainly intended for tea wares. A number of the prints appear to date from before 1836, a typical early example being shown in Plate 2.6. This was probably intended for use on a teapot or sucrier. These Bat Prints are considered in Chapter Eleven.

In addition to the pattern books, there are a number of old source prints in the archives which could have been used as a basis for early Minton designs. One plain covered book[11] has numerous old prints pasted into it, taken from several different publications. An example is shown in Plate 2.7. It depicts Ludlow Castle and was engraved by S. Middiman from an original painting by J.J. Ibbertson and was published on 1 January 1813 in the *Select Views in Great Britain*.[12] Importantly this print has had a faint pencil grid superimposed, no doubt as an aid to the

Plate 2.6. Print included in the Minton Bat Print book (MS 3580). Some of the prints in the book date from the end of the nineteenth century, but this is an early engraving, c.1820, probably intended for use on a teapot or sucrier. The design is a faithful copy of the engraving of Ludlow Castle shown in Plate 2.7. Width 145 mm.

engraver transferring the design to a copper plate. Similar grids are found on many of the prints at the factory, confirming their use as sources for engraved patterns. The Ludlow Castle print in Plate 2.7 has clearly been used as the source for the bat print engraving shown in Plate 2.6.

Shape Books

The earliest remaining shape book[13] is drawn on paper watermarked for 1827. It starts with details of 50 tableware designs, followed by separate sections for tea wares and then jugs. Each design is lettered, A to Z then AA to ZZ, although some letters were not used. The first 31 dinner ware entries are by the same hand and most may have been entered when the book was started to represent the designs available at that time. This initial set of entries is not in chronological order and some of the shapes would appear to have been introduced much earlier than

Plate 2.7. Ludlow Castle engraved by S. Middiman and published in 1813. A faint pencil grid has been superimposed over part of the print as a guide to producing the engraving shown in Plate 2.6. This is one of many early source prints pasted into a plain covered book (MS 1987). Width 182 mm.

1827. The later designs in the book are entered in a different style, probably by other draughtsmen. The typical layout for each dinnerware design (see Appendix) includes details of the soup and sauce tureens, the covered dish, the salad bowl and a plan of the basic profile. An attempt at dating the period of the designs in the book was made by Godden[14] who noted that the thirty-seventh entry, NN, was used during the Minton & Boyle period (1836 to 1841) and that a shape registered in 1846 was not included in the book. A much later Minton shape book,[15] published in 1884, was reproduced in full by Atterbury and Batkin.[16] Although this predominantly shows much later designs it also includes a few shapes introduced prior to 1836.

Attribution of Patterns to Minton

When impressed factory marks were not used, the attribution of early printed wares to a particular factory is made difficult not only because very similar designs were often used by a number of different manufacturers, but also because there was significant intertrading between factories. It has been suggested that this may have included sale of undecorated wares to help complete orders and perhaps even the lending of engravings.[17] Copper plates could also be bought in from factories on their closure, either for continued production or for re-engraving. Given that the Minton factory had its own engraving shops and a significant amount of copper was being purchased for new patterns, it is less likely that old engravings would be sold or engravings bought from other factories for direct use. In attributing patterns it is, however, necessary to be aware of the possibility that Minton copper plates may have been used by other factories or that Minton bought and utilised engravings previously used elsewhere. This requires attribution to be based not just upon details of the design but also upon the quality and characteristics of ceramic body and glaze, the potting characteristics such as shape and stilt marks, and printed or impressed workman's marks, all of which should be more directly associated with a specific factory. Furthermore several characteristic shapes and workman's marks should be linked to an individual pattern to account for the possibility that workers or moulds transferred to another factory. It should be noted, however, that although numerous patterns and shapes have been identified which are close copies of Minton wares and designs, there are always sufficient minor differences in the engravings or the mouldings to confirm that different copper plates or moulds had been used.

Of the available archive material reviewed in this chapter, the few remaining early copper plates, the early engravings illustrated in pattern books and the surviving source prints are probably the most important with respect to attribution of Minton wares. These contain sufficient detail of Minton patterns to distinguish them from the often very similar designs used by other factories. These patterns have been used as the foundation for attribution of the early Minton printed wares. The subsequent identification of a wide range of wares in these key patterns has enabled characteristic Minton shapes, potting characteristics and workman's marks to be established. These have permitted further Minton patterns to be identified, some of which were also used on Minton porcelain. In identifying the early Minton printed wares, matching the pattern to the appropriate contemporary factory name is often very difficult. Where a reasonable link can be made the original pattern name will be adopted. In other cases, either pattern names which have become established in the literature will be retained or, as necessary, new names introduced.

All the patterns which have been attributed to Minton are summarised in the next chapter. This is followed by five chapters which form an illustrated catalogue where each pattern is presented and discussed individually, including the current evidence for its attribution and comparison with any similar designs used by other manufacturers. The patterns are presented in approximately chronological order. The earliest patterns, introduced up to about 1810 and inspired primarily by original Chinese designs, are considered in two groups. The chinoiserie landscape designs are presented in Chapter Four, with the remaining, mainly floral, early designs in Chapter Five. By about 1810 a European influence was becoming more evident in new designs and Chapter Six considers the earliest of these, which were introduced up to about 1820 on a basic pearlware body. Chapter Seven considers the patterns first introduced on the Semi-China body, which was probably produced by Minton between about 1820 and 1825. Chapter Eight considers the patterns introduced on Opaque China, Stone China and Improved Stone China bodies during the 1825 to 1836 period, by which time designs had started to exhibit a more romantic influence.

The illustrations used in cataloguing the patterns are primarily aimed at showing the basic Minton designs and distinguishing them from any other factory versions. For many patterns further illustrations are also included in Chapter Nine in which the main emphasis is on documenting the Minton shapes and potting characteristics and linking these to the available evidence of Minton shapes identified in this chapter.

References

1. G.A. Godden, *Minton Pottery & Porcelain of the First Period* (Barrie & Jenkins, 1968), p. 141.
2. A. Eatwell and A. Warner, 'A London Staffordshire Warehouse', *Journal of the Northern Ceramic Society*, Vol. 8, 1991, p. 120.
3. Minton MS 1257, 1259, 1260, 1261, 1262, Early Sales Accounts (Minton Archives).
4. Minton MS 1228, Inventory and Valuations for Minton Factory 1810–13 (Minton Archives).
5. Minton MS 1282, Inventory and Valuations for Minton Factory 1817–26 (Minton Archives).
6. T.A. Lockett, 'Minton in 1810', *Journal of the Northern Ceramic Society*, Vol. 4, 1981, pp. 1–26.
7. Minton MS 277, Minton's Notebook (Minton Archives).
8. Minton MS 2419, 1870 Printed Pattern Book (Minton Archives).
9. Minton MS 2576, 1886 Printed Pattern Book (Minton Archives).
10. Minton MS 3580, Bat Print Book (Minton Archives).
11. Minton MS 1987, Book of Various Source Prints (Minton Archives).
12. S. Middiman, *Select Views in Great Britain* (London: Boydell & Co, 1813).
13. Minton MS 1584, Shape Book (Minton Archives).
14. Godden, *Minton Pottery*, p. 40.
15. Minton MS 1336, Shape Book (Minton Archives).
16. P. Atterbury and M. Batkin, *The Dictionary of Minton* (Antique Collector's Club, 1990)
17. R. Copeland, *Spode's Willow Pattern and other Designs after the Chinese*, 3rd ed. (Studio Vista, 1999), p. 8.

Chapter Three

Pattern Reference Guide

Early Landscapes

*Plate 3.1. **Hermit or Bridgeless Chinoiserie**, c.1800 (p. 49). A direct copy of a design found painted on Chinese porcelain. Used on dinner and dessert wares. Two original copper plates remain at the factory. The same basic design was used by numerous factories. Dish width 370 mm. Mark P1.*

*Plate 3.2. **Hermit and Boat**, c.1800 (p. 54). Used on hollow ware such as jugs, bowls and mugs, the basic design is distinguished from the Hermit pattern by the beached boat in the foreground. At least one other factory used this design. Bowl diameter 254 mm.*

Plate 3.3. Chaplin, c.1810 (p. 63). An unusual chinoiserie design used on mugs and possibly jugs. Produced by at least one other factory. Mug height 88 mm. Mark P9.

Plate 3.4. Pearl River House, c.1800 (p. 74). The design is a direct copy of a pattern used on Chinese export porcelain. It is found mainly on tea wares and was produced by several factories. Cup height 66 mm. Mark P10.

Plate 3.5. Bird Chinoiserie, c.1800 (p. 55). Used on jugs and bowls, on which it can be found in combination with the Hermit and Boat pattern. A similar design was probably used by at least one other factory. Bowl diameter 254 mm.

Plate 3.6. Fig Tree Chinoiserie, c.1800 (p. 56). Used on jugs and bowls. One original engraving remains at the factory. A similar type of design was used by Stevenson. Bowl diameter 233 mm.

Plate 3.7. One Man Chinoiserie, c.1800 (p. 57). A direct copy of a design found painted on Chinese porcelain. It is found on tea wares and was produced by several factories. This print is from the inside of a Fig Tree Chinoiserie pattern bowl. Print diameter 116 mm.

Plate 3.8. Nankin, c.1800 (p. 77). Found on both normal and toy-sized tea wares. Possibly also used by other factories. Toy saucer, diameter 102 mm. Mark P1.

Plate 3.9. Willow, c.1800 (p. 59). This famous standard Willow design was possibly originally designed by Minton for Spode. It was recorded as being used by Minton in 1798, with subsequent continuous production into the twentieth century. Over 40 Willow engravings remain at the factory. The same basic design was used by most factories. Baking dish width 362 mm. Mark P1.

Plate 3.10. Dagger Border with Temple, c.1800 (p. 70). An early tableware pattern. The same basic design was used by Spode and Barker. Meat dish width 417 mm.

27

Plate 3.11. Chinese Family, c.1805 (p. 72).
An early teaware pattern with a very similar border to the Fisherman pattern. The same basic design was used by at least one other factory. Saucer dish diameter 203 mm. Mark P4.

Plate 3.12. Chinese Garden, c.1805 (p. 76).
The pattern is found on both normal and toy-sized tea wares. No other factory version is known. Saucer dish diameter 210 mm. Mark P3.

Plate 3.13. Fisherman, c.1805 (p. 72).
Found on both table wares and jugs. The design shows some similarities to the Fisherman pattern used on early porcelain at Caughley and Worcester. Sixteen-inch meat dish width 420 mm.

Plate 3.14. Chinaman with Rocket, c.1800 (p. 82). An early teaware pattern. The same basic design was produced by many factories, including Stevenson and, on porcelain, by Turner. Teapot length 245 mm. Mark P1.

Plate 3.15. Chinese Sports, c.1810 (p. 80).
Used on both table and tea wares and often found painted over in coloured enamels. The same design was used painted on bone china as Pattern No. 539, which was introduced in 1810. Plate diameter 250 mm. Mark P6.

Plate 3.16. Oriental Family, c.1810 (p. 81).
A teaware pattern similar in type to Chinese Family. At least one other factory used the same basic design. Creamer length 148 mm. Mark P9.

Plate 3.17. Broseley, c.1810 (p. 64). Perhaps the most famous and widely used printed teaware pattern. Originally christened by Minton during his apprenticeship at the Caughley china works and engraved by him as an early Spode pattern. Minton used the pattern on both china and earthenware, including some use on table wares. Twenty-six copper plates remain at the factory. Almost identical versions of the design were used by most factories. China teapot stand width 192 mm.

Plate 3.18. Bridge, c.1805 (p. 78). A teaware pattern which was also produced at several other factories, including Spode who also used a version on china table wares. Teapot length 222 mm.

29

Plate 3.19. China Pattern, c.1800 (p. 84). *The pattern is a direct copy of a design found painted on Chinese porcelain. It was used on both table and tea wares, including use on early bone china. No other factory version is known. Wicker plate diameter 181 mm. Mark P1.*

Early Floral Designs

Plate 3.20. Star, c.1805 (p. 92). *Used on table and toilet wares. The pattern is occasionally found painted over in coloured enamels. Star is listed as a pattern in the 1810 inventory. No other factory version is known. Soup plate diameter 238 mm.*

Plate 3.21. Lily, c.1800 (p. 87). *One of the earliest patterns used on both table and tea wares. Also used on bone china as Pattern No. 123. The pattern was still being produced at the end of the nineteenth century. Some 40 copper plates remain at the factory. Several other factories used very similar designs. Dessert dish width 247 mm.*

Plate 3.22. Stylised Floral, c.1800 (p. 90). *Used on tea wares and produced by several factories on a range of wares. Saucer diameter 138 mm. Mark P4.*

Plate 3.23. Dragon, c.1810 (p. 110). Used on tea wares and listed in the 1817 inventory. The pattern was produced by several factories, normally on bone china. Pearlware coffee can diameter 65 mm.

Plate 3.24. Trophy, c.1800 (p. 106). Listed in 1810 as both a table and a teaware pattern. The design is a direct copy of an original found painted on Chinese porcelain. The same basic pattern was used by numerous factories. Plate diameter 241 mm.

Plate 3.25. Pinwheels, c.1805 (p. 92). Used on tablewares. An almost identical pattern was produced by at least one other factory. Dessert dish width 248 mm.

Plate 3.26. Basket, c.1805 (p. 94). Used on both table and tea wares, this popular design was still being produced at the end of the nineteenth century. Thirty-two copper plates remain at the factory, some of which can be dated to c.1805. A different flower arrangement was used for each engraving. Basket was listed in both 1810 and 1817 inventories. The pattern was also used on early bone china. Several other factories used the same design with very similar flower arrangements. Meat dish width 472 mm.

Plate 3.27 (top left). Plant, c.1810 (p. 109).
A relatively rare pattern found on dinner and dessert wares. Note the distinctive border which helps to distinguish this from similar botanical patterns produced at other factories, including Wedgwood. Plate diameter 241 mm. Mark P4.

Plate 3.29 (left). Dahlia, c.1810 (p. 107).
Used on both table and tea earthenwares, and on first period bone china as Pattern No. 124. An almost identical pattern was produced by Coalport and probably other factories. Basket width 242 mm.

European Influence

Plate 3.28 (top right). Queen of Sheba, c.1810 (p. 113). Used on both normal and toy-sized octagonal dinner wares. Another factory used a very similar version on jugs. Plate width 235 mm. Mark P11.

Plate 3.30 (bottom left). Roman, c.1810 (p. 114). A series of designs, copied from engravings of Greek and Roman figures by Kirk published in 1804, and used on dinner and dessert wares. Similar series were produced by Spode, Knottingly and possibly Herculaneum. Sauce tureen stand width 197 mm. Mark P7.

Plate 3.31. Camel and Giraffe, c.1815 (p. 127). An unusual design with a chinoiserie-type landscape incorporating an Arabian Camel and a Cameleopard or Giraffe from Bewick engravings. Used on dinner and dessert wares. Plate width 247 mm. Mark P4.

Plate 3.32. Bewick Stag, c.1815 (p. 125). Both the stag and animals in the border are based on Bewick engravings. Used on dinner and dessert wares. Also used painted on first period bone china. Plate width 246 mm. Mark P2.

Plate 3.33. Bird or Ornithological Series, c.1810 (p. 120). A series of finely engraved birds based on Bewick engravings. Used on dinner and dessert wares. Very similar series were produced by other factories, including Stevenson. Basket width 244 mm. Mark P2.

Plate 3.34. Shepherd, c.1810 (p. 111). A teaware pattern which was probably also produced by at least one other major factory. Teapot length 244 mm.

Plate 3.35. Castle Gateway, c.1815 (p. 137).
A toiletware pattern with a deep border similar in some respects to that found on Monk's Rock series jugs. Bowl diameter 330 mm. Mark P14.

Plate 3.36. Ruined Abbey, c.1820 (p. 140).
An attractive toiletware pattern with a deep floral border. Bowl diameter 300 mm. Mark P13.

Plate 3.37. Monk's Rock series, c.1815 (p. 127).
A series of fine rural landscape scenes within a floral border. Original source prints for most of the scenes remain at the factory. Used on dinner and dessert wares and jugs. Eighteen-inch size meat dish. Width 471 mm.

Plate 3.38. Dove, c.1815 (p. 139). A floral type pattern used on dinner and dessert wares. The pattern was probably contemporary with the Monk's Rock series, and represents relatively late use of an oriental type design. Sauce tureen stand width 193 mm.

Plate 3.39. Benevolent Cottagers, c.1815 (p. 148). A fine pattern featuring a cottage scene, used on dinner and dessert wares. The design is based on a painting called 'The Benevolent Cottagers'. Plate width 187 mm. Mark P4.

Plate 3.40. Maypole, c.1815 (p. 138). A rural scene with floral border used on jugs, mugs and vases. Maypole is listed in the 1817 inventory copper plate list. Height of mug 125 mm.

Plate 3.41. Cottage and Cart, c.1815 (p. 146). A rural scene used on toy-sized tea wares. Teapot length 145 mm.

Plate 3.42. Cottage and Cows, c.1815 (p. 143). A relatively rare teaware pattern featuring a typical rural scene. Teapot length 243 mm. Mark P2.

Plate 3.43. Farmyard, c.1813 (p. 144). *A teaware pattern featuring a farmyard scene. Farmyard is mentioned as a teaware pattern in factory accounts for 1813, and included in the 1817 inventory. Essentially the same pattern was also produced by another factory. Saucer diameter 142 mm. Mark P9.*

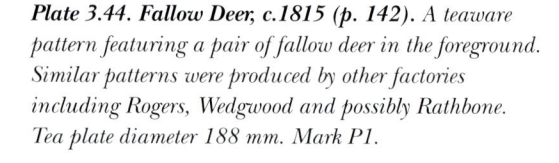

Plate 3.44. Fallow Deer, c.1815 (p. 142). *A teaware pattern featuring a pair of fallow deer in the foreground. Similar patterns were produced by other factories including Rogers, Wedgwood and possibly Rathbone. Tea plate diameter 188 mm. Mark P1.*

Plate 3.45. Domed Building, c.1815 (p. 143). *The pattern features a distinctive building with a domed roof and was used on toy-sized tea wares. Teapot length 138 mm. Mark P12.*

Plate 3.46. Apple Tree, c.1815 (p. 147). *A teaware pattern featuring a family picking apples. Apple Tree is mentioned as a teaware pattern in 1816 factory accounts and listed in the 1817 inventory. Coffee pot height 272 mm. Mark P12.*

Plate 3.47. Carisbrooke Castle, c.1815 (p. 141). A fine toiletware pattern featuring a view of Carisbrooke Castle, Isle of Wight, within a deep border. The original source print for the central design remains at the factory. Bowl diameter 254 mm.

Plate 3.48. Japan Vase, c.1815 (p. 149). A Japan-type pattern with an outline print featuring a central vase, painted over in coloured enamels. Used on dinner and dessert wares. Plate diameter 217 mm.

Plate 3.49. Fruit, c.1815 (p. 148). A dessertware pattern featuring various fruit and foliage on a blue ground. Often found painted over in coloured enamels. Dish width 262 mm.

Plate 3.50. Forbes Castle, c.1820 (p. 145). A teaware pattern featuring a view of Forbes Castle, Aberdeenshire. Teapot length 237 mm.

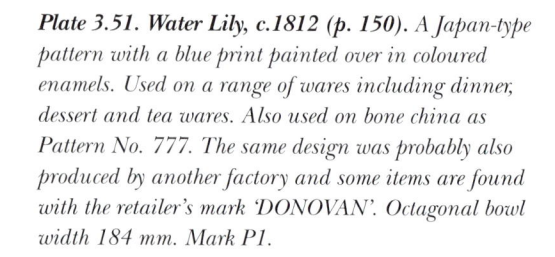

Plate 3.51. Water Lily, c.1812 (p. 150). A Japan-type pattern with a blue print painted over in coloured enamels. Used on a range of wares including dinner, dessert and tea wares. Also used on bone china as Pattern No. 777. The same design was probably also produced by another factory and some items are found with the retailer's mark 'DONOVAN'. Octagonal bowl width 184 mm. Mark P1.

Plate 3.52. Exotic Birds, c.1815 (p. 149). A Japan-type pattern with a print painted over in coloured enamels. Used on toilet wares. Potpourri jar foot diameter 192 mm.

Semi-China

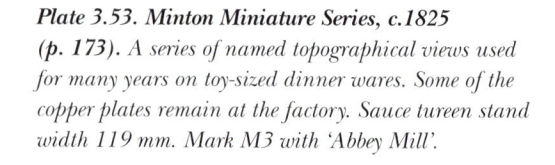

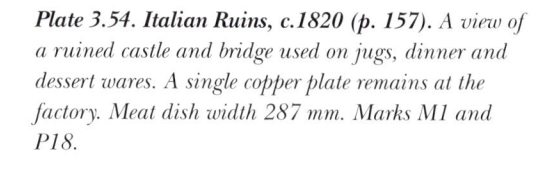

Plate 3.53. Minton Miniature Series, c.1825 (p. 173). A series of named topographical views used for many years on toy-sized dinner wares. Some of the copper plates remain at the factory. Sauce tureen stand width 119 mm. Mark M3 with 'Abbey Mill'.

Plate 3.54. Italian Ruins, c.1820 (p. 157). A view of a ruined castle and bridge used on jugs, dinner and dessert wares. A single copper plate remains at the factory. Meat dish width 287 mm. Marks M1 and P18.

Plate 3.55. Girl with Puppies, c.1820 (p. 176).
A relatively rare teaware pattern. Saucer dish diameter 200 mm. Marks M1 and P13.

Plate 3.56. Dying Tree, c.1818 (p. 156).
A teaware pattern, perhaps introduced on pearlware. Saucer diameter 143 mm. Mark P15.

Plate 3.57. English Scenery, c.1824 (p. 160).
A series of landscape views within a floral border used for many years, mainly on dinner and dessert wares. Thomas Minton is reputed to have assisted in the engraving. Some source prints remain at the factory. Sixteen-inch meat dish width 416 mm. Mark M2.

Plate 3.58. Riverside Cottage, c.1820 (p. 156).
A relatively rare teaware pattern featuring rural views with a floral border. Slop bowl diameter 160 mm. Mark M1.

Plate 3.59. Botanical Groups, c.1825 (p. 176). Featuring distinct bunches or groups of flowers on a blue ground with a distinctive edging border. Used on toiletwares in the 1820s and 1830s. Similar patterns were produced by other factories. Ewer height 242 mm. Mark M1.

Plate 3.60. Leaf, c.1825 (p. 182). Probably a teaware pattern. Ewer-shaped milk jug height 104 mm. Marks M1 and P2.

Plate 3.61. Floral Vases, c.1825 (p. 179). Featuring various vases of flowers on a blue ground. Used on a range of tea wares and jugs. Also used on bone china tea wares. Close copies of the design were produced by at least two other factories. Teapot length 239 mm. Marks M1 and P16.

Plate 3.62. Botanical, c.1825 (p. 178). Featuring finely engraved flowers on a blue ground with a simple edging border. Used on jugs and mugs. Similar in some respects to the Botanical Groups patterns. Similar designs were produced by other factories. Roman shape jug height 201 mm. Mark P16.

Plate 3.63. Botanical Vase, c.1820 (p. 182).
An impressive dinnerware pattern featuring a vase of flowers on a blue ground. Possibly introduced at the end of the pearlware period. A single copper plate engraving remains at the factory. A variant of the design was used on toilet wares. Soup plate diameter 243 mm.

Plate 3.64. Floral Cottage, c.1820 (p. 176).
A floral teaware design with a border containing panels decorated with cottage scenes. The example shown has been overpainted in coloured enamels, but this may not always have been done. Plate diameter 167 mm. Marks M1 and P2.

Plate 3.65. Filigree, c.1823 (p. 184). A relatively common pattern featuring a series of floral arrangements within a vase. Used on dinner and dessert wares for many years. Copied by at least one other factory. Similar to the Spode design introduced in 1823. Sixteen-inch meat dish width 421 mm. Mark M1.

Plate 3.66. Bamboo and Flowers, c.1820 (p. 153).
A relatively common pattern which was used on a wide variety of wares, including jugs, mugs, dinner, dessert and tea wares. Sixteen-inch meat dish width 426 mm. Marks M1 and P4.

Plate 3.67. Dresden, c.1825 (p. 191).
A distinctive floral design used on dinner and dessert wares. Soup plate diameter 247 mm. Mark M5.

Opaque China

Plate 3.68. Dresden Embossed, c.1825 (p. 191). The main floral design exactly matches that used on the Dresden pattern in Plate 3.67, indeed common engravings seem to have been used. This second version of the pattern uses a different border, however, and is found on table and toilet wares of distinctive shapes with embossed mouldings. Dresden Embossed wares are listed in the 1825 and 1826 factory inventories. Opaque China plate diameter 226 mm. Mark M6.

Plate 3.69. Dresden Flowers, c.1825 (p. 200). A floral design used on toy tea and table wares and produced over many years. Some copper plates remain at the factory, including the characteristic printed mark. Opaque China cup and saucer, diameter 110 mm, marks M9 and P2.

Plate 3.70. Chinese Marine, c.1827 (p. 212). A series of oriental landscapes within a floral border. Used on a wide variety of table and toilet wares. Close copies were produced by many other factories. Opaque China soup tureen stand width 428 mm. Mark M15.

Plate 3.71. Florentine, c.1827 (p. 195).
A distinctive floral design used on a wide variety of table and toilet wares and produced over many years. One copper plate remains at the factory. A version with additional floral border elements is found on embossed wares. Plate diameter 251 mm. Marks M7 and M31.

Plate 3.72. Swiss Cottage, c.1827 (p. 201). A teaware pattern featuring alpine type cottage views. Opaque China broth bowl stand, diameter 154 mm. Mark M11.

Plate 3.73. Flora, c.1827 (p. 201). A floral design used on tea wares and associated items. Opaque China cup and saucer, diameter 137 mm. Mark M10.

Plate 3.74. Genevese, c.1827 (p. 206). A series of romantic landscape views featuring alpine chalets within a floral border. Used on table and toilet wares and produced over many years. Close copies were produced by other factories. Copper plates remain at the factory and some prints are included in a factory pattern book. Opaque China meat dish, width 428 mm. Mark M14.

Plate 3.75. Corinthian, c.1827 (p. 203). An elaborate floral design used on embossed tablewares. Also used on Stone China tea wares as Corinthian Embossed. Opaque China soup plate diameter 259 mm. Marks M12 and P15.

Stone China

Plate 3.76. Wreath, c.1830 (p. 220). A floral design featuring a central rose spray surrounded by a floral wreath border. Introduced on Stone China dinner wares. Improved Stone China soup plate diameter 262 mm. Marks M17 and M31.

Plate 3.77. Claremont, c.1830 (p. 224). A floral design introduced on Stone China toilet wares, with later use on tea wares. Copper plate engravings remain at the factory. Stone China toilet box, length 202 mm, mark M20.

Plate 3.78. British Views c.1830 (p. 225). A series of landscape views within a floral border. Despite having an apparently authentic Minton printed mark, an example of this pattern is yet to be attributed to Minton. Several factories used the same border and landscape scenes. Earthenware 16-inch meat dish, width 425 mm, mark M21.

Plate 3.79. Berlin Roses, c.1830 (p. 220). A floral design with roses and similar to the Wreath pattern. Introduced on Stone China dinner wares. A copper plate engraving remains at the factory. Stone China stand, diameter 312 mm, mark M18.

Plate 3.80. Berlin Chaplet, c.1830 (p. 220). An elaborate floral pattern perhaps inspired by embroidery designs published in Berlin. Introduced on Stone China dinner wares. The pattern, mark and basic shapes were copied by at least one other factory. Stone China plate, diameter 262 mm. Marks M19 and P14.

Plate 3.81. Royal Persian, c.1827 (p. 218). A floral design which includes a fence and a flying insect. Used on dinner wares with a characteristic printed mark which can include 'Stone China' or 'Opaque China'. The same design was probably also used by at least one other factory. Opaque China sauce tureen stand, width 207 mm, mark M16a.

Plate 3.82. Japan type patterns, c.1825 (pp. 226–28). Examples of early overpainted printed patterns from the new number series introduced by Minton in c.1825, and used on both china and earthenware. Pattern No. 53 mug (Plate 8.71). Pattern No. 59 Chinese Marine Opaque China plate, diameter 266 mm. Pattern No. 62 Amhurst Japan sauce tureen (Plate 8.67). Pattern No. 89 plate (Plate 8.72).

45

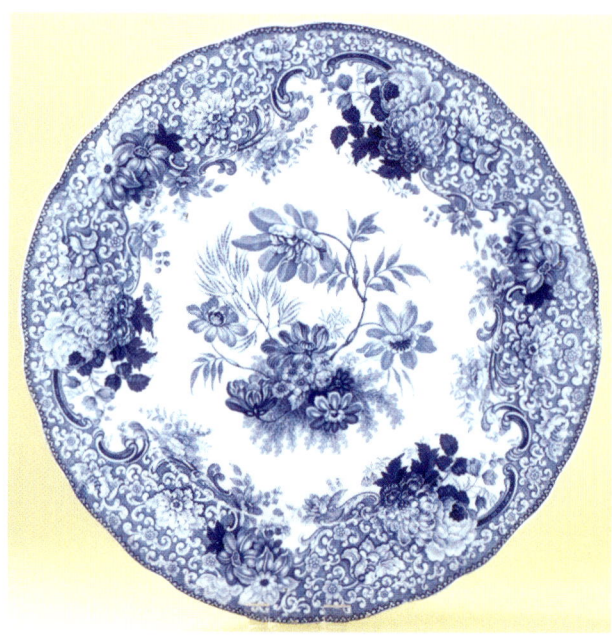

Improved Stone China

Plate 3.83. Chinese Fence, c.1835 (p. 232). Copied from a design found painted on Chinese porcelain and used on dinner wares. The outline print on this example has been painted in with underglaze blue. A version in a Minton pattern book is painted in coloured enamels. Improved Stone China dinner plate, diameter 251 mm. Mark M31.

Plate 3.84. Arabesque, c.1835 (p. 230). A delicate design featuring various central floral arrangements surrounded by a floral border. Used on dinner wares. Improved Stone China dinner plate diameter 263 mm. Marks M24 and M31.

Plate 3.85. Trellis and Plants, c.1830 (p. 228). A series of botanical specimens surrounded by a trellis border. Used on dinner wares. Sauce tureen stand, width 201 mm, mark M23.

Plate 3.86. Lace Border, c.1835 (p. 232). A distinctive floral design with a lace border. Used on dinner wares. Improved Stone China 11-inch baking dish. Width 300 mm. Marks M25 and M31.

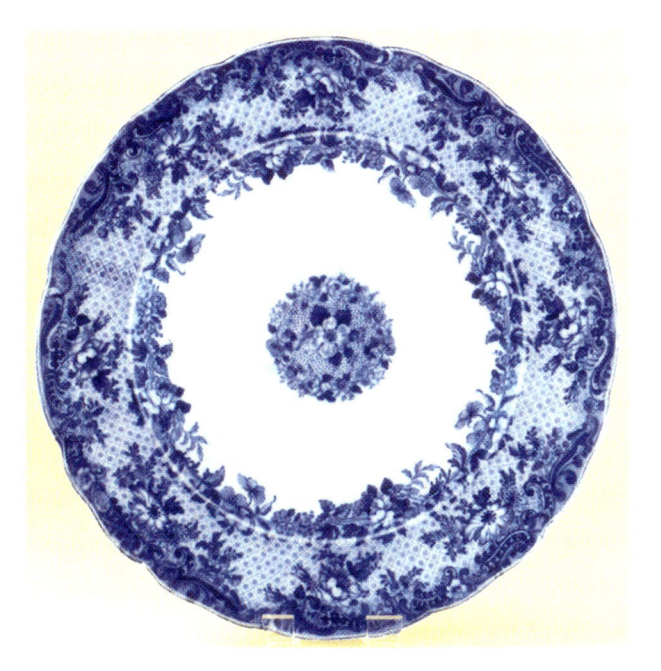

Plate 3.87. Rose and Violet Star, c.1835 (p. 235).
A simple design with a relatively small central floral print surrounded by the same floral border as used with the Rose and Violet Wreath pattern. Used on dinner wares. Improved Stone China plate, diameter 200 mm. Marks M27 and M31.

Plate 3.88. Sicilian, c.1833 (p. 240). A series of stylised romantic landscapes within a floral border. Used on dinner and dessert wares. A very similar pattern with the same printed mark was used by Pountney and Allies. Improved Stone China dinner plate diameter 264 mm. Marks M29 and M31.

Plate 3.89. Verona, c.1833 (p. 236). A series of stylised romantic landscapes within a floral border. Used on a wide range of wares. Several copper plate engravings and an original pencil drawing remain at the factory. Stone China 14-inch dish, width 383 mm. Mark M28.

Plate 3.90. Rose and Violet Wreath, c.1833 (p. 234).
An attractive series of Eastern landscape views within a border incorporating a wreath of roses and violets. Used on dinner wares. A copper plate engraving remains at the factory. Improved Stone China 18-inch gravy dish, width 469 mm. Marks M26, M31 and impressed size mark '18'.

Plate 3.91. Floweret (tureen base only), c.1835 (p.246). A distinctive floral type pattern introduced on dinner wares probably in the early 1830s. A copper plate engraving remains at the factory, including the usual printed cartouche mark. Soup tureen with replacement Rose and Violet Wreath pattern lid. Stone China or Improved Stone China body. Length 350 mm. Mark M30.

Plate 3.92. Pattern No. 252, c.1827 (p.246). Minton used this distinctive dragon design on bone china tea wares. Copper plate engravings remain at the factory, including the characteristic printed seal mark normally found with the pattern. Bone china tea plate, diameter 198 mm.

Black and Bat Prints

Plate 3.93. Bat printed pearlware spill vase, c.1820. Minton used black and bat printing on both pearlwares and bone china. A bat print book remaining at the factory includes many of the early designs used. Details are given in Chapter Eleven. This spill vase is decorated on one side with the view of Fulham illustrated (see also Plate 11.3), and on the other side with a print titled Gray's Cliffe (print B36). Height 120 mm.

Chapter Four

Catalogue of Patterns
1. Early Landscapes

Bridgeless Chinoiserie or Hermit

As with most of the early landscapes considered in this chapter, this pattern is a direct copy of a design found painted in blue on Chinese export porcelain, as illustrated in Plate 4.1. It was used by numerous manufacturers and is traditionally referred to as Bridgeless Chinoiserie. The Minton examples found show variation in body and of engraving style indicating production over many years. The earliest examples use line engraving for ground areas suggesting that the pattern was introduced around 1800. A likely factory name is Hermit, this being the only appropriate tableware pattern mentioned both in the early accounts, where significant sales to Chamberlain's are recorded between 1804 and 1811 with a plate recorded as returned from Chamberlain's in 1825, and also in the 1810 and the 1817 inventory copper plate lists. Only two copper plates with this early design remain at the factory, each having a pen number 203. One, which has no outer border, is detailed in Plate 4.2. It has fine line engraving of the ground area and a plate number of 5945, which forms part of the Broseley series of Minton coppers. The other engraving, shown in Plates 2.4 and 4.3, is complete with border and has

Plate 4.1. Chinese export porcelain dinner plate, painted in blue, c.1790. This is the original design for the Bridgeless Chinoiserie pattern, as produced by several factories in the 1800 to 1820 period. Minton closely copied both the pattern details and the plate shape and probably referred to this as the Hermit pattern. Diameter 242 mm. Single recessed foot ring.

Plate 4.2. Detail of an early Minton copper plate engraving of a chinoiserie design, c.1805. This is assumed to correspond to the Hermit tableware pattern mentioned in the 1804 sales accounts and included in the 1810 and 1817 inventories. Fine line engraving has been used in the foreground. There is no outer border and the engraving is too large for use on a dinner plate, so it may have been intended for use on a circular stand. Diameter of engraving 223 mm.

Plate 4.3. Detail of the only other copper plate engraving of the Hermit pattern found at the factory, c.1810. It was probably produced several years after the example in Plate 4.2 as stipple engraving has been used for the foreground. This engraving, which would have been used on a table plate, clearly illustrates the outer border design. Comparison of the two Hermit pattern copper plates highlights the important common features which help to identify the Minton version of this pattern. These include the arrangement of the seven birds to the left of the sky, the absence of a solid pillar at the left of the main building and the detail of the figure inside the door. Despite being different sizes and probably engraved at different times, the correspondence in detail between the two engravings is very good. The only main difference is in the pair of trees at the left of the upper island, with the later engraving having a distinctive angular design of the foliage. Width of engraving 224 mm, diameter to the outer edge of the inner border 159 mm.

stipple engraved ground, so probably post-dates the other copper. Sufficient examples of this version of the pattern have been found on wares of characteristic early Minton shape, and with a range of Minton workman's marks, to confirm that these were original Minton copper plates.

The Hermit pattern was produced by a number of factories and the various versions can be placed in two groups, distinguished by the absence or presence of a solid pillar on the left corner of the main building. Minton used a pillarless

Plate 4.4. *Minton Hermit pattern pearlware plate c.1805. Note the distinctive arrangement of seven birds and the absence of a solid pillar on the left of the main building. This pattern is similar to the engraving shown in Plate 4.2, although the hard glassy glaze makes it difficult to determine if fine line engraving has been used in the foreground. Diameter 240 mm. Mark P1.*

version with a distinctive arrangement of seven birds in the sky. It was used on Trophy shape dinner wares with plain circular plates as shown in Plates 4.4 and 4.5. The dinner plate in Plate 4.4 has a hard glassy glaze, typical of early Minton wares, and could have been made around 1805. The example illustrated in Plate 4.5 has a clearer glaze and was probably made between 1815 and 1820. The most commonly found marked examples of this pattern were produced by Davenport, as illustrated in Plate 4.6. Compared to the Minton version, the main distinguishing feature of the Davenport plate is the absence of an inner border, though numerous other differences in detail are apparent. A fine quality plate by an unknown maker decorated in another pillarless version is shown in Plate 4.7. Further examples of the Hermit pattern are found impressed 'STEVENSON'. These can be either without a pillar, as in Plate 4.8, or with a pillar.[1] They have been linked to the brothers Andrew and Ralph Stevenson potting in Staffordshire.[2] Given the early date of the illustrated plate it is possible that it was the product of Ralph Stevenson potting in Corbridge in partnership with John Dale.[2] Distinguishing between Minton and Stevenson Hermit wares is made more difficult by a common use of plain circular and oval shapes, whereas other manufacturers appeared to have used plain octagonal shapes. The Stevenson plate in Plate 4.8 also has the same potting characteristics as Minton Trophy shape plates, with a single recessed foot ring and three single stilt marks beneath the rim, although the Minton eight-inch plate was, however, slightly bigger with a diameter of about 215 mm. This highlights the difficulty in distinguishing between different factory versions of the early chinoiserie patterns. Don also used a pillarless version, as shown in Plate 4.9, but again this is clearly distinguished from the Minton design by minor variations, including the absence of birds. Plate 4.10 shows a pillared version which in other respects closely matches the Don design. Further examples of pillared versions by unknown makers are shown in Plates 4.11 and 4.12, the latter being interesting as its bird arrangement closely matches that used by Minton. A further version of the Hermit pattern was found on earthenware dinnerware shards excavated from the Coalport pottery site.[3]

Plate 4.5. Minton pearlware Hermit pattern plate, c.1815. A slightly later version very similar to the engraving shown in Plate 4.3, with stipple engraving to the foreground and the distinctive treatment of the island trees. In other respects the design corresponds closely to that shown in Plate 4.4. Diameter 244 mm.

Plate 4.6. Davenport Hermit pattern pearlware plate, c.1810. Compared to the Minton version many differences in detail can be found. Note also the absence of an inner border. The good quality print uses line engraving for the foreground. No foot ring, three triple rear and single front stilt marks. Width 239 mm. Impressed 'Davenport' over an anchor.

Plate 4.7. Fine quality pearlware plate by an unknown maker, c.1810. The print differs from all attributed versions. The border is distinctive with the feature at one o'clock having the outer scrolls complete. A similar border is used on Longbridge pattern plates illustrated by Morton-Nance as Swansea.[4] No foot ring, three single stilt marks on base. Width 238 mm.

Plate 4.8. Stevenson Hermit pattern pearlware eight-inch plate, c.1805. Line engraved ground areas. Although this pillarless version is seen to have no birds, other Stevenson examples illustrated, both with[1] and without[2] a pillar, have birds present. Single recessed foot ring, three single stilt marks under rim. Diameter 205 mm. Impressed 'STEVENSON' (mark 24 mm long).

Plate 4.9. *Don Hermit pattern pearlware plate, c.1815. Note the more cramped appearance compared to the other illustrated pillarless examples and the absence of birds. The plate is quite heavily potted. Single recessed foot ring, three triple rear and single front stilt marks. Width 234 mm. Impressed 'DON POTTERY'.*

Plate 4.10. *Pillared Hermit pattern earthenware plate by an unknown maker, c.1820. Apart from the pillar, it closely matches the Don design, perhaps indicating a Yorkshire origin. The plate is quite heavily potted and of poor quality. No foot ring, three triple rear and single front stilt marks. Width 252 mm.*

Plate 4.11. *Very distinctive pillared version of the Hermit pattern on a pearlware plate by an unknown maker, c.1810. Line engraved ground. No foot ring, three single rear stilt marks. Width 241 mm.*

Plate 4.12. *Pearlware plate with a pillared version of the Hermit pattern by an unknown maker, c.1810. Note that the arrangement of the birds closely matches that used by Minton. Line engraved ground. Single recessed foot ring, three single front stilt marks. Width 210 mm.*

Plate 4.13. Minton Hermit and Boat pattern pearlware bowl, c.1805. The pattern closely resembles the Hermit dinnerware pattern, but has an extension to the main building and a distinctive boat in the foreground. These extra features help to adapt the pattern to use on hollow wares. In decorating bowls, factories sometimes used several patterns in combination. In this case the other side of the bowl has a different chinoiserie design, as shown in Plate 4.15. The inner border corresponds to that used on the mug shown in Plate 4.14. Diameter 254 mm.

Hermit and Boat

This would seem to be the version of Hermit used by Minton on mugs, jugs and bowls. It is essentially the same as Hermit but with the addition of a grounded boat in the foreground and a stilted building to the left of the normal main pillarless building. The bowl illustrated in Plate 4.13 gives a good illustration of the overall pattern. The border is different from that used on Hermit, as shown on the mug in Plate 4.14. The pattern is attributed to Minton based on the distinctive handle forms used on mugs and jugs, and printed workman's marks. Apparently the only other factory to use this pattern was at Coalport[3] where shards from a mug were found decorated with a very similar design. The Coalport version shows several minor variations to the main design and border, including a pillar to the main building.

Plate 4.14. Two views of a Minton Hermit and Boat pattern pearlware mug, c.1800. The distinctive border normally found with this design is clearly shown, as are the unusual trees to the left of the main buildings, which are not clear on the bowl illustrated in Plate 4.13. The mug can be attributed to Minton based on the distinctive moulded handle form, which was used with several patterns into the 1820s. Height 143 mm. Mark P4.

Plate 4.15. *The opposite side of the bowl shown in Plate 4.13, showing the distinctive Bird Chinoiserie design used by Minton on jugs and bowls, c.1805. The design in the centre of the bowl is shown in Plate 4.16. Although often found in combination with the Hermit and Boat pattern, this unusual chinoiserie design has a different border, as illustrated in Plate 4.17. Diameter 254 mm.*

Bird Chinoiserie

This is another early pattern used on jugs and bowls. It is attributed to Minton based on its use in conjunction with the Hermit and Boat pattern on bowls, as illustrated in Plate 4.15. The pattern is seen to be a very nondescript chinoiserie design and the only inspiration for a name comes from the two strange birds. The inner bowl design and characteristic border are shown in Plates 4.16 and 4.17. Apart from bowls, the only other piece found to date is an early spill vase of characteristic Minton shape. A similar design has been seen on early earthenware tea wares, possibly made by Wedgwood.

Plate 4.16. *Detail of the central decoration inside the Minton bowl shown in Plates 4.13 and 4.15. Although the birds are missing and boats have appeared, the design is clearly associated with the Bird Chinoiserie pattern.*

Plate 4.17. *Inside of an early Minton pearlware footed bowl decorated with both the Bird Chinoiserie and the Hermit and Boat patterns, c.1805. The border is that specifically associated with the Bird Chinoiserie pattern. Diameter 190 mm. Mark P10.*

Plate 4.18. Minton Fig Tree Chinoiserie pattern, printed from an early line engraving on the reverse of the Hermit copper plate illustrated in Plate 4.2. This is the only engraving of the pattern found at the factory. Areas of damage incurred during reworking of the copper plate can be clearly seen. Found on jugs and bowls, this is probably one of the first patterns produced by the factory at the end of the eighteenth century. This engraving was probably intended for use inside the centre of a bowl. Engraving diameter 151 mm.

Fig Tree Chinoiserie

It had been hoped that some evidence of early patterns would be found on the back of reworked copper plates. A significant find was on the reverse of the Hermit pattern engraving, shown in Plate 4.2, where there is the rather damaged but very interesting early line-engraved chinoiserie scene illustrated in Plate 4.18. The pattern takes its name from the distinctive tree in the foreground. To date the pattern has only been noted on jugs and bowls, although examples are rarely found so it is possible that other items such as mugs were also produced. Typical early Minton wares decorated in this pattern are shown in Plates 4.19 and 4.20. Both pieces are of fine quality with extensive use of line engraving. A barrel-shaped jug of Minton form decorated in this pattern is illustrated by Henrywood,[5] where it is wrongly identified as the 'Chinaman with Rocket pattern' as shown at the end of this chapter.

The border used by Minton with the Fig Tree Chinoiserie pattern is clearly illustrated in Plates 4.19 and 4.21. A very similar border was used on a bowl decorated with a different chinoiserie pattern,[6] but close inspection of original photographs of that bowl reveal a number of differences of detail, sufficient to make it probable that the bowl was made by another manufacturer. In addition to an almost identical border being used elsewhere, a similar Fig Tree pattern was used by Stevenson,[2] although in this case there are sufficient differences to easily distinguish the two designs in addition to the border being different.

Plate 4.19. Two views of a fine Minton pearlware jug decorated with the Fig Tree Chinoiserie pattern, c.1800. Although the overall layout of the pattern has been adapted to fit the jug, the main features correspond closely to the engraving found at the factory and shown in Plate 4.18. Note the characteristic Minton handle shape. Height 217 mm.

One Man Chinoiserie

The Fig Tree Chinoiserie pattern bowl shown in Plate 4.20 is particularly interesting in that a completely different pattern has been used inside at its centre, as shown in Plates 4.21 and 4.22. The pattern is traditionally called One Man Chinoiserie, referring to the single person crossing the bridge, and is based on an original Chinese design, as shown in Plate 4.23. The attribution of the pattern to Minton is currently based solely on its use in conjunction with the Fig Tree Chinoiserie pattern on the illustrated bowl and the coffee can illustrated in Plate 4.24, which has a typical Minton handle and workman's mark. Hopefully further examples can be found to confirm the attribution.

The pattern was used on tea wares by several manufacturers, notably by Shorthouse and Co. for whom marked examples are known.[7] Earthenware

Plate 4.20. Early Minton Fig Tree Chinoiserie bowl, c.1800. As with the jug in Plate 4.19, the piece is well potted in a fine compact pearlware body and the print shows extensive use of line engraving. A different print is used on the other side of the bowl, as shown in Plate 9.106. The border inside the bowl can be seen in Plate 4.21 to correspond to that on the jug. Diameter 233 mm.

Plate 4.21. Inside of the Minton Fig Tree Chinoiserie bowl shown in Plate 4.20. The distinctive border matches that used on the jug in Plate 4.19. The central print is particularly interesting as it is a different pattern, as detailed in Plate 4.22.

Plate 4.22. Detail of a line engraved print found inside a Minton Fig Tree Chinoiserie bowl, c.1800. Traditionally called One Man Chinoiserie, this pattern was used on tea wares by several manufacturers. Print diameter 116 mm.

teaware shards with this pattern have also been found at Coalport.[8] Careful attention to minor detail within the print is required to distinguish the different versions. The print shown in Plate 4.22 appears to correspond to that recorded on a fine Argyll.[9] The pattern is normally found on earthenwares; although it is found on a teapot described as blue painted on porcelain in Miller,[10] this description is subject to some doubt and the shape closely matches the pearlware teapot shown in Plate 4.82.

Plate 4.23. Hand-painted Chinese export porcelain saucer, c.1790. This original oriental design has clearly been used as the basis for the One Man Chinoiserie pattern. Diameter 157 mm.

Plate 4.24. Pearlware One Man Chinoiserie coffee can, possibly Minton, c.1800. Note the typical angular moulded handle. Gilded rim. Height 60 mm. Mark P5.

Plate 4.25a&b. Detail of Willow pattern prints included on page 2 of the factory pattern book of 1886 (see also Plate 2.5). The dark gable ends on the building at the water's edge are clearly shown on print (a). This feature is characteristic of Minton Willow and is rarely found on other factory versions. The simple design of the birds in print (b) is typical of the earliest Willow pattern engravings.

Willow

The standard Willow pattern is undoubtedly the most famous design ever used on blue printed pottery. In Chapter One it was speculated that Thomas Minton may have been involved in its original design whilst working for Spode in the early 1790s. The sales accounts discussed in Chapter Two mention Willow pattern services being supplied by Minton in 1798. Copper plates for this pattern are listed in both 1810 and 1817 inventories. Willow printed wares are listed separately in the inventories between 1817 and 1826, and typically represented up to a quarter of the printed wares in stock. Clearly the production of the popular Willow pattern tablewares was a major part of the Minton business throughout its early history, as was no doubt also the case at other manufactories. Over 40

Plate 4.26. Pull taken from a Minton Willow pattern engraving probably produced around 1820 and intended for use on a meat dish or drainer. The characteristic Minton dark gable ends are clearly shown. Other features which are typical of Minton, but are also often found on other versions, include the narrow garden path, the curved lantern handle of the rear man on the bridge and the wavy base of the boat. Note the more intricate and later bird design compared to the print in Plate 4.25b. Width 310 mm.

Plate 4.27. *Pull taken from a Minton Willow pattern engraving probably produced around 1820. The print exhibits all the main Minton characteristics shown in Plate 4.26 and shows a similar treatment of the birds. Note how the border feature at the top has a light outer half to the pair of scrolling leaves. This is typical of the slightly later engravings and can also be seen on the plate shown in Plate 4.29 which has been printed from a very similar but slightly smaller engraving. The shading of these border leaves is reversed in the earliest engravings, such as in Plate 4.28. Width 258 mm.*

standard Willow copper plates were found at the factory, mainly in three separate pens. As expected these indicated use over a long period of time with both thin early coppers and later thicker ones, sometimes steel plated. Several of the plates had capital A, C and L marks engraved and some 'BURNELL LONDON' around a sword, perhaps a retailer. Many of the thinner early copper plates were designed for octagonal plates and dishes.

All the copper plates found were well engraved with fine stippled ground areas. Most had several features in common. The garden path tended to be narrow, the rear man on the bridge carried a lantern on a curved stick and the boat had a wavy base. Although these features are common to other makers, there was one uncommon and distinctive feature found on all the coppers, in that the two roofs of the small central building at the water's edge had dark shading of the gable end. Normally this is light with the roof sides being dark, such as in the Rogers (Plate 4.31) and later Spode (Plate 4.34) versions illustrated. This Minton characteristic, together with the others noted, can be seen on the prints shown in Plates 4.25 to 4.27. The dark gable ends are very occasionally found on non-Minton wares of lesser quality and some early Spode examples can be confused on this basis. Indeed the early Spode Willow pattern is similar to Minton's in many respects, as can be seen on the Spode basket shown in Plate 1.6, tending to support the speculation that Minton was associated with the initial engraving of this pattern for Spode. Identification of Minton Willow pattern wares should therefore not rely solely on the printed design but also upon potting characteristics, shapes and any workman's marks.

Plate 4.28. Minton pearlware plate decorated with perhaps the earliest version of the Willow pattern, c.1800. Note the simple birds and early border features. The hard glassy glaze makes it difficult to determine if the ground areas have been engraved by fine lines or stippling. Width 236 mm. Mark P1.

Plate 4.29. Minton pearlware plate decorated with a slightly later Willow engraving than Plate 4.28, c.1815. Although the print has been taken from a slightly smaller engraving than the pull shown in Plate 4.27, the detail of the design matches closely. Width 239 mm.

Plate 4.30. Pearlware soup plate decorated with a slightly later version of the Minton Willow pattern, c.1825. Note the more elaborate birds. Width 247 mm. Mark P17.

Plate 4.31. Rogers Willow pattern pearlware plate, c.1820. The light gable ends of the water side building are typical of non-Minton Willow, although other features are very similar. Single recessed foot ring, three triple rear and single front stilt marks. Width 250 mm. Impressed 'ROGERS' and '6'.

Plate 4.32. *Minton earthenware Willow pattern plate, c.1835. Although produced almost 40 years after the pattern had been introduced at the factory, the main Minton characteristics are still present, including the dark gable ends. Width 193 mm. Impressed 'Improved Stone China' seal mark M31.*

Plate 4.33. *Minton earthenware Willow pattern plate on a plain circular shape, c.1900. Note the use on this relatively late piece of the dagger border, first introduced at the factory some 100 years earlier on different patterns. Diameter 262 mm. Impressed 'MINTONS' and printed globe mark with 'ENGLAND'.*

Examples of Minton Willow are shown in Plates 4.28, 4.29, 4.30, 4.32 and 4.33. These confirm the continued production of this pattern throughout the nineteenth century and help to illustrate how certain features in the pattern evolved as new copper plates were engraved. The most obvious are the birds, which are of relatively plain design in early versions (Plates 4.25b and 4.28) but become more elaborate in later engravings (Plates 4.30 and 4.32). Another early feature common to several factory versions is that the pairs of scrolling leaves in the border feature, found at 45 degrees to the vertical and horizontal, have their outer halves shaded (Plate 4.28), whereas the later versions have the inner half shaded. The early outer leaf shading was found on only three of the Minton coppers. One was a small border section which had a floral pattern re-engraved on its reverse, and the others were engravings for small indented octagonal gravy boat stands.

Minton originally used the Willow pattern on plain octagonal dinner and dessert wares. Plate 4.33 shows much later use of the pattern on a circular plate with a dagger border. The 1810 inventory also lists Willow teaware copper plates. This is surprising in that although Minton produced Willow pattern tea sets towards the end of the nineteenth century, there is no evidence of the Standard Willow pattern having been used by any factory on tea wares in the early 1800s. It is quite possible, however, that these teaware copper plates were actually engraved with the very similar Mandarin pattern (Plates 1.4 and 1.5) as used by Spode and other factories on early tea wares. Mandarin was one of the most popular teaware patterns used on early pearlwares and it is likely that a version was produced by Minton. To date, however, no examples of tea wares in the Mandarin pattern have been positively attributed to Minton.

Plate 4.34. Spode Willow pattern pearlware concave-octagonal plate of fine quality, c.1820. Although the basic design remains the same as when it was introduced some 30 years earlier, this plate shows how the pattern evolved to become rather more elaborate. No foot ring, three single stilt marks beneath rim. Width 250 mm. Impressed 'SPODE' (9 mm long) over '21'.

Plate 4.35. Chaplin pattern pearlware mug, probably Minton, c.1810. The piece is linked to Minton by the characteristic moulded handle and the printer's mark. The same basic design is found on wares which are not typical of Minton, suggesting use by another factory. Height 88 mm. Mark P9.

Chaplin

This distinctive chinoiserie-type design is illustrated on the mug shown in Plates 3.3 and 4.35. The pattern name derives from the 'Charlie Chaplin' figure with a cane and hat appearing to be tightrope-walking along the top of a fence over a river. This piece has a moulded handle of characteristic Minton form, exactly matching those used on mugs decorated with known Minton patterns. It also has a typical Minton printer's mark. This is, however, the only piece so far recorded in this pattern which has Minton characteristics. A jug has been illustrated[11] with a very similar main design combined with the border normally used with the Ornithological Series, but neither the jug form nor the border detail were typical of Minton. It is therefore likely that this relatively uncommon design was used by both Minton and at least one other manufacturer. A further example of the pattern has been illustrated[12] on a mug also printed with the Georgian Coat of Arms in use from 1814 to 1837, and having a loop handle with both ends splayed into leaf finials.

Plate 4.36. A fine quality Minton pearlware Broseley pattern teapot, c.1810. This plain circular shape has a deep cape around the lid, a distinctive handle form and a plain nine-hole strainer. Minton was known to be supplying round cap¹ teapots to Wedgwood in 1806. The spout is taken from the same mould as used with Minton new oval shape china teapots. Although the Broseley pattern was used by most factories of the time on china tea wares, its use on earthenwares appears to have been much less common. Length 230 mm. Mark P14 to base and lid.

Broseley

The Broseley pattern was first introduced at Caughley (Plate 1.2) in 1782 where it was adapted from a painted Chinese porcelain design and reputedly christened after the adjacent town by Minton. It was adopted by many factories and became probably the most popular printed teaware pattern, with continued use throughout the nineteenth century. A total of 26 Broseley pattern tea and tableware copper plates were found at the factory. These were mainly thin early coppers though a few had been nickel or steel plated. Twenty three of the coppers had been impressed with a pen number 77, and 15 had smaller plate numbers impressed, all in the range 5934 to 5951. All the coppers showed strong similarity of engraving with fine stipple groundwork and shading. A set of three copper plates, for 10, 12 and 14-inch oval dishes, had 'J. Harlow, Lane End', the name of the copper plate maker, impressed on the reverse. Directories list John Harlow as a brazier, tin and copper plate worker at Lane End in 1818 and 1823.[13] He later moved to Stoke and amended his mark. Some copper plates were found for 'Dresden Flowers' with a 'Felspar China' mark incorporating '24' and 'M' and 'J. Harlow Stoke' on the reverse, indicating a move to Stoke not long after 1823. One of the Broseley copper plates had 'J. Wayte NC' on the back and another had 'China' scraped on it, indicating its use on china. One plate had the mark 'J. Allsup 16 St Pauls Church Yard, Albion'. Similar marks are recorded with London instead of Albion, so it would be interesting to know when the form of their address changed. Godden notes a letter sent to retailers Messrs Allsup in 1838.[14]

As detailed in Plate 2.2, the 1810 Minton inventory lists eight Broseley pattern teaware copper plates. The relatively high value of these plates, together with the note that work was in progress on additional Broseley plates, probably indicates that the pattern was being updated or introduced around this time. This may have been to replace an earlier similar pattern, perhaps Chinese Temple or Pagoda, or because the pattern was to be used on new teaware shapes. The 1817 inventory lists 11 plates, again only for tea wares. It could be significant that the

Plate 4.37. Royal fluted bone china Minton tea bowl printed with the Broseley pattern and gilded rim, c.1810. The 1811 factory inventory includes 66 'not handled tea cups' at 5d. each in a section of 'China Printed Fluted'. Diameter 88 mm. Blue Sevres-type mark.

Plate 4.38. Minton pearlware Broseley pattern coffee can, with gilding, c.1815. The engraving used is the same as that on the Minton bone china can in Plate 4.41. Note the distinctive moulded handle. Height 63 mm.

work on Broseley plates noted in 1810 is followed by the appearance in the 1811 inventory of the following section of tea wares:

China printed fluted.

13 hand^d bowls	10½	11s 4d
168 Saucers for tea cups	6	£4 4s
13 han^d breakfast cups	8	8s 8d
40 han^d tea cups	6	£1
66 not han^d tea cups	5	£1 7s 6d
12 saucers for bowls	10½	10s 6d
14 Slop bowls	1/4	18s 8d
16 Sugar bowls	1/2	18s 8d
1 Sugar box		2s 5d
33 Milks	1/3	£2 1s 3d
16 large teapots	5/-	£4
16 large B & B plates	2/1	£1 13s 4d
24 small B & B plates	1/10	£2 4s
28 Cans	10	£1 3s 4d
39 7 in Muffins	1/-	£1 19s
66 breakfast saucers	8	£2 4s

The earliest Minton Broseley pattern pieces recorded to date are bone china tea wares with the blue painted Sevres mark. A Royal fluted Minton tea bowl is shown in Plate 4.37, a plain saucer in Plate 4.39 and a coffee can in Plate 4.41. Plate 4.36 illustrates the pattern on a fine pearlware Minton teapot and the pearlware coffee can shown in Plate 4.38 uses the same engraving as the china can in Plate 4.41. Plates 4.40 and 4.43 illustrate Minton Broseley pattern wares of a slightly later date. The two Minton saucers shown in Plates 4.39 and 4.40 have clearly been decorated from different engravings. Although the saucer in Plate 4.40 was probably made around 1840, the engraving has a 'Semi-China' mark indicating production in the early 1820s. The corresponding engraving for the tea cup is shown in Plate 4.44 and clearly shows the 'Semi-China' seal marks. Although a new set of Broseley coppers was probably originally introduced for Semi-China wares, they were soon also being used on the bone china body introduced in about 1824, as illustrated by the china teapot in Plate 4.43, which corresponds to the Minton Cottage shape.

Plate 4.39. Minton bone china saucer decorated with the Broseley pattern and gilded rim, c.1810. This early engraving was replaced by the later design shown in Plate 4.40, probably in the 1820s. Marked Minton Broseley pattern first period china is surprisingly uncommon. Blue Sevres-type mark.

Plate 4.40. Minton Broseley pattern fluted saucer, c.1840. Heavily potted clear glazed earthenware body. The engraving probably dates from c.1820 and is included in the 1886 print book. Note the similar form of the school name to that shown in Plate 4.44. Diameter 148 mm. Printed 'Semi-China' seal mark.

Plate 4.41. Minton bone china coffee can decorated with the Broseley pattern and gilded rim, c.1810. Note the typical china ring handle and the unusual slight outward flaring of the rim. The engraving is the same as that used on the pearlware can shown in Plate 4.38. Height 62 mm. Blue Sevres-type mark.

Close comparison of the early Broseley pieces with those produced in the 1820s shows one particular significant difference in the borders. In all of the early pieces the individual semicircular flower head, at the periphery of the border and surrounded by dark ground, is relatively small and plain. In the later pieces the flower is larger and has a pair of stamens. This is perhaps clearest to see by comparing the pulls from Broseley pattern plates included in the printed pattern book for 1886, some of which are shown in Plate 4.42. The coffee cup print has the early border whereas the other prints all have the later border design, as did nearly all the copper plates found at the factory.

Following its introduction at Caughley, the Broseley pattern became popular with many factories, and amongst the most prolific producers during the early period were Coalport and Miles Mason. By about 1810 Broseley was probably being used by most manufacturers producing bone china tea wares, initially on the new oval shape and later on the London shape. Differentiating between the various factory versions is very difficult, with the early Miles Mason pattern[15] being particularly close to that used by Minton.

66

Plate 4.42. Selection of Broseley pattern teaware prints included in the Minton 1886 pattern book. The coffee cup engraving shows strong similarities to the print on the tea bowl in Plate 4.37, and the simple semicircular flower heads in the border are characteristic of the earliest Broseley wares. The other border prints all have the later larger flowers with the pair of stamens. These were probably engraved c.1820 for use on Semi-China wares, although they were also used on the bone china introduced c.1824, such as the teapot in Plate 4.43. A note at the bottom of the page shown indicates that engravings were also available for bowls, ewers, dishes, an egg cup and a chamber pot.

Plate 4.43. Minton Broseley pattern bone china teapot with gilding, c.1825. This 'Cottage' shape is illustrated in the Minton shape book of c.1830 and was also used for earthenwares. The copper plate engraving remains at the factory and part of the border print is included in Plate 4.42. Plain strainer of 15 holes in triangular arrangement. Length of teapot 270 mm. There are no marks, which is typical of much of the early second period bone china.

Plate 4.44. Pull from a Broseley pattern copper plate engraving at the Minton factory, c.1820. The engraving appears to be that used for the teacup included in the print book shown in Plate 4.42. The small engravings at the bottom of the plate would be intended for use inside the cup and on the handle. Note the later version of the border. The engravings for Birch Sunday School would probably have been applied over the main print, as on the saucer shown in Plate 4.40, which also has the distinctive 'Semi-China' seal mark applied. An engraving for Norfolk Hotel was also found on several Minton Broseley coppers. Width of upper border strip 260 mm.

Plate 4.45. Minton Broseley pattern copper plate, c.1820. One of 26 coppers found at the factory for this pattern, this was intended for use on the large bread and butter plate, presumably originally on a plain circular plate. The same copper is seen to have been used, however, with the later, more elaborate, plate shape shown in Plate 4.46. Height of engraving 260 mm.

Plate 4.46. Minton Broseley pattern bone china bread and butter plate, c.1840. It can be seen how the circular engraving shown in Plate 4.45 has been made to fit this later plate shape. Width 243 mm.

Plate 4.47. Blue painted Chinese export porcelain soup plate, c.1790. Clearly the original design for the Temple printed pattern used by several factories and illustrated in Plate 4.48. Width 239 mm.

Temple

The only evidence that Minton may have produced this pattern is the copper plate engraving shown in Plate 4.48, and the inclusion of 'Chinese Temple' teaware copper plates in the 1810 inventory. It is important to distinguish between Temple and the very similar Broseley pattern. They are based on two distinct Chinese export porcelain designs with significant differences in both the border and the main design. Furthermore several factories used both patterns, mainly on porcelain tea wares, including Caughley, Spode and Miles Mason. Versions of both patterns produced by several factories are illustrated by Copeland.[16]

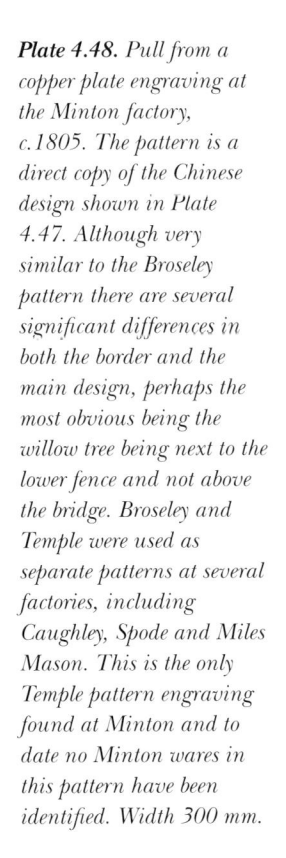

Plate 4.48. Pull from a copper plate engraving at the Minton factory, c.1805. The pattern is a direct copy of the Chinese design shown in Plate 4.47. Although very similar to the Broseley pattern there are several significant differences in both the border and the main design, perhaps the most obvious being the willow tree being next to the lower fence and not above the bridge. Broseley and Temple were used as separate patterns at several factories, including Caughley, Spode and Miles Mason. This is the only Temple pattern engraving found at Minton and to date no Minton wares in this pattern have been identified. Width 300 mm.

Plate 4.49. Dagger Border with Temple pattern pearlware plate, probably Minton, c.1800. The body, shape and potting characteristics exactly match Minton plates. The pattern is very similar to one produced by Spode in the 1790s, the main differences being the willow tree at the bottom of the landscape, and the W-shaped panels in the inner border, both absent in the Spode version. Furthermore the distinctive diamond-shaped panel above the temple door is oval in the Spode pattern. Three single stilt marks beneath the rim, no foot ring. Width 236 mm.

Dagger Border with Temple

This distinctive chinoiserie landscape pattern features a temple with a panel above the door standing at the water's edge, as illustrated on the finely potted dinner plate in Plate 4.49. The current evidence to link this pattern to Minton is the correspondence of the shape and potting characteristics of the wares found to known Minton wares, including the shell dish illustrated in Plate 4.50 and the covered vegetable dish with moulded fiddlestick knob shown in Plate 9.34. Given that very similar items were also made by other factories, however, the attribution must currently remain open to some doubt.

As illustrated by Copeland,[17] the same basic pattern was produced by other factories, with that introduced by Spode, probably around 1790, being very similar. The Spode pattern has the same dagger border but does not have the willow tree at the base of the landscape nor the W-shaped panels in the inner border, and the distinctive panel above the temple door is oval and not diamond-shaped. The version by Barker shown in Plate 4.51 has a different border, as does a similar pattern produced by Joshua Heath. A version very similar to Spode, but with the main landscape in reverse, is also known.

If this pattern was produced by Minton it would be one of their earliest designs, for the examples found show significant use of line engraving. Of the patterns mentioned in 1798 accounts, it could corresponding to either Dagger Border or Nankeen (Nankeen Temple in 1801).

Plate 4.50. Dagger Border with Temple pattern pearlware shell dish, probably Minton, c.1800. The shape and potting characteristics exactly match known Minton wares, as does the treatment of the handle decoration (see Plate 9.72). Almost identical shell dishes were, however, produced by other factories. Line engraving of ground areas. Width 186 mm.

Plate 4.51. This landscape design is very similar to the Dagger Border with Temple Pattern, but the border design is different, c.1800. The pattern is mainly line engraved. Pearlware plate with three sets of quadruple stilt marks on the base and three single stilt marks on the face. No foot ring. Width 198 mm. Impressed mark 'BARKER' (16 mm long).

Plate 4.52a&b. Pair of Minton Fisherman pattern pearlware plates, c.1805. The central figure on the boat holding a fish is reminiscent of the Fisherman pattern used at Caughley and Worcester on porcelain. The plate on the right (b) is seen to have additional features and shading compared to that on the left (a). Close examination of the two prints seems to indicate that the original engraving used for plate (a) was reworked and then used for plate (b). Width 236 mm. Plate (b) Mark P6.

Plate 4.53. Minton Fisherman pattern pearlware jug, c.1805. The handle and body shape are both characteristic of early Minton jugs. Height 183 mm. Mark P10.

Plate 4.54. Chinese Family pattern pearlware saucer dish, probably Minton, c.1805. The border and some of the figures are very similar to those in the Fisherman pattern. Diameter 203 mm. Mark P4.

Fisherman

Illustrated on the pair of plain octagonal pearlware plates shown in Plate 4.52 and the jug in Plate 4.53, this pattern is attributed to Minton based on its use on a range of wares of characteristic Minton shape, and with various Minton workman's marks. It is interesting to note how the detail of the pattern was changed between the two plates illustrated in Plate 4.52, apparently by modifying the original engraving. The same print as used on Plate 4.52b has been found on a later Minton concave-octagonal Opaque China plate, c.1825. The pattern has some similarities with the Fisherman pattern introduced on porcelain at Caughley, perhaps when Minton was working there, and at Worcester. No other factory versions of the pattern have been found.

The use of this pattern on early jug forms indicates that it was probably introduced around 1800. There is a possibility that it is the pattern referred to as Image in factory accounts for 1804 and in the 1810 inventory, where both tea and tableware copper plates are listed.

Chinese Family

This pattern is illustrated on the saucer dish shown in Plate 4.54. It is seen to have a similar assembly of Chinese figures or 'Images' to the Fisherman pattern and also uses a very similar border design, so this may be the Image teaware pattern referred to in factory records. The arrangement of the figures is changed when a longer engraving is required, such as for cups, cans, bowls and presumably teapots. This can be seen on the coffee can and cups illustrated in Plates 4.55 and 4.56. The pattern is attributed to Minton based on its use on characteristic Minton shapes with several known workman's marks. The bowl in Plate 4.57 indicates production by another factory of a very similar version of the pattern, but with an ochre painted rim.

Plate 4.55a&b. Chinese Family pattern pearlwares, probably Minton, c.1805. The coffee can (a) above left is gilded, has 24 flutes, a characteristic Minton square handle and is 63 mm high. The coffee cup (b) has a distinctive handle form, and is 61 mm high with mark P9. The same engraving appears to have been used for both pieces.

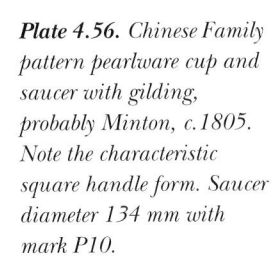

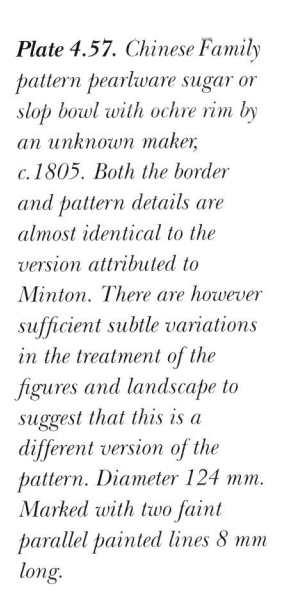

Plate 4.56. Chinese Family pattern pearlware cup and saucer with gilding, probably Minton, c.1805. Note the characteristic square handle form. Saucer diameter 134 mm with mark P10.

Plate 4.57. Chinese Family pattern pearlware sugar or slop bowl with ochre rim by an unknown maker, c.1805. Both the border and pattern details are almost identical to the version attributed to Minton. There are however sufficient subtle variations in the treatment of the figures and landscape to suggest that this is a different version of the pattern. Diameter 124 mm. Marked with two faint parallel painted lines 8 mm long.

Plate 4.58. Pearl River House pattern pearlware fluted coffee cup, probably Minton, c.1800. Note the willow tree above the bridge and the detail behind the fisherman, which help to distinguish this version of the pattern. Twenty-two flutes. Height 65 mm.

Plate 4.59. Pearl River House pattern pearlware coffee cup with gilding, probably Minton, c.1800. The print has line engraving of ground areas and matches that used on the cup in Plate 4.58. The distinctive handle is from the same mould as used for the cup in Plate 4.55b. Height 66 mm. Mark P10.

Pearl River House

Several versions of this pattern are illustrated in Plates 4.58 to 4.64. Copeland discusses the pattern and suggests that the building is typical of those found on the banks of the Pearl River at that period.[18] The design is known to be a direct copy of one used on Chinese export porcelain. The distinctive moulded handle form and workman's mark on the cup shown in Plate 4.59 indicate that this version of the pattern was probably produced by Minton. The same print has been used on the cup in Plate 4.58 and one illustrated by Copeland. The version

Plate 4.60. Pearl River House pattern earthenware coffee can, attributed to Spode, c.1800. The distinctive tree arrangement beside the bridge distinguishes this from the Minton version. Height 59 mm. Marked with two parallel painted lines.

Plate 4.61. Pearl River House pattern porcelain fluted sugar bowl with gilding, attributed to New Hall, c.1800. A close copy of the original design found on Chinese porcelain. Twenty-eight flutes. Diameter 114 mm.

Plate 4.62. Pearl River House pattern pearlware fluted tea bowl with gilding, probably Minton, c.1800. Note the same design of trees behind the fisherman to that on the cup in Plate 4.58. Twenty-four flutes. Diameter 85 mm. Mark P3.

Plate 4.63. Detail of the teabowl shown in Plate 4.64 clearly showing the different tree arrangement behind the fisherman, compared to the version attributed to Minton shown in Plate 4.62. Twenty-four flutes. Diameter 87 mm.

Plate 4.64. Pearl River House pattern pearlware fluted tea bowl and saucer with gilding, by an unknown maker, c.1800. This version of the pattern is very similar to that attributed to Minton, but can be distinguished by the distinctive trees behind the fisherman, as shown in Plate 4.63. Thirty-two flutes to saucer and 24 to cup. Diameter of saucer 129 mm.

produced by Spode is shown in Plate 4.60 and is seen to have a distinctive tree arrangement. A further version,[19] probably produced by Ralph Wedgwood, is very similar to the Spode design. Porcelain pieces in the pattern, such as shown in Plate 4.61, can normally be attributed to New Hall.

The pattern on the fine quality tea bowl and saucer illustrated in Plates 4.63 and 4.64 is very similar to the version attributed to Minton, but there are several variations in the design, with the different treatment of the trees behind the fisherman being perhaps the most obvious.

Plate 4.65. Chinese Garden pattern pearlware saucer dish, probably Minton, c.1805. This pattern has a distinctive border and bearded gardener. It was also used on toy tea wares such as the teapot in Plate 4.67, and could correspond to the Chinese Figures copper plates listed in the 1810 Minton inventory. Diameter 201 mm. Mark P3.

Chinese Garden

This chinoiserie garden scene is illustrated in Plates 4.65 to 4.67. It features a bearded gardener and has a distinctive border. As is normal with tea patterns the arrangement of the design varies between the circular engravings for saucers and the longer engravings used on teapots, jugs, cups and bowls. The pattern is found on tea wares of characteristic Minton shape and potting characteristics and with

Plate 4.66. Sparrow beak pearlware milk jugs printed with the Chinese Garden and Nankin pattern, probably Minton, c.1805. Both would have been used as part of tea services, probably with plain globular teapots such as in Plates 4.67 and 4.68. The larger Chinese Garden jug, height 67 mm, is probably for normal size wares with the smaller Nankin jug, height 54 mm, being from a toy service.

Plate 4.67. Toy-sized Chinese Garden pattern pearlware globular teapot, probably Minton, c.1805. For such a small piece it has been very well potted. Distinctive eight-sided moulded spout and plain four-hole diamond-shaped strainer. Length 130 mm.

Plate 4.68. Toy-sized Nankin pattern pearlware teapot, probably Minton, c.1800. The eight-sided spout and four-hole strainer correspond to those on the pot in Plate 4.67. Length 130 mm.

Plate 4.69. Two views of a fine quality Nankin pattern pearlware coffee can with gilding, possibly Minton, c.1800. The border matches that used on the toy-sized pieces in Plates 4.66 and 4.68, as do the characteristic boats, buildings and bridge, which is opposite the can handle so only the ends can be seen below. Line engraving of ground areas. Height 59 mm.

Minton printed workman's marks. Occasionally the pattern is found with blue painted rims, which could correspond to the 'blue top' printed tea wares listed in early inventories. Both normal size and toy size tea wares were produced in this pattern. The sparrow beak jug in Plate 4.66 and the globular teapot in Plate 4.67 are both typical of the early 1800s. Of the three patterns in the 1810 copper plate list for 'Tea & Toy', Chinese Figure seems to be more appropriate than either Naking or Pagoda. No versions of the pattern by other factories are known.

Nankin

A typical early chinoiserie landscape pattern found on both normal and toy-sized tea wares and illustrated in Plates 4.66, 4.68, 4.69 and 9.115. The attribution of the pattern to Minton is based on the close correspondence of the wares to those decorated with the Chinese Garden pattern, and the use of characteristic printer's

Plate 4.70. Bridge pattern Minton old oval shape pearlware teapot, c.1805. This well-printed pot clearly illustrates the Minton version of this popular pattern. Note how the foliage on the main tree in the foreground is represented by light and dark half shading. Although a similar effect is found on Spode china tableware in this pattern, the version used by Spode on pearlware tea wares, such as in Plate 4.75, has all dark foliage. Length 222 mm.

Plate 4.71. Pair of Minton Bridge pattern pearlware coffee cans with gilding, c.1805. Characteristic early square-edged moulded Minton handle. Stipple engraved ground areas. Height 66 mm. Mark P4.

Plate 4.72. Bridge pattern pearlware coffee can, probably Minton, c.1815. The moulded handle exactly matches those on known Minton cans of the 1810 to 1820 period. There are some minor differences in the engraving compared to that used on the cans in Plate 4.71, suggesting that some new copper plates had been engraved for this popular pattern. Height 64 mm.

marks, including the distinctive crown mark P1. The jugs in Plate 4.66 are of identical basic form and body, and the teapots shown in Plates 4.67 and 4.68 have spouts from probably the same mould. Some difference in the profile of the teapot bodies is apparent, but this can be attributed to variations in turning the pieces, as another Nankin pattern teapot with the same spout, handle and print shows an even greater variation of body form. The pattern has extensive use of line engraving and was probably introduced around 1800. It could well correspond to the 'Naking Tea & Toy Set' (presumably a misspelling on Nankin) copper plates listed in 1810. Versions of this pattern may have been produced by other factories.

Bridge

This early chinoiserie landscape is most frequently found on wares produced at the Spode factory, where it was originally referred to as the Bridge pattern. Spode produced two early versions, one on earthenwares, as illustrated here, and referred to as Bridge I, and another on bone china which had butterflies in the border in place of the rosettes, Bridge II. Several examples are illustrated by

Plate 4.73. Bridge pattern oval shape pearlware teapot with dark ochre painted rims, probably Harley, c.1810. Although unmarked, the distinctive shape and moulding matches teapots found impressed 'HARLEY', normally taken to be by Thomas Harley of Lane End. This version of the pattern is very similar to those of Minton and Spode. Note, however, the relatively deep and horizontal brickwork at the base of the main building and the more elaborate semicircular floral rosettes in the border.

Plate 4.74. Bridge pattern pearlware tea bowl and saucer, probably Minton, c.1815. Note the characteristic light and dark shading on the tree. Diameter of saucer 137 mm. Mark P3.

Plate 4.75. Bridge pattern fluted pearlware tea bowl with gilding, attributed to Spode, c.1810. Twenty-four flutes. Diameter 85 mm. Marked with two painted lines 4 mm long forming a 'T'.

Copeland[20] and Drakard.[21] Spode continued production of the pattern into the twentieth century and renamed it Queen Charlotte. A version of the pattern is attributed to Minton based on its use on tea wares of known Minton form with characteristic workman's marks. The Minton examples shown in Plates 4.70 and 4.71 are typical of quite early products, although the pattern uses stipple engraving. Other Minton examples found indicate a later date of c.1815, suggesting use of the pattern over a number of years.

In addition to Spode and Minton, a version of the pattern was also produced by Thomas Harley (Plate 4.73) and probably others. The various factory versions are very similar. A guide to the Minton pattern is the foliage on the main tree in the foreground which is represented by light and dark half shading. Although a similar effect is found on some Spode china tablewares in this pattern, the version used by Spode on pearlware tea wares, Bridge I, has all dark foliage. There is no mention of Bridge as a teaware pattern in the 1810 copper plate list, indicating that a different factory name was used for the pattern. The Bridge pattern mentioned in the Wyllie sales accounts in 1820 and 1822 is probably a different design, perhaps Italian Ruins.

Plate 4.76. Chinese Sports pattern pearlware meat dish, Minton, c.1815. This design was introduced by Minton hand painted on bone china as pattern 539 in c.1810. This was the largest standard size of meat dish included in the table service. The pattern on each piece in the service has a different arrangement of children playing various sports and games. Minton also used the design on pearlware tea wares. The pattern is often found overpainted in coloured enamels. Width 534 mm. Mark P5.

Chinese Sports

This pattern is found on earthenwares of characteristic Minton shape with a range of workman's marks. It corresponds to the hand-painted pattern number 539 used on Minton bone china. This was the highest pattern number included in the 1810 inventory, indicating introduction of the design at that time. Its use as a printed pattern on earthenwares may be contemporary with this or could be linked to the cessation of china production a few years later. It was used on the circular and oval concave-shaped dinner wares listed in 1817, such as the large meat dish shown in Plate 4.76, and on tea wares as in Plate 4.77. It is often found overpainted or 'clobbered' in enamel colours. No versions of the pattern by other factories are known.

Plate 4.77. Chinese Sports pattern pearlware Minton cup and saucer, c.1815. Note the rounded cross section of the moulded handle. This handle form probably replaced the more angular handles used on the earlier cups and cans (e.g. Plate 4.56) around 1810. Diameter of saucer 138 mm. Marks P7 on saucer and P1 on cup.

Plate 4.78. Pearlware teacup decorated with the Oriental Family pattern, maker unknown, c.1815. The cup is not a known Minton form and, compared to the Minton pattern, there are several minor differences in the design, sufficient to suggest that this is a separate version of the pattern and not produced by Minton. Note the coarser honeycomb pattern in the central panel in the building. Recessed foot ring. Diameter 80 mm.

Plate 4.79. Pearlware Minton Oriental Family pattern teacup, c.1815. The moulded handle exactly matches that used on the Chinese Sports cup in Plate 4.77. Diameter 77 mm. Mark P9.

Oriental Family

This pattern features a typical Chinese family scene and is illustrated in Plates 4.78 to 4.80. It may have been introduced as a replacement for the very similar 'Chinese Family' pattern, although the borders are different and the dog has been replaced by extra figures. It is attributed to Minton based on its use on pearlware tea wares of characteristic Minton shape with known workman's marks. The cup in Plate 4.79 is of the same form and body as the Chinese Sports teacup in Plate 4.77, and has an identical moulded handle, despite the cup being of a smaller size. The shape of the creamer in Plate 4.80 corresponds to Minton new oval shape china tea wares, which were probably introduced between 1805 and 1810. Plate 4.78 shows a teacup printed with a the same basic pattern but probably by another factory. It is very similar to the Minton design, but is seen to have a coarser honeycomb pattern on the central panel in the building. For this second version an accompanying saucer has been illustrated,[22] and shards have been found at the site of an Exeter shop trading in the 1820s.[23]

Plate 4.80. Pearlware Minton Oriental Family pattern creamer, c.1810. This new oval shape was probably introduced around 1805 and is normally found in Minton bone china. Length 148 mm. Mark P9.

81

Plate 4.81. Chinaman with Rocket pattern Minton old oval shape pearlware teapot, c.1800. A fine quality piece of characteristic Minton form with the distinctive printed crown workman's mark. Numerous factories produced very similar versions of this design, making attribution of wares based on pattern alone very difficult. Length 245 mm. Mark P1.

Chinaman with Rocket

This is a relatively common early chinoiserie pattern used by a number of factories on tea wares in the 1800 to 1810 period. The similarity of the basic design and border of the various factory versions of this pattern can be seen from the examples illustrated here, including the teapot of fine quality pearlware shown in Plate 4.82 and the four tea bowls in Plate 4.83. This makes attribution very difficult unless a marked piece or distinctive shape is found. A version of the design can be attributed to Minton based on its use on the fine quality pearlware old oval shape teapot of characteristic Minton form illustrated in Plate 4.81. A version has been attributed to Stevenson based on a drum-shaped pearlware teapot impressed

Plate 4.82. Chinaman with Rocket pattern pearlware teapot, maker unknown, c.1800. This version of the design appears to be different from those attributed to Minton, Stevenson or Turner. The distinctive body, spout and handle seem to match that of a teapot illustrated by Miller[10] and decorated with a version of the One Man Chinoiserie pattern. Plain 10-hole strainer. Length 241 mm.

Plate 4.83. Examples of wares decorated with the Chinaman with Rocket pattern, c.1800. The four tea bowls illustrated above highlight the difficulty of attributing this design, each bearing a slightly different version of the same basic pattern. The first tea bowl, top left, is of finely potted porcelain with a slightly flared and gilded rim and may have been produced by the Staffordshire Turners of Lane End. The Turners may also have produced the porcelain creamer shown right; this silver shape is normally found in a pearlware body. The other tea bowls are pearlware by unknown makers. The fourth tea bowl, middle right, is distinctive in having an unusually orange tinted ochre painted rim. Tea bowl diameters, 88 mm, 86 mm, 91 mm and 87 mm. Creamer height 130 mm.

'Stevenson'.[24] Godden[25] attributes a version found on porcelain to the Turners of Lane End, based on the characteristic form of a teapot. A mirror image version of the design can be attributed to Dawson's Low Ford Pottery, Sunderland, based on an earthenware jug in the Sunderland Museum collection inscribed 'Hylton Low Ford Pottery May 1801'.[26]

Plate 4.84. Minton China Pattern first period porcelain teapot with gilding of characteristic old oval shape, c.1800. Octagonal profile spout, domed strainer, heart-shaped pouring guard and flat base. The pattern is seen to be a direct copy of the design used on the Chinese plate illustrated in Plate 4.85. Length 245 mm.

Plate 4.85. Chinese export porcelain dinner plate painted in blue, c.1790. This original oriental design has clearly been used as the basis for the Minton China Pattern, as used on both tea wares (Plate 4.84) and dinner and dessert wares (Plate 4.86). Width 237 mm.

Plate 4.86. Minton pearlware China Pattern wicker plate, c.1805. Note the close correspondence with the original Chinese design. Minton also used the pattern on plain octagonal dinner wares with the same border as used on tea wares. Diameter 181 mm. Mark P1.

China Pattern

This pattern was originally attributed to Minton through its use on first period porcelain tea wares,[27] Plate 4.84 showing a teapot of characteristic Minton shape. The design, including the border, is a close copy of a pattern found painted on Chinese export porcelain, as shown in Plate 4.85. Minton also used the pattern on earthenware dessert wares and plain octagonal dinner wares. Plate 4.86 shows a wicker plate of characteristic Minton shape bearing the distinctive small crown printer's mark. The name China Pattern has been adopted as it is listed in 1810 as used on both tea and tablewares, the listing for tea wares being grouped with Broseley and Chinese Temple, perhaps because of common usage on bone china. In any event, given its use on china tea wares, the name seems appropriate. No versions of this design by other factories have been recorded.

References

1. *Friends of Blue Bulletin*, No. 3, 1973, p. 7.
2. A. Bunce, *NCS Newsletter*, No. 97, 1995, pp. 8–10.
3. J. and S. Wyatt, *NCS Newsletter*, No. 92, 1993, pp. 41–45.
4. E.M. Nance, *The Pottery and Porcelain of Swansea and Nantgarw* (Batsford, 1942), Plate XIII.
5. R.K. Henrywood, *An Illustrated Guide to British Jugs* (Swan-Hill Press, 1997), p. 64.
6. *Friends of Blue Bulletin*, No. 58, 1988, p. 3.
7. A.W. Coysh and R.K. Henrywood, *The Dictionary of Blue and White Printed Pottery* (Antique Collectors Club, 1982), p. 337.
8. J. and S. Wyatt, *NCS Newsletter*, No. 91, 1993, pp. 14-15.
9. *Friends of Blue Bulletin*, No. 99, 1998, p. 10.
10. P. Miller and M. Berthoud, *An Anthology of British Teapots* (Micawber Publications, 1985), plate 818, p. 137.
11. *Friends of Blue Bulletin*, No. 108, 2000, p. 9.
12. *Friends of Blue Bulletin*, No. 81, 1993, p. 5.
13. D. Drakard and P. Holdway, *Spode Printed Ware* (Longman, 1983), p. 27.
14. G.A. Godden, *Minton Pottery & Porcelain of the First Period* (Barrie & Jenkins, 1968), p.158.
15. G.A. Godden, *Mason's China and the Ironstone Wares* (Antique Collectors Club, 1980), p. 62.
16. R. Copeland, *Spode's Willow Pattern and other Designs after the Chinese*, 3rd ed. (Studio Vista, 1999), p.53.
17. Copeland, *Spode's Willow Pattern*, p. 83.
18. Copeland, *Spode's Willow Pattern*, p. 75.
19. *Friends of Blue Bulletin*, No. 91, 1996, p. 3.
20. Copeland, *Spode's Willow Pattern*, p. 92.
21. Drakard and Holdway, *Spode Printed Ware*, p. 198.
22. *Friends of Blue Bulletin*, No. 89, 1995, p. 6.
23. *Friends of Blue Bulletin*, No. 88, 1995, p. 6.
24. *Friends of Blue Bulletin*, No. 106, 2000, p. 6.
25. G.A. Godden, *Staffordshire Porcelain* (Granada Publishing, 1983), p. 94.
26. J.C. Baker, *Sunderland Pottery*, 5th ed. (Thomas Reed Ind. Press, 1984), p. 2.
27. G.A. Godden, *Encyclopaedia of British Porcelain Manufacturers* (Barrie & Jenkins, 1988), p. 536.

Chapter Five

Catalogue of Patterns
2. Early Floral Designs

Lily

In common with the early landscape patterns considered in the previous chapter, the earliest floral patterns produced by Minton were often based on designs found on imported hand-painted Chinese porcelain. One of the most popular of these was the Lily pattern, known also as Royal Lily, Queen's Lily or King's Lily. About 40 copper plates for this pattern remain at the factory. A majority are thin plates, consistent with early use, but there are about a dozen thicker plates, some of which have been steel plated. All the coppers have the same basic design, as shown in Plates 5.1 and 5.2. Some of the plates have engraved marks, including a Minton globe mark with 'Queen's Lily' and a Minton mark with 'King's Lily', indicating use at least into the second half of the nineteenth century. The pattern is normally found on Minton earthenwares, such as the dinner plate shown in Plate 5.3, but the same copper plates were used to print on first period bone china as pattern No. 123,[1] although examples are very rare.[2] This use on first period china confirms that some of the copper plates date from the early years of the nineteenth century. Other plates must, however, have been engraved at a slightly later date. On the back of one of the thicker coppers is impressed 'J. WAYTE' with 'NC' beneath. A commercial directory for 1828–29[3] lists James Wayte as a brazier and tin plate worker in High Street, Newcastle-under-Lyme, 'NC' being the

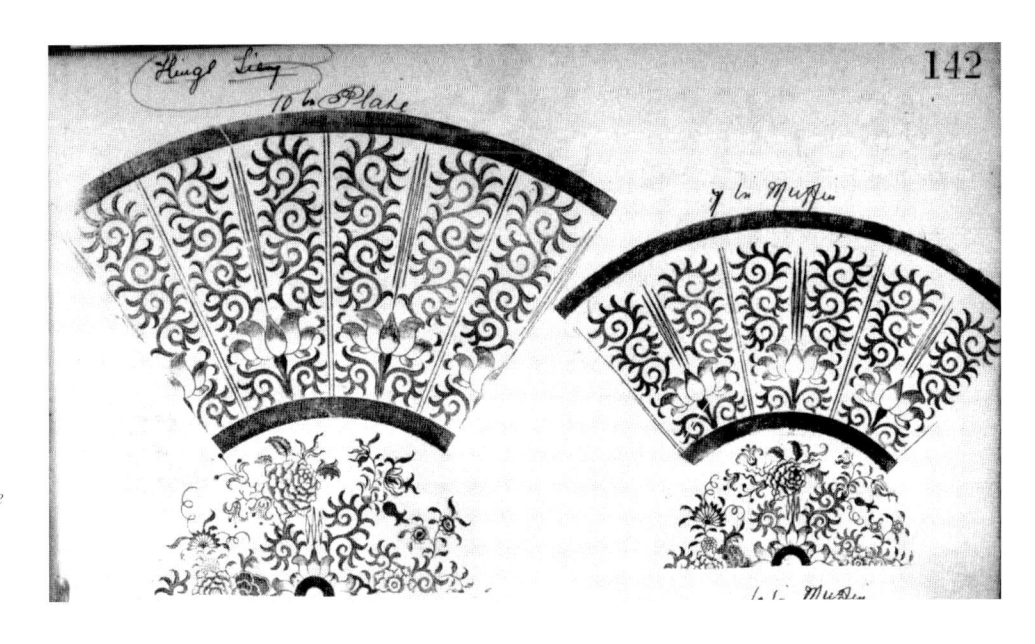

Plate 5.1. Extract from page 142 of the Minton printed pattern book MS 2576, compiled in 1886, showing details of the Lily pattern. This popular design was still in production at the end of the nineteenth century, and has been noted on pieces impressed 'MINTONS'.

Plate 5.2. Copper plate engraved with the Minton Lily pattern, one of over 40 with this pattern found in the factory copper plate room, c.1800. The pattern is mentioned in sales accounts for 1804 and included in the copper plates listed in the 1810 and 1817 inventories. Engraving diameter 229 mm, copper plate width 257 mm.

Plate 5.3. Minton earthenware plate decorated with the Lily pattern, c.1810. The print exactly matches one of the engravings still held at the factory. The pattern is normally found on the plain circular and oval Trophy shape wares, although an example on a plain octagonal plate is also known. Diameter 241 mm. Mark P2.

Plate 5.4. The intricate central decoration appears to be unique to Minton. It is clearly illustrated here on the centre of an octagonal earthenware plate, c.1810 (width 209 mm) and the corresponding copper plate engraving. Other factory versions had either a plain centre or a much simpler central design.

Plate 5.5. Porcelain bute shape teacup and saucer with plain loop handle, c.1800. Possibly made by Coalport or Turner. Note how the centre of the saucer is left plain. Saucer diameter 135 mm.

Plate 5.6. Earthenware coffee can and saucer decorated with the Minton version of the Lily pattern, c.1810. The elaborate central design on the saucer easily distinguishes this from the version in Plate 5.5. The print on the saucer matches one of the pulls included on page 144 of the Minton 1886 print book, as shown below. Saucer diameter 138 mm. Mark P9.

abbreviation for Newcastle. One of the thinner copper plates has a number of capital 'C' marks engraved, perhaps intended for use as printed marks.

The pattern is included and named in the factory pattern books from c.1870[4] and 1886,[5] as shown in Plate 5.1. A further pattern book of 1886[6] illustrates the pattern with various gilt or enamelled embellishments. Lily was a popular pattern on porcelain at the end of the eighteenth and beginning of the nineteenth century. It was certainly used at Caughley and Worcester, and in Staffordshire by Spode and Turner. The main distinguishing feature of the Minton version is the elaborate central design which is detailed in Plate 5.4. Other factory versions used either a very simple central decoration or left the centre plain, as in Plate 5.5. Both Minton and Spode used the Lily pattern on early earthenware tea wares. Copeland[7] illustrates a creamer which is attributed to Spode and a teapot stand is known impressed Spode.[8] Plate 5.6 shows an earthenware coffee can and saucer attributed to Minton.

Plate 5.7. Pearlware Stylised Floral pattern cup and saucer of fine quality and gilding, probably Minton, c.1805. Both the cup and saucer are of typical Minton form and have known printer's marks. The moulded angular handle exactly matches those on Minton cups. A slightly different version of the pattern is shown in Plate 5.8 on wares which are not typical of Minton. Saucer diameter 138 mm with recessed foot ring and mark P4. Cup diameter 79 mm and mark P7.

Plate 5.8. Pearlware Stylised Floral pattern coffee can and tea bowl with ochre rim by an unknown maker, c.1805. Although the design is very similar to that found on the cup and saucer in Plate 5.7, there are numerous minor differences in the detail of the prints. The moulded handle on the coffee can has a smaller and more rounded cross section than Minton handles. Bowl diameter 86 mm, can height 62 mm.

Stylised Floral

This early chinoiserie-type floral design was probably produced by several factories and is found on a range of earthenware tablewares, tea wares, bowls, jugs and mugs,[9] as well as on bone china tea wares.[10] The pattern is commonly referred to as Stylised Floral. A first suggestion that a version of the pattern was produced by Minton was made by Godden,[11] who illustrates an early pearlware milk jug, now known to be of characteristic Minton form, and a slop bowl. Although no archive evidence that Minton produced this pattern has yet been found at the factory, further early pearlware tea wares of typical Minton form with characteristic printer's marks are illustrated in Plate 5.7. At least one other factory produced earthenware tea wares in this pattern, as the pieces shown in Plate 5.8 are not typical of Minton wares and have a slightly different version of the pattern.

The fine teapot shown in Plate 5.9 shows a superficial resemblance to the Minton old oval shape, as shown in Plate 4.70. Common features include the octagonal profile spout, the basic handle form with imitation rivet at its base, the

Plate 5.9. Stylised Floral pattern pearlware teapot by an unknown maker, c.1800. Although this piece superficially resembles the Minton old oval teapot shape, the body profile, handle cross section and details of the lid, knob and base are all different. Although there is some possibility that it could be a very early Minton teapot form, it was probably the product of a different factory. Octagonal spout, recessed base, domed strainer, heart-shaped pouring guard, fluted knob with distinctive cross-wise groove at its tip. Relatively thin body profile with slightly concave sides. The teapot shown in Plate 5.10 is possibly by the same factory. Length 249 mm.

domed strainer and heart-shaped pouring guard and the finely fluted knob. Closer inspection, however, reveals several significant differences. The body plan profile is thinner than the Minton pot and the base is recessed and not flat. The handle is from a different mould, being thinner and more angular. The knob has a distinctive cross-wise groove at its tip and the lid has remains of forward sloping pieces at the front of its rim, apparently designed to lock under the pouring guard. Although it is possible that this represents an early form of the Minton old oval shape, on balance current evidence points to production by a different factory. It is of note that the very distinctive knob and lid design and the thin profile and recessed base are also found on the Violin pattern teapot shown in Plate 5.10.

Plate 5.10. Violin pattern pearlware teapot by an unknown maker, c.1800. Although the spout and handle are different from the teapot in Plate 5.9, both pieces have the same distinctive knob and lid design. Although smaller, the main body has the same slender profile with slightly concave sides, a domed strainer and a recessed base. This pattern was produced by several factories on earthenwares, and is most often found on tea wares, sometimes with an ochre rim. There is currently no evidence that Minton used this pattern. Length 230 mm.

Plate 5.11. Star pattern pearlware plate, probably Minton, c.1810. This distinctive design probably corresponds to the Star pattern copper plates listed in the 1810 inventory. Although used here on a concave shape plate, the pattern is also found on the plain circular Trophy shape, both of characteristic Minton shape. Three single stilt marks beneath the rim, no foot ring. Diameter 217 mm. Impressed '7', 5 mm high.

Star

This pattern is found on both Trophy and concave shape dinner wares of characteristic Minton form. The concave plate illustrated in Plate 5.11 corresponds exactly to known Minton plates and bears the distinctive impressed '7'. The pattern is also used on the supper set section of known Minton form illustrated in Plate 9.41 and has been noted on a ewer. The pattern is also sometimes found overpainted in enamel colours and gilding (Plate 3.20). The design is assumed to correspond to the dinnerware pattern called Star listed in the 1810 inventory copper plate list. No versions of Star by other factories are known.

Pinwheels

Several versions of this distinctive pattern are found, all on earthenwares. One version is found on octagonal dinner wares of known Minton form and with characteristic workman's marks, including the distinctive crown mark P1. A typical Minton meat dish decorated with this version is shown in Plate 5.13. The dessert dish in Plate 3.25 is also a typical Minton form. The same basic pattern was used by other factories, possibly including Harley,[12] and distinguishing different factory versions based on pattern alone is difficult. Those wares in this pattern with an enamelled ochre rim such as the example in Plate 5.12b are not characteristic of Minton. This ochre rimmed version is traditionally associated with Swansea, although a marked example has yet to be recorded.

Plate 5.12a&b. *Pinwheels pattern pearlware octagonal dinner plates, c.1810. The example (a) on the left is of characteristic Minton form with no foot ring and single stilt marks beneath the rim, width 233 mm. The other smaller plate, width 184 mm, three triple rear and single front stilt marks and no foot ring, shows essentially the same design used by another factory. This version has an ochre enamelled rim, a well-defined double row of shapes in the border and is more commonly found than Minton examples.*

Plate 5.13. *Pinwheels pattern pearlware octagonal 20-inch meat dish, attributed to Minton, c.1810. The pattern name derives from the similarity of some of the flower heads to the American fireworks called Pinwheels, known as Catherine Wheels in England.[13] Width 524 mm. Mark P1.*

Plate 5.14. Minton Basket pattern 18-inch meat dish, c.1810. This is an early example, the pearlware body having a thick glassy glaze. The copper plate used to print this dish is detailed above, and is one of the 32 plates for this pattern found at the Minton factory. Also illustrated is the back stamp coppersmith's mark which was used by Whittow & Harris between 1805 and 1808. Width 472 mm. Impressed workman's mark '2', 4 mm high.

Basket

This popular pattern was produced by Minton over many decades. Thirty-two table and nine teaware Basket pattern copper plates were listed in the 1810 inventory and the 1817 inventory included 33 table coppers (Plates 2.2 and 2.3). Prints for the pattern are included in the 1886 pattern book, where it is referred to as 'Old Basket', as shown in Plate 5.16. Importantly 32 of these early copper plates were found in the copper plate room, providing valuable evidence for the attribution of early Minton wares. The coppers were relatively thin and had

Plate 5.15. Minton pearlware Basket pattern 16-inch meat dish c.1820. The corresponding copper plate was found at the factory and is detailed below. Note how each engraving has a different flower arrangement in the basket. Width 427 mm. Impressed size mark 16.

Plate 5.16. The first of two pages in the Minton printed pattern book for 1886 which show details of Basket pattern engravings. The corresponding copper plates were found at the factory and could be dated to c.1805. Together with the copper plates, these prints have enabled a range of early Minton Basket pattern wares to be identified. Note that the prints are not always correctly labelled: the 10-inch plate actually corresponds to the copper plate for a nine-inch plate (see Plate 5.17).

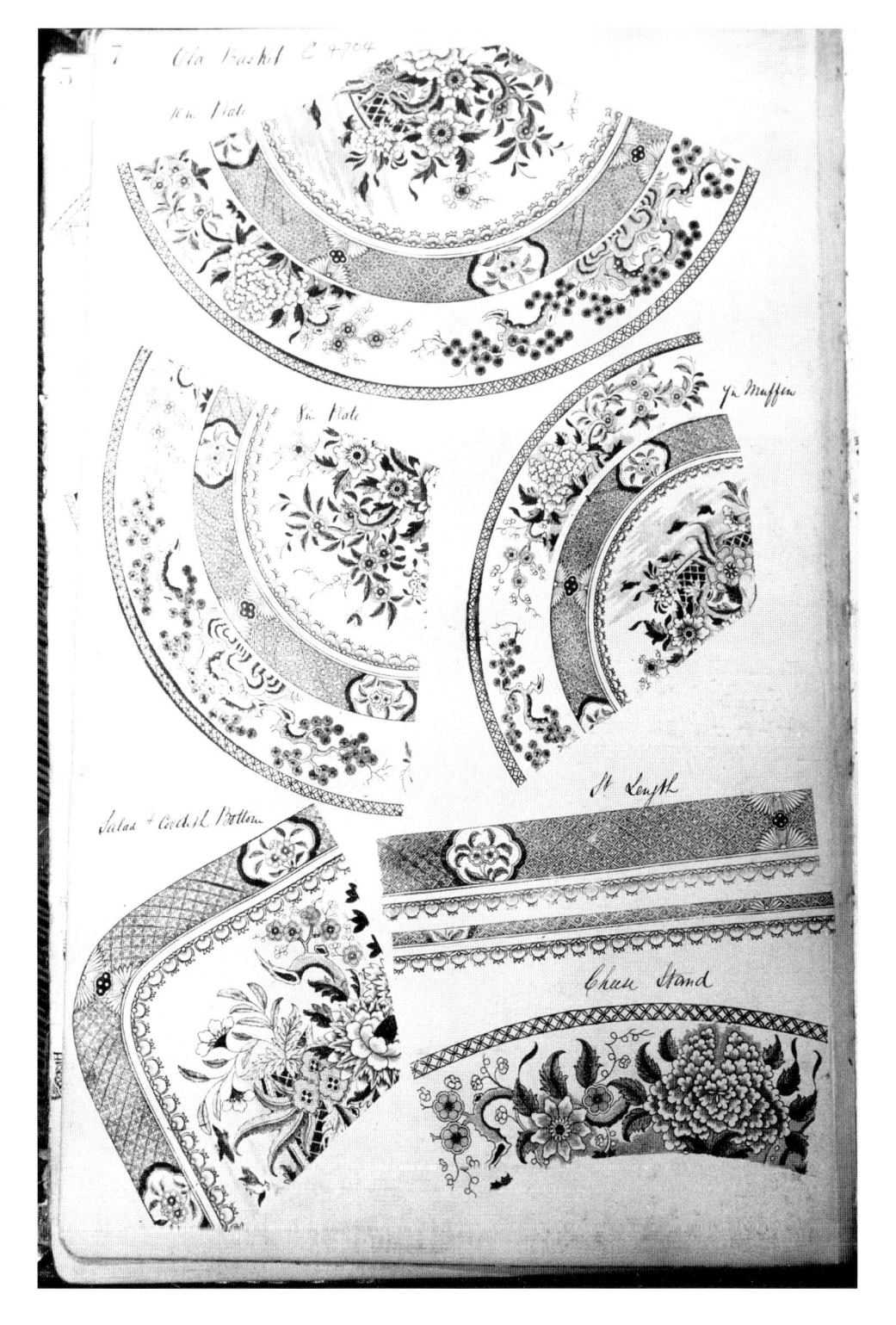

impressed numbers, consistent with the other early coppers found. About a third of the coppers had been metal plated. Three coppers are particularly important as they have coppersmith marks stamped on the reverse. One has 'B.WHITTOW & SON, No.31 SHOE LANE, HOLBORN, LONDON', and the other two 'WHITTOW & HARRIS, No 31 SHOE LANE, LONDON', as shown in Plate 5.14. These copper plate makers were researched by Drakard and Holdway,[14] who indicate that the first mark was used between 1798 and 1804, and the second between 1805 and 1808. Thus the pattern was probably engraved and introduced around 1805.

Plate 5.17. *Detail of the Minton Basket pattern copper plate engraving for the nine-inch dinner plate. It is seen to correspond to one of the pulls included in the 1886 print book, where it is wrongly labelled as for a 10-inch plate. It is of note, however, that the standard nine-inch plate, such as that illustrated in Plate 5.35, is significantly larger than nine inches. The illustrations clearly show the half light and half dark shading on several of the leaves, which is characteristic of the Minton version of this pattern. Engraving diameter 178 mm to the outer edge of the inner border.*

The Basket prints included in the 1886 Minton print book included both tea and tablewares. In addition to several 'straight lengths', parts of prints are illustrated for '10 inch plate, 8 inch plate, 7 inch muffin, salad & cov'dish bottom, cheese stand, soup tureen side, sauce tureen, ladle, sauce cover, can, coverdish, and pelican'. An additional note indicates that plates were also held for '10 in plate, 10 in soup, sauce stand, boat, soup stand and dishes 8, 9, 10, 12, 14, 16, 18 & 20'. The prints were compared with the surviving copper plates and found to correspond, although two of the prints would seem to have been wrongly labelled in the book. The print labelled '10 in Plate', and illustrated in Plate 5.16, was found to actually correspond to the copper plate for a nine-inch plate, as detailed in Plate 5.17. This explains the note in the book referring to an additional copper for a 10-inch plate. Although this copper could not be found, it presumably was that used to print the plate illustrated in Plate 5.18. The second problem is the print labelled 'sauce tureen', as the copper from which it was taken is inscribed 'tea cup'. The survival of several of the early teaware copper plates listed in 1810 supports the suggestion made in Chapter Two that the copper plate listing for 1817, which only listed the Basket tableware plates, did not include all the coppers held, probably omitting those not in regular use at that time.

Minton originally used Basket on the plain circular and oval Trophy shape dinner wares and dessert wares, which are included in the factory shape book of c.1830 as Shape G, as indicated in Plate 5.21. The earliest wares are normally found on pearlware, although occasional first period bone china tablewares are found, normally gilded and sometimes with the blue Sevres mark. This use on bone china is further confirmation that the coppers were original early Minton plates and not bought in on the closure of another factory. Basket pattern wares of clear-glazed Opaque China or Stone China body are found, indicating production throughout the 1820s. The concave-circular dinnerware plate illustrated in Plate 5.18 confirms that Basket was still in production in the 1860s, and early twentieth-century dinner wares are also occasionally found.

A range of Minton Basket pattern wares, attributed based on direct comparison with the surviving copper plates, is shown in Plates 5.14 to 5.34. Not only do these wares illustrate details of the Minton version of the pattern but also

Plate 5.18. Minton Basket pattern 10-inch earthenware dinner plate, 1868, showing relatively late use of the pattern on a clear glazed concave-shaped plate. Although the 10-inch plate copper plate is listed in the 1886 pattern book, it could not be found at the factory. Diameter 262 mm. Impressed 'MINTON' and year cypher for 1868.

Plate 5.19. Minton Basket pattern pearlware bowl, c.1820. The print corresponds to the copper plate used for the seven-inch Muffin plate, as included in the 1886 pattern book. Note how the main flower can be mistaken for a bunch of pears. Diameter 187 mm.

97

Plate 5.20.
Minton Basket pattern soup tureen, c.1825. Characteristic tureen shape used by Minton with Trophy shape dinner wares, seen in Plate 5.21 to correspond to factory Shape G of c.1830. Finely potted in a clear glazed Opaque China body. The main print used on each side of the tureen is seen to correspond to a print included in the 1886 pattern book, as shown below. The print used to decorate the base inside the tureen is seen to have been taken from the Minton copper plate illustrated above, which is inscribed '10', indicating normal use on the 10-inch meat dish. The print on the lid is taken from the 12-inch dish copper plate, as used on the serving dish shown in Plate 5.26. Length 256 mm. Mark P14.

Plate 5.21. *Minton Basket pattern sauce tureen, c.1820. Finely potted in a Semi-China body. Note the correspondence with Shape G in the factory shape book of c.1830. The main print used on the sides of the tureen corresponds to that used on the early Minton dessert comport shown in Plate 5.23. It does not correspond to the print in Plate 5.25, which is shown in the 1886 pattern book as for a sauce tureen. The print used on the lid corresponds to a small section of print labelled 'Sauce Cover' in the pattern book. The inside of the tureen is decorated with the circular print shown below. This is seen to correspond to the Ladle print in the pattern book. Note that the lion head handle applied to each side of the tureen has a flatter profile than that normally found on Minton Trophy shape tureens, such as used on the soup tureen in Plate 5.20. Length 176 mm.*

Plate 5.22. Minton Semi-China Basket pattern sauce tureen stand, c.1820. The print is taken from a copper plate found at the factory for the eight-inch dish. Width 193 mm.

Plate 5.23. Minton pearlware Basket pattern dessert comport, c.1810. The print used on the sides is the same as that used on the sauce tureen shown in Plate 5.21. The inner print can be seen to correspond to the Minton copper plate engraving for the 14-inch meat dish, as detailed below. Width 287 mm. Mark P7.

Plate 5.24. Minton pearlware Basket pattern radish tray, c.1815. The sides are decorated with the print shown in Plate 5.25 and the inside print corresponds to that used inside the soup tureen in Plate 5.20. Length 285 mm.

Plate 5.25. Print included in the 1886 pattern book labelled 'Sauce Tureen', but taken from a copper plate inscribed 'Tea Cup'. It is used on the radish tray in Plate 5.24 and the serving dish in Plate 5.26, but not the sauce tureen in Plate 5.21.

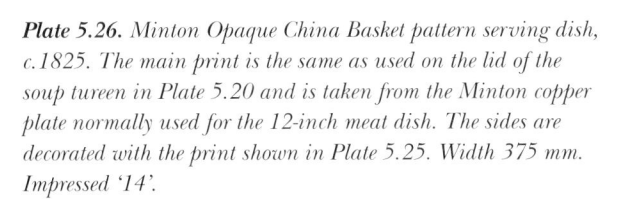

Plate 5.26. Minton Opaque China Basket pattern serving dish, c.1825. The main print is the same as used on the lid of the soup tureen in Plate 5.20 and is taken from the Minton copper plate normally used for the 12-inch meat dish. The sides are decorated with the print shown in Plate 5.25. Width 375 mm. Impressed '14'.

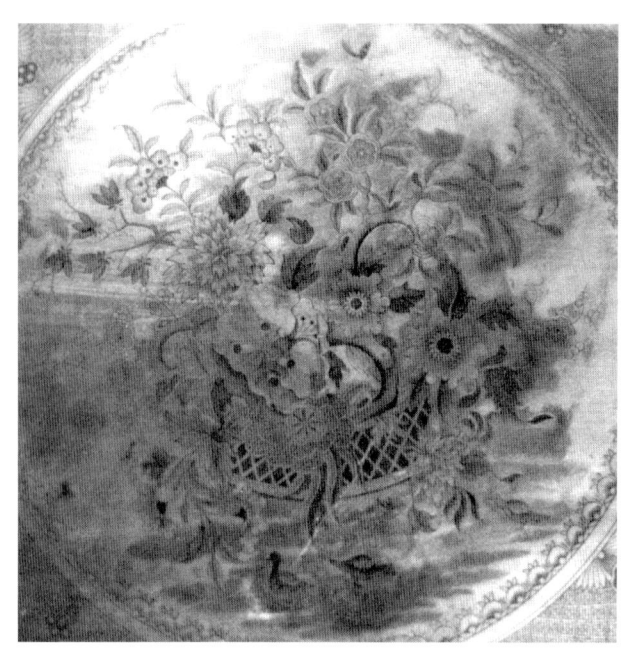

Plate 5.27. *Detail of the Minton Basket pattern copper plate inscribed 'soup' indicating normal use on a soup bowl. Width of engraving to outer edge of main border 267 mm.*

Plate 5.28. *Minton pearlware dessert dish, c.1810. Details of the print correspond exactly to the engraving in Plate 5.27, although some additional features in the copper indicate that some subsequent minor re-engraving must have been carried out. Minimum width 156 mm. Mark P7.*

Plate 5.29. *Minton Basket pattern pearlware broth bowl stand, c.1815. Printed from the Minton copper plate inscribed '6', indicating normal use on a six-inch plate. Diameter 170 mm. Impressed '5'.*

Plate 5.30. *Minton Basket pattern earthenware covered vegetable dish base, c.1830 (see also Plate 9.35). The print corresponds to that included in the 1886 pattern book labelled 'Salad & Covdish Bottom', as shown in Plate 5.16. Minimum width 226 mm.*

Plate 5.31. Pair of Basket pattern prints from the 1886 Minton pattern book. One labelled 'Can', presumably referring to a coffee can, and the other apparently labelled 'Pelican'. Note the different basket design and basic flower arrangement compared to the previously illustrated prints. The source print for this design, shown above, was found in the Minton archives.[15] *This was probably the design used primarily on tea wares.*

Plate 5.32. Minton Basket pattern pearlware broth bowl and cover, c.1815. The lid is decorated with the same print used on the stand illustrated in Plate 5.29. The main print on the side is seen to be of the same basic design as the 'teaware type' prints above. Width 187 mm.

Plate 5.33. Pearlware Basket pattern saucer, probably Minton, c.1810. The print on this fine quality piece shows strong similarities with the Minton designs illustrated above. Diameter 128 mm.

103

provide valuable confirmation of a range of early shapes. It is interesting to note the variation between engravings of the arrangement of flowers within the basket. Plates 5.31 to 5.33 detail the version of the pattern used by Minton on tea wares, which is seen to have a different basket design. Plate 5.31 includes the source print found in the factory archives,[15] which was published on 12 May 1794 by Laurie & Whittle, 53 Fleet Street, London. Plates 5.35 and 5.36 show further wares which are probably Minton but for which exactly matching engravings could not be found.

The Basket pattern was also produced by several other manufacturers, including Bathwell and Goodfellow, for whom marked pieces are occasionally found. Distinguishing between the various versions of the pattern is not straightforward as the factories often used essentially the same flower arrangements. This close correspondence of the designs suggests that the intention was to directly copy what was clearly a popular pattern. Close examination of other factory versions, such as the two illustrated here in Plates 5.37 and 5.38, and examples marked Bathwell & Goodfellow illustrated elsewhere,[16,17] reveals sufficient variation of detail to distinguish them from Minton wares. A useful indicator is that in the Minton engravings several of the leaves have half dark and half light shading, as can be clearly seen in Plate 5.17, whereas some other versions have plain dark leaves, sometimes with darker short dashes superimposed. The insect descending into the basket from the right is another feature which shows significant variation. The basic shape of the plates and their potting characteristics can also be helpful in distinguishing between factories, although the use of tureens with lion head handles seems common to most examples.

Plate 5.34. Minton pearlware Basket pattern wicker basket, c.1810. The main print is taken from the Minton copper plate normally used on the nine-inch meat dish. Detail of part of the engraving, which is in poor condition, is shown below. Width 247 mm. Mark P5.

Plate 5.35. Pearlware Basket pattern plate, probably Minton, c.1810. The plate is of characteristic Minton shape and the print corresponds closely to the Minton design in Plate 5.17. There are some minor differences in the fine detail of the engraving, however, indicating either that there were originally two engravings for this standard plate size, or that it was re-engraved after 1810, both of which are likely. Diameter 246 mm.

Plate 5.36. Pearlware Basket pattern plate, possibly Minton, c.1815. The print is different from that included in the 1886 print book for an eight-inch plate (see Plate 5.16). However, the plate is of characteristic Minton shape and many details of the print are typical of the Minton basket designs. It is possible that this is an early Minton version of the print for this plate size. Diameter 216 mm. Mark P17.

Plate 5.37. Pearlware Basket pattern plate, maker unknown, c.1820. The basic design is a close copy of the Minton version used on this standard plate size, but significant variation in detail is apparent. Note the unusual insect above the flowers. Well-potted concave-octagonal shape. Single recessed foot ring. Three single stilt marks to front of the rim. Diameter 243 mm.

Plate 5.38. Pearlware Basket pattern plate, maker unknown, c.1820. The same basic shape and design as used by Minton. Differences in detail distinguish this quite common version from the others, especially the dark specks used on some of the leaves. Plain circular shape with single recessed foot ring. Three triple rear and single front stilt marks. Diameter 249 mm. Impressed '6'.

Plate 5.39. Hand-painted Chinese export porcelain saucer dish, c.1790. This original oriental design was used as the basis for the Trophy pattern, and was produced by several factories; the example shown in Plate 5.41 was probably made by Minton. Diameter 210 mm.

Plate 5.40. Minton Trophy pattern plate, c.1850. Relatively late use of the design originally introduced some 50 years earlier. The use of Flow Blue tends to obscure details of the pattern. Rounded foot ring. Diameter 227 mm. Impressed marks 'BB' over 'New Stone'.

Trophy

Evidence that a version of this commonly found pattern was made by Minton is found in the 1810 inventory copper plate list which includes 24 Trophy pattern tableware coppers and six for tea wares. The pattern is a direct copy of a Chinese design normally found on plain circular wares, such as the saucer dish shown in Plate 5.39. A detailed discussion of the origins of this and related patterns is given by Copeland.[18] In the version illustrated here the central feature is surrounded by four groups of flowers mixed with objects representing symbolic treasures. Trophy is also listed in the 1817 inventory as one of the standard shapes for dinner plates. The first tentative attribution of a Minton version of this pattern was by Broughton[19] who illustrates two plain circular Trophy shape dinner plates of common form and impressed workman's mark, one bearing the Minton Hermit pattern and the other the Trophy pattern. This version of Trophy is illustrated in Plate 5.41 on another plate of characteristic Minton shape. As detailed in Plate 5.41, Minton may have re-engraved some of its early Trophy pattern copper plates, refining the lattice work in the border and central feature.

Based on the print alone, it is not easy to distinguish this possible Minton version of Trophy from that used by other factories, such as Spode, Heath,[20] Harrison[21] and no doubt others. Close attention must be paid to minor differences in border or pattern detail, combined with examination of potting characteristics and shape. Minton examples should be found on plain circular plates having a single recessed foot ring and three single stilt marks beneath the rim. However, very similar plates may well have been produced by other factories, such as the example by Stevenson in Plate 4.8. Note that Minton also used the Trophy pattern with the later 'New Stone' body, as shown in Plate 5.40.

Plate 5.41. Trophy pattern plate, probably Minton, c.1815. The pattern is seen to be a very close copy of the design shown in Plate 5.39 on Chinese porcelain. It was produced by several factories at the beginning of the nineteenth century. Minton Trophy copper plates are listed in 1810 for both tea and tablewares. This plain circular plate, which Minton referred to as the Trophy shape, corresponds exactly to known Minton plates. Another plate of the same shape and size, but dating from c.1800, has an almost identical print, differing primarily in the size of lattice engraving in the border and centre. The later engraving (top detail) has a finer lattice compared to the earlier one (lower detail). Both engravings can probably be attributed to Minton. Three single stilt marks under the rim, single recessed foot ring. Diameter 238 mm.

Dahlia

This oriental floral design was used by Minton on first period china as pattern 124. Coalport[22] also used the design on porcelain, so attribution cannot rely upon pattern alone; the plate shown in Plate 5.44 is possibly a Coalport example. The design is reminiscent of Chinese Lotus scrolls, but Dahlia pattern has become commonly used to describe it, perhaps from its use by Godden.[22]

The pattern is commonly found on earthenwares. Trophy shape dinner wares, dessert wares and tea wares have all been found which can probably be attributed to Minton based on shape, potting characteristics and workman's marks. The wicker basket shown in Plate 5.42 has potting characteristics and mouldings, including the distinctive handles, which exactly match known Minton examples, such as that shown in Plate 5.34. The saucer dish shown in Plate 5.43 has a typical Minton printer's mark. Although earthenware examples of this pattern have yet to be positively attributed to any other factory, a version may have been produced by Wedgwood[23] and possibly others.

Plate 5.42. Dahlia pattern pearlware wicker basket, probably Minton, c.1810. Although very similar baskets were made by other factories, the moulding, potting characteristics and handles on this example exactly match known Minton pieces, such as that illustrated in Plate 5.34. Width 242 mm.

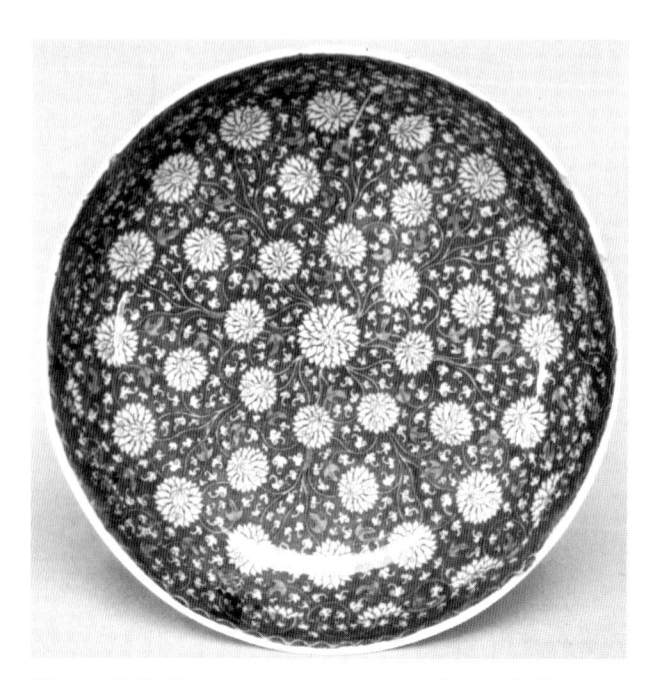

Plate 5.43. Dahlia pattern pearlware saucer dish, probably Minton, c.1810. Fine quality compact body with hard glassy glaze. Diameter 180 mm. Mark P7.

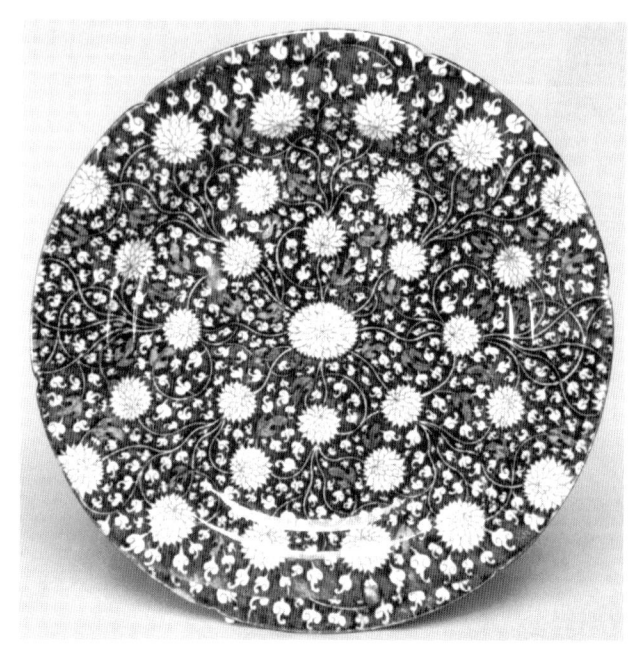

Plate 5.44. Dahlia pattern porcelain plate, c.1805. This piece could have been made by Coalport who included this design in their printed pattern book.[22] Single foot ring. Diameter 211 mm.

Plate 5.45. Plant pattern pearlware wicker basket, probably Minton, c.1810. The pattern is illustrated on a typical Minton Trophy shape dinner plate and wicker dessert wares. This basket exactly matches the body form, potting characteristics and moulded handles of the Minton Willow pattern basket in Plate 9.89. The pattern illustrates botanical specimens in a very similar manner to the Wedgwood botanical flowers series. Width 269 mm.

Plate 5.46. Plant pattern pearlware Trophy shape plate, probably Minton, c.1810. Note the Convolvulus and twine wreath border, similar to that used by Wedgwood shown in Plate 5.47. Diameter 241 mm. Mark P4.

Plate 5.47. Wedgwood clear-glazed earthenware concave shape Botanical pattern plate, c.1830. This Wedgwood version of the pattern is less common than that with the border of interlacing rings. Diameter 247 mm. No foot ring. Impressed 'WEDGWOOD' and 'H'.

Plant

This relatively rare botanical type pattern has been found on the typical Minton Trophy shape dinner plate shown in Plate 5.46, and the early wicker basket and stand in Plates 5.45 and 5.48. The basket exactly matches other Minton examples. A wicker plate in this pattern has also been illustrated.[24] The distinctive border features a wreath of Convolvulus with twine running through. The most commonly found botanical series was that produced by Wedgwood with a simple border of interlacing rings, easily distinguishable from the Minton border. Wedgwood did, however, also produce a later and less common botanical series with a Convolvulus border similar to but different from that used by Minton, as shown in Plate 5.47. This may be the Plant tableware pattern listed in 1810.

Plate 5.48. Plant pattern wicker basket stand, probably Minton, c.1810. This stand accompanies the basket shown in Plate 5.45. The edge has been painted underglaze in blue. Width 287 mm.

Plate 5.49. Dragon pattern pearlware coffee can, probably Minton, c.1815. The moulded handle exactly matches those found on known Minton cans, such as the Broseley pattern example shown in Plate 4.38. Several factories produced this pattern, normally on bone china tea wares. Diameter 65 mm.

Dragon

This popular pattern is most commonly found on bone china tea wares produced by several factories, including Spode, Coalport and Miles Mason. Although no Minton china is recorded in this pattern, it is listed as a teaware pattern in the 1817 factory inventory, and the pearlware coffee can shown in Plate 5.49 can probably be attributed to Minton based on its distinctive moulded handle form. This version of the pattern seems to closely match an example illustrated[25] on a tea saucer bearing a painted 'DONOVAN' retailer's mark. James Donovan was a china dealer in Dublin who bought wares from various Staffordshire manufactories, including Minton.

References

1. Minton MS 2287, Minton first period China Pattern Book 1 (Minton Archives).
2. G. Langford, *NCS Newsletter*, No. 100, 1995, pp. 75–76.
3. Pigot & Co's *National Commercial Directory* for 1828–29, Staffordshire, p. 717.
4. Minton MS 2419, 1870 Printed Pattern Book (Minton Archives).
5. Minton MS 2576, 1886 Printed Pattern Book (Minton Archives).
6. Minton MS 2313, 1886 Printed Pattern Book (Minton Archives).
7. R. Copeland, *Spode's Willow Pattern and other Designs after the Chinese*, 3rd ed. (Studio Vista, 1999), p. 149.
8. *Friends of Blue Bulletin*, No. 70, 1990, p. 7.
9. *Friends of Blue Bulletin*, No. 73, 1991, p. 2.
10. *Friends of Blue Bulletin*, No. 74, 1991, p. 2.
11. G.A. Godden, *Minton Pottery & Porcelain of the First Period* (Barrie & Jenkins, 1968), Plate 2.
12. *Friends of Blue Bulletin*, No. 46, 1984, p. 6.
13. A.W. Coysh and R.K. Henrywood, *The Dictionary of Blue and White Printed Pottery Volume 2* (Antique Collectors Club, 1989), p. 158.
14. D. Drakard and P. Holdway, *Spode Printed Ware* (Longman, 1983), p. 26.
15. Minton MS 1988, Book of Various Source Prints (Minton Archives).
16. D. Kay, *NCS Newsletter*, No. 87, 1992, p. 14.
17. *Friends of Blue Bulletin*, No. 55, 1987, p. 10.
18. Copeland, *Spode's Willow Pattern*, p. 130.
19. *Friends of Blue Bulletin*, No. 84, 1994, p. 3.
20. A.W. Coysh and R.K. Henrywood, *The Dictionary of Blue and White Printed Pottery* (Antique Collectors Club, 1982), p. 174.
21. R. Pomfret, *NCS Newsletter*, No. 107, 1997, p. 28.
22. G.A. Godden, *Coalport and Coalbrookdale Porcelains* (Herbert Jenkins, 1970), fig. 79.
23. *True Blue Transfer Printed Earthenware, Exhibition Catalogue* (Friends of Blue, 1998), p. 118.
24. Coysh and Henrywood, *Dictionary of Blue and White Vol. 2*, p. 221.
25. Coysh and Henrywood, *Dictionary of Blue and White*, p. 113.

Chapter Six

Catalogue of Patterns
3. Early European Influence

Shepherd

This teaware pattern is a good illustration of how the early chinoiserie designs soon evolved to display a more European influence. The basic layout is still very similar to early imported Chinese designs, such as the Broseley and Bridge patterns, but the buildings, trees and figures are in a European style and the border more floral. The pattern is shown in Plate 6.1 on a pearlware teapot of characteristic Minton form. A prominent feature is a shepherd standing in the foreground addressing a reclining lady.

Attribution of the pattern to Minton is based on its use on the teapot shown in Plate 6.1, and another of smaller size bearing the characteristic printer's mark P2. It is of note that the 1810 inventory includes a set of teaware copper plates for a 'Shephard' pattern. Further examples of the pattern on wares of very good quality with a well-fitting lustrous glaze are shown in Plates 6.2 to 6.4. These were probably not made by Minton: although the basic design is essentially the same as in Plate 6.1 the layout is slightly different, which would not be expected on similar sized teapots from the same factory. There are also subtle differences in the treatment of the figures, trees and border, and the secondary spout and handle prints are also different. Furthermore, the shapes have not been positively linked to any other Minton teaware pattern, nor has the use of ochre rims. They are probably from a major factory which may also have produced the teapot in Plate 6.5 and used the Dahlia and Lyre pattern.

Plate 6.1. Minton pearlware Shepherd pattern old oval teapot, c.1810. Attribution of this pattern to Minton is based on its use on this teapot of characteristic Minton form, and another with the same print but of a slightly smaller size. Length 244 mm. Unmarked, but the smaller pot has mark P2.

Plate 6.2. *Shepherd pattern pearlware teapot with ochre painted rims, maker unknown, c.1810. A fine quality piece, very well potted with a lustrous glaze, in a basic shape used by many factories. Compared to the version in Plate 6.1 there are subtle differences in the treatment of the figures, trees and border. The secondary patterns on the spout and handle are also different. This second version of the pattern is used on the coffee pot and tea bowl in Plates 6.3 and 6.4. Domed strainer. Length 251 mm.*

Plate 6.3. *Shepherd pattern pearlware coffee pot with ochre painted rims, maker unknown, c.1810. Replacement lid. The main pattern design and the decoration to handle and spout are the same as on the teapot in Plate 6.2. It is interesting to note that a coffee pot of the same form, including the distinctive moulded spout, has been noted decorated with the pattern illustrated on the teapot in Plate 6.5. This Shepherd print has also been noted on a coffee pot of a simpler body form, but with apparently the same handle and spout, such as illustrated by Copeland[1] decorated with a version of the Lyre pattern, and as also seen decorated in the Dahlia pattern. Nine-hole diamond-shaped plain strainer. Height to top of spout 213 mm.*

Plate 6.4. *Shepherd pattern pearlware tea bowl with ochre rim, maker unknown, c.1810. Finely potted with a body and glaze matching the teapot in Plate 6.2. Diameter 81 mm.*

112

Plate 6.5. Pearlware blue printed teapot of fine quality with ochre painted rims, maker unknown, c.1810. The body and glaze match the coffee pot in Plate 6.3, and this pattern has been seen on a coffee pot apparently of the same shape. The border appears very similar to that used by Wedgwood on the Chinese Vase pattern.[2] Nine-hole diamond-shaped plain strainer. Length 250 mm. Indistinct printer's mark.

Queen of Sheba

This familiar early pattern is sometimes referred to as Indian Procession. The central figures appear to be based on a design used on shop signs in London during the eighteenth century,[3] with titles such as Indian Queen, Old Indian Queen or Indian Queen and Star. The castle is similar to that in the Shepherd pattern and in Spode's Gothic Castle pattern. Minton used this pattern on plain octagonal dinner wares, and the example shown in Plate 6.6 is on a baking dish of identical form to the Minton Willow pattern dish shown in Plate 3.9 – both bear the same crown printer's mark P1. A dinner plate of standard Minton form is shown in Plate 6.7. The same version of the pattern is also found on toy dinner

Plate 6.6. Minton Queen of Sheba pattern 14-inch baking dish, c.1810. This dish has the same moulded body form and deep foot ring as the Willow pattern dish in Plate 3.9. Width 365 mm. Mark P1.

Plate 6.7. Minton Queen of Sheba pattern pearlware dinner plate, c.1810. The distinctive central figures, probably based on a popular eighteenth-century shop sign design, are combined with a gothic type castle. Width 235 mm. Mark P11.

Plate 6.8. Queen of Sheba pattern pearlware jug, maker unknown, c.1810. Compared with the Minton version, this pattern is seen to show significant differences in the detailed design, especially the central figures. The jug is not a typical Minton form. Height 220 mm.

wares. Another version of the pattern is used on the jug illustrated in Plate 6.8. This jug differs from the normal Minton shape and there are numerous significant differences in the pattern detail, especially the figures in the foreground, indicating that the jug is by another factory which also used this basic pattern.

It is possible that this is the pattern in the 1810 copper plate list called 'Windsor Castle'. Although the Minton English Scenery series does feature Windsor Castle on the largest meat dish (Plate 7.25), this was not produced until after 1820 at the earliest.

Roman or Kirk Series

Roman is listed in the 1810 Minton inventory as a pattern used on tablewares, and is no doubt the pattern referred to in 1873 by the long-standing factory employee Mr Hassels in saying, 'I forgot to mention a pattern that was done in the Old gentleman's days, it consisted of a variety of Roman and Grecian figures with a dark ground and was thought very good.'[4] Four main dinnerware series were made which fit this description. One is the famous Greek pattern introduced by Spode in about 1806[5] and based[6] on the drawings published by Kirk[7] and Tischbein[8] of ancient vases in the collection of Sir William Hamilton. An example from this series is shown in Plate 6.9. The second series was made at the Knottingly Pottery[9,10] by Wedgwood & Co. around 1800. The third series, as illustrated in Plate 6.10, is normally found with an ochre painted rim on wares that do not match those of Minton, and is traditionally attributed to Herculaneum,[11] although this attribution is questionable as a marked piece is still to be reported. The fourth version is also based on the drawings of Kirk, and is commonly referred to as the Kirk Series. Examples of this previously unattributed series are given by Coysh and Henrywood.[12] It is this version which has been shown to be the Minton 'Roman' pattern.

Evidence for attributing the Kirk series to Minton is that all examples examined to date are on dinner and dessert wares of known Minton form and potting characteristics, often bearing known Minton printer's marks. Furthermore

Plate 6.9. *Spode pearlware Greek pattern eight-inch plate, c.1810. This popular pattern was produced by Spode over many years. Each type of ware has a different central design and different figures within the four border panels, although details of the four vases remain the same. The design is easily distinguished from the Minton Roman pattern, even though both series are based largely on the drawings of Kirk. No foot ring, three single stilt marks beneath the rim. Width 210 mm. Impressed 'Spode' (12 mm long).*

Plate 6.10. *Pearlware Greek pattern eight-inch plate with ochre painted rim, possibly Herculaneum, c.1810. This version, sometimes termed the Etruscan design, is characterised by a central pattern, typically featuring chariots and figures, surrounded by a border of oval figure medallions on a Greek key background. An ochre painted rim is also normally used. Although traditionally attributed to Herculaneum, no marked piece has yet been recorded. No foot ring, three triple rear and single front stilt marks. Width 204 mm.*

a copy of the original 1804 publication of the drawings by Kirk[7] from which the designs were taken is still in the Minton archives.

A range of Minton Roman pattern wares are illustrated in Plates 6.11 to 6.17, together with some of the corresponding original designs from Kirk. The Minton version is seen to be easily distinguishable from other versions, a particular point to note being the dark blue ground which is engraved with fine jig-jag lines. The series is characterised by a central group of Greek or Roman figures surrounded by a distinctive design incorporating acanthus type leaves surmounted by birds and fan-like motifs. A different central design is used for each of the various sized plates and dishes in the service and the arrangement of Greek figures used in the outer border also varies. The most commonly found dinner plate is the 10-inch size shown in Plate 6.11, suggesting that this was the standard size used in the service. This is slightly unusual at this early period when other contemporary Minton tableware patterns used the nine-inch plate as standard. Another interesting point to note in Plate 6.11 is that two subtly different plate designs were available for this size, one being slightly more discreet than the other with extra robes being draped around the figures.

Although the Spode Greek pattern remained popular for many years, the Roman pattern is normally found only on wares of a pearlware body, suggesting that it was not produced after about 1820; indeed it is not listed as a stock pattern in the 1817 copper plate list. The same basic design as shown in Plate 6.14 has, however, been found on a dinner plate of twentieth-century production, though a different and slightly larger engraving was used for the modern version.

Plate 6.11. Pair of Minton Roman pattern 10-inch dinner plates, c.1810. Note the characteristic design of acanthus type leaves and fan motifs surrounding a central feature of Greek or Roman figures on a dark ground. Different figures were used in the centre and border for the various pieces in the dinner service. The pattern is traditionally known as the Kirk Series, after the 1804 publication from which the designs were taken. The central design of this size of plate is taken from Kirk's Plate 59, shown right, which features Act 4 of the Tragedy of Euripedes, Iphigenia being told of the death of Agamemnon. Interestingly Minton used two versions of the design, one can be seen as a direct copy whereas the other uses extra robes to make the scene more discreet. The figures in the border also come from Kirk, with two examples shown below, including Jupiter in a chariot with thunder in his hand and myrtle around his head. Width of each plate 249 mm. Mark P7 on right plate.

Plate 6.12 (above left). Minton Roman pattern six-inch plate, c.1810. This was probably the smallest of five different sized plates available in the series. The central design is taken from Kirk Plate 30. Width 164 mm.

Plate 6.13 (above right). Minton Roman pattern seven-inch plate. The main design is seen to be based on Kirk Plate 51, shown right, which features Acratus, the genius of drunkards, with a female carrying myrtle. Width 183 mm. Mark P5.

Plate 6.14. Minton Roman pattern nine-inch dinner plate, c.1810. The design is seen to be based on Kirk Plate 54, shown right. Note the addition of a circular cartouche containing various symbols. Similar additions are found on several of the designs in the series. The same engraving is used to decorate inside the base of the vegetable tureen shown in Plate 6.17. Significantly this print has also been noted on the early concave-octagonal nine-inch plate shape, as used by Minton for the Bird pattern. Width 236 mm. Mark P6.

Plate 6.15. *Minton Roman pattern root dish base and cover, c.1810. The design on this fine piece is seen to be based on several of Kirk's illustrations, two of which are shown above. Note the distinctive jig-jag engraving used for the dark ground. This piece is missing its inner liner used for containing the vegetables, which would have had a rim to take the lid and may have been divided to form two or four sections. Root dishes were listed in the 1810 inventory in three sizes, 10, 11 and 12-inch, with options for single or double divided. They were amongst the most expensive items listed at 8s. for the 12-inch size double divided, reflecting the cost of the multiple parts. Overall length 290 mm.*

Plate 6.16. *Minton Roman pattern sauce tureen, c.1810. Note the detail of the 'fiddlestick' knob and the 'ears' providing handles to the base. These are typical for the plain octagonal dinner wares. The design used along the side of the tureen is based on Kirk Plate 27 and the chariot design seen on the lid is based on Kirk Plate 12. Overall length 180 mm.*

Plate 6.17. Minton Roman pattern covered vegetable dish, c.1810. In common with most of the examples found in this pattern this piece is of excellent quality, being relatively thinly potted with a hard glassy glaze. Minimum width of base 228 mm.

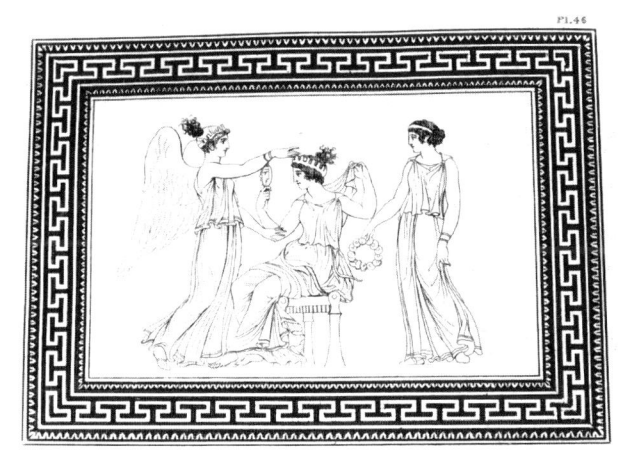

Plate 6.18. Some further examples of Kirk's illustrations used by Minton in its Roman series. Plate 46 above is the basis of the main design used on the eight-inch plate (Plate 9.1). Plate 17 was used on a meat dish and drainer[13] and Plate 61, shown right, on the large 20-inch dish.[14]

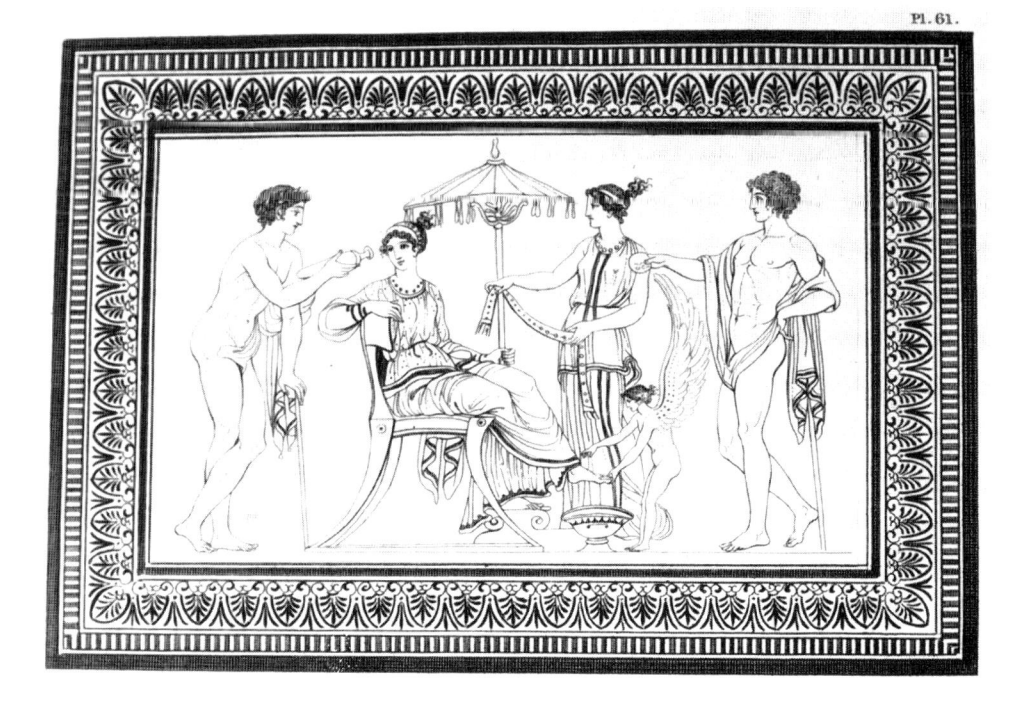

119

Plate 6.19. *Minton Bird pattern pearlware wicker basket featuring a pair of Grebes, c.1810. As illustrated above, this basket closely matches that printed with a known Minton Basket pattern engraving and illustrated in Plate 5.34. Although very similar Baskets were produced by other factories, examination of Minton baskets has identified several features which, when found together, indicate Minton manufacture. The base is flat with three stilt marks, the moulded bow handles are the same on a given basket size (note however the variation shown in Plate 9.90) and there are distinctive hand repairs to the moulding at each end beneath the handles. Despite these features, it is still normally necessary to make a direct comparison to be sure of a Minton shape. Width 244 mm. Mark P2.*

Ornithological Series or Bird

This series of patterns depicts a variety of birds within a common border of floral panels, with different birds being used on each of the main pieces in the dinner service. Examples of the series are occasionally found marked 'Stevenson', but it is apparent that several factories used the same basic design, including Minton. A version is attributed to Minton based on its use on wares of characteristic Minton shape with typical Minton printer's marks. The pattern is traditionally referred to as the 'Ornithological Series', but the Minton factory name was probably 'Bird', this being listed in the 1810 copper plate list as both a tableware pattern and one for ewer and basin. Distinguishing between the various factory versions is difficult as they use an almost identical border design, very similar shapes and sometimes very similar bird arrangements. Identifying the Minton Bird pattern must therefore rely heavily upon close attention to shape, potting characteristics and the minor variations which inevitably occur between the engravings used by different manufacturers.

Plate 6.19 shows the pattern on a wicker basket of Minton form. Details of the basket exactly match the piece printed with a known Minton Basket pattern engraving (Plate 5.34), as can be seen from the comparison of the moulded bow handles. Minton used the pattern on concave-octagonal dinner wares, such as the dinner plate illustrated in Plate 6.20. This plate has single stilt marks and no foot ring, in common with the plain octagonal wares. To date the only other patterns found on this early concave-octagonal shape of plate with no foot ring are some examples of the Roman pattern and a small plate printed with the Bewick Stag pattern. The concave-octagonal plate shape was probably changed c.1815 to the more commonly found version with a double foot ring. Other examples of the Minton Bird pattern are shown in Plates 6.23, 6.25 and 6.26.

There was a strong interest in natural history at this period with publications featuring illustrations of quadrupeds and birds being particularly popular. Amongst the most skilled of engravers of such illustrations was Thomas Bewick (1753–1828) and Minton drew upon Bewick engravings to produce several fine patterns at this period. Many of the designs used in the ornithological series are based on illustrations found in Bewick's *A History of British Birds*

Plate 6.20. Minton Bird pattern pearlware concave-octagonal nine-inch dinner plate, c.1810. The plate has a fine quality lustrous glaze on a relatively thinly potted body. The design is based directly on the Bewick prints shown below. Essentially the same pattern, but printed in reverse, was used by another manufacturer, as shown in Plate 6.21. Width 238 mm. Mark P4.

Plate 6.21. Ornithological series pearlware concave-octagonal nine-inch dinner plate, maker unknown c.1815. A mirror image of the same basic design as used by Minton. The border has a peripheral engraved line running around the edge of the rim. Slightly more heavily potted than the Minton example in Plate 6.20. Single recessed foot ring. Three single stilt marks beneath the rim. Diameter 246 mm. Impressed 'T' (4 mm high).

Plate 6.22. Bewick engravings of the Peacock and the Turkey, taken from his BRITISH BIRDS.[16] The bird pattern design used by Minton in Plate 6.20 is seen to be based on direct copies of these prints. Width of prints, Turkey 83 mm, Peacock 88 mm.

Plate 6.23. Minton Bird pattern pearlware concave-octagonal eight-inch dinner plate c.1810. Width 213 mm. Mark P4.

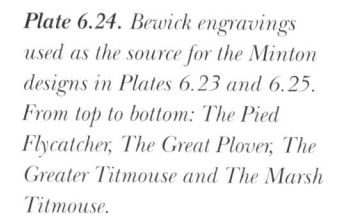

Plate 6.24. Bewick engravings used as the source for the Minton designs in Plates 6.23 and 6.25. From top to bottom: The Pied Flycatcher, The Great Plover, The Greater Titmouse and The Marsh Titmouse.

Plate 6.25. Minton Bird pattern pearlware custard cup, c.1810. A fine quality piece of distinctive Minton form. Although decorated inside the rim, it would originally have had a lid. Height 56 mm. Mark P4.

Plate 6.26. Minton Bird pattern footed pickle dish stand, c.1810. Although other factories made very similar pickle sets, this stand corresponds exactly to other known Minton pieces. The pattern includes the Kestrels shown in Plate 6.27 and the Greater Titmouse (Plate 6.24). The engraving seems to correspond to that used on a supper set section and lid illustrated by Coysh and Henrywood,[15] which also includes the Kingfisher shown below. Width 298 mm. Mark P4.

Plate 6.27. Bewick engravings of the male (upper) and female (lower) Kestrel, used on the Minton design in Plate 6.26. The Kingfisher and the Dusky Grebe have also been used in the series, probably by Minton.

Plate 6.28. Ornithological series 20-inch pearlware concave-octagonal meat dish, maker unknown, c.1815. A fine quality piece with a well-fitting lustrous glaze. The dimensions and shape of this dish do not match Minton dishes of this basic shape and size. The peripheral engraved line around the border may link this to the plate shown in Plate 6.21. No foot ring. Three single stilt marks beneath the rim. Width 515 mm.

Plate 6.29. Stevenson Ornithological series pearlware six-inch plate, c.1815. Note the distinctive dark edges surrounding the five-petal border flower heads. Three triple rear and single front stilt marks. No foot ring. Diameter 162 mm. Impressed 'Stevenson' above a three-masted ship.

Plate 6.30. Ornithological series pearlware vegetable dish base, maker unknown, c.1815. The body and glaze and the impressed mark link this piece to the plate in Plate 6.21. Width 216 mm. Impressed 'I' (4 mm high).

(1797–1804).[16,17] The examples in Plates 6.22, 6.24 and 6.27 show how closely Minton copied the Bewick engravings, no doubt enhancing the appeal of the series.

Plate 6.29 shows an example of the Stevenson version of the pattern. In common with the Stevenson plate illustrated by Coysh and Henrywood,[18] a dark edging to the five-petaled flowers can be identified as a distinctive border feature. Further marked Stevenson examples are required to see how representative this is. Coysh and Henrywood link these pieces to Andrew Stevenson potting at Cobridge. Plate 6.21 shows a further version of the pattern by an unknown maker on a dinner plate of fine quality and the same basic size as the Minton example in Plate 6.20. The central design is seen to be an almost exact mirror image of the

Minton design, although several minor variations are apparent. The border is also very similar to Minton, as are the plate shape and potting characteristics, including use of single stilt marks beneath the rim. The use of a foot ring and fairly thick potting, however, help to distinguish this from the Minton plate. The same factory probably also produced the very good quality examples shown in Plates 6.28 and 6.30. The plate and vegetable dish base have an identical impressed workman's mark. The fine meat dish in Plate 6.28 can easily be mistaken as a Minton piece, especially given the basic shape and the use of three single rear stilt marks. The dimensions do not, however, correspond exactly to known Minton concave-octagonal dishes of this size and the piece is heavier than would be expected for Minton. Furthermore a matching 20-inch dish has been seen with the three single stilt marks on the face, not known on Minton wares of this period. The dish can be linked to the version shown in Plate 6.21 as both engravings have a line running around the rim at the outer border edge. No line is present on the Minton or Stevenson versions.

Bewick Stag

This distinctive pattern corresponds to a hand-painted design used by Minton on bone china.[19] The pattern name derives from the Stag being based on a woodcut by Thomas Bewick from his *General History of Quadrupeds* (1790),[20] as illustrated in Plate 6.32. The same source is seen to have been used for some of the animals in the border. The pattern was used on distinctive indented concave-octagonal dinner wares, as illustrated in Plate 6.33. Note, however, that a smaller six-inch plate is known (see Plate 9.4) of non-indented concave-octagonal shape with no foot ring, as used with the Bird pattern, and bearing the distinctive crown printer's mark P1. The tureen shape has the same oval base as used for the Basket pattern, but with an indented octagonal lid, as used with the Camel and Giraffe pattern (see Plate 9.29). The fine ewer shown in Plate 6.31 indicates that use of the Bewick Stag pattern was not confined to dinner wares.

Plate 6.31. Minton Bewick Stag pattern pearlware ewer, c.1815. The main transfer has been cut to make it fit the rounded profile near the ewer base, indicating that the engraving may have been designed for a flatter-sided piece, perhaps a soup tureen. Height 208 mm.

Plate 6.32. Bewick engravings of the Stag, the Grey Squirrel and a tailpiece, from his HISTORY OF QUADRUPEDS and used by Minton in the Bewick Stag pattern.

Plate 6.33. Minton Bewick Stag pattern pearlware indented concave-octagonal nine-inch dinner plate, c.1815. This distinctive design, based on the engravings of Thomas Bewick, was also used by Minton hand-painted on bone china. Double recessed foot ring. Width 246 mm. Mark P2.

Plate 6.34. Bewick engravings of the Arabian Camel and the Cameleopard, from his HISTORY OF QUADRUPEDS. These appear to have been the source of the animals in Minton's Camel and Giraffe pattern. The use of the name Cameleopard to describe the Giraffe perhaps explains the rather unusual combination of animals used in this design.

Plate 6.35. Minton Camel and Giraffe pattern indented concave-octagonal nine-inch dinner plate, c.1815. A distinctive and rather exotic design, it was used on the same plate shape as the Bewick Stag pattern. Note that although some examples of this pattern are found on plates with no foot ring, such as that shown here, it is also found on those with double foot rings, such as the Bewick Stag piece in Plate 6.33. Width 247 mm. Mark P4.

Camel and Giraffe

This distinctive pattern is illustrated in Plate 6.35 and is seen to be an unusual combination of chinoiserie and European design. The inspiration for the animals is again seen to be Bewick engravings, as shown in Plate 6.34. It is attributed to Minton based on its use on dinner and dessert wares of typical Minton form with a range of characteristic printer's marks. It is found on the same indented concave-octagonal dinner wares as used by Minton for the Bewick Stag pattern. These distinctively-shaped plates were produced both with no foot ring and, probably at a slightly later date, with a double foot ring. The pattern has also been recorded on a dessert dish of the same distinctive shape as that decorated with the Chinese Sports pattern illustrated by Heywood,[21] both dishes bearing the printed mark P4. The pattern seems to be unique to Minton, although a giraffe is featured in similar types of design by other makers.

Monk's Rock Series

This is a finely engraved pattern consisting of a series of rural views with a common border and which is traditionally referred to as Monk's Rock, this being the first view to be identified.[22] Although no copper plates have been found at the factory, the original source prints for eight of the designs have been found amongst old engravings pasted into a book[23] – these are illustrated in Plates 6.36 to 6.46 together with corresponding printed wares. Importantly each of the source prints has had a pencil grid superimposed, no doubt as an aid to the engraver transferring the design to the copper plate. Similar grids are found on other source prints at the factory for some later designs. The source prints appear to have been collected from several publications. The only two which are dated, January 1813, were published in Middiman's *Select Views in Great Britain*.[24] One is the view of Monk's Rock, Tenby, and the other a view of Beeston Castle. Each of the Middiman views is accompanied by a brief but interesting caption:

The great insulated rock of Beeston, composed of sandstone, is very lofty and precipitous on three sides, affording the most curious birds-eye prospect imaginable; on the other side it slopes down 366 feet to Beeston Brook from the summit. The castle has been a place of very great strength; the access about midway of the slope was defended by a great gateway, and a strong wall, fortified with round towers, which ran from one edge of the precipice to the other, across the slope, but never surrounded the hill. The line within may be about four or five acres. The castle on the summit is defended on one side by an amazing ditch cut out of the live rock, on the other by an abrupt precipice: within is a square chapel and a draw well sunk through the highest part of the rock to the level of Beeston Brook below. The ruins belong to Sir Roger Mostyn, Bart. Beeston gives name to an ancient family, of whom was Sir William Beeston, Govenor of Jamaica. In the highest part of the hill, within the walls, was a well 91 yards deep. In the patents of Henry III it is called the castle on the rock.

Interestingly the grid superimposed on the Monk's Rock scene omits much of the sky, which is consistent with the view actually used in the series. The caption accompanying the original publication gives some detail of the view:

Tenby is a neat walled town on a dry rock, commanding the sea, very considerable for its port and plenty of fish (whence it is called Tenby-y-Piscoid): it is governed by a major and bailiff. The shore retreating to the west, one sees the poor remains of Manober Castle, which Giraldus called Pyrrhus' Mansion, and which in his time was, as he tells us, 'excellently furnished with towers and bulwarks, having on the west a spacious harbour, on the north and north west close under its walls a fine fish pond, considerable both for its beauty and depth of water in it'. The romantic rock which makes one of the most prominent features in the anexed engraving, seen from Tenby, presents a very curious and grotesque appearance, and seems to shelter the beach, where the bathing machines are in readiness for the visitors.

Minton normally used this pattern on plain octagonal meat dishes and concave-octagonal plates with a double foot ring. The tureen shape is unusual and would seem to be unique to this pattern, although the distinctive knob was used with other patterns. The floral border as used on the meat dish was used on the

Plate 6.36. Beeston Castle, Cheshire, engraved by S. Middiman and published in January 1813 by Boydell & Co.. This was used as the basis for the engraving used by Minton on the 20-inch meat dish in the Monk's Rock series, as well as a smaller engraving used later on black printed tea wares (see Plate 11.2). Note the faint pencil grid, presumably used as an aid to the engraver copying the print. MS 1987. Width 182 mm.

Plate 6.37. Minton Monk's Rock series pearlware 18-inch meat dish, c.1815, and source print. The view of Monk's Rock, Tenby used on this dish is based on the Middiman engraving published in January 1813. The original print from the Minton archives is illustrated here. The pencil grid superimposed by the engraver clearly defines the part of the scene used for the copper plate. Although each main piece in this series uses a different central design, the pattern is commonly referred to as the Monk's Rock series after this distinctive view. Width of dish 471 mm. Width of source print 182 mm.

Plate 6.38. *Minton Monk's Rock series pearlware 16-inch meat dish, c.1815, and source print. The main view of a River Crossing is based directly on the print shown here. This was one of five related source prints used by Minton for this series (see also Plates 6.39, 6.40, 6.42 and 6.44), all cut out and pasted into a book (MS 1987) with no reference to their origin. Width of dish 422 mm, mark P6. Width of print 191 mm.*

Plate 6.39. Minton Monk's Rock series pearlware 14-inch meat dish, c.1815, and source print. This rural scene is referred to as the Anonymous Inn as the original source print is seen to feature an inn or tavern sign which has been omitted from the copper plate engraving. Width of dish 376 mm, mark P4. Width of print 199 mm.

Plate 6.40. *Minton Monk's Rock series pearlware nine-inch dinner plate, c.1815, and source print. The Watermill scene is taken directly from the illustrated source print. As with several Minton patterns, two similar engravings were used for the standard plate size. The other engraving is shown in Plate 6.41 and is seen to include additional animals grazing in the foreground. This Watermill scene was also used on Minton dessert wares in this series. The plate shape is concave-octagonal with a double foot ring. This is in contrast to the meat dishes used in the series, which were of a plain octagonal shape with no foot ring. This corresponds to the 1817 inventory entry for block moulds which includes concave-octagonal plates but only plain octagonal meat dishes. Width of plate 247 mm, mark P5. Width of print 198 mm.*

Plate 6.41. Minton Monk's Rock series pearlware soup plate, c.1815. The animals grazing in the foreground distinguish this version of the Water Mill scene from that shown in Plate 6.40, though clearly both engravings are derived from the same source print. Width 241 mm. Impressed '7'.

Plate 6.42. Minton Monk's Rock series pearlware eight-inch plate, c.1815, and source print. This attractive Thatched Cottage design is again a faithful copy of the original source print. Plate width 221 mm, mark P4. Print width 205 mm.

tureen lid, but the main design is framed by another distinctive floral arrangement which is also found on other hollow ware items in this series such as the covered jug in Plate 6.50. It is likely that the pattern was introduced shortly after the publication of Middiman's prints in 1813. The earlier wares found are on a pearlware body, but there is some later use on Semi-China. The tureen shape is not listed in the factory shape book of c.1830. This series may correspond to the Landscape pattern listed in the 1817 inventory. Alternatively, given that the predominant feature in the majority of the prints is a cottage, it may have been listed as 'Cottage'. These were easily the most valuable copper plates at that time (see Plate 2.3), consistent with the detailed engraving required for such elaborate scenic designs.

The jug illustrated in Plate 6.51 is not a typical Minton form and the pattern detail differs from that used on Minton pieces. The indication is that the pattern was copied by another factory, but perhaps only on hollow wares such as jugs and mugs, as no dinner wares have yet been found that cannot be attributed to Minton.

Plate 6.43. Minton Monk's Rock series pearlware six-inch plate, c.1815. The main feature on this, the smallest plate size normally supplied in the dinner service, is the Thatched Barn. Note how the bushes to the left resemble an animal. Width 160 mm, mark P6.

Plate 6.44. Minton Monk's Rock series Semi-China dessert dish, c.1820, and source print. This fine Family Cottage scene was used on both dessert dishes and the 10-inch meat dish. The example illustrated is a relatively late use of the pattern on a Semi-China handled dessert dish shape apparently unique to Minton and used with many patterns during the 1820s. Earlier Monk's Rock series dessert wares used the traditional pearlware shapes (see Plate 9.71). Dish width 264 mm. Print width 208 mm.

Plate 6.45. Minton Monk's Rock series Semi-China square dessert dish, c.1820. This Riverside Picnic scene was also used inside the salad bowl. Width 217 mm.

Plate 6.46. Source print, titled 'View of Bengrove, Gloucestershire', used by Minton for the seven-inch Monk's Rock series plate. Further named views pasted into the same book, but apparently not used by Minton, are a view near Bengrove, one of Beckford, Gloucestershire and one of Ashton Church, Worcestershire. Each appears to have been washed over in sepia paint in aquatint style and all are probably from the same source. Width 229 mm.

Plate 6.47. Minton Monk's Rock series pearlware sauce tureen, c.1815. A distinctive tureen shape which appears to be unique to this pattern, although the handles and knob were also used on the Dove pattern tureen (Plate 6.59), and a similar knob is found on Minton teapots. The shape is not included in the early Minton shape book (MS 1584), indicating that it had been discontinued by about 1830. The view decorating the tureen sides is contained within a frame of scrolls surrounded by a distinctive floral border. The same border is found on Monk's Rock series supper sets (Plate 6.49) and jugs (Plate 6.50), though with a different view. The normal border for this series is used on the tureen lid (Plate 6.55) and stand (Plate 6.48). Length 183 mm.

Plate 6.48. Minton Monk's Rock series pearlware sauce tureen stand, c.1815. The same scene is used on the sauce tureen lid. Width 192 mm, mark P5.

Plate 6.49. Minton Monk's Rock series pearlware supper set section base. c.1815. This piece combines use of the floral border used on flat ware such as plates and dishes, with the floral border with scrolls as used on hollow ware. The scene within the border differs from that on the tureen above, but was used on jugs as shown in Plate 6.50. The supper set lid uses the same distinctive blue painted knob as found on the tureen (Plate 9.43). Width 375 mm.

135

Plate 6.50. *Minton Monk's Rock series pearlware covered jug, c.1815. This design is particularly well suited to hollow ware shapes such as this jug, though it is also found on the flat supper set base shown in Plate 6.49. The print shown right is from the Minton Bat Print book and features a very similar rural scene. Note the jug in Plate 6.51 which suggests use of the same basic design by another factory. Jug height 168 mm. Mark P14. Print width 91 mm.*

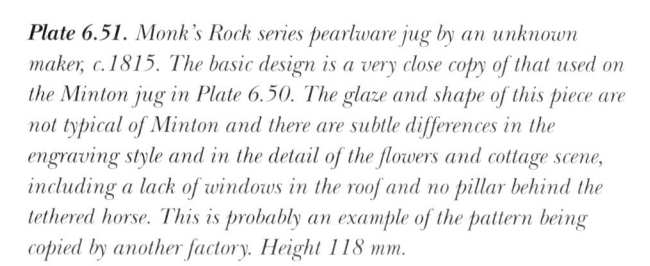

Plate 6.51. *Monk's Rock series pearlware jug by an unknown maker, c.1815. The basic design is a very close copy of that used on the Minton jug in Plate 6.50. The glaze and shape of this piece are not typical of Minton and there are subtle differences in the engraving style and in the detail of the flowers and cottage scene, including a lack of windows in the roof and no pillar behind the tethered horse. This is probably an example of the pattern being copied by another factory. Height 118 mm.*

Plate 6.52. Minton Castle Gateway pattern pearlware ewer, c.1815. The floral border enclosing rural scenes has strong similarities with the border used on Monk's Rock series jugs and tureens. The distinctive flared base to the strap handle, detailed left, matches that found on the Bewick Stag ewer shown in Plate 6.31. Height 191 mm. Mark P12.

Castle Gateway

This fine toiletware pattern features a view of a castle on rocks above a bridge and is illustrated on the ewer and bowl shown in Plates 3.35, 6.52 and 6.53. The broad floral border with enclosed rural scenes is very similar to that used on hollow ware decorated in the Minton Monk's Rock series, such as the jug in Plate 6.50, and the ewer handle decoration is the same as that used on the Monk's Rock series jug. The ewer has a distinctive flared base to its strap handle, as detailed in Plate 6.52, which closely matches that found on the Bewick Stag pattern ewer shown in Plate 6.31. This pattern may be the 'Castle' ewer, basin and chambers pattern listed in 1817, or it may have been introduced shortly after 1817. A bourdaloue decorated with this pattern is illustrated by Coysh.[25]

Plate 6.53. Minton Castle Gateway pattern Semi-China flared footed wash bowl, c.1820. An attractive feature of this design is the deep floral border containing several rural scenes and buildings. The main pattern in the centre of this bowl is shown in Plate 3.35. Diameter 330 mm. Mark P14.

137

Plate 6.54. Minton Maypole pattern pearlware jug, c.1815. The maypole is seen at the front of the jug, with rural scenes on either side, the whole view being printed from a single engraving. Height 207 mm. Mark P14.

Maypole

This distinctive pattern is found on jugs and mugs and other hollow ware items such as spill vases and loving cups. It is well illustrated on the large jug shown in Plate 6.54 and is seen to consist of a cleverly composed rural scene stretching around the pot, from thatched buildings and ducks on one side, past a central maypole to more buildings, animals and a rustic figure beside a tree on the other side. The design includes a floral border which is clearly visible around the top of the illustrated jug, together with a slightly different floral border used inside the rim. The pattern was originally attributed to Minton based on its use on spill vases in combination with a border section taken directly from the Monk's Rock series, as detailed in Plates 6.55 and 6.56. Confirmation of the attribution has come from its use with Minton printer's marks and on wares of known Minton form, such as the mug with the distinctive Minton handle form shown in Plates 3.40 and 9.95. No doubt this is the Maypole jugs pattern listed in 1817. Although other factories produced patterns featuring a maypole, they all differ significantly from this Minton design.

Plate 6.55. Detail of the Minton Monk's Rock series sauce tureen from Plate 6.47, c.1815. Note the distinctive blue painted knob and handle and the usual border design.

Plate 6.56. Detail of the Minton Maypole pattern spill vase shown in Plate 6.57. Note the use of the Monk's Rock series border around its base, where it gives the effect of ground flowers and foliage.

Plate 6.57. Minton Maypole pattern pearlware spill vase. Height 130 mm. Mark P13.

Plate 6.58. Minton Dove pattern pearlware eight-inch concave-octagonal plate, c.1815. Although the design is seen to have a mainly oriental influence it is conveniently included here. It shows some resemblance to the Spode Grasshopper pattern. Width 223 mm.

Dove

This pattern is illustrated on the plate shown above and the sauce tureen with stand and ladle shown in Plate 6.59. The tureen is a combination of two other Minton shapes: the distinctive knob and handles correspond exactly to those used for the Monk's Rock series as detailed in Plate 6.55, whilst the lid, base and stand correspond exactly to those on a Roman pattern tureen in Plate 6.16. The plate is the standard Minton concave-octagonal shape with double foot ring, and several pieces are known with Minton printer's marks. The pattern would seem to be contemporary with the Monk's Rock series, and is assumed to be that listed as Dove in 1817.

Plate 6.59. Minton Dove pattern pearlware sauce tureen ladle and stand, c.1815. This represents an unusual combination of parts used on two separate Minton tureen shapes. The knob and handles correspond exactly to those used on the Monk's Rock series tureen in Plates 6.47 and 6.55, whilst the base, lid and stand are from the standard octagonal wares, exactly matching the example found with the Roman pattern shown in Plate 6.16. Length of stand 193 mm.

Plate 6.60. Minton Ruined Abbey pattern pearlware wash bowl, c.1820. A toiletware pattern which incorporates a deep floral border with prominent roses. The pattern is also shown in Plate 9.108 on a pearlware flared wash bowl similar to that shown in Plate 6.53. Diameter 300 mm. Mark P13.

Ruined Abbey

This toiletware pattern is illustrated on the bowl in Plate 6.60. It is seen to feature a ruined abbey, possibly Kirkstall Abbey, standing beside a river and bridge surrounded by a deep floral border including prominent rose flowers and buds. It is attributed to Minton based on its use on typical Minton shapes bearing known Minton printer's marks. In addition to toilet wares, the pattern is also recorded on an interesting perforated cylindrical lidded vessel,[26] resembling a steamer. Significantly a matching lid for such a vessel has been noted decorated with the Minton Botanical Vase pattern. Note that Abbey (1820) and Rose Bud (1819) are both recorded as Minton Pattern names in the accounts of Robert Wyllie discussed in Chapter Two.

Plate 6.61. Minton Ruined Abbey pattern covered soap box and tray. The tray is Semi-China c.1825 and the soap box Opaque China, c.1830. Exactly matching shapes are found in other known Minton patterns. Box length 105 mm. Tray length 170 mm. Mark P13.

Plate 6.62. *Minton Carisbrooke Castle pattern Opaque China wash bowl, c.1825. Relatively late use of a toiletware pattern introduced on pearlware in c.1815. The pattern is a fine example of the Minton excellence in both design and engraving at this period. The main scene, taken from the source print shown in Plate 6.63, is cleverly complemented by the deep border with its rural waterside scenes. The same border is used to decorate the outside of the bowl. Diameter 254 mm.*

Carisbrooke Castle or Covered Wagon

This stunning toiletware pattern shown in Plate 6.62 was originally attributed to Minton based on its use on known Minton shapes, including a large potpourri vase with the distinctive lion handles. Further confirmation of the attribution came with the discovery in the Minton archives of the original source print, as shown below. This is another candidate for the Castle pattern listed in 1817.

Plate 6.63. Original source print for the Carisbrooke Castle pattern from the Minton Archives, MS 1987. Titled 'Carisbrooke Castle from the Calbourn Road', it was published by J. Murray, London, on 1 October 1814. Carisbrooke is close to Newport on the Isle of Wight. Width of engraving 175 mm.

Plate 6.64. *Rogers Fallow Deer pattern plate, c.1820. This relatively common version of the pattern, with its distinctive crocus border, was first produced by Rogers and later copied by Wedgwood. Diameter 166 mm. Impressed 'ROGERS'.*

Plate 6.65. *Fallow Deer pattern pearlware tea plate, probably Minton, c.1815. Note the distinctive floral border which helps to distinguish this from other versions of the pattern. Three single stilt marks beneath the rim and single recessed foot ring. Diameter 188 mm. Mark P1.*

Fallow Deer

Plate 6.66. Fallow Deer pattern pearlware porringer-shaped creamer, probably Minton, c.1815. Length 112 mm. Mark P11.

Plate 6.67. Fallow Deer pattern pearlware teacup, possibly by Thomas Rathbone, c.1825. Note the border with deer and buildings. Rim diameter 81 mm.

This is a familiar pattern, the most common version of which uses a crocus border and is shown in Plate 6.64. It is found on tea and table wares produced originally by Rogers and later copied by Wedgwood. At least two other versions of the pattern were produced, however, both apparently just on tea wares. The version shown on the cup in Plate 6.67 has been linked to shards found at the Scottish factory of Thomas Rathbone.[27] Note the distinctive border design including deer and buildings. The third version, again with a different border, is illustrated in Plates 6.65 and 6.66. This version is relatively uncommon and can probably be attributed to Minton based on the teaware shapes and the use of characteristic Minton printer's marks, including the distinctive crown mark. A teacup and saucer in this version have also been illustrated.[28]

Plate 6.68. Cottage and Cows pattern pearlware new oval shape teapot, attributed to Minton, c.1815. A close copy of the shape introduced around 1808 in bone china. The moulded spout is particularly distinctive and was also used on the Broseley pattern pearlware teapot shown in Plate 4.36. Heart-shaped pouring guard, flat 14-hole triangular strainer. Blue painted knob and rims. Length 243 mm. Mark P2.

Cottage and Cows

This typical rural scenic pattern is attributed to Minton based on the teapot shown in Plates 3.42 and 6.68. The fine quality pearlware pot is a close copy of the Minton new oval shape normally found in bone china, including the distinctive spout also used on the Broseley teapot in Plate 4.36. This may correspond to the Cottage teaware pattern listed in 1810.

Domed Building

This unusual pattern found on toy tea wares is attributed to Minton based on the shape and printer's mark on the toy teapot shown in Plate 3.45. The eight-sided moulded spout, four-hole strainer and handle match those used on the plain globular teapots shown in Plate 4.68, whilst the body is a miniature version of the Broseley teapot in Plate 4.36. The toy teacup and saucer in Plate 6.69 show a typical Minton cup and handle shape, such as that in Plate 6.75.

Plate 6.69. Domed Building pattern pearlware toy teacup and saucer, probably Minton, c.1815. Note the typical Minton cup and handle form. Saucer diameter 102 mm.

Plate 6.70. Minton Farmyard pattern pearlware London shape teapot, c.1815. Note the distinctive blue painted knob, also used by Minton on contemporary dinner wares (Plate 6.55) and later tea wares (Plate 4.43). The moulded handle is unusual for London shape teapots and helps to identify this Minton form. This is a larger size than most of the Minton teapots found in this shape. Length 265 mm. Mark P2.

Farmyard

This teaware pattern is illustrated in Plates 3.43 and 6.70. It is attributed to Minton based on its use on wares of characteristic Minton form bearing typical Minton printer's marks. The London shape teapot shown above is found with numerous Minton patterns, and was probably used during the 1815 to 1825 period. The distinctive handle is unusual for this basic shape and is different from that used by Minton on bone china London shape teapots. The knob design matches that used on Monk's Rock series and Dove pattern dinner wares (Plates 6.55 and 6.59) and was retained on the next London or 'cottage' shape teapots used with both bone china (Plate 4.43) and earthenware (Plate 11.2). It is assumed that this is the Farmyard pattern listed in the 1817 inventory, with earlier mention of a Farm pattern in Wyllie accounts for 1813. The same basic pattern is used on the pearlware teapot shown in Plate 6.71 and also illustrated by Miller.[29] Close inspection of this teapot reveals no evidence of Minton manufacture and the print is not the same as that used on the Minton teapot above. Thus it is likely that another factory also produced this pattern.

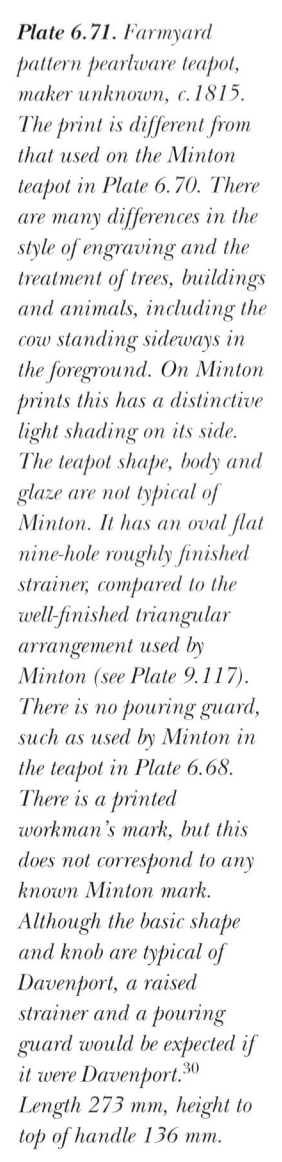

Plate 6.71. Farmyard pattern pearlware teapot, maker unknown, c.1815. The print is different from that used on the Minton teapot in Plate 6.70. There are many differences in the style of engraving and the treatment of trees, buildings and animals, including the cow standing sideways in the foreground. On Minton prints this has a distinctive light shading on its side. The teapot shape, body and glaze are not typical of Minton. It has an oval flat nine-hole roughly finished strainer, compared to the well-finished triangular arrangement used by Minton (see Plate 9.117). There is no pouring guard, such as used by Minton in the teapot in Plate 6.68. There is a printed workman's mark, but this does not correspond to any known Minton mark. Although the basic shape and knob are typical of Davenport, a raised strainer and a pouring guard would be expected if it were Davenport.[30] Length 273 mm, height to top of handle 136 mm.

144

Plate 6.72. Minton Forbes Castle pattern teapot, c.1820. The body is of a fine quality earthenware matching the Semi-China wares discussed in the next chapter. This London shape with distinctive spout, handle and knob, is a slightly smaller size than the Farmyard pattern example in Plate 6.70, but exactly matches the Minton examples shown in Plates 7.4 and 7.58. The same view is used for a print in the Minton Bat Print book, as shown above (see also Chapter Eleven, print B10). Length 237 mm.

Forbes Castle

This pattern is illustrated on the teapots shown in Plates 6.72 and 6.73 and features a view of Castle Forbes, Aberdeenshire, the ancestral seat of the chiefs of the clan of the Forbes. The structure is made from granite and was rebuilt starting in 1814. The same basic view was used by Enoch Wood & Sons on dinner wares in the Grapevine Border Series. Its use by Minton on tea wares is confirmed by the teapot shown in Plate 6.72 which exactly matches teapots of this characteristic shape found in other known Minton patterns. The same view was also used for a print in the Minton Bat Print book, including the title 'Forbes Castle', as shown in Plate 6.72.

The use of the same pattern on the teapot shown below in Plate 6.73 is important in that it identifies a further Minton teapot shape. It was probably introduced to replace the earlier round caped shape as used with the Broseley pattern (Plate 4.36), which interestingly used the same distinctive handle form.

Plate 6.73. Minton Forbes Castle pattern Semi-China teapot, c.1820. This distinctive round caped shape was probably introduced to replace the earlier round form shown in Plate 4.36, which interestingly used the same handle form. Lid missing. Length 220 mm. Mark P15.

Plate 6.74. Cottage and Cart pattern Semi-China toy teapot of fine quality, probably Minton, c.1820. The teapot shape shows strong similarities to the full size teapot shown in Plate 6.73. The plain loop handle matches those found on earlier Minton toy teapots, such as in Plate 3.45. Plain four-hole diamond-shaped strainer. Length 145 mm.

Plate 6.75. Cottage and Cart pattern Semi-China toy teacup and saucer, probably Minton, c.1820. The teacup shape exactly matches other Minton teacups, including the characteristic handle form. The pieces both have a typical Minton printer's mark, and mark P13 has been noted on a sucrier. Saucer diameter 101 mm, with mark P2. Cup diameter 62 mm, with mark P16.

Cottage and Cart

This attractive rural pattern is found on toy tea wares, such as those shown in Plates 6.74 and 6.75. Examples are relatively common and are found both on the fine quality Semi-China body and occasionally in Opaque China, probably indicating production throughout the 1820s. Its attribution to Minton is based on the shape of the wares and the use of several typical Minton printer's marks. The teapot shape is very similar to the full size Forbes Castle piece in Plate 6.73, although the plain loop handle is taken from the earlier toy shapes such as in Plates 3.45 and 4.68. The cup shown in Plate 6.75 is typical of Minton and has the characteristic round cross section moulded handle.

Plate 6.76. Apple Tree pattern pearlware vase-shaped coffee pot, probably Minton, c.1815. There are certain similarities with the coffee pot shape used with Minton bone china, especially the handle. The same pattern is used on a teapot matching that shown in Plate 6.73. Apple Tree is listed in the 1817 copper plate list. Height 272 mm. Mark P12.

Apple Tree

Apple Tree is listed in the 1817 copper plate list as a teaware pattern and also mentioned in the Wyllie accounts in 1816. It seems that this corresponds to the pattern used on the fine coffee pot shown above in Plate 6.76. Attribution is based firstly on an illustrated[31] teapot decorated with this pattern and of the same shape as the Forbes Castle teapot shown in Plate 6.73, including the distinctive thumb rest to the handle. The vase-shaped coffee pot in Plate 6.76 has a typical Minton printer's mark and shows certain similarities to the coffee pot shape used with bone china,[32] in particular the shape of the handle. Other patterns are known featuring apple picking, but these are easily distinguished from this version.

Plate 6.77. Benevolent Cottagers pattern nine-inch pearlware concave-octagonal plate, probably Minton, c.1820. The pattern has been recorded on Minton shapes with typical workman's marks and potting characteristics. Furthermore this plate has a retailer's mark also used on a dish with the Minton Semi-China seal mark M1. Width 249 mm. Three single stilt marks beneath the rim. Double recessed foot ring. Mark P6. Impressed '3'. Blue printed retailer's mark as above 27 mm long.

Plate 6.78. Fruit pattern pearlware shell-shaped dessert dish, attributed to Minton, c.1815. The pattern is normally found painted over in coloured enamels (Plate 3.49), but this example has been left plain. It is found on characteristic Minton dessertware shapes. Minton also used a very similar design hand painted on first period bone china. Width 190 mm.

Benevolent Cottagers

This fine pattern is illustrated in Plate 6.77. Each piece in the service uses the same design and floral border. The scene originates from a painting 'The Benevolent Cottagers' by Sir Augustus Wall Callcott RA.[33] It is recorded on a sauce tureen matching that in Plate 5.21 and a wicker basket similar to that in Plate 9.90.[34] It has also been noted on octagonal meat dishes matching those used for the Bamboo and Flowers pattern. Examples of the pattern have potting characteristics and workman's marks typical of Minton. The most significant evidence for a Minton attribution, however, is the Hillcock and Walton retailer's mark used on the example in Plate 6.77, as this mark was also used on a dish with floral decoration in the British Museum which has the Minton Semi-China seal mark M1.[35] Interestingly the retailer's mark was only used between 1817 and 1823,[36] indicating a transition from pearlware to Semi-China during this period. This pattern could correspond to the Cottage tableware pattern listed in 1817.

Fruit

This distinctive pattern features an arrangement of fruit on a blue ground and is found on dessert wares. It is usually found overpainted in coloured enamels, such as on the dessert dish shown in Plate 3.49, but the shell dish in Plate 6.78 shows that the pattern was sometimes left uncoloured. Although both these dishes are typical Minton forms, very similar shapes were also produced by other factories. The pattern can be attributed to Minton based on its use on more distinctive shapes: it has been recorded on early dessert dish forms matching those used on first period porcelain and thought to be unique to the factory.[37] The pattern has also been noted on the later Minton earthenware dessert shape matching that shown in Plate 6.44. Further evidence for this as a Minton pattern comes from the recollections of the early factory worker Mr Hassels[4] who refers to 'two dirty impressions of patterns, the one with the fruit was done I understand in Mr Minton's days of engraving'. Interestingly a very similar design was used by Minton hand painted on an early bone china ink stand.[38]

Plate 6.79. Japan Vase pattern eight-inch concave Trophy shape pearlware plate, attributed to Minton, c.1815. The basic pattern outline and blue ground areas have been printed then the pattern finished by elaborate overpainting in a range of coloured enamels. The plate exactly matches the Star pattern plate shown in Plate 5.11. Diameter 217 mm. Impressed '7'.

Plate 6.80. Exotic Birds pattern covered pearlware potpourri jar, attributed to Minton, c.1815. A large piece with distinctive open-mouthed lion handles exactly matching those found on other Minton jars. Unfortunately the upper flared section of the body has been broken off and the domed perforated outer lid is also missing. The original inner lid has been mounted in a metal rim to form the replacement cover. Diameter of base 192 mm.

Early Japan Patterns

Certain printed patterns were completed by being overpainted in coloured enamels. These are traditionally referred to as Japan patterns. The early Minton inventories of the 1812 to 1826 period included sections of Japan tea, table and toilet wares (see Table 2.2). As the inventories used value (and hence production cost) as a main guide to categorisation, it is likely that some of the Japan wares listed were overpainted traditional patterns such as Fruit or Chinese Sports, which were also produced plain. The following are truer Japan patterns in which the engravings mainly acted to only outline the design and thus were always intended to be coloured in.

Japan Vase

This pattern is illustrated in Plates 3.48 and 6.79, and is seen to feature birds perching on a plant contained in an oriental-style vase, all surrounded by an elaborate border. The pattern requires quite intricate painting in a range of coloured enamels. It is attributed to Minton based on the characteristic shape of wares and the use of typical workman's marks. It is found on both dinner and dessert wares, and used the distinctive concave Trophy shape plates and dishes.

Exotic Birds

This design is shown on the large but damaged potpourri jar shown in Plates 3.52 and 6.80. A relatively open design combined with restrained overpainting produce an overall effect of lightness to this pattern, which is normally found on toilet wares. It is attributed to Minton based on the characteristic shape of the wares.

Plate 6.81. Minton Water Lily pattern bone china Bute shape teacup with gilding, c.1812. This is Minton pattern number 777 and was used on new oval shape tea wares. Diameter 85 mm. Blue Sevres-type mark

Plate 6.82. Minton Water Lily pattern pearlware teacup and saucer, c.1815. Minton used some of the engravings on both earthenware and china tea wares. Saucer diameter 141 mm. Cup diameter 85 mm.

Water Lily

This distinctive Japan-type floral design, with an underglaze blue print overpainted in coloured enamels, was introduced by Minton on first period china as Pattern No. 777, probably in about 1812. It was used on new oval shape china tea wares, such as the teacup in Plate 6.81, the sucrier in Plate 6.83 and the saucer dish in Plate 6.85, all of which bear the blue painted Sevres-type mark. It is apparent that Minton also used the same pattern on earthenware tea and tablewares. The pearlware cup and saucer shown in Plate 6.82 and the sucrier in Plate 6.84 were decorated with some of the same engravings as used on the corresponding china pieces, and there is also seen to be close correspondence between the basic shapes. Note however the different handle form on the pearlware teacup. The pattern was also used by Minton on dinner and dessert wares, such as the small octagonal soup bowl shown in Plate 3.51, which bears the distinctive crown printer's mark, and the dessert dish in Plate 6.86. A dinner plate has also been noted with the Minton 'Improved Stone China' impressed seal mark (mark M31), indicating production in the 1830s, perhaps as a special replacement order.

Plate 6.83. Minton Water Lily pattern bone china new oval sucrier with gilding, c.1812. The lid has been printed from the same engraving as used on the earthenware example in Plate 6.84. Length 184 mm. Blue Sevres mark.

Plate 6.84. Minton Water Lily pattern pearlware new oval shape sucrier, c.1815. Note the same basic shape as the china example in Plate 6.83, although the earthenware body is slightly larger and more heavily potted. Length 192 mm. Mark P6.

Plate 6.85. Minton Water Lily pattern bone china saucer dish with gilding, c.1812. Diameter 201 mm. Blue Sevres mark.

Plate 6.86. Minton Water Lily pattern pearlware dessert dish. The main engraving is the same as that used on the dish shown in Plate 3.51. Maximum width 180 mm.

Attribution of wares in this pattern is not straightforward as the same design appears to have been produced by at least one other factory, dinner wares being found with both potting characteristics and impressed workman's marks which are not typical of Minton. Some pieces in this pattern are found marked impressed or painted 'Donovan', representing the Dublin retailer and decorator James Donovan. Factory accounts indicate that Minton supplied large quantities of first period bone china and earthenwares to Donovan from as early as 1799. Interestingly the accounts also include cash payments back to Donovan, such as entries in 1809 and 1810 in respect of overcharging or crazing of wares supplied. It is known that 'DONOVAN' was added as a retailer's mark to china made at and supplied by several manufactories, including Minton. Thus it is possible that some Minton earthenwares could be found marked Donovan. Indeed a saucer illustrated[39] with a painted Donovan mark appears to be very similar to the Minton version of the Dragon pattern (Plate 5.49). The examples of Water Lily pattern dinner ware marked 'Donovan' which have been examined to date, however, were not typical of Minton manufacture. This raises the possibility that Donovan were using their own set of Water Lily engravings to decorate wares supplied from another factory. Alternatively Donovan may simply have bought in finished wares in this pattern from another factory.

References

1. R. Copeland, *Spode's Willow Pattern and other Designs after the Chinese*, 3rd ed. (Studio Vista, 1999), p. 152.
2. A.W. Coysh, *Blue Printed Earthenware 1780-1840* (David & Charles, 1970), p. 92.
3. *True Blue Transfer Printed Earthenware, Exhibition Catalogue* (Friends of Blue, 1998), p. 59.
4. Minton MS 277, Minton's Notebook (Minton Archives).
5. D. Drakard and P. Holdway, *Spode Printed Ware* (Longman, 1983), p. 164.
6. M. Buxton, *Friends of Blue Bulletin*, No. 52, 1986, p. 7.
7. Kirk, *Outlines from the Figures and Compositions upon the Greek, Roman and Etruscan Vases of the late Sir William Hamilton, Drawn and engraved by the late Mr Kirk* (London: 1804).

8. W. Tischbein, *Collection of engravings from ancient vases, mostly of pure Greek workmanship, discovered in sepulchres in the Kingdom of the Two Sicilies, but chiefly in the neighbourhood of Naples during the course of the years 1789 to 1790, now in the possession of Sir William Hamilton*, 3 vols. (Naples: 1791–95).
9. A.W. Coysh, *Blue Printed Earthenware 1800-1850* (David & Charles, 1972), p. 32.
10. *Friend of Blue Bulletin*, No. 8, 1975, p. 5.
11. A. Smith, *The Illustrated Guide to the Liverpool Herculaneum Pottery* (Barrie and Jenkins, 1970), p. 49.
12. A.W. Coysh and R.K. Henrywood, *The Dictionary of Blue and White Printed Pottery Volume 2* (Antique Collectors Club, 1989), p. 120.
13. *Friends of Blue Bulletin*, No. 59, 1988, p. 9.
14. *Friends of Blue Bulletin*, No. 67, 1990, p. 8.
15. A.W. Coysh and R.K. Henrywood, *The Dictionary of Blue and White Printed Pottery* (Antique Collectors Club, 1982), p. 268.
16. T. Bewick, *A History of British Birds, Vol. 1. History and Description of Land Birds* (Newcastle, 1797) (extracted illustrations from 1805 edition).
17. T. Bewick, *A History of British Birds, Vol. 2. History and Description of Water Birds* (Newcastle, 1804) (extracted illustrations from this edition).
18. Coysh and Henrywood, *Dictionary of Blue and White*, p. 43.
19. G.A. Godden, *Minton Pottery & Porcelain of the First Period* (Barrie & Jenkins, 1968), Plate 32.
20. T. Bewick, *A General History of Quadrupeds* (London, 1790) (extracted illustrations from 1807 edition).
21. J. Heywood, *NCS Newsletter*, No. 82, 1991, p. 23.
22. Coysh and Henrywood, *Dictionary of Blue and White*, p. 250.
23. Minton MS 1987, Book of Various Source Prints (Minton Archives).
24. S. Middiman, *Select Views in Great Britain* (London: Boydell & Co, 1813).
25. Coysh, *Blue Printed Earthenware*, p. 104.
26. *Friends of Blue Bulletin*, No. 82, 1993, p. 7.
27. *Friends of Blue Bulletin*, No. 68, 1990, p. 10.
28. *Friends of Blue Bulletin*, No. 57, 1987, p. 5.
29. P. Miller and M. Berthoud, *An Anthology of British Teapots* (Micawber Publications, 1985), Plate 1318, p. 220.
30. T.A. Lockett and G.A. Godden, *Davenport, China, Earthenware and Glass 1794–1887* (Barrie & Jenkins, 1989), pp. 156 and 215.
31. *Friends of Blue Bulletin*, No. 61, 1988, p. 7.
32. R. Cumming and M. Berthoud, *Minton Patterns of the First Period* (Micawber Publications, 1997), cover illustration.
33. Coysh and Henrywood, *Dictionary of Blue and White Vol. 2*, p. 26.
34. *Friends of Blue Bulletin*, No. 104, 1999, p. 12.
35. W.L. Little, *Staffordshire Blue* (Batsford, 1969; repr. 1987), p. 73.
36. Coysh and Henrywood, *Dictionary of Blue and White*, p. 175.
37. Godden, *Minton Pottery*, Plate 31.
38. Godden, *Minton Pottery*, Plate 60.
39. Coysh and Henrywood, *Dictionary of Blue and White*, p. 113.

Chapter Seven

Catalogue of Patterns
4. The Semi-China Period

Bamboo and Flowers

This pattern is usually found marked with what is probably the earliest of the formal printed marks used by Minton, the 'Semi-China' seal mark detailed in Plate 7.1. The mark is attributed to Minton based on its use on several Broseley pattern copper plates remaining at the factory, a pull from such an engraving being shown in Plate 4.44. A copper plate for another pattern commonly found with this mark, Italian Ruins, has also been found at the factory. Further confirmation of the attribution is in the characteristic Minton form of the wares found with this mark, as well as the associated use of typical Minton printer's marks. Similar 'Semi-China' marks were of course used at other factories, with some clearly being intended as direct copies of the Minton mark (U2a and U2b in Table 10.4). Fortunately, apart from some variation in size, the detailed design of the Minton mark is very consistent.

The Bamboo and Flowers pattern is found on a wide range of wares, including jugs, bowls, dinner, tea, and dessert wares, examples being shown in

Plate 7.1. Minton Bamboo and Flowers pattern Semi-China plate, c.1820. This concave-octagonal shape of plate with double recessed foot ring was used by Minton with many patterns during the 1820 to 1825 period. The design shows some oriental influence and in some respects resembles the slightly earlier Dove pattern. It seems to have been popular over many years and is found on a wide variety of wares. The pattern is almost invariably found with the 'Semi-China' seal mark shown above. This Minton mark was consistently reproduced on a range of patterns. Note in particular the detail of the symbols within the octagonal frame and the use of upper and lower case lettering. Note that very similar marks were used at other factories, such as in Plates 7.63 and 7.88. Plate diameter 254 mm. Mark M1. Impressed 'T' (4 mm long).

Plate 7.2. *Detail of the dinnerware shapes used by Minton with the Bamboo and Flowers pattern. Taken from the earliest extant factory shape book, MS 1584, which contains some 50 designs. Although the book probably dates from around 1830, many of the shapes were clearly introduced at an earlier date. The first 30 designs are not in chronological order and seem to have been drafted by the same hand. Many were probably entered when the book was first compiled to represent the shapes then in production. Comparison with the corresponding sauce tureen in Plate 7.3 illustrates the accuracy with which the shapes were drawn, including the detail of moulded parts such as handles and knobs.*

Plates 7.1 to 7.7. The dinner wares correspond to design BB in the shape book of c.1830. The dinner plate was the standard concave-octagonal shape with double foot ring, but the meat dishes were of a relatively angular and heavily potted plain octagonal shape (Plate 3.66). Wicker-type dessert wares are found, and some tea wares are typical of the pre-1820 period. It is likely that the pattern was introduced in about 1820. Although 'Baboe' is listed as a teaware pattern in 1810, perhaps a misspelling of Bamboo, this presumably refers to a different design.

Plate 7.3. *Minton Bamboo and Flowers pattern Semi-China sauce tureen, c.1820. Note the close correspondence with Shape BB in the Minton shape book shown in Plate 7.2, including the moulded handle form. This piece is typical of the Minton Semi-China body, having a well-fitting lustrous glaze of excellent quality with little sign of crazing. The glaze has a pale blue coloration often with occasional trapped black kiln dirt or small air bubbles where it has gathered around mouldings or in corners. Length 190 mm. Mark M1 to cover and base.*

Plate 7.4. Minton Bamboo and Flowers pattern Semi-China teapot, c.1820. Note the detail of the spout, knob and handle on this characteristic shape which was introduced by Minton in about 1815 and used with a range of patterns. Length 235 mm. Marks M1 and P2.

Plate 7.5. Minton Bamboo and Flowers pattern Semi-China cup and saucer, c.1820. Relatively thinly potted London shape. The saucer has a double rounded profile and a single rounded foot ring (Plate 9.131). Cup diameter 87 mm, mark M1. Saucer diameter 143 mm, marks M1 and P15, and impressed '8' (3 mm high).

Plate 7.6. Minton Bamboo and Flowers pattern Semi-China footed bowl, c.1820. Diameter 235 mm. Marks M1 and P13.

Plate 7.7. Minton Bamboo and Flowers pattern Semi-China coffee can, c.1820. Note the distinctive moulded handle form which was used at the factory for many years with a wide range of patterns, such as in Plates 4.38, 4.72 and 5.49. Height 67 mm. Marks M1 and P2.

Plate 7.8. Dying Tree pattern Semi-China cup and saucer, attributed to Minton, c.1820. These pieces have exactly the same Semi-China body, moulded shape, potting characteristics and workman's marks as the Bamboo and Flowers cup and saucer shown in Plate 7.5. There is no Semi-China seal mark, perhaps indicating that the pattern was originally introduced just prior to 1820, during the pearlware period. Cup diameter 87 mm, mark P9. Saucer diameter 143 mm, mark P15 and impressed '8' (3 mm high).

Dying Tree

This teaware pattern is attributed to Minton based on the cup and saucer in Plate 7.8, which correspond exactly with respect to body, shape and workman's marks to the Bamboo and Flowers pattern cup and saucer in Plate 7.5.

Riverside Cottage

This attractive teaware pattern comprising rural views with a floral border is illustrated on the London shape slop bowl shown in Plates 3.58 and 7.9. It is attributed to Minton based on the use of the Semi-China seal mark.

Plate 7.9. Riverside Cottage pattern Semi-China slop bowl, attributed to Minton, c.1820. Interestingly the same ruined church is seen to be featured by Minton in the English Scenery pattern soup plate shown in Plate 7.20. The other side of the bowl has a cottage scene, as shown in Plate 3.58. It is likely that several different rural views were used for the different pieces in the tea service. The shape is typical of London shape wares produced by many factories. The attribution to Minton is based on the distinctive seal mark. Diameter 160 mm. Mark M1.

Plate 7.10. Minton Italian Ruins pattern Opaque China concave-octagonal plate, c.1830. Later use of a pattern introduced on Semi-China. It is normally found with the 'Semi-China' seal mark. The small print above is included in the factory Bat Print book, and an engraving remains at the factory. This could be the Bridge pattern first referred to in the Wyllie accounts in 1820. Plate diameter 248 mm, mark M1.

Plate 7.11. Minton Italian Ruins pattern Semi-China dessert dish, c.1820. This piece differs slightly from the normal shape as the holes usually found either side of the handle (e.g. Plate 7.38) have been formed into grooves. Width 196 mm. Mark M1.

Plate 7.12. Minton Italian Ruins pattern Semi-China Roman shape jug, c.1820. Height 180 mm. Marks M1 and P18.

Italian Ruins

This fine pattern features a ruined castle overlooking a bridge and river. The castle and other buildings have not been identified, but they reportedly[1] correspond to those illustrated in an unsigned oil painting hanging in an Oxford college. The design appears to have remained popular for many years, being found on a range of dinner, dessert and toilet wares, jugs and other articles in both Semi and Opaque China bodies, examples being shown in Plates 7.10 to

Plate 7.13. Detail of the dinnerware shape used by Minton for Italian Ruins pattern wares. Examples are shown in Plates 7.14 and 7.15. Note that very similar shapes were used by other factories, including Spode. The tureen in Plate 7.16 indicates that Minton also used a different shape with the Italian Ruins pattern.

7.16. The pattern is attributed to Minton as it is almost invariably found with the Semi-China seal mark, and because a single small engraving remains at the factory. A print featuring this design is also included in the Minton Bat Print book, as shown in Plate 7.10. All the wares found in this pattern are typical Minton shapes, and there is no evidence for the design being used by any other factory. The dinnerware shapes commonly found correspond to factory Shape K, as shown in Plates 7.13 to 7.15. Similar shapes were used at other factories, including Spode. The soup tureen in Plate 7.16 indicates that the pattern was also used, and perhaps introduced on, a more unusual and seemingly rare factory shape, which is not included in the shape book.

Plate 7.14. Italian Ruins pattern Semi-China covered vegetable dish, c.1820. The design corresponds to Shape K from the factory shape book, as shown in Plate 7.13. Width 247 mm. Mark M1.

Plate 7.15. Minton Italian Ruins pattern Semi-China sauce tureen, ladle and stand, c.1820. The design corresponds to Shape K from the factory shape book, as shown in Plate 7.13. Width of stand 227 mm. Width of tureen base 184 mm. Mark M1 to cover, base and stand.

Plate 7.16. Minton Italian Ruins pattern Semi-China soup tureen and stand, c.1820. This impressive and rare round tureen shape with fish handles is not included in the Minton shape book of c.1830. It is possible that Italian Ruins was originally introduced on this shape but then produced on the perhaps more popular Shape K. Width of stand 332 mm. Width of tureen base 346 mm. Mark M1 to cover, base and stand.

Plate 7.17. Minton English Scenery pattern Semi-China concave-octagonal dinner plate, c.1825. An early example of the pattern with typical lustrous pale blue glaze. Thomas Minton reputedly developed this fine Semi-China body and helped in the engraving of the pattern. The series uses this attractive floral border with a variety of central views, each featuring a boat and central building surrounded by trees. It is almost invariably found with the printed mark shown above. The building in this engraving appears to be based on a view of a windmill at Charenton near Paris, a locality featured by Enoch Wood & Sons in the French series, and by unknown makers in the Pineapple Border series[2] and the Passion Flower Border series.[3] Plate diameter 251 mm. Mark M2.

English Scenery

This fine tableware pattern features a series of landscape views within a floral border. As can be seen in the range of wares illustrated in Plates 7.17 to 7.41, each view is characterised by having trees and a boat on water in the foreground with a background featuring a prominent building. A range of buildings was used including churches, castles and country mills and houses. The series can be recognised by the characteristic border and the printed mark illustrated in Plate 7.17, which is almost always found with this pattern. Many of the buildings featured can be identified, and indeed the original source prints for Ripon and Grantully Castle have been found at the factory, as shown in Plates 7.22 and 7.30. It is apparent from these source prints that the overall views are not directly copied from prints but have been individually composed at the factory, with each building being set within an imaginary landscape of trees and water. In addition to finding source prints at the factory, the pattern can be attributed to Minton based on the characteristic shape of the dinner and dessert wares. Minton used Shape E for the dinner wares, as shown in Plate 7.34, and the dessert dish shown in Plate 7.38 is characteristic of the Minton Semi-China wares of this period.

This fine pattern is no doubt the 'Old English Scenery' pattern referred to by Thomas Smith, a factory worker of the time (see page 19). Smith estimated that the design was introduced in about 1824 and goes on to say that not only was Thomas Minton responsible for some of the engraving, but that Minton had also developed the Semi-China body. Smith also indicated that the popularity of the design kept it in production for some 40 years. This is consistent with examples of the pattern being found on Opaque China and Improved Stone China, and

Plate 7.18. *Minton English Scenery pattern Semi-China concave-octagonal plate, c.1825. Featuring an unidentified building, this print was also used on the dessert dish shown in Plate 7.38. Diameter 221 mm. Mark M2. Impressed '6' (6 mm high)*

Plate 7.19. *Minton English Scenery pattern Opaque China concave-octagonal plate, c.1830. Unidentified buildings. Diameter 164 mm. Mark M2.*

Plate 7.20. *Minton English Scenery pattern Semi-China soup plate, c.1825. The unidentified ruined church was also used by Minton on the Riverside Cottage pattern slop bowl shown in Plate 7.9. Diameter 247 mm. Mark M2.*

indeed occasionally being found impressed 'Minton'. In addition to dinner and dessert wares, the pattern was also used by Minton on toilet wares, such as the ewer in Plate 7.24.

Several factories produced similar landscape series at this time, each being characterised by their own distinctive border. The same buildings are often featured in the views, and occasionally the entire central scene was copied directly. An example is the view of Ripon, shown in Plate 7.21. Given the existence of the Ripon source print (Plate 7.22) at the factory, it is likely that Minton originated the overall design. The very close copy of the view used on the Passion Flower Border series dish in Plate 7.23 must therefore have been based directly on the Minton engraving.

Plate 7.21. Minton English Scenery pattern Semi-China 16-inch meat dish, c.1825. The scene features Ripon and is copied directly from the source print still at the factory, shown in Plate 7.22. Note that although the building design has been faithfully copied, it has been incorporated into an imaginary landscape. This typifies the designs created by Minton for this series. Width 416 mm. Mark M2. Impressed '16'.

Plate 7.22. Original source print of Ripon used by Minton in creating the landscape used on the dish in Plate 7.21. The print is one of many pasted into a book at the Minton factory, MS 1987, including similar views of church buildings at Lancaster, Shrewsbury and York, with no indication of the original source. Minton also used this print as the basis of hand-painted decoration on a bone china vase.[4] Width of print 144 mm.

Plate 7.23. *Fine quality pearlware 16-inch meat dish with a view of Ripon, maker unknown, c.1825. This dish is from the Passion Flower Border series of views in England and Ireland. Several of the views are direct copies from other manufacturers, including Ralph Stevenson's Acorn and Oak Leaf Border series. This view is copied directly from the Minton English Scenery dish shown in Plate 7.21. Minor differences between the two engravings can be found, in particular the treatment of the sky. Three triple rear and single front stilt marks. Width 434 mm. Printed floral ribbon mark U1 shown below. Impressed '16' (6.5 mm high).*

Plate 7.24. *Minton English Scenery pattern Semi-China ewer, c.1825. The illustration shows Ripon Cathedral on one side. The other side of the ewer (Plate 9.103) features the unidentified ruined abbey shown in Plate 7.41. Height 240 mm. Mark M2.*

163

Plate 7.25. Minton English Scenery pattern 20-inch well and tree Semi-China meat dish, c.1825. This was the largest standard size dish produced in the dinner service. It features a view of Windsor Castle, a location used by several manufacturers. Interestingly this Minton design was closely copied by Ralph Stevenson in his Acorn and Oak Leaf Border series,[5] using the same inner stringing as found on the copy of Ripon in Plate 7.23. Width 524 mm. Mark M2. Impressed '20'.

Plate 7.26. Minton English Scenery pattern Opaque China 14-inch meat dish, c.1830. The featured mill has not been identified. Width 368 mm. Marks M2 and P16. Impressed '14'.

Plate 7.27. Minton English Scenery pattern Improved Stone China 12-inch meat dish, c.1835. The featured church building has not been identified. Width 318 mm. Mark M2. Impressed mark M31 and '12'.

Plate 7.28. Minton English Scenery pattern Opaque China 11-inch meat dish, c.1830. Featuring a view of Worcester similar to that used by Herculaneum in their Cherub Medallion Border series.[6] Width 296 mm. Mark M2. Impressed '11'.

Plate 7.29. Minton English Scenery pattern clear glazed earthenware 18-inch well and tree meat dish, c.1840. The scene features Castle Grantully, taken from the original source print shown below. Width 472 mm. Impressed '18'.

Plate 7.30. Source print of Castle Grantully used by Minton in creating the landscape on the dish in Plate 7.29. The print is one of many pasted into a book at the Minton factory, MS 1990, where it forms one of a set of four, with no indication of the original source. Grantully is a Stewart house on the south side of the Tay. Prominent in the engraving is the unusual stair tower on the outer face of the building capped with a seventeenth century ogee roof. Width of print 63 mm.

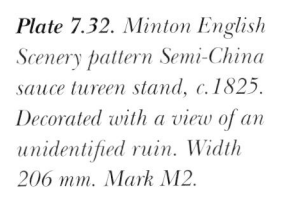

Plate 7.31. Minton English Scenery pattern Opaque China sauce tureen, c.1830, corresponding to Minton Shape E (Plate 7.34). Each side is decorated with the same engraving featuring Gloucester cathedral. A similar view was used by Harvey in his Cities and Towns series.[4] The base inside the tureen is decorated with a view of Faulkbourn Hall, as shown in Plate 7.39. Length 189 mm. Mark M2.

Plate 7.32. Minton English Scenery pattern Semi-China sauce tureen stand, c.1825. Decorated with a view of an unidentified ruin. Width 206 mm. Mark M2.

Plate 7.33. Minton English Scenery pattern Opaque China soup tureen, c.1830, corresponding to Minton Shape E. The lid, sides and inner base are each decorated with different views. The scene shown features Canterbury Cathedral. A similar view was used by Enoch Wood & Sons[8] in the Grapevine Border series. Length 365 mm. Mark M2 to lid and base.

Plate 7.34. Shape E from the Minton shape book of c.1830. Minton used this shape with several patterns, including English Scenery, Filigree and Dresden.

Plate 7.35. *The opposite side of the Minton English Scenery pattern soup tureen shown in Plate 7.33. This view features Fonthill Abbey, built by Thomas Beckford in the early nineteenth century at the Fonthill Estate, Wiltshire. The 275-foot high tower collapsed in 1825 and destroyed much of the Abbey. Fonthill Abbey was featured in several series of views on pottery, with a very similar design being used in the Passion Flower Border series.*[9]

Plate 7.36. *Detail of the unidentified view printed inside the soup tureen shown in Plates 7.33 and 7.35. Width of print 166 mm.*

Plate 7.37. Minton English Scenery pattern Opaque China sauce boat, c.1830. The two illustrations to the left show that each side has a different print, with a further view being used inside, as shown above. None of the views have been identified, although the church building shows some similarity to the view of Gloucester Cathedral used on the sauce tureen and salad bowl (see Plates 7.31 and 7.40). Length 141 mm. Mark M2.

Plate 7.38. Minton English Scenery pattern Opaque China dessert dish, c.1830. The same engraving as used on the eight-inch plate shown in Plate 7.18, with an unidentified view. This basic dessert shape was used by Minton with several patterns. Width 197 mm. Mark M2.

Plate 7.39. Detail of print inside the Minton English Scenery pattern sauce tureen shown in Plate 7.31. The view shows Faulkbourn Hall, after an engraving from Grey's excursions through Essex, published in 1818. The same basic view of the Hall was used by Andrew Stevenson in his Rose Border series.[10] Width of print 80 mm.

Plate 7.40. Minton English Scenery pattern Opaque China Shape E salad bowl, c.1830. The outside is decorated with four prints from the same engraving of Gloucester cathedral used on the sauce tureen (Plate 7.31). Length 280 mm. Mark M2.

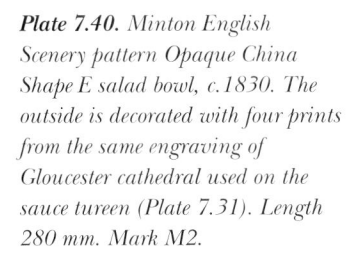

Plate 7.41. Minton English Scenery pattern Opaque China Shape E covered vegetable dish, c.1830. Detail of the decoration inside the base is shown below right. The same unidentified ruined abbey engraving was used inside the salad bowl shown above. The same abbey is also used as a basis of an engraving on the ewer in Plates 7.24 and 9.103. Width of base 278 mm. Mark M2.

Plate 7.42. Minton Miniature series Semi-China sauce tureen stand, c.1825. An early example of a pattern which was produced over many decades. Note the characteristic floral border and typical rural scene. Sixteen different views have been identified, some of which were also used by Minton on tea wares. The round print shown below is for a saucer (Plate 11.8a) and is reproduced from the Minton Bat Print book. Many of the views are named in the characteristic printed cartouche mark normally found with this series. Several copper plates for the series remain at the factory, including the engraving used on the stand. Width of stand 119 mm, print width 82 mm. Mark M3 with 'Abbey Mill'.

Plate 7.43. Minton Miniature series Semi-China soup tureen, c.1825. A small version of factory Shape E, as used with the English Scenery series (Plate 7.34). The view of Bysham Monastery is taken from Grose's ANTIQUITIES.[12] The lid has an unidentified windmill scene. Length 151 mm. Marks M3 with 'Bysham Monastery' and P17.

172

Plate 7.44. Minton Miniature series Semi-China sauce tureen and ladle, c.1825. The main print is probably based on a view of Brandenburg House from VIEWS ON THE THAMES by Cooke & Cooke. Although the actual source print was not found at the factory, Minton had copied it for the teaware engraving shown below in Plate 7.45. The lid is decorated with a view of Corf Castle. Length 108 mm. Mark M3 with 'Corf Castle'.

Minton Miniature Series

This fine series of toy dinner wares features a variety of scenes, based largely on topographical views of England, contained within a characteristic floral border. Typical examples are shown in Plates 7.42 to 7.46, with Plates 7.47 to 7.49 showing some of the original source prints found at the factory. Attribution of the series to Minton is based not only on the discovery of these early prints, but also on the finding of several of the original copper plate engravings. Furthermore, the series was produced over many decades, and later pieces can be found impressed with

Plate 7.45. Print from the Minton Bat Print book featuring Brandenburg House. It was possibly intended for use on a teapot or sucrier. This is a direct copy of a print included in VIEWS ON THE THAMES by Cooke & Cooke published in 1811. This was probably also the source of the engraving used by Minton on the sauce tureen in Plate 7.44.

Plate 7.46. Minton Miniature series meat dish, c.1900. This clear glazed earthenware dish shows that the pattern was still being produced by Mintons some 75 years after its introduction. The view of Lanercost Priory is taken from THE BEAUTIES OF ENGLAND AND WALES, by Britton, Brayley and Brewer.[13] The copper plate engraving is still held at the factory. Width 152 mm. Mark M3 with 'Lanercost Priory'. Impressed 'MINTONS', plus workman's marks and a partly indistinct year cypher, probably representing 1901.

Minton marks, such as on the dish shown in Plate 7.46. Pieces are normally found with a printed mark naming the view, such as that shown in Plate 7.42. Early examples of the series are found on the typical Minton Semi-China body, indicating introduction of the pattern in around 1825. This is consistent with the relatively thin copper plate used for the engravings found at the factory. These coppers each had engraved marks naming the following views: Abbey Mill, Embdon Castle, Kenilworth Priory, Lanercost Priory, Lechlade Bridge and

Plate 7.47. Print titled 'Mr Keene's Richmond, late S.t Ch.s Asgill's', drawn by S. Owen and engraved by W. Cooke. The print has been pasted into a book of various engravings at the Minton factory (MS 1987). It was included in both the 1811 and the 1822 editions of VIEWS ON THE THAMES by Cooke & Cooke. Featuring Asgill House, the scene was copied directly to produce an engraving included in the Minton Bat Print book and used on an early black printed Minton teapot (Plate 11.4). A very similar view, probably based on this print, was used on the salad bowl in the Minton Miniature series. Width of print 172 mm.

Plate 7.48. Print titled 'Lechlade', drawn by S. Owen and engraved by W. Cooke. The print has been pasted into a book of various engravings at the Minton factory (MS 1987). It is included in the 1822 edition of VIEWS ON THE THAMES *by Cooke & Cooke. The view was copied for the engraving used inside the covered vegetable dish of the Minton Miniature series. The same scene was copied by Minton for a print in the Bat Print book probably intended for tea ware. Width of print 199 mm.*

Tewksbury Church. Further named views used in the series include Bysham Monastery, Donnington Park, Corf Castle, Entrance to Blaize Castle, deGaunt Castle and St Mary's Dover. These views are illustrated by the Milbourns,[11] who detail a total of 16 different views and identified many of the original source prints. These had been taken from a several publications[12-15] published between 1780 and 1822, consistent with introduction of the pattern in the mid 1820s. Three of these source prints, found at the factory, are shown in Plates 7.47 to 7.49.

Minton also used some of the same views as a basis for additional engravings for use on tea wares. These are included in the factory Bat Print book, examples being shown in Plates 7.42 and 7.45 and in Chapter Eleven.

It is interesting to note that this Minton series of toy wares used a miniature version of Minton dinnerware Shape E (Plate 7.34), the same as was used for the English Scenery series which was introduced at about the same time.

Plate 7.49. Print titled 'St Mary's Church, Dover', drawn by L. Clennell and engraved by George Cooke. The print has been pasted into a book of various engravings at the Minton factory (MS 1987). Published in London on 1 March 1814 by J. Murray, the view was copied for the engraving used inside the salad bowl of the Minton Miniature series. The same scene was copied by Minton for a print in the Bat Print book and found on a tea saucer (Plate 11.8b).

Plate 7.50. Girl with Puppies pattern Semi-China saucer dish, probably Minton, c.1825. This is the only example of this pattern recorded to date. Diameter 200 mm. Marks M1 and P13.

Plate 7.51. Floral Cottage pattern tea plate, probably Minton, c.1825. This example has been painted over in coloured enamels, but it may also have been used plain. Diameter 167 mm. Marks M1 and P2. Single recessed foot ring and three single stilt marks beneath the rim.

Girl with Puppies

This pattern is illustrated on the saucer dish in Plate 7.50. To date this is the only piece that has been identified, and it is likely that the pattern was just used on tea wares. Other examples should use the same border but the central design may vary within the tea service from piece to piece. The attribution to Minton is based solely on the use of the distinctive Semi-China seal mark and typical printed workman's mark.

Floral Cottage

As with the previous pattern, only one example of this design has been recorded to date, the small plate shown in Plate 7.51. Again the attribution is based on the Semi-China seal mark, although in this case there is also a known printer's mark and the plate is typical of Minton having a single recessed foot ring and single stilt marks beneath the rim. It is probable that the plate is from a tea service. The example illustrated has been overpainted with coloured enamels, but until further examples are found it remains uncertain whether the design was a true 'Japan' painted pattern, or if it was normally left unpainted.

Botanical Groups

One of several similar patterns produced by Minton in the 1820s which consisted of a mainly floral design on a blue ground. It is illustrated in Plates 3.59, 7.52 and 7.53 and is seen to feature distinct groups or bunches of flowers. Note also the distinctive border, which helps to distinguish it from the other similar designs. This Botanical Groups pattern is found on toilet wares of characteristic Minton form, normally marked with the Semi-China seal mark. It is often found on the clear-glazed Opaque China body, and production probably continued into the 1830s. Similar designs were used by Spode and other factories.

Plate 7.52. Minton Botanical Groups pattern Opaque China ewer, c.1830. Note the use of distinct bunches or groups of flowers on a blue ground consisting of finely engraved circles. The characteristic border helps to distinguish this design from the Minton Botanical pattern, shown in Plates 7.54 and 7.55, and the several other similar botanical designs produced by other factories. The pattern is normally found on toilet wares with the Semi-China seal mark, although examples are often found on the later Opaque China body. Height 242 mm. Mark M1.

Plate 7.53. Minton Botanical Groups pattern toilet wares. Note the distinct floral groups and characteristic border. Opaque China oblong covered toilet box, c.1830. Length 200 mm. Mark M1. Semi-China tray, c.1825, length 173 mm. Mark M1. Opaque China round covered box, c.1830, diameter 84 mm. Mark '4 oz' impressed.

Plate 7.54. Minton Botanical pattern Opaque China Roman jug, c.1830. Differences in the border and the floral arrangement distinguish this from the similar Botanical Groups pattern. Although normally found with the Semi-China seal mark, this example has only a printer's mark. Height 201 mm. Mark P16.

Plate 7.55. Minton Botanical Pattern Semi-China mug, c.1825. The lustrous glaze of the Semi-China body increases the effectiveness of this pattern. Note the characteristic Minton handle form. Height 85 mm. Mark M1.

Botanical

This fine floral pattern is illustrated in Plates 7.54 and 7.55. It is distinguished from the similar Botanical Groups pattern shown in Plate 7.52 by the different border and edging and the greater spread of flowers. It is found on jugs and mugs of characteristic Minton form and normally with the Semi-China seal mark. It was probably introduced in about 1825 and the design is at its most vibrant when found on the lustrous Semi-China. Examples are often found on Opaque China, and production probably continued into the 1830s. Very similar floral patterns were produced by other factories.

Plate 7.56. *Minton Floral Vases pattern Opaque China Roman jug, c.1830. The other side is decorated with a mirror image of the print shown. Minton also used the pattern on mugs and tea wares. The jug shown below in Plate 7.57, and the tea wares in Plates 7.62 and 7.63, illustrate use of the same pattern by other, as yet unidentified makers. Height 160 mm. Mark M1.*

Plate 7.57. *Floral Vases pattern jug, maker unknown, c.1830. The Stone China body is relatively thinly potted. Note the distinctive moulding at the base of the handle with a body firing tear beneath. The printed mark is similar to an Iron Stone China mark recorded by Lawrence[16] as used by the Swillington Bridge pottery in Yorkshire. Height 175 mm. Printed mark 51 mm wide, as detailed below.*

Floral Vases

This design was used for both jugs, mugs and tea wares and is perhaps the most commonly found of the Minton botanical type patterns. It is illustrated on the fine Roman jug in Plate 7.56 and the tea wares in Plates 7.58 to 7.61. These clearly show the unusual arrangement of a box containing a vessel or lamp with vases of flowers on either side. Note that on both the Minton jug and teapot the engraving has an opposite left-to-right arrangement of these items on each face. Minton probably introduced the design in the early 1820s, and pieces normally have the Semi-China seal mark. Examples are often found on Opaque China and the bone china cup and saucer in Plate 7.61 are probably Minton.

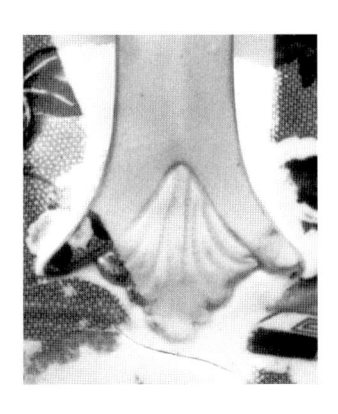

Plate 7.58. Minton Floral Vases pattern Semi-China teapot, c.1825. Note the characteristic Minton shape. The relatively light print is typical of the Minton version of this pattern. This contrasts the darker prints found on the non-Minton pieces shown in Plates 7.62 and 7.63. Length 239 mm. Marks M1 and P16.

Plate 7.59. Minton Floral Vases pattern Semi-China toy milk jug, c.1825. This typical Minton jug confirms that the pattern was used on both normal and toy-sized tea wares. Height 73 mm. Mark M1.

Plate 7.60. Minton Floral Vases pattern Semi-China coffee can, c.1825. Note the distinctive Minton handle form. Height 66 mm. Marks M1 and P14.

Plate 7.61. Floral Vases pattern bone china cup and saucer, c.1830. Details of the print and the profile of the cup and its handle all point to Minton manufacture. Saucer diameter 147 mm, cup diameter 91 mm.

Plate 7.62. *Floral Vases pattern earthenware teapot, maker unknown, c.1825. Although very similar to the Minton version, the print is darker and clearly different in its detail from that used on the teapot in Plate 7.58. This variant of the London teapot shape is normally found in bone china and was produced by several factories, including Ridgway. Length 256 mm. Ten-hole plain triangular strainer. Impressed Staffordshire knot (10 mm long) and '18' (4 mm high).*

Plate 7.63. *Floral Vases pattern earthenware slop bowl, c.1825. Possibly by the same factory as the teapot in Plate 7.62, although some variation in pattern detail is apparent. Diameter 159 mm. 'Semi China' seal mark (24.5 mm long) as detailed below, clearly in imitation of the Minton mark.*

Plate 7.64. Minton Leaf pattern Opaque China jug, c.1830. This small ewer-shaped jug is probably from a tea service. 'Ewer creams' are listed in the 1817 inventory (Plate 2.1). Height 104 mm. Marks M1 and P2.

Plate 7.65. Minton Opaque China covered sponge dish base, decorated with a version of the Botanical Vase pattern, c.1830 (see also Plate 9.113). The main floral arrangement is the same as used on the soup plate shown in Plate 7.66, but the vase design is taken from the Minton Filigree pattern. The floral border is probably only used on this toiletware version of the pattern. Width 218 mm. Mark P10.

Plates 7.57, 7.62 and 7.63 all illustrate examples of this pattern produced by other manufacturers. Although each has some form of marking, none have yet been attributed. The seal mark used on the bowl in Plate 7.63 is clearly intended as a direct copy of the Minton mark, differing mainly in the use of all upper case 'SEMI-CHINA'. The tea wares in Plates 7.62 and 7.63 may be from a common maker. Both are of good quality and have relatively dark prints. An earthenware teapot apparently matching the shape of that illustrated in Plate 7.62 has been recorded[17] printed with a country lodge scene.

Leaf

This pattern has been recorded on the small ewer-shaped jug shown in Plate 7.64, which is probably the milk jug from a tea service. It has also been noted on a Semi-China egg cup stand of the characteristic Minton shape shown in Plate 9.138. This would indicate that this was a teaware pattern, although the possibility remains that it was also used for toilet wares or jugs.

Botanical Vase

This fine floral pattern is illustrated on the soup plate in Plate 7.66. Examples have been found on Semi-China but the wares are not normally marked, so the pattern may have been first introduced on pearlwares in around 1820. The design features various floral arrangements in a distinctive decorative vase or basket. Attribution to Minton was initially based on the discovery of a typically thin early copper plate at the factory. A pull from the engraving is shown in Plate 7.67. It was probably intended for use on an octagonal meat dish. A soup tureen in this pattern has been noted corresponding to Minton factory Shape E, as detailed in Plate 7.34. Examples of this pattern are not common, and it may have been quickly superseded by the similar and popular Filigree pattern.

The Minton covered sponge dish shown in Plates 7.65 and 9.113 shows a variant of the Botanical Vase pattern, probably used exclusively on toilet wares. The central floral arrangement on blue ground is the same as used on the soup plate (Plate 7.66), but the vase design is taken from the Minton Filigree pattern (Plate 7.68). The sponge dish also uses a special floral border design.

Plate 7.66. *Minton Botanical Vase pattern Semi-China concave-octagonal soup plate, c.1825. The relatively thin geometric border helps to emphasise the impressive botanical engraving. Plate 7.67 shows a pull from the single engraving for this pattern found at the factory. Note the variation of the floral arrangement. Plate 7.65 shows that the same basic pattern was used on toilet wares but with a different border and the vase design from the Filigree pattern. Diameter 243 mm.*

Plate 7.67. *Pull taken from an engraving of the Botanical Vase pattern found in the Minton copper plate room. The engraving may have been originally intended for use on a meat or baking dish. It might have been retained for use with another pattern, perhaps inside a footbath. Width 370 mm.*

Plate 7.68. Minton Filigree pattern Semi-China 20-inch concave-octagonal meat dish, c.1825. This fine floral pattern used a series of different arrangements within a common border. Spode produced a Filigree pattern which was very similar but used a more rounded vase. Minton produced the pattern for many years and examples are normally found with the distinctive printed mark shown above. Width of mark 40 mm, but note a slightly larger width of 45 mm was also used. Width of dish 524 mm. Mark M4 and impressed '20'.

Filigree

This pattern features a variety of finely engraved floral arrangements within an angular vase or basket, surrounded by a distinctive floral border. It is very similar to the Spode Filigree pattern, reputedly introduced in 1823.[18] Minton introduced the design on Semi-China dinner and dessert wares at about the same time. Typical examples are illustrated in Plates 7.68 to 7.81 and bear the 'Nankeen Semi China' printed mark shown in Plate 7.68. The pattern must have proved to be popular as examples are relatively common and are found on Semi, Opaque and Improved Stone China. Pieces are also occasionally found dating from the 1860s and impressed 'MINTON'. The wares are of characteristic Minton form and often bear typical Minton printed or impressed workman's marks. The dinner wares are seen to correspond to factory Shape E (Plate 7.34) and the dessert wares were the standard Minton shapes of the 1820s. A pull from an engraving still held at the factory is shown in Plate 7.75, which includes the standard mark. The same vase design was used in the Minton Botanical Vase toiletware pattern shown in Plate 7.65.

The Minton Filigree pattern is easily distinguished from the corresponding Spode version, but at least one other factory produced a direct copy, as illustrated in Plate 7.76. The engraving is less fine than the Minton original, and although the printed mark was also copied, maker's initials were added. Recent non-Minton modern reproductions of the pattern are also found.

Plate 7.69. Minton Filigree pattern Semi-China 18-inch meat dish, c.1825. Note how an insect has been incorporated into the engraving. Width 471 mm. Mark M4 and impressed '18'.

Plate 7.70. Minton Filigree pattern Opaque China 12-inch meat dish, c.1830. Although introduced on Semi-China, Minton continued to produce this pattern on various earthenware bodies into the 1860s. Width 318 mm. Mark M4 and impressed '12'.

Plate 7.71a&b. *Minton Filigree pattern Semi-China concave-octagonal dinner plates, c.1825. This was the standard size of dinner plate supplied in the service. As was the case with several Minton patterns, two slightly different designs are seen to have been used for the same size plate. The plates illustrated above and those in Plate 7.72 are all taken from the same service. This contained a mixture of the various plate engravings with no indication of one design having predated the other. Diameter of (a) above left, 250 mm with marks M4 and P4. Diameter of (b) above right, 251 mm with mark M4.*

Plate 7.72a&b. *Minton Filigree pattern Semi-China eight-inch concave-octagonal dinner plates, c.1825. As with the standard sized plates shown in Plate 7.71, two different engravings are seen to have been used for this smaller sized plate. Diameter of (a) above left, 221 mm with marks M4 and P14 and impressed '6'. Diameter of (b) above right, 222 mm with mark M4.*

Plate 7.73. Minton Filigree pattern Semi-China concave-octagonal six-inch plate, c.1825. The smallest standard plate size produced in the service. Diameter 161 mm. Mark M4.

Plate 7.74. Minton Filigree pattern Semi-China concave-octagonal soup plate, c.1825. Note that this engraving has been copied by another factory and used on the circular dish shown in Plate 7.76. Diameter 238 mm. Mark M4.

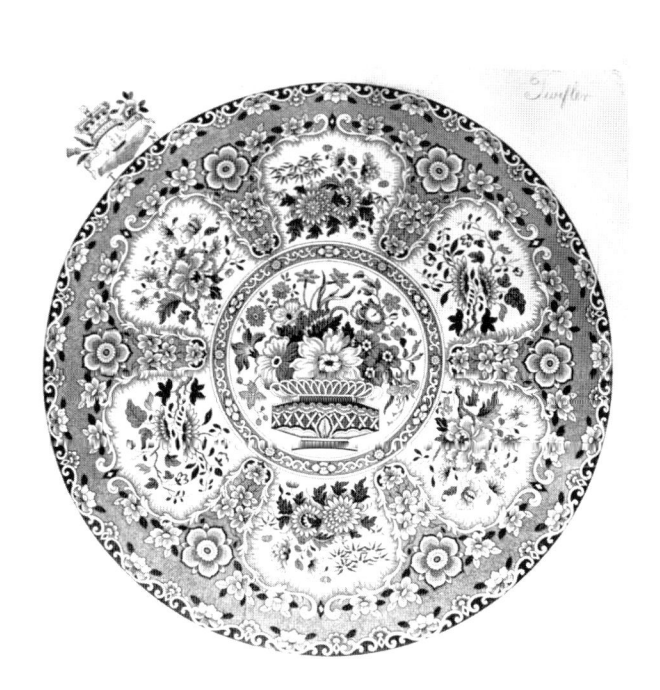

Plate 7.75. Mirror image of pull taken from an engraving of the Minton Filigree pattern at the factory. Although essentially the same as the design used on the eight-inch plate or 'twifler' in Plate 7.72b, variation in detail indicates that this is from a different engraving. Re-engraving of plates is to be expected for a pattern produced over several decades. The significance of the initials 'TM' beneath the mark is not clear, but may signify involvement of Thomas Minton in the original design or engraving of the pattern.

Plate 7.76. Black printed Filigree pattern dish, maker unknown, c.1830. Heavily potted clear-glazed earthenware decorated from an engraving copied directly from the Minton design shown in Plate 7.74, though minor differences of detail can be seen. The printed mark has also been copied with addition of makers initials 'J.C. & S.' as detailed above (see also Table 10.4 for detail of an associated impressed mark). Diameter 248 mm. Printed mark 47 mm long.

Plate 7.77. Minton Filigree pattern Semi-China soup tureen, c.1825. Minton used Shape E dinner wares for this series, as shown in Plate 7.34 and as used with the English Scenery series. Note how the border design has been cleverly adapted, following the moulded ridges on the tureen sides and framing the central floral design. Length 369 mm. Mark M4.

Plate 7.78. Minton Filigree pattern Semi-China Shape E covered vegetable dish, c.1825. Length 283 mm. Mark M4.

Plate 7.79. Minton Filigree pattern Opaque China soup tureen stand, c.1830. The same print was used on the 16-inch meat dish (see Plate 3.65). Width 382 mm. Mark M4.

Plate 7.80. Minton Filigree pattern Opaque China dessert dish, c.1830. The floral arrangement is used to particularly good effect on this piece. Note that Minton used several patterns on this popular design of dessert wares. Width 213 mm. Mark M4.

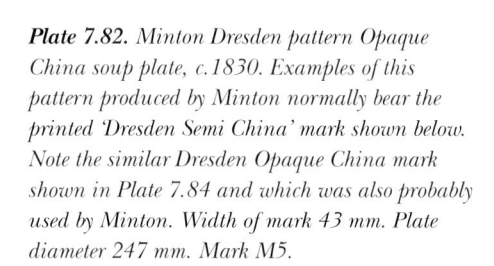

Plate 7.81. Minton Filigree pattern Semi-China dessert dish, c.1825. A characteristic Minton dessert dish form used with several patterns during the 1820s. The same central print was used on the 10-inch meat dish. Width 264 mm. Mark M4.

Plate 7.82. Minton Dresden pattern Opaque China soup plate, c.1830. Examples of this pattern produced by Minton normally bear the printed 'Dresden Semi China' mark shown below. Note the similar Dresden Opaque China mark shown in Plate 7.84 and which was also probably used by Minton. Width of mark 43 mm. Plate diameter 247 mm. Mark M5.

Plate 7.83. Minton Dresden pattern Semi-China dessert dish, c.1825. This characteristic dessert dish shape exactly matches those produced by Minton in several other patterns (see Plates 6.44 and 7.81). Note that the same engraving appears to have been used to print the central design on the embossed Dresden pattern dessert dishes in Plates 7.84 and 7.85. Width 265 mm. Mark M5.

Dresden

Plates 7.82 and 7.83 show a version of this floral pattern produced by Minton on tablewares. Attribution is based on the distinctive shape of the wares, in particular the characteristic form of the dessert wares, such as the dish in Plate 7.83. The pattern has a floral border and uses the printed Semi-China mark shown in Plate 7.82. A further version of the pattern is shown in Plate 7.84. It uses an apparently identical central design but a different border and an 'Opaque China' printed mark.

Plate 7.84. Dresden pattern embossed Opaque China dessert dish, probably Minton, c.1826. This version of the Dresden pattern is normally found on embossed wares with the Opaque China mark illustrated below. Although the border design is different, the central floral design appears to have been printed from the same engraving as used for the Minton dish in Plate 7.83. Minton listed Dresden Embossed table and toilet wares in 1825 and 1826 inventories. Width of mark 42 mm. Width of dish 281 mm. Mark M6.

Plate 7.85. Dresden pattern embossed Opaque China dessert dish, probably Minton, c.1826. Note the different embossed handle design compared to the dish in Plate 7.84. Both dishes come from the same service and were printed from the same engraving. Width of dish 223 mm. Mark M6.

It is found on embossed table and toilet wares of good quality and with certain potting characteristics typical of Minton. The distinctive embossed shapes appear to have been used exclusively with this pattern, making attribution more difficult. Significantly, however, the central design on the embossed dessert dishes in Plates 7.84 and 7.85 appear to have been printed from the same engraving as used on the Minton dish shown in Plate 7.83. Given that the soup plate shown in Plate 7.82 has an Opaque China body, and so is probably contemporary with the embossed wares, it is unlikely that the copper plates had been sold on by Minton. It therefore seems probable that the embossed Opaque China Dresden pattern wares were produced by Minton. Indeed these may be the wares listed in the 1825 and 1826 factory inventories as Dresden Embossed. The items listed in January 1825 included jugs, ewers, chambers, square soaps, brush boxes, foot pans, plates and various dinner and dessert wares. During the 1825 to 1835 period Minton

Plate 7.86. Dresden pattern embossed Opaque China toilet tray, probably Minton, c.1826. Length 181 mm. Mark M6.

Plate 7.87. Dresden pattern embossed Opaque China dessert plate, probably Minton, c.1826. Diameter 226 mm. Three single stilt marks beneath the rim. Double recessed foot ring. Mark M6.

used Dresden to describe a range of ornamental porcelains, typically modelled on original Dresden designs, and sometimes marked with the painted Dresden crossed swords. The inventory entry could therefore refer to the embossed design and not the pattern name. The entry for 1826 does not support this possibility, however, as it refers to Embossed Dresden and other patterns. In the next chapter it is seen that versions of the Florentine and Corinthian patterns were both produced on embossed wares. Interestingly the appearance of the entry for Dresden embossed wares in the 1825 inventory, together with the corresponding change of the Dresden pattern mark, may indicate that Opaque China was being introduced around that time.

The Dresden pattern has also been recorded on a milk jug with a typical Minton handle and bearing the mark M6, indicating use of the design by Minton on non-embossed tea wares. Griffin illustrates the pattern on a large teapot

Plate 7.88. Two views of an earthenware jug by an unknown maker, c.1825. The jug is printed in blue and painted over in enamel colours. It is marked with the Semi-China seal mark U2b shown above, which is seen to be very similar to the mark M1 used by Minton. Note however the difference in the symbols within the octagonal border. Height of jug 118 mm. Width of mark 21 mm.

produced by the Don Pottery, bearing a printed mark very similar to M6 but without the pair of symbols within the cartouche.[19] Griffin also reports use of a very similar mark and pattern by Dixon, Austin and Co. of the Garrison Pottery, Sunderland. Other factories, including Ridgeway and Clews, produced Dresden patterns, but these were different basic designs from the pattern illustrated here.

References

1. *Friends of Blue Bulletin*, No. 45, 1984, p. 12.
2. A.W. Coysh and R.K. Henrywood, *The Dictionary of Blue and White Printed Pottery* (Antique Collectors Club, 1982), p. 78.
3. *Friends of Blue Bulletin*, No. 40, 1983, p. 9.
4. G.A. Godden, *Minton Pottery & Porcelain of the First Period* (Barrie & Jenkins, 1968), Plate 112.
5. N. Hudson Moore, *The Old China Book* (New York: Tudor Publishing Co., repr. 1946), fig. 79.
6. *Friends of Blue Bulletin*, No. 88, 1995, p. 4.
7. Coysh and Henrywood, *Dictionary of Blue and White* , p. 155.
8. A.W. Coysh and R.K. Henrywood, *The Dictionary of Blue and White Printed Pottery Volume 2* (Antique Collectors Club, 1989), p. 58.
9. Coysh and Henrywood, *Dictionary of Blue and White* , p. 143.
10. Coysh and Henrywood, *Dictionary of Blue and White Vol. 2*, p. 81.
11. M. and E. Milbourn, *Understanding Miniature British Pottery & Porcelain, 1730–Present Day* (Antique Collectors Club, 1983), pp. 92–102.
12. F. Grose, *The Antiquities of England, Wales, Scotland & Ireland*, 12 vols. (London: 1785–97).
13. J. Britton, E.W. Brayley and J. Brewer, *The Beauties of England and Wales*, 26 vols. (London, 1801–08).
14. J. Storer and I. Greig, *The Antiquarian and Topographical Cabinet*, 10 vols. (London: W. Clarke, 1807–11).
15. G. Cooke and W.B. Cooke, *Views on the Thames* (London: 1811 and 1822).
16. H. Lawrence, *Yorkshire Pots and Potteries* (David & Charles, 1974), p. 244.
17. *Friends of Blue Bulletin*, No. 65, 1989, p. 6.
18. D. Drakard and P. Holdway, *Spode Printed Ware* (Longman, 1983), p. 146.
19. J.D. Griffin, *The Don Pottery 1801–1893* (Doncaster Museum Service, 2001), p. 114.

Chapter Eight

Catalogue of Patterns
5. Opaque China, Stone China and Improved Stone China

Florentine

This distinctive floral design was used by Minton on a wide range of table and toilet wares, examples being illustrated in Plates 8.1 to 8.11. It is normally found with the printed mark shown in Plate 8.1. The pattern was introduced on Opaque China, probably in the mid 1820s. Examples are relatively common, including some use on the later Improved Stone China body, indicating continued production for many years. Dinner wares were produced in factory Shape F, with a distinctive floral knob to the tureen. Dessert wares, jugs and mugs were all produced in standard Minton shapes of the 1820 period. A single small copper

Plate 8.1. Minton Florentine pattern Improved Stone China concave-octagonal dinner plate, c.1835. This distinctive floral design was introduced by Minton on Opaque China in the mid-1820s. Production continued for many years and examples such as this plate can be found impressed with the later Improved Stone China seal mark. The pattern is almost invariably found with the printed mark M7, as shown above. No evidence has been found to support a traditional attribution of this pattern to Gordon's pottery at Prestonpans. Width of mark 52 mm. Three small single stilt marks to front of rim. Plate diameter 251 mm. Printed mark M7. Impressed mark M31.

Plate 8.2. Minton Florentine pattern Opaque China sauce tureen, c.1827. Minton used Shape F dinner wares for this pattern as shown below. The Minton Opaque China body and glaze were of excellent quality and produced crisply potted moulded features. Note the use of underglaze blue painting to highlight the moulding around the feet. Length 172 mm. Mark M7.

Plate 8.3. Minton dinnerware design F from the factory shape book of c.1830. Minton seems to have used this shape exclusively with the Florentine pattern.

Plate 8.4. Minton Florentine pattern Opaque China Shape F covered vegetable dish, c.1827. Length 318 mm. Mark M7.

plate engraving of this pattern remains at the factory. It has been claimed that this pattern was produced by the Gordon's pottery at Prestonpans. Although it is certainly possible that this popular design was copied by other factories, all the examples found to date seem to be of Minton origin, and it is possible that some confusion between 'GORDON' and 'MINTON' impressed marks may have occurred. Florentine is known to have been used as a pattern name at other factories, but these were different basic designs.

Plate 8.5. Minton Florentine pattern Opaque China sauce tureen stand, c.1827. Width 207 mm. Mark M7.

Plate 8.6. Minton Florentine pattern Opaque China jug, c.1827. A characteristic Minton jug form, also used with the Chinese Marine pattern. Height 195 mm. Mark M7. Inscribed size mark 9.

Plate 8.7. Minton Florentine pattern Opaque China covered jug, c.1827. The lid is secured by two lugs which locate beneath an inner rim. Fifteen-hole plain triangular strainer. Height 175 mm. Marks M7 and P20

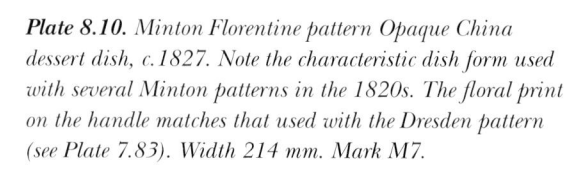

Plate 8.8. Minton Florentine pattern Opaque China mug, c.1827. Note the handle form. Height 81 mm. Marks M7 and P14.

Plate 8.9. Minton Florentine pattern Opaque China small handled pot, c.1827. Outer rim diameter 120 mm. Mark M7.

Plate 8.10. Minton Florentine pattern Opaque China dessert dish, c.1827. Note the characteristic dish form used with several Minton patterns in the 1820s. The floral print on the handle matches that used with the Dresden pattern (see Plate 7.83). Width 214 mm. Mark M7.

Plate 8.11. Minton Florentine pattern Opaque China potpourri jar, c.1827. Note the detail of the knobs and the open-mouthed lion handles, matching those on the larger pot shown in Plate 6.80. The main print matches that used on the jug in Plate 8.6. Height 242 mm. Diameter of base 134 mm. Marks M7 and P13.

Florentine Embossed

As illustrated on the jug shown in Plate 8.12, the main design of this pattern is essentially the same as the Florentine pattern. It is distinguished by having a different printed mark and being found on wares with applied or 'embossed' mouldings.

It is possible that wares in this pattern were part of the section headed 'embossed Dresden & other patterns' included in the 1826 Minton factory inventory. As shown in Plate 8.12, the detail of the embossed reliefs corresponds to those included on ewer Shape D of the factory shape book of c.1830. The fine white body and the lustrous and well fitting glaze of this piece match those of the Dresden Embossed pattern wares shown in Plates 7.84 and 7.85.

Plate 8.12. Minton Florentine Embossed pattern Opaque China ewer c.1827, with corresponding design from the 1830 shape book. Note the additional floral border design used with the embossed wares. Height 239 mm. Marks M8 and P4.

Plate 8.13. Minton Dresden Flowers pattern Opaque China toy tea wares, c.1827. Wares in this pattern usually bear the mark shown above. Note the inclusion of the cursive M indicative of Minton. Slop bowl diameter 112 mm. Sucrier width 105 mm. Saucer diameter 110 mm. All wares with mark M9. Saucer also mark P2.

Dresden Flowers

A floral pattern found on toy tea and table wares and introduced by Minton on Opaque China in the mid 1820s. Examples are not uncommon, suggesting production for many years. They usually bear the printed mark incorporating a cursive M shown in Plate 8.13, which also shows typical wares. Several copper plate engravings for this pattern, including the printed mark, remain at the factory.

Plate 8.14. Minton Flora pattern Opaque China cup and saucer, c.1827. This attractive floral pattern is illustrated on a full size version of the toy teacup and saucer shown above in Plate 8.13. Saucer diameter 137 mm. Mark M10, as shown below. Note that as with mark M9, a cursive M has been included in the mark.

Plate 8.15. Minton Flora pattern Opaque China tea plate, c.1827. An unusually small size of plate. It may be a cup plate as this pattern is not normally associated with toy-sized wares. Diameter 137 mm. Marks M10 and P2.

Plate 8.16. Minton Swiss Cottage pattern Opaque China stand, c.1827. Probably a broth bowl stand. The cottage-type building from which the pattern name derives is clearly shown. The sucrier in Plate 8.17 indicates that other scenes were also used in this teaware pattern. Wares usually bear the printed mark shown below. Diameter 154 mm. Mark M11.

Plate 8.17. Minton Swiss Cottage pattern Opaque China sucrier (lid missing), c.1827. The other side bears the normal Swiss cottage scene. Probably matching the Minton Cottage teapot shape, such as that shown in Plate 4.43. Length 188 mm. Mark M11.

Flora

An attractive floral pattern introduced by Minton in the mid 1820s on Opaque China tea wares, examples of which are shown in Plates 8.14 and 8.15. The cup and saucer in Plate 8.14 are the same basic design as the toy Dresden Flowers pattern cup and saucer. A Flora pattern teapot has been recorded in the cottage shape shown in Plate 4.43. The corresponding sucrier was probably of the shape shown in Plate 8.17 below. The characteristic printed mark is shown in Plate 8.14 and includes a typical Minton cursive M. Flora was also used as a pattern name by other factories, but for different basic designs.

Swiss Cottage

A teaware pattern introduced on Opaque China in the mid 1820s and featuring a Swiss-type chalet (see Plate 8.16), similar to those used in the Genevese pattern. Other cottage scenes were also used, as shown in Plate 8.17, which also illustrates the printed mark, including the characteristic cursive M.

Plate 8.18. Minton Corinthian pattern Opaque China sauce tureen, c.1827. This corresponds to the basic Minton dinnerware Shape H, as shown below, with the addition of some embossed mouldings. Length 195 mm. Mark M12.

Plate 8.19. Minton dinnerware design H taken from the factory shape book of c.1830. The basic shape used by Minton for the Corinthian pattern. Note the similarity with Shape D, shown in Plate 8.31. Differences in the moulding of the feet and the base of the knob help to distinguish the two designs.

Plate 8.20. Minton Corinthian pattern Opaque China sauce tureen stand, c.1827. Note how the floral border prints are housed within embossed panels. This pattern is normally found with the printed mark with cursive M shown above. Width of mark 35 mm. Width of stand 224 mm. Mark M12.

Corinthian

This pattern is typical of the elaborate floral designs being produced during the late 1820s. It was introduced by Minton on Opaque China dinner wares, examples being shown in Plates 8.18 to 8.22. It is seen to have a central floral arrangement surrounded by a moulded embossed border containing four floral printed panels. It is found on wares corresponding to basic factory Shape H, as shown in Plate 8.19, with the addition of an embossed border. Wares normally have the printed mark shown in Plate 8.20, including the characteristic cursive M. Other factories used Corinthian and Corinthia as pattern names, but for different basic designs.

Corinthian Embossed

This floral pattern was probably introduced by Minton on Stone China teawares in the late 1820s. It is illustrated on the tea plate and saucer shown in Plates 8.23 and 8.24. The central design is basically the same as that used on Corinthian, but only two of the four border panels have floral prints, the others featuring birds. The embossed mouldings also differ to those used on Corinthian wares. This teaware pattern was probably introduced to accompany the Corinthian dinnerware pattern, and is normally found with the printed mark with cursive M shown in Plate 8.24. The change from Opaque to Stone China in the mark is perhaps indicative that Corinthian and the Stone China body were both introduced at around the same time. Given that both Corinthian designs are found on embossed wares, it is unclear why 'embossed' is only incorporated into one of the marks.

Plate 8.21. Minton Corinthian pattern Opaque China salad bowl, c.1827. A piece of fine quality with crisp potting and an excellent glaze and body. It corresponds to the factory Shape H, as shown in Plate 8.19, with the additional embossed mouldings. Width 277 mm. Marks M12 and P16.

Plate 8.22. Minton Corinthian pattern Opaque China soup plate, c.1827. Diameter 259 mm. Printed marks M12 and P15.

Plate 8.23. Minton Corinthian Embossed pattern Stone China tea plate, c.1830. Diameter 176 mm. Mark M13.

Plate 8.24. Minton Corinthian Embossed pattern Stone China tea saucer, c.1827. This teaware pattern is very similar to the Corinthian table ware pattern, but uses different border prints and embossed moulding. The pattern is normally found with the printed mark with cursive M shown below. Diameter 142 mm. Mark M13.

Plate 8.25. Minton Genevese pattern Improved Stone China dinner plate, c.1835. Later use of a design introduced in the mid 1820s. The series uses a variety of romantic landscape views surrounded by a typical floral border. It remained in production for many years and was used on a wide range of wares. The same design was copied by other factories. Minton examples are found with the printed mark shown above, including the characteristic cursive M. Width of mark 53 mm. Three small single stilt marks to front of rim. Plate diameter 257 mm. Printed marks M14 and P16. Impressed seal mark M31.

Genevese

This pattern features a series of romantic landscape views containing alpine chalets surrounded by a characteristic floral border. Examples are illustrated in Plates 8.25 to 8.39. It was introduced by Minton on Opaque China jugs, table and toilet wares in the mid 1820s and examples are normally found with the printed mark with cursive M shown in Plate 8.25. The design proved very popular and remained in production for many years. The copper plates for this pattern are still at the factory and some prints were included in a factory printed pattern book from 1886,[1] examples being shown in several Plates between 8.28 and 8.40. Minton used this design on factory Shape D, as shown in Plate 8.31. The basic tureen design was very similar to Shape H, as used with the Corinthian pattern and shown in Plate 8.19.

Although originally introduced by Minton, the popularity and longevity of the design resulted in copies being produced by several other factories, including Thomas & Benjamin Godwin,[2] Clews,[3] Reed Taylor & Co.[4] and Edge Malkin & Co..[5] The Minton examples can normally be distinguished by their superior quality and the inclusion of the cursive M in the printed mark.

Plate 8.26. Minton Genevese pattern Opaque China six-inch plate or 'Muffin', c.1827. This design is included in the Minton printed pattern book, as illustrated below in Plate 8.28. Diameter 166 mm. Mark M14.

Plate 8.27. Minton Genevese pattern Opaque China soup plate, c.1827. As with the majority of Minton pieces produced during the Opaque China period, the quality of the print, body and glaze is excellent. Diameter 259 mm. Mark M14.

Plate 8.28. Genevese pattern print used on the six-inch 'Muffin' plate (see Plate 8.26 above) taken from the factory printed pattern book of 1886.

Plate 8.29. Minton Genevese pattern Opaque China 10-inch meat dish, c.1827. Note the profile and moulding on the rim, which is also found on the plates. Width 320 mm. Printed marks M14 and P10. Impressed size mark '12'.

Plate 8.30. *Minton Genevese pattern Opaque China sauce tureen, c.1827. The print used on the sides of the tureen is included in the Minton printed pattern book, as shown in Plate 8.33. Tureen length 197 mm. Mark M14.*

Plate 8.31. *Minton dinnerware design D from the factory shape book of c.1830. The shape used by Minton for the Genevese pattern. Note the similarity with Shape H, shown in Plate 8.19.*

Plate 8.32. *Minton Genevese pattern Opaque China 18-inch meat dish, c.1827. Width 472 mm. Mark M14 and impressed size mark '18'.*

Plate 8.33. *Genevese pattern print as used on the sauce tureen in Plate 8.30, taken from the Minton pattern book of 1886.*

Plate 8.34. *Genevese pattern toiletware prints taken from the factory printed pattern book of 1886.*

Plate 8.35. *Minton Genevese pattern Opaque China covered soap box, c.1827. The prints correspond to those included in the factory print book, as illustrated above in Plate 8.34. The shape of this three-piece box matches the Ruined Abbey pattern example shown in Plate 9.112, although the perforations in the inner tray are different. Length 105 mm. Marks M14 and P10.*

Plate 8.36. *Minton Genevese pattern Opaque China jug, c.1827. Minton produced a range of jug sizes in this distinctive shape with the Genevese pattern. Height 106 mm. Printed marks M14 and P19. Indistinct inscribed size mark, possibly '36'.*

Plate 8.37. *Genevese pattern print for the size 30 jug, from the factory pattern book of 1886.*

Plate 8.38. Minton Genevese pattern Opaque China size 4 footed wash bowl, c.1827, with the corresponding print from the factory pattern book shown right. The outside of the bowl is decorated with a deep floral border. Diameter 329 mm. Printed marks M14 and P19. Impressed '4'.

Plate 8.39. Minton Genevese pattern Opaque China size 24 jug, c.1827. This example is printed in brown. Height 136 mm. Printed marks M14 and P19. Inscribed '24'.

Plate 8.40. Genevese pattern print for the size 4 ewer from the factory pattern book. Such a ewer would be included in the typical toilet set, together with the wash bowl shown above.

Plate 8.41. Minton Chinese Marine pattern Opaque China gadroon-edged plate, c.1827. One of the most successful designs introduced by Minton, probably around 1825. Note the characteristic floral border which is used with a series of stylised Chinese landscapes. Minton examples normally bear the printed mark M15, as shown above, including the characteristic cursive M. Many factories copied the pattern and mark, though with a different initial letter. The plate shown in Plate 8.42 shows how closely the engravings and moulded shapes could be reproduced. Plate diameter 265 mm. Marks M15 and P16. Width of mark 36 mm.

Chinese Marine

This familiar pattern consists of a series of stylised Chinese landscapes within a floral border, typical examples being shown in Plates 8.41 to 8.54. As with many of the patterns introduced by Minton during the 1820s, the design proved highly successful and was produced over several decades. Its popularity also ensured that close copies of the design were produced by many factories. The pattern was introduced by Minton on factory dinnerware Shape B (see Plate 8.46) with plates and dishes having a moulded gadroon edge. This was probably around 1825, when Spode is reported[6] to have also introduced gadroon-edge wares with the Jasmine pattern. Minton also used the pattern with dessert and toilet wares, jugs and various other items. These wares normally bear the printed mark shown in Plate 8.41, including the characteristic cursive M. In addition Minton produced the pattern painted over in coloured enamels, the printed mark then being accompanied by a painted pattern number 59 (see Plate 3.82).

The various versions of this pattern produced by other factories used the same basic shapes and printed mark and very similar engravings. Comparison of the plates in Plates 8.41 and 8.42 highlights how closely the engraved designs and shapes could be copied. Minton examples can normally be distinguished by their superior quality and by the cursive initial M in the mark. Other initial marks found to date include the following: B, unattributed; B&G, unattributed;[7] B&S, possibly Barker & Son (see Plate 8.42); F, Ferrybridge or Swillington Bridge Pottery;[8] G, Bell Vue Pottery, Hull;[9] L.W., possibly Lewis Woolf, Ferrybridge Pottery;[10] O, unattributed; no letter, Fell & Co. Newcastle and probably others.

Very similar patterns produced by other factories include Canton Views by Elkin, Knight & Bridgewood, Chinese Porcelain by John Rogers & Son, and Chinese Scenery recorded on a large presentation jug[11] dated May 1828 and

Plate 8.42. Chinese Marine pattern Opaque China dinner plate, c.1830. Many factories used the Chinese Marine pattern and comparison of this fine quality copy with the Minton example in Plate 8.41 shows how closely the engraving and moulded shape could be reproduced. Double recessed foot ring, three triple rear and single front stilt marks. Diameter 268 mm. Mark width 36 mm.

Plate 8.43. Minton Chinese Marine pattern Opaque China eight-inch plate, c.1827. Diameter 219 mm. Marks M15 and P21.

Plate 8.44. Minton Chinese Marine pattern Opaque China soup plate, c.1827. Diameter 259 mm. Marks M15 and P16.

printed with a mark incorporating a non-cursive M. The floral border from Chinese Marine was also used by Minton with other central designs. Plate 8.52 shows a print in the Minton archives with a different central landscape design. The same border was also used for armorial wares, including the Minton Lizard Armorial pattern.

Plate 8.45. Minton Chinese Marine pattern Opaque China soup tureen, c.1827. The lustrous glaze, white body and crisp moulding is characteristic of the fine quality of Minton wares of this period. The tureen is seen to correspond to factory Shape B. Note that the same basic shape and mouldings were used by other factories copying this pattern. Length 365 mm. Mark M15.

Plate 8.46. Minton dinnerware design B from the factory shape book of c.1830. The shape was used for Chinese Marine and Royal Persian pattern wares.

Plate 8.47. Minton Chinese Marine pattern Opaque China low footed stand, c.1827. Note the fine moulding to the handles, which was also used on the tureen stands and vegetable dishes. These mouldings were copied by other factories producing this pattern. The same engraving is used on the vegetable dish base, which is smaller, deeper and with a rim to accommodate a lid. Width 366 mm. Height 58 mm. Mark M15.

Plate 8.48. Minton Chinese Marine pattern Opaque China sauce tureen stand, c.1827. Width 207 mm. Marks M15 and P15.

Plate 8.49. Minton Chinese Marine pattern Opaque China sauce boat, c.1827. Although the view is essentially the same as that used on the lid of the box in Plate 8.53, different engravings appear to have been used. Length 157 mm. Mark M15.

Plate 8.50. Minton Chinese Marine pattern Opaque China footed bowl, c.1827. A basic round profile, but with eight U-shaped grooves around the outside. The side view shows how the border design has been developed to give an attractive floral decoration around the bowl. Diameter 248 mm, height 115 mm. Mark M15.

Plate 8.51. Minton Chinese Marine pattern Opaque China jug, c.1827. The same shape as used by Minton for the Florentine pattern, as shown in Plate 8.6. Height 168 mm. Mark M15. Inscribed size mark '12'.

Plate 8.52. Print titled 'Arabian' from a pattern book (MS 1943) in the factory archives, showing the border of the Chinese Marine pattern being used with an alternative central romantic landscape.

Plate 8.53. Minton Chinese Marine pattern Opaque China covered toilet box, c.1827. Inside is divided by a single length-wise low partition. Length of base 193 mm, length of lid 199 mm. Mark M15.

Plate 8.54. Minton Chinese Marine pattern Opaque China chamber pot, c.1827, with detail of inner print below. Note the detail of the moulded handle. Outer diameter of upper rim 240 mm, height 139 mm. Marks M15 and P19.

Plate 8.55. Royal Persian pattern Stone China dinner plate, c.1830, probably Minton. This pattern is found on wares exactly matching Minton Chinese Marine pattern dinner wares. Examples are also found impressed with the Minton Improved Stone China seal mark M31 (see Plate 9.92). This moulded plate matches that shown in Plate 8.41. The pattern is normally found with the printed mark shown above, although occasionally the mark incorporates 'Opaque China'. The same basic design and shape may well have been produced by other factories, including Meigh. Double recessed foot ring and three single stilt marks beneath the rim. Plate diameter 264 mm. Width of mark 44 mm. Mark M16.

Lizard Armorial

An armorial design[12] used on dinner wares in which the border from Chinese Marine is used with a central design in which a pair of lizards support the coat of arms for the Worshipful Company of Ironmongers. The shape of the wares is the same as for Chinese Marine. This printed design was reportedly[12] used continuously from around 1825, and supplied to the Ironmonger's Company by both Minton and Copeland Spode, with the back of later pieces sometimes bearing the name of the Warden of the Company in office at the time of purchase.

Royal Persian

An attractive floral pattern found on dinner wares corresponding to Minton Shape B, as used with the Chinese Marine pattern, examples being illustrated in Plates 8.55 to 8.57. Attribution of these wares to Minton is based on their exact correspondence to the Chinese Marine factory shapes, including minor detail in the moulded knobs and handles. The glaze, body and potting characteristics are also typical of Minton. Examples of the pattern are also found with the Minton 'Improved Stone China' seal mark. It should be noted, however, that other factories closely copied these dinnerware shapes, as is apparent from the example in Plate 8.42. Furthermore a plate of the same basic shape and pattern as that shown in Plate 8.55 has been recorded[13] on which the printed mark incorporates the initials 'J M & S', as used by Job and Charles Meigh. Royal Persian copper plates are also included in the 1861 auction sale at the Phoenix Pottery of Thomas Goodfellow.[14] The printed cartouche mark used with this pattern normally includes Stone China, but occasionally Opaque China is used, perhaps indicating that the pattern was being introduced at a time of simultaneous production of the two types of body.

Plate 8.56. Royal Persian pattern Stone China soup tureen, c.1830, probably Minton. Factory Shape B exactly matching the Chinese Marine tureen shown in Plate 8.45, including the detailed moulding of the knob, handles and feet. Length 364 mm. Mark M16.

Plate 8.57. Royal Persian pattern Opaque China sauce tureen stand, c.1830, probably Minton, and matching the example in Plate 8.48. The accompanying sauce tureen had the normal 'Stone China' mark M16. Printed mark M16a as shown below. Width 207 mm. Width of mark 33 mm.

Plate 8.58. Minton Wreath pattern Improved Stone China soup plate, c.1835. This pattern was introduced on Stone China, probably around 1830. The pattern name relates to the floral wreath border. Examples normally bear the printed mark shown above. The plate shape, moulding and outer string border were also used with the contemporary patterns Berlin Chaplet and Berlin Roses. Mark width 54 mm. Three small single stilt marks to front of rim. Diameter 262 mm. Printed mark M17. Impressed mark M31.

Wreath

An attractive floral tableware design featuring a central rose print surrounded by a floral wreath border, as shown in Plate 8.58. The pattern is attributed to Minton as the pattern is sometimes found with the characteristic impressed Improved Stone China mark, such as on the example shown above. Furthermore the moulding and string decoration around the periphery and other potting characteristics exactly match those found with the Minton Berlin Roses and Berlin Chaplet patterns.

Berlin Roses

The pattern uses a very similar floral decoration to the Wreath pattern, as shown on the examples illustrated in Plates 8.59 and 8.61. Minton used the design on dinnerware Shape AA, as shown in Plate 8.62. A single copper plate engraving of this pattern remains at the factory, including an engraving of the cartouche mark M18, but without the heraldic lion, which may have been applied separately.

Berlin Chaplet

Berlin patterns were probably inspired by the floral embroidery designs published in Berlin. Berlin Chaplet, illustrated in Plate 8.60, is a typical example featuring chaplets, which were floral wreaths for the neck or head. The white body, clear glaze and the fine engraving used for this piece are all characteristic of the Minton Stone China wares. Minton probably used this design on factory Shape L, as shown in Plate 8.62, which differs from Shape AA in having an oval instead of a

Plate 8.59. Minton Berlin Roses pattern Stone China low footed stand, c.1830. The sparse floral decoration complements the fine white body. The moulding and string border were also used by Minton on the Wreath and Berlin Chaplet patterns. Minton used this pattern on Shape AA dinner wares. A single copper plate engraving for this design remains at the factory, including the printed cartouche mark above, but without the heraldic lion. Mark width 55 mm. Stand diameter 312 mm, height 63 mm. Printed mark M18.

Plate 8.60. Minton Berlin Chaplet pattern Stone China dinner plate, c.1830. Minton probably used this pattern on Shape L dinner wares. The pattern is normally found with the printed mark shown below, sometimes including the characteristic cursive initial M. Width of mark 55 mm. Plate diameter 262 mm. Printed marks M19 and P14.

221

Plate 8.61. Minton Berlin Roses pattern Stone China covered vegetable dish, c.1830, with gilding to handle. The dish is of the usual excellent quality Minton Stone China with a hard clear glaze on a fine white body. The circular plan of this dish corresponds to factory Shape AA, as shown in Plate 8.62. Plan widths 280 mm by 280 mm. Mark M18.

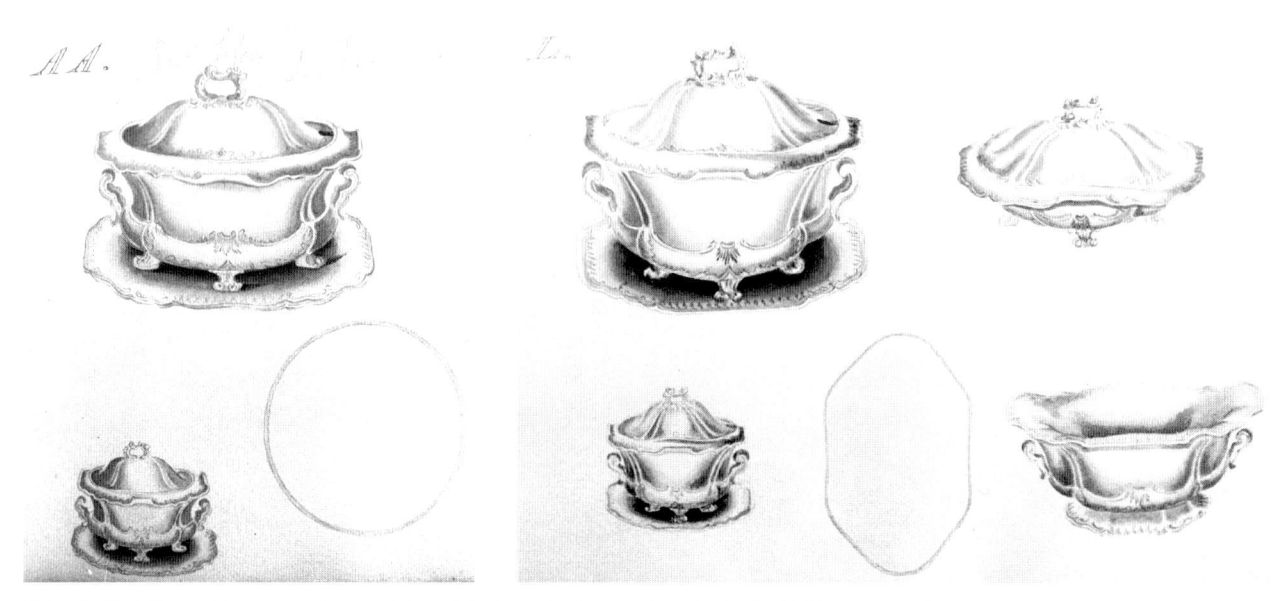

Plate 8.62. Minton dinnerware designs AA and L, from the factory shape book of c.1830. The two designs differ mainly in their plan view, AA being circular and L being oval. The shape book does not give details of the vegetable dish or salad bowl for Shape AA, but a note is seen to make reference to Shape L. Shape AA was used with the Berlin Roses pattern, as shown in Plate 8.61. Shape L was probably used for Berlin Chaplet. Note however that the vegetable dish of this basic shape shown in Plate 8.63 is probably not of Minton manufacture.

Plate 8.63. *Berlin Chaplet pattern earthenware covered vegetable dish by an unknown maker, c.1830. The basic shape is a close copy of the Minton Shape L shown in Plate 8.62. Although the dish is of good quality, the glaze appears relatively soft with a definite pale blue tint, unknown on Minton Stone China wares. The details of the mouldings to the handle and rims differ slightly from those on the dish in Plate 8.61. The engravings are also less crisp and with different treatment of the flowers compared to Minton. The mark, shown right, is a close copy of the Minton version, but smaller. The pole on which the lion stands is only 22 mm long, compared to 30 mm on all the Minton examples. Dish plan widths 280 mm by 230 mm. Mark U6.*

round plan. The pattern is normally found with the printed mark shown in Plate 8.60 which, as in the example shown, sometimes includes the characteristic cursive M. Plate 8.63 shows a good quality Berlin Chaplet covered vegetable dish corresponding to Shape L, but which is probably not Minton: the detail of the moulding to the rims and handle do not match the Minton example in Plate 8.61, the body and glaze are also not typical of Minton Stone China, the glaze being much softer and with a bluish tint compared to the relatively hard and clear glaze

Plate 8.64. Minton Claremont pattern Stone China toilet box lid, c.1830. This typical floral design was used by Minton on both toilet wares and tea wares. The toilet box (see Plate 3.77) has two internal crosswise partitions or supports. The pattern is normally found with the printed mark shown above, including the cursive initial M. Copper plates for the design remain at the factory, and some later wares were produced in this design around 1900, such as the cup shown below. Width of mark 43 mm. Lid length 202 mm. Mark M20.

Plate 8.65. Minton Claremont pattern earthenware teacup, c.1908. Relatively late use of the pattern, first introduced in about 1830. Diameter 115 mm. Impressed cyphers and date mark for 1908.

found on Minton wares, and the decoration differs from the Minton plate in the treatment of the flowers. Also, a Berlin Chaplet covered dish of the same basic shape has been illustrated[15] with slightly different dimensions and with apparently different floral prints. It therefore seems likely that another factory copied the Berlin Chaplet pattern on the same basic shapes and using a very similar mark.

Claremont

A typical floral pattern used by Minton on toilet and tea wares, and probably introduced in around 1830. Detail of the design is shown in Plate 8.64 on the lid of a toilet box (see also Plate 3.77). The teacup shown in Plate 8.65 is a later product, indicating use of the design in the early 1900s. The earlier pieces normally bear the printed cartouche mark shown in Plate 8.64, including the cursive M. The copper plates for this pattern remain at the factory, and examples are included in the factory printed pattern book of 1886 (MS 2576). Claremont is also recorded as a pattern name for potters Beardmore and Edwards[16] and Baker & Son.[17]

Plate 8.66. British Views pattern 16-inch meat dish, c.1830, featuring The Rookery, Surrey. Despite bearing the printed mark shown above, including a characteristic cursive initial M and a lion passant, this dish is very unlikely to be a Minton product. The quality of the body and glaze, and the shape and size do not match other Minton 16-inch concave-octagonal dishes. The impressed size mark is also very different from that used by Minton. Furthermore it has triple stilt marks beneath the rim, unknown on Minton wares of this period. Apparently exactly the same engraving as used on this dish was used by the potters Griffiths, Beardmore & Birks on a large mug as part of their Light Blue Rose Border series. If these potters produced this meat dish, it is unclear why an imitation Minton mark was used instead of their usual series mark. No foot ring, three triple rear and single front stilt marks. Width of mark 56 mm. Width of dish 425 mm. Mark M21. Impressed size mark '16' (4 mm high).

British Views

A series of landscape views within a floral border, an example being shown on the meat dish in Plate 8.66. A further view has been illustrated on a nine-inch meat dish.[18] Both pieces bear the printed cartouche mark M21 shown in Plate 8.66 including the characteristic cursive initial M and a lion passant. At this time, the only link between Minton and this pattern is the cursive initial M in this mark and its strong similarity to the other Minton Stone China marks with a lion passant, M18 and M19, as shown in Plates 8.59 and 8.60 respectively. The dish illustrated in Plate 8.66, however, was very probably not produced by Minton. Its quality, shape, size and potting characteristics, including triple rear stilt marks, the body and glaze and the impressed size mark are all atypical and indicative of another manufacturer. It is possible that the pattern was originally produced by Minton, using the characteristic Minton mark, but that either the design and mark were copied by, or the engravings sold on to, another factory. The mark, being on the engravings, would also pass to the new owner. Alternatively, the pattern and mark could have been produced by a factory completely independently of Minton, although the inclusion of a copy of a Minton mark makes this unlikely.

This series is very similar to the Wedgwood Blue Rose Border series, including the same border design.[19] There are even stronger similarities with the Light Blue Rose Border series produced by Staffordshire potters of Griffiths, Beardmore & Birks.[20] Indeed these potters may have produced the dish in Plate 8.66, as what appears to be the same engraving was used by them on a large mug.[21] If this was the case, it remains unclear why they should use the imitation Minton mark, instead of the mark[20] normally used by them on their own series. Until the British Views pattern and mark is found on wares characteristic of Minton, it cannot be considered as a Minton pattern. Note that series titled British Views were also produced by Henshall & Co. and by another factory,[22] but both of these used different borders from that shown here.

Plate 8.67. Amhurst Japan pattern no. 62 Improved Stone China sauce tureen, c.1835. This popular design was used by Minton on a wide variety of wares for at least 70 years from the late 1820s. Normally found with the printed mark M22 shown above, with a painted number dependant on the colouration of the overpainted enamels. Mark width 36 mm. Tureen length 190 mm. Mark M22 including '62' and impressed mark M31.

Amhurst Japan

This is a Japan-type pattern, with a blue print painted over in coloured enamels. It is normally found with the printed mark shown in Plate 8.67, indicating introduction of the design on Stone China in the mid- to late 1820s. A number is painted into the mark to indicate the coloration used. The earliest and most common version was No. 62, which is seen in Plate 3.82 to have a predominance of iron red. This version was still in use in 1896 when the small jug shown in Plate 8.68 was made. Other colour combinations include pattern numbers 3768, 3769 and 9437. Plate 8.70 shows a version included in a Minton printed pattern book.

Minton used this pattern on a wide range of wares, including dinner, dessert, toilet and tea wares, jugs, and various other items such as the fine potpourri jar shown in Plate 8.69. The tureen shown in Plate 8.67 is interesting in that the basic factory Shape M (Plate 8.96) has been used with the knob design from the similar Shape D, as used with the Genevese pattern (Plate 8.31). Minton produced numerous such coloured-in printed designs from the late 1820s onwards, other examples being shown in Plates 8.71 and 8.72. Many of these are recorded in factory pattern books, and some have been published.[22] Very similar designs were of course produced by other factories at this time.

Plate 8.68. Amhurst Japan pattern no. 62 earthenware face jug, c.1896. Relatively late use of this popular design. This basic shape of jug was probably introduced in the 1820s and was made by numerous factories. Height 134 mm. Mark M22 with '62'. Impressed 'MINTONS' and year cypher for 1896.

Plate 8.69. Amhurst Japan pattern no. 62 Stone China potpourri jar, c.1830. A large jar with a flat inner lid fitted just below the domed perforated lid. Note the similarity of form to the jug Shape H from the factory shape book of c.1830 and shown below. Height 325 mm. Mark M22 with '62'.

Plate 8.70. Print of the Amhurst Japan pattern included in a Minton pattern book (MS 1946).

Plate 8.71. Minton Japan-type pattern No. 53 Opaque China mug, c.1826. Blue printed outline coloured with enamels (see also Plate 3.82). The low pattern number indicates that this is a relatively early Minton design. The shape matches the mug in Plate 8.8. Height 79 mm. Printed mark M6a as shown below, 43 mm wide.

Plate 8.72. Minton Japan-type pattern No. 89 gadroon-edged Improved Stone China dinner plate, c.1835. Printed outline coloured with enamels (see also Plate 3.82) The low pattern number indicates that this is a relatively early Minton design. The plate matches that used with Chinese Marine and other patterns. Three small single stilt marks on front of rim. Diameter 266 mm. Impressed mark M31. Painted pattern number, 'N.89'.

Pattern Nos. 53 and 89

Pattern number 53 was a floral printed design coloured over in enamels. It is illustrated on the mug shown in Plates 8.71 and 3.82. The mug is a characteristic Minton form, matching the Florentine pattern example in Plate 8.8. The same prints were used for pattern number 1860. The mark for pattern number 53 is seen to be very similar to the Dresden Opaque China mark. A clue to the dates at which these early numbered patterns were introduced, probably on Opaque China, is provided by the factory inventory of January 1826 which includes £83 worth of 'Ironstone No. 53'.

Pattern number 89 is another Japan-type pattern consisting of a printed outline coloured in with enamels. It is illustrated in Plates 8.72 and 3.82. Unlike Amhurst Japan, this design has no pattern name, simply the number 89. It is attributed to Minton as the example shown in Plate 8.72 is impressed with the characteristic Minton Improved Stone China seal mark. The plate matches the gadroon-edged shape used by Minton for the Chinese Marine and other patterns.

Trellis and Plants

An attractive floral design consisting of various botanical specimens within a trellis border. Examples are shown in Plates 3.85 and 8.73, which also shows the printed mark with cursive M normally found with the pattern. The mark does not include Opaque or Stone China. The pattern was used on dinner wares, with the salad bowl shown in Plate 8.73 possibly corresponding to Shape MM. The handles on the salad bowl match those found on the Minton tray decorated with the Basket pattern shown in Plate 5.26.

Plate 8.73. Minton Trellis and Plants pattern salad bowl, c.1835. This salad bowl possibly corresponds to factory Shape MM. The handles match those used on the Basket pattern tray shown in Plate 5.26. The pattern is normally found with the printed mark M23 shown above, including the cursive M. Width of mark 47 mm. Bowl height 120 mm, plan 290 mm by 250mm. Printed mark M23. Impressed size mark '11'.

Plate 8.74. Minton Arabesque pattern Improved Stone China dinner plate, c.1835. A fine floral design on a plate of excellent quality. The pattern is normally found with the printed cartouche mark M24 shown above. It was used by Minton on Shape C dinner wares. Width of mark 58 mm. Three small single stilt marks on front of rim. Diameter of plate 263 mm. Printed mark M24. Impressed mark M31.

Arabesque

An attractive pattern which uses a series of floral groups within an elaborate border of flowers and scrolls, examples being shown in Plates 8.74 and 8.75. It was used by Minton on dinner wares using factory Shape C, as detailed in Plate 8.76. The pattern is normally found with the printed cartouche mark shown in Plate 8.74. The mark does not contain reference to the type of body, nor the characteristic cursive M. Examples are typically found on wares with the Minton Improved Stone China impressed seal mark.

The design was probably introduced in the early 1830s. In common with the Trellis and Plants pattern salad bowl in Plate 8.73, the soup tureen in Plate 8.75 has no marks to indicate the type of earthenware body. It is unclear why Minton ceased to include the body type in the printed mark, unless these patterns were intended for use with the new Improved Stone China body. The plate shown above is interesting in that it has three single stilt marks on the face of the rim, with no stilt marks on the rear of the plate. The same arrangement is found on all of the plates impressed Improved Stone China. This contrasts strongly with all the earlier Minton plates and dishes, which invariably have the three single stilt marks on the back of the rim. Presumably in both cases the plates were stacked vertically with each plate supported by three thimble type stilts, for the Improved Stone China body face down but for all earlier bodies face up. The reason for this change is not obvious, but it may have been related to some difference in the behaviour of the Improved Stone China glaze or body during firing.

Plate 8.75. *Minton Arabesque pattern soup tureen, c.1830. This tureen corresponds to factory Shape C, as detailed in Plate 8.76. Length 350 mm. Mark M24 with printed workman's marks P22 to base and P16 to lid.*

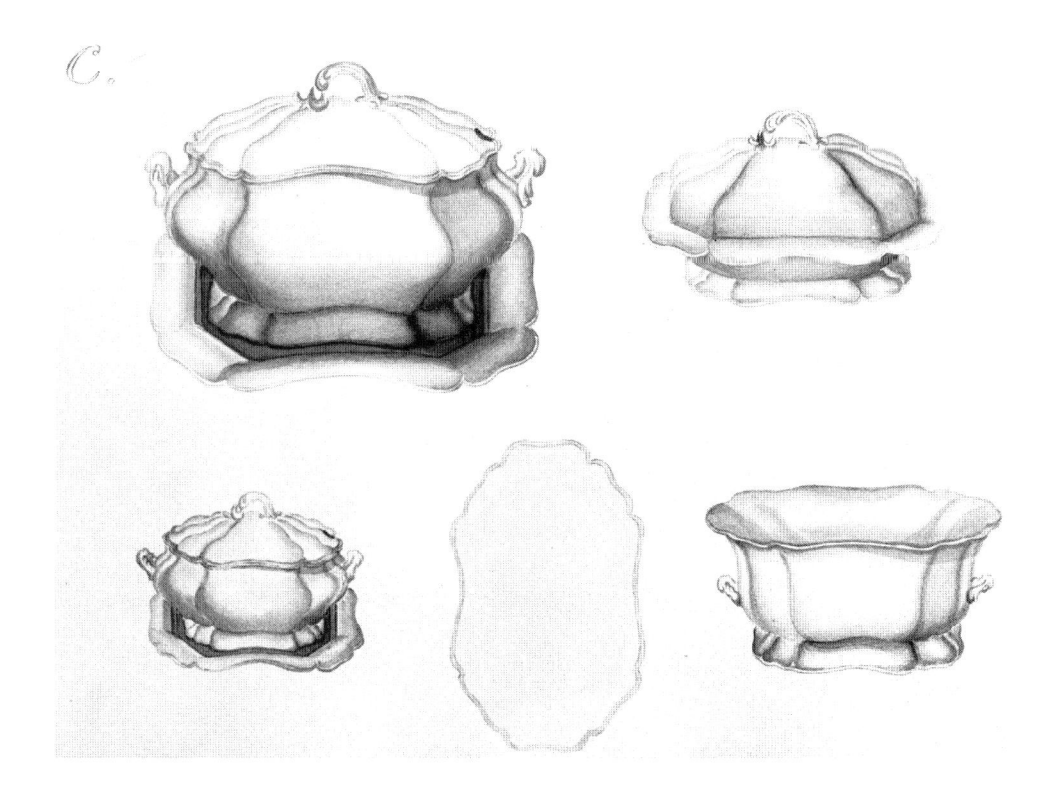

Plate 8.76. *Dinnerware design C from the factory shape book of c.1830. This design was used by Minton for several patterns, including Arabesque, Verona and Rose and Violet Wreath.*

231

Plate 8.77. Minton Chinese Fence pattern Improved Stone China concave-octagonal dinner plate, c.1835. The design is a direct copy of one found painted on Chinese export porcelain. Although the plate has the appearance of having been entirely hand painted in underglaze blue, the same outline print was used for Minton polychrome pattern No. 4435. Three small single stilt marks on front of rim. Diameter 251 mm. Impressed mark M31.

Chinese Fence

This typical chinoiserie design is illustrated in Plate 8.77. The dinner plate is attributed to Minton based on the characteristic impressed Improved Stone China seal mark, and was probably made around 1835. The pattern is a direct copy of a design found hand-painted on Chinese export porcelain.[23] Indeed the plate shown above gives the appearance of being entirely hand painted in underglaze blue, in direct imitation of the Chinese. It is likely, however, that the outline of the design was in fact printed, as this basic design is included in a Minton pattern book[24] as pattern 4435, an outline print painted in with coloured enamels.

Lace Border

A distinctive floral pattern with a lace border design. It was used by Minton on dinner wares, such as the examples shown in Plates 8.78 and 8.79. The pattern is normally found with the printed mark with characteristic cursive M shown in Plate 8.78. It was probably introduced in the early 1830s. No versions of this pattern are known by other makers, but Ralph Stevenson produced a 'Lace Border' series featuring views from England, India and America.

Plate 8.78. Minton Lace Border pattern Improved Stone China dinner plate, c.1835. This distinctive floral design was used by Minton on dinner wares. It is normally found with the printed mark M25, as shown above. Width of mark 53 mm. Three small single stilt marks on front of rim. Plate diameter 260 mm. Printed mark M25. Impressed mark M31.

Plate 8.79. Minton Lace Border pattern gravy boat, c.1835. Length 165 mm. Mark M25.

Plate 8.80. Minton Rose and Violet Wreath pattern vegetable dish base, c.1835. An attractive dinnerware pattern consisting of a series of eastern views within a floral border. This vegetable dish base corresponds to factory Shape C, as detailed in Plate 8.76. Minton also used the pattern on the round version of this design, Shape P (Plate 8.82). The pattern is normally found with printed cartouche mark M26, as shown above. A single copper plate engraving of this pattern, including the associated mark, remains at the factory. Length of mark 40 mm. Width of dish 302 mm. Mark M26.

Rose and Violet Wreath

This attractive pattern features a series of Eastern landscape views within a stylised border incorporating a wreath of roses and violets. Examples are shown in Plates 8.80 to 8.83. It was used by Minton on dinner wares with factory Shapes C and P, as detailed in Plates 8.76 and 8.82. The two designs are seen to differ mainly in the plan profile, Shape P being a round version of Shape C. The pattern was probably introduced in the early 1830s. Examples are normally found with the printed mark shown in Plate 8.80 and sometimes also with the characteristic impressed Improved Stone China mark. A copper plate engraving of this pattern and incorporating the printed mark M26 remains at the factory.

Plate 8.81. Minton Rose and Violet Wreath pattern soup tureen lid, c.1835. This lid shape exactly matches that on the Arabesque pattern Shape C tureen shown in Plate 8.75. Note the detail of the moulded handle. Length 270 mm.

Plate 8.82. Dinnerware design P from the Minton factory shape book of c.1830. This appears to be a round version of the factory Shape C, detailed in Plate 8.76. Minton used both shapes with the Rose and Violet Wreath pattern.

Rose and Violet Star

This pattern is shown in Plate 8.84 and is seen to use the same border as the Rose and Violet Wreath pattern, but with a simple floral print for the main central design. It was used by Minton on dinner wares and examples normally have the printed mark shown in Plate 8.84. The characteristic impressed Improved Stone China mark is also sometimes found. The pattern was probably introduced in the early 1830s and perhaps produced as a slightly plainer alternative to the Rose and Violet Wreath pattern.

Plate 8.83. Minton Rose and Violet Wreath pattern salad bowl, c.1835. The bowl has a round plan and corresponds to factory Shape P, as detailed above. The landscape scene printed inside the bowl is detailed below. Diameter 265 mm. Mark M26.

Plate 8.84. Minton Rose and Violet Star pattern Improved Stone China plate, c.1835. This dinnerware pattern is seen to use the same border as the Rose and Violet Wreath pattern, but with a simple floral central design. It is normally found with the printed cartouche mark M27, as detailed above. Width of mark 45 mm. Plate diameter 200 mm. Printed mark M27. Impressed mark M31.

Verona

A series of romantic landscape views, often featuring ruined buildings, contained within a stylised floral border. Minton used the pattern on a wide range of wares, examples being illustrated in Plates 8.85 to 8.90. There is various evidence for attribution of this pattern to Minton. Plate 8.86 shows an original pencil drawing from the factory archives which has clearly been the inspiration for the design on the dinner plate shown in Plate 8.85. Some of the original copper plate engravings also remain at the factory. These include the characteristic printed cartouche mark normally found with the series, as detailed in Plate 8.85. As with several other printed marks, Minton used it both with and without the cursive initial M. Also found on one of the copper plates was an indistinct four-line coppersmith's back-stamp 'Wm ?ONT?EE&SONS+WOOD, No 46 47 48 + 49, Shoe Lane London, B'. An engraving illustrating a large copper and brass works at this address in the 1820s is given by Drakard & Holdway.[25]

Other potters recorded[26] as producing Verona patterns include Cork & Edge, Lockhart & Arthur, David Methven & Sons and George Phillips. Typically these consist of one or more romantic scenic views, but are all basically different designs. All may have been inspired by the reputation of the northern Italian city of Verona, which was a favoured destination of young men on their grand Tour.

Plate 8.85. *Minton Verona pattern Improved Stone China plate, c.1835. A series of romantic European landscape views within a stylised lace and floral border. Used by Minton on a variety of wares. The pattern is normally found with the printed cartouche mark M28, as shown above, often but not always including the characteristic cursive initial M. The design used on this plate is seen to be based on the pencil drawing from the Minton archives shown below. Width of mark 42 mm. Three single stilt marks to front of rim. Plate diameter 262 mm. Printed marks M28 and P22. Impressed mark M31.*

Plate 8.86. *Pencil drawing found in the Minton archives (MS 1945). This seems to have been the inspiration for the very similar design used on the Verona pattern dinner plate shown above.*

237

Plate 8.87. *Minton Verona pattern low footed circular stand, c.1835. Fine white clear-glazed body, probably Improved Stone China. Diameter 280 mm and height 60 mm. Printed marks M28 with no cursive M, and P22.*

Plate 8.88. *Minton Verona pattern Improved Stone China 10-inch oval baking dish, c.1835. Width 272 mm. Printed marks M28 and P22. Impressed mark M31, size mark '10' and workman's mark '6'.*

Plate 8.89. Minton Verona pattern round teapot, c.1835. An unusually large teapot with a handle normally found on Roman shape jugs, such as that shown in Plate 7.12. Note that a different landscape scene is used on each side. The body matches that of the Improved Stone China dish in Plate 8.88. Plain 19-hole 'V'-shaped strainer. Length 313 mm. Height 160 mm. Mark M28 without cursive M.

Plate 8.90. Minton Verona pattern vegetable dish lid, c.1835. This corresponds to factory Shape C, as detailed in Plate 8.76. Indeed this lid fits the Rose and Violet Wreath pattern dish base shown in Plate 8.80. Probably an Improved Stone China body. Width 226 mm. Mark P22.

Plate 8.91. Minton Sicilian pattern Improved Stone China plate, c.1835. This series of romantic landscapes was used by Minton mainly on dinner wares. It is normally found with the printed cartouche mark M29 shown above. As with other patterns of this period, examples were also produced printed in brown. The same basic pattern and mark was also used by Pountney & Allies at Bristol, an example being shown in Plate 8.93. Width of mark 50 mm. Three small single stilt marks to front of rim. Plate diameter 264 mm. Printed marks M29 and P22. Impressed mark M31.

Sicilian

A series of stylised romantic landscapes within a floral border, similar in style to the Verona pattern, examples being shown in Plates 8.91 to 8.101. Introduced by Minton on tablewares, probably in the early 1830s, it is found on two different

Plate 8.92. Minton Sicilian pattern basket, c.1835. Detail of the print inside the basket shown in Plate 8.94.

Plate 8.93. Bristol Pottery Sicilian pattern plate, c.1833. The border and style of the central scene are very similar to the Minton pattern shown in Plate 8.91. The printed cartouche mark is almost identical to the Minton mark, though with a slightly less elaborate 'S'. The clear-glazed earthenware body is creamier than Minton's white Improved Stone China. This example has an impressed mark for Pountney & Allies, indicating production before 1835. Later examples are marked for Pountney & Goldney. Three single stilt marks beneath the rim. Double recessed foot ring. Mark 52 mm wide. Plate diameter 265 mm. Printed mark U7. Impressed 'POUNTNEY & ALLIES' in horseshoe shape around a cross (GM3124).

Plate 8.94. Minton Sicilian pattern basket, c.1835. A fine quality piece, probably Improved Stone China. Details of the inner print are shown in Plate 8.92. Length 268 mm. Marks M29 and P22.

factory dinnerware Shapes M and W. It is normally found with the printed cartouche mark without a cursive M, as shown in Plate 8.91. Wares are often also marked with the Minton impressed Improved Stone China seal mark. The same basic design and printed mark is found on wares impressed with marks for both Pountney & Allies and Pountney & Goldney of the Bristol pottery, an example being shown in Plate 8.93. This change of ownership at Bristol occurred in March 1835, confirming introduction of the design in the early 1830s.

Plate 8.95. Minton Sicilian pattern Improved Stone China sauce tureen, c.1835, corresponding to factory Shape M as detailed left. Minton also used this pattern on the more elaborate Shape W, shown in Plate 8.99. Length 191 mm. Marks M29 and P22. Impressed mark M31.

Plate 8.96. Minton dinnerware design M from the factory shape book of c.1830, as used with the Sicilian pattern.

Plate 8.97 (opposite). Minton Sicilian pattern Improved Stone China covered vegetable dish, c.1835. Factory Shape M. Width 315 mm. Marks M29 and P15. Impressed mark M31.

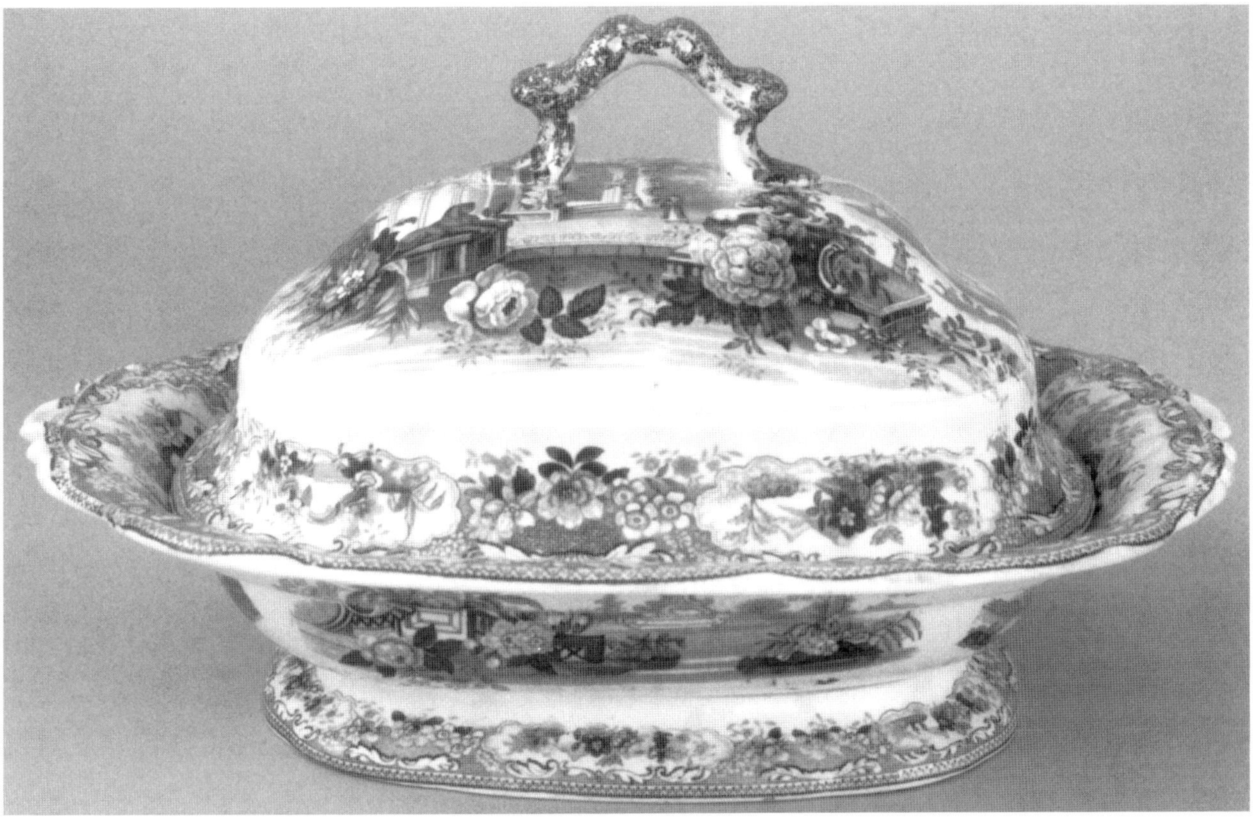

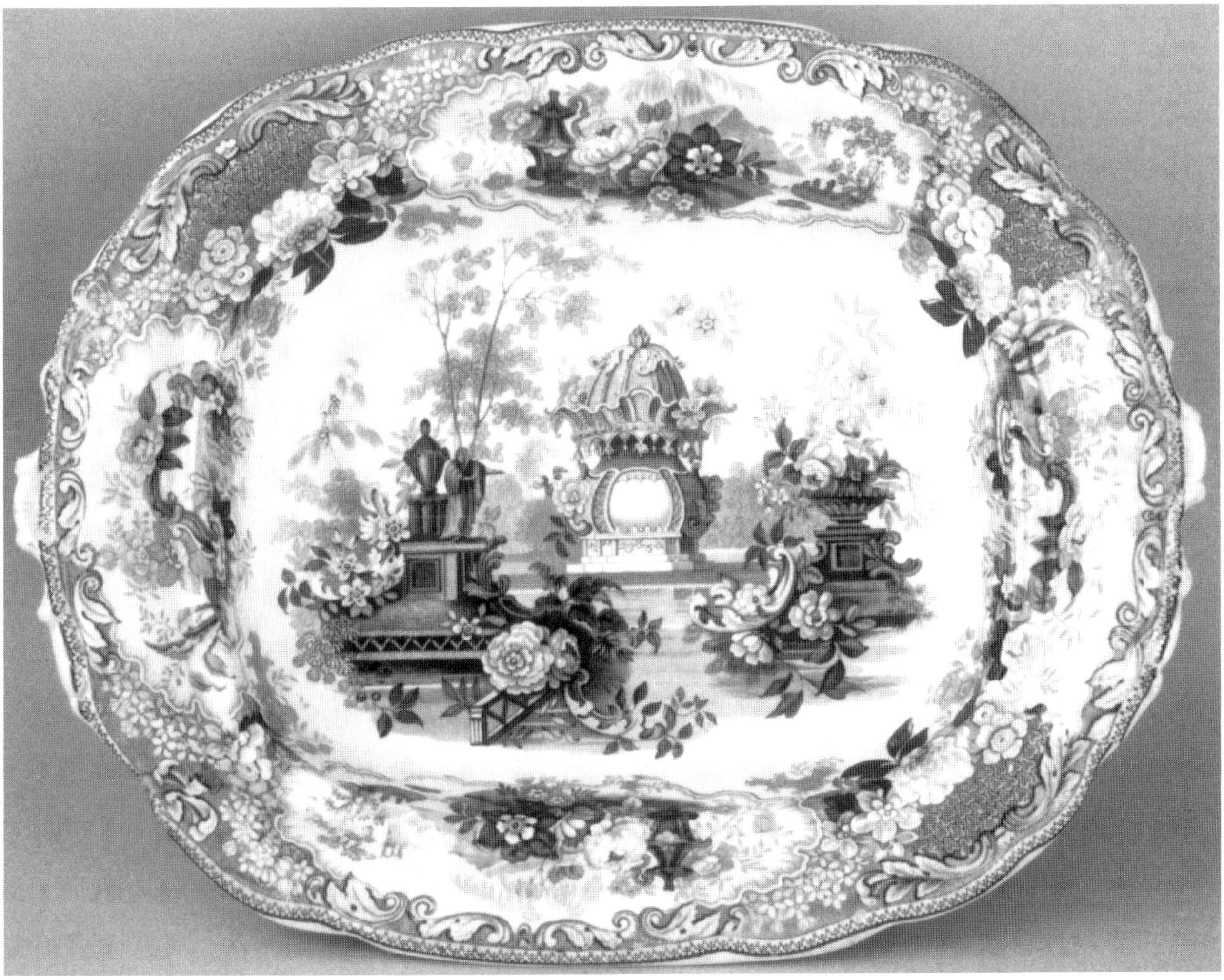

Plate 8.98. Minton Sicilian pattern soup tureen. c.1835. Factory Shape W, as detailed below. Probably Improved Stone China. A large and impressive piece with elaborate moulded handles to the base. Length 405 mm. Printed marks M29 and P22.

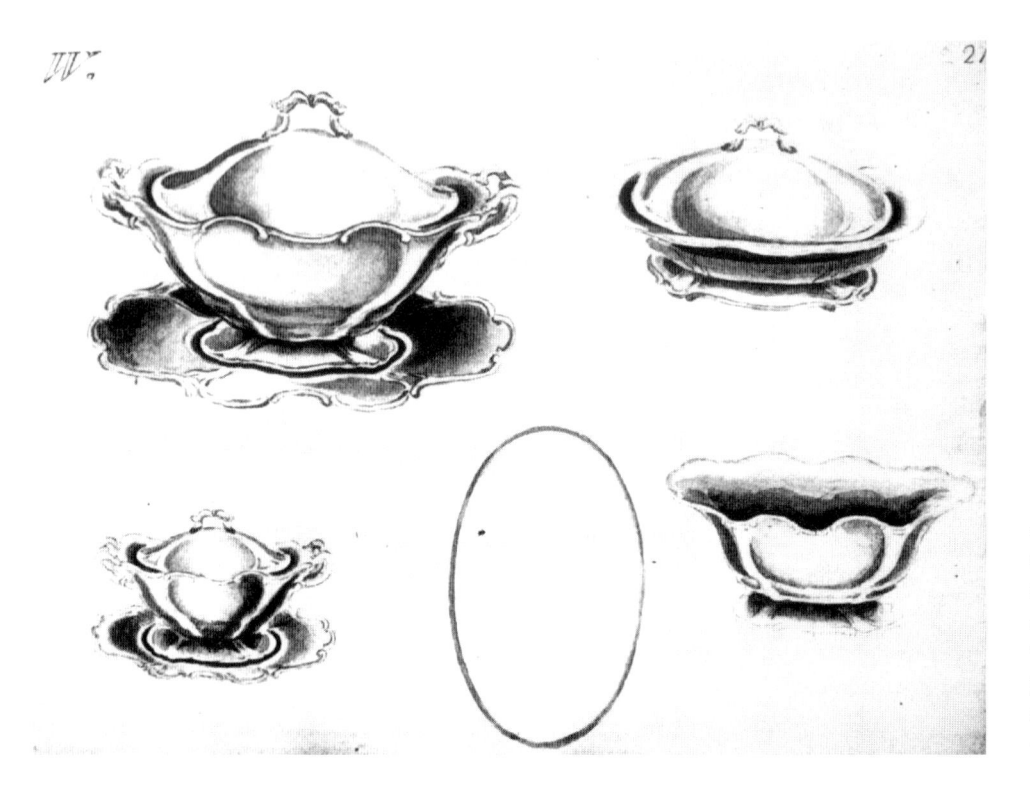

Plate 8.99. Minton dinnerware design W from the factory shape book of c.1830. One of the shapes used with the Sicilian pattern, examples being shown in Plates 8.98 and 8.100.

Plate 8.100. *Minton Sicilian pattern Improved Stone China covered vegetable dish, c.1835. Factory Shape W, as detailed in Plate 8.99. Note that the prints are different from those used by Minton for the other vegetable dish shape used with the Sicilian pattern, as shown in Plate 8.97. Width 310 mm. Printed marks M29, P22 lid and P15 base. Impressed mark M31.*

Plate 8.101. Minton Sicilian pattern handled tray, c.1835. Probably Improved Stone China. Width 352 mm. Printed marks M29 and P4.

Floweret

A distinctive floral design probably introduced c.1830 on Shape C dinner wares, such as the tureen in Plate 8.103. Details of the design are shown in Plate 8.102, together with the usual printed mark. Some copper plates remain at the factory.

Pattern 252

A chinoiserie-type dragon design probably introduced in the late 1820s and normally found on bone china tea wares. As shown in Plate 8.104, it is usually found with a distinctive printed seal mark. Copper plates remain at the factory.

Plate 8.102. Detail of Minton Floweret pattern print used inside the soup tureen shown in Plate 8.103. The design was probably introduced c.1830 on Stone China or Improved Stone China. Some copper plate engravings remain at the factory, including the printed mark M30 shown below which is normally found with this pattern. Width of print 240 mm. Width of mark 47 mm.

Plate 8.103. *Minton Floweret pattern tureen base, c.1835. Probably Improved Stone China. This corresponds to factory Shape C, as shown in Plate 8.76. It is illustrated with a Rose and Violet Wreath pattern replacement lid (see Plate 8.81). Length 350 mm. Mark M30.*

Plate 8.104. *Minton pattern number 252 bone china bread and butter plate, c.1840. Some copper plates remain at the factory, including the characteristic seal mark normally found with this pattern. Note that details of the mark symbols can vary. Given the low pattern number the design was probably introduced c.1826. It is normally found on bone china tea wares. Width 248 mm. Printed '252' seal mark, width 12 mm.*

References

1. Minton MS 2576, 1886 Printed Pattern Book (Minton Archives).
2. G.A. Godden, *Mason's China and the Ironstone Wares* (Antique Collectors Club, 1980), p. 226.
3. J.B. Snyder, *Romantic Staffordshire Ceramics* (Schiffer, 1997), p. 47.
4. A.W. Coysh and R.K. Henrywood, *The Dictionary of Blue and White Printed Pottery Volume 2* (Antique Collectors Club, 1989), p. 89.
5. A.W. Coysh and R.K. Henrywood, *The Dictionary of Blue and White Printed Pottery* (Antique Collectors Club, 1982), p. 151.
6. D. Drakard and P. Holdway, *Spode Printed Ware* (Longman, 1983), p. 124.
7. Coysh and Henrywood, *Dictionary of Blue and White Vol. 2*, p. 55.
8. A.W. Fields, *Friends of Blue Bulletin*, No. 5, 1974, p. 4.
9. H. Lawrence, *Yorkshire Pots and Potteries* (David & Charles, 1974), p. 223.
10. A.W. Fields, *Friends of Blue Bulletin*, No. 4, 1974, p. 3.
11. Coysh and Henrywood, *Dictionary of Blue and White Vol. 2*, p. 164.
12. *Friends of Blue Bulletin*, No. 9, 1975, p. 4.
13. *Friends of Blue Bulletin*, No. 21, 1978, p. 9.
14. R. Hampson, *Northern Ceramic Society Newsletter*, No. 65, 1987, p. 32.
15. I. MacDonald, *Friends of Blue Bulletin*, No. 89, 1995, p. 9.
16. Coysh and Henrywood, *Dictionary of Blue and White*, p. 86.
17. Snyder, *Romantic Staffordshire Ceramics*, p.38.
18. Coysh and Henrywood, *Dictionary of Blue and White Vol. 2*, p. 38.
19. Coysh and Henrywood, *Dictionary of Blue and White*, p. 46.
20. Coysh and Henrywood, *Dictionary of Blue and White Vol. 2*, p. 125.
21. *Friends of Blue Bulletin*, No. 65, 1989, p. 4.
22. Coysh and Henrywood, *Dictionary of Blue and White*, p. 60.
22. H. Davis, *Chinoiserie Polychrome Decoration on Staffordshire Porcelain 1790–1850* (Rubicon Press, 1991), pp. 88–119.
23. R. Copeland, *Spode's Willow Pattern and other Designs after the Chinese*, 3rd ed. (Studio Vista, 1999), p. 137.
24. Davis,*Chinoiserie Polychrome Decoration*, p. 111.
25. Drakard and Holdway, *Spode Printed Ware*, p. 26.
26. Coysh and Henrywood, *Dictionary of Blue and White*, p. 377.

Colour Plate 1. *Portrait of Thomas Minton (Courtesy of Royal Doulton).*

Colour Plate 2. *The early Minton patterns and shapes were based on Chinese export painted porcelain such as these plates (Plates 4.1 and 4.85).*

Colour Plate 3. Chinese Sports pattern 20-inch meat dish (Plate 4.76).

Colour Plate 4. Monk's Rock series 14-inch meat dish, based on an engraving of a riverside tavern (Plate 6.39).

Colour Plate 5. *English Scenery series 20-inch gravy dish, featuring a view of Windsor Castle (Plate 7.25).*

Colour Plate 6. *Filigree pattern 20-inch meat dish (Plate 7.68).*

Colour Plate 7. Willow pattern soup tureen (Plate 9.24).

Colour Plate 8. English Scenery series soup tureen featuring a view of Fonthill Abbey (Plate 7.35).

Colour Plate 9. Basket pattern soup tureen (Plate 5.20).

Colour Plate 10. Filigree pattern soup tureen (Plate 7.77).

Colour Plates 11 to 15. Collection of dessert dishes. Monk's Rock series (Plates 9.71, 6.44 and 6.45); Basket pattern (Plate 5.28); Italian Ruins pattern (Plate 9.82).

Colour Plates 16 to 19. *Collection of sauce tureens. Italian Ruins pattern (Plate 7.15); Filigree pattern (length of stand 208 mm); Monk's Rock series (Plate 6.47) and Dove pattern (Plate 6.59).*

255

Colour Plate 20.
Hermit and Boat pattern mug (Plate 9.94) and Fig Tree Chinoiserie pattern jug (Plate 4.19).

Colour Plate 21.
Maypole pattern jug (Plate 6.54) and spill vase (Plate 6.57). Botanical pattern mask jug (height 160 mm, mark M1).

Colour Plate 22.
Chinese Sports pattern sauce tureen and coffee can (Plates 9.28 and 9.125).

256

Chapter Nine

Catalogue of Printed Wares

Archive material containing information about the range of early Minton products was reviewed in Chapter Two. This included sales accounts dating from 1798, factory inventories for the periods 1810 to 1813 and 1817 to 1826, and factory shape books of c.1830 and 1884. The sales accounts confirm that extensive dinner services were being produced at least by 1798, and also mention several early teaware shapes.

The range of early wares produced by the Minton factory is indicated by the surviving early price list[1] reproduced overleaf. Although undated, the list refers to Thomas Minton's Factory and includes no reference to China Wares, so may just predate the partnership formed in 1817 with Thomas's sons. The prices for the printed wares are seen to be significantly higher than for the other wares, which would have either been left plain or given simple painted decoration. Note that prices for certain wares, such as Plates, Bowls, Teapots and non-printed dishes, are given 'per dozen', whilst for others, such as tureens and printed dishes, they are given for single items. The Willow printed tablewares are listed separately, being sold at a lower price than wares with other printed patterns. The price list includes only the typical basic range of items, common to most large earthenware manufactories of the period. The sizing methods used were also standardised. These are discussed in detail by Drakard and Holdway[2] and Edwards and Hampson,[3] so only an outline of the basic system is given here. Items such as plates, dishes and tureens, were distinguished by a characteristic dimension, either diameter or length. Certain items such as gravy boats had size numbers, with increasing number corresponding to decreasing size. Cup sizes were given names, such as London or Norfolk. Most hollow ware items, such as teapots and jugs, were distinguished by 'number per dozen'. The reference size was 12, appropriately giving the standard 12 to the dozen. This size historically contained one pint of fluid, although factories tended to exceed standard volume, sometimes significantly, to give them a market edge. Volume was inversely proportional to size, so 24's in theory held only half a pint, and were priced at 24 to the dozen. The price for a 'dozen' sometimes varied slightly with size, to account for the extra cost of producing the larger number of smaller items. The prices given for mugs and jugs illustrate this. The largest printed mugs listed, 6's, cost one shilling each and 12's cost sixpence, whereas the smallest half pint size, 24's, cost threepence three farthings.

Although the price list provides a useful summary of the standard wares being produced at that time, it gives no real evidence to help distinguish the Minton products from those of competitors such as Spode, Ridgeway and Davenport, whose price lists would have been very much the same. The lists of wares included in the factory inventories are also largely unhelpful with regard to attribution, with similar generic descriptions being used. The inventories do, however, include some further detail of both the design and the range of wares in production, as indicated in Table 9.1 which lists various types of blue printed wares included in the inventories. It is clear from this extensive and varied list that the

PRICE CURRENT,
AT
THOMAS MINTON'S MANUFACTORY,
STOKE-UPON-TRENT.

		Cream Coloured	Best concave Cr. Coloured	Edged.	Under Glaze Lined.	PRINTED. Willow pattern.	PRINTED. Other patterns.			Cream Coloured	Edged.	Under Glaze Lined.	PRINTED. Willow pattern.	PRINTED. Other patterns.
		s. d.	s. d.	s. d.	s. d.	s. d.	s. d.			s. d.	s. d.	s. d.	s. d.	s. d.
Table Plates	in. 10	1 9	2 0	2 0	2 6	4 0	5 0	Compotiers	in. 8	0 3	0 4			1 3
Supper ditto	- 9	1 9	1 9	2 0	2 6	4 0	5 0	Ditto	- 9	0 4	0 6			1 6
Twifler ditto	- 8	1 4	1 6	1 6	2 0	3 6	4 0	Ditto	- 10	0 6	0 8			1 9
Muffin ditto	- 7	1 2	1 4	1 4	1 8	3 0	3 6	Ditto	- 11	0 8	0 10			2 0
Ditto	- 6	1 0	1 2	1 2	1 6	2 6	3 0	Ditto	- 12	0 10	1 0			2 6
Ditto	- 5	0 10	1 1	1 0	1 4	2 0	2 6	Centre pieces, for desserts		2 0	2 6			3 6
Ditto	- 4	0 8		0 10	1 2	1 9	2 0	Cheese Stands, round high feet	10	1 0	1 6		2 6	3 0
Flat Oval Dishes	- 9	2 0	2 6	2 6	3 0	0 6	0 9	Ditto	- 11	1 3	1 9		3 0	3 6
Ditto	- 10	2 6	3 0	3 0	4 0	0 9	1 0	Ditto	- 12	1 6	2 0		3 6	4 0
Ditto	- 11	3 0	4 0	4 0	5 6	1 0	1 3	Egg Cups		1 3	1 6	1 9	3 0	
Ditto	- 12	4 0	5 0	5 6	7 0	1 3	1 9	Pudding Bowls		2 9				
Ditto	- 13	5 0	6 0	7 0	9 0			Pickle sets, flat					3 0	3 6
Ditto	- 14	6 0	8 0	9 0	12 0	1 9	2 6	Ditto, high foot					3 6	4 0
Ditto	- 15	8 0	10 0	11 0	15 0			Egg Stands, 6 Cups		1 4				3 0
Ditto	- 16	10 0	12 0	14 0	18 0	2 9	3 6	Ditto, 5 ditto		1 2				2 9
Ditto	- 17	12 0	15 0	17 0	21 0			Ditto, 4 ditto		1 0				2 6
Ditto	- 18	15 0	18 0	20 0	24 0	4 0	4 6	Ditto, 3 ditto		0 10				2 3
Ditto	- 19	18 0	24 0	24 0	27 0					Cream Coloured	Painted.	Printed plain and topt		
Ditto	- 20	24 0	30 0	28 0	30 0	5 0	5 6							
Oval Baking Dishes	7	1 6	2 0	2 6	3 0			Bowls, all sizes		2 6	4 0	7 0		
Ditto	- 8	2 0	2 6	3 0	4 0			Chamberpots down to 6's		2 6	4 0	7 0		
Ditto	- 9	2 6	3 0	4 0	5 0	1 0	1 3	Hand Basins		2 6	4 0	8 6		
Ditto	- 10	3 6	4 0	5 0	6 0	1 3	1 6	Ewers		3 0				
Ditto	- 11	4 6	5 6	7 0	8 0	1 6	2 0	Mugs, 6s. & 12s.		1 9	4 0	6 0		
Ditto	- 12	6 0	7 0	9 0	10 0	1 9	2 6	Ditto, 24s.		1 9	4 0	7 6		
Ditto	- 13	8 0	9 0	11 0	12 0			Jugs, 3s. 4s. & 6s.		2 0	4 0	6 0		
Ditto	- 14	10 0	12 0	13 0	15 0			Ditto, 12s.		2 0	4 0	7 6		
Round Bakers, Nappies and Turtles, one size higher in price.								Ditto, 24s.		3 0		9 0		
								Dutch Jugs, to 12s.		3 0				
Soup Tureens,	- 9	1 6	2 0	2 0	2 6	4 6	5 0	Ditto, 24s.		4 0				
Ditto	- 10	2 0	2 6	2 6	3 0	5 0	6 0	Toast Mugs, Porringers and Chambers less than 6s.		3 6				
Ditto	- 11	2 6	3 0	3 0	4 0	6 0	7 0							
Ditto	- 12	3 6	4 0	4 0	5 0	7 0	8 0	London Teas, not handled		1 6	2 3	4 6		
Ditto Stands	- 9	0 3				1 6	1 9	Norfolk ditto, ditto			2 3	4 0		
Ditto	- 10	0 4		0 6		1 9	2 0	Irish ditto ditto		2 0	2 9	5 6		
Ditto	- 11	0 5		0 7		2 0	2 6	Bowls and Saucers, ditto		3 0	4 6	7 6		
Ditto	- 12	0 6		0 8		2 6	3 0	Handled Teas, 1s. per doz. extra						
Ditto Ladles		0 10	1 0	1 0		1 3	1 6							
Sauce Tureens, complete, 1st size		1 2	1 6	1 9				Fluted ditto, 1s. per doz. extra						
2nd ditto		1 0	1 3	1 6		2 6	3 0	Round Teapots and Sugars, to 24s.		6 0	8 0	12 0		
3d ditto		0 10		1 3				Ditto, 30s.		7 0	9 0	14 0		
Sauce Boats,	No. 1	4 0	4 0	4 0	5 0	6 0	7 0	Oval Teapots and Sugars		16 0	24 0			
Ditto	2	2 6	3 6	3 6	4 6	5 6	6 0	Chair-pans	- 5 6 7 8 9 10 11 12 in.					
Ditto	3	2 0	3 0	3 0	4 0	5 0	5 6		5d. 6d. 8d. 10d. 1s. 1s. 2d. 1s. 4d 1s. 6d. each.					
Ditto	4	1 9	2 6	2 6	3 0	4 6	5 0	Feet-pans	in. 17	9 0		15 0		
Ditto	5	1 6		2 0	2 6	4 0	4 6	Ditto	15	7 6		12 6		
Ditto	6	1 4		1 9	3 6	4 0		Ditto	13	6 0		10 6		
Covered Dishes -	- 10	1 0	1 3	1 6	1 9	2 6	3 0	Potting Pots, round		2 3		6 6		
Ditto	- 11	1 3	1 6	1 9	2 0	3 0	3 6	Ditto, oval		3 0	5 0	8 0		
Ditto	- 12	1 6	2 0	2 0	2 6	3 6	4 0	Patty-pans, round		2 6		6 6		
Salads	- 10	0 8	1 2	1 0		2 6	3 0	Ditto, oval		4 0		9 0		
Ditto	- 11	0 10	1 6	1 3		3 0	3 6							
Ditto	- 12	1 0	1 9	1 6		3 6	4 0							
Round Butters		6 0		9 0		12 0								
Ditto and Stands	24s.					0 9								
Ditto	30s.					0 7								
Root Dishes	in. 10	2 0	2 6	3 0		4 0	5 0							
Ditto	- 11	2 6	3 0	3 6		5 0	6 0							
Ditto	- 12	3 0	4 0	4 0		6 0	7 0							
Sixpence more for each partition														
Gravy Dishes	- 16	2 6	3 6	3 6	4 0	5 6	6 0							
Ditto	- 18	3 6	4 0	4 6	5 6	6 6	7 6							
Ditto	- 20	4 6	5 0	6 0	7 0	7 6	9 0							
Pans the same as Gravy Dishes														
Water Plates		1 0												

TOMKINSON, PRINTER, STOKE.

Table 9.1. Minton Wares listed in Early Inventories

Dinner wares

Dinner plate, Soup plate, Twifler plate
Muffin plate   7, 6, 5, 4 inch
Meat dish   21, 20, 18, 16, 14, 12, 11, 10, 9 inch
Gravy dish   20, 18, 16 inch
Gravy dish, cover and pan   14 inch
Gravy tureen
Soup dish and cover   18 inch
Baker   13, 12, 11, 10, 9, 8, 7, inch
Drainer   20, 18, 16, 14 inch
Covered dish   12, 11, 10 inch
Water pans   18, 16, 14 inch
Water plate
Square salad   12, 11, 10, 9 inch
Oval salad   12, 11, 10 inch
Soup tureen and stand   13, 12, 11 inch
Soup tureen ladle, Sauce tureen ladle
Sauce tureen and stand
Small sauce tureen and stand
Root dish   12, 11, 10 inch
Root dish and drainer   10 inch
Root dish divided   12, 11, 10 inch
Root dish double divided   12 inch
Broth bowl and stand   24's, 30's, 36's
Asparagus tray
Gravy boats   2nd, 3rd, 4th, 5th, 6th, 7th size
Gravy boat stands
Turtle dish   13, 11, 10 inch
Round supper set covered   small, large
Oval supper set covered   small, large
Pepper, Round salt
Mustard, Flat mustard
Round pattie, Oval pattie
Pap boat
Knife rest
Single covered muffin
Double covered muffin
Cheese stand   12, 11, 10, 9 inch
Square cheese stand
Single cheese toaster, Double cheese toaster
Pickle stand on foot
Pickle stand flat, Pickle set flat
Diamond pickle
Oval pickle
Oval pickle divided
Pickle leaf   1st, 2nd, 3rd size
Radish tray, Radish tray with butter tubs
Scalloped shell   1st, 2nd, 3rd, 4th size
Covered custard, Upright custard
Bell custard   36's
Custard cup handled
Egg cup
Egg stand   3, 4, 5, 6 cup
Egg drainer

Dessert wares

Dessert centre
Basket and stand   10, 9, 8, 7 inch
Wicker plate
Cream bowl
Comports (Comportiers)   11, 10, 9, 8 inch

Toilet wares & jugs

Ewer and bowl
Mug, Mug covered
Jug, Jug covered
Chamber pot
Shaving box
Toothbrush tray large
Toothbrush box small, large
Square soap box small, large
Round soap box not covered
Round soap box covered
Toilet box   1st, 2nd, 3rd size

Tea wares

Round teapot
Oval teapot   12's, 18's, 24's
Coffee pot vase shape
Round sugar box   24's
Oval sugar box, Oval sugar box fluted
Oval cream (milk)   24's, 30's, 36's
Ewer cream (milk)   36's
Round cream (milk)
Round flat milk
Plain bowl and saucer
Handled bowl and saucer
Plain breakfast, Handled breakfast
Plain tea
Handled tea   London, Norfolk, Irish size
Plain Tea   London, Norfolk, Irish size
Cans   36's
Bowl   24's, 30's
Bowl fluted   24's, 30's
Chocolate
Toast rack
Bread and butter plate   small, large
Butter tub and stand
Oval butter tub and stand, covered
Water pot
Toy teapot, sugar box, cream, cup & saucer, slop bowl

Miscellaneous

Round potting pots
Centre for Plynth not covered
Green banded flower pots and stands
Punch bowls and dip bowls
Snuffer trays
Extinguishers

Table 9.2. Block Moulds Included in the 1817 Factory Inventory

Plates

1 Set of plates Thumb patt^n grafs edge 6 moulds
1 Set of plates Thumb patt^n plain 7 moulds
1 Set of plates grafs edge 10 moulds
1 Set of plates Bath 6 moulds
1 Set of plates Royal 8 moulds
1 Set of plates Paris 12 moulds turned
1 Set of plates Octagon 11 moulds
1 Set of plates Concave 9 moulds turned
1 Set of plates Concave Octagon 6 moulds
1 Set of plates Trophy 11 moulds turned
2 Wicker plates 8 & 7 In

Meat Dishes, Bakers, Gravy dishes etc.

7 Sizes of Octagon cov^d dishes 9 10 11 12 14 16 18
5 Sizes of Trophy cov^d dishes 11 12 14 16 18
12 Paris dishes in sizes
13 Grafs edge dishes in sizes
13 Concave dishes in sizes
5 Paris round dishes flat
4 Paris round dishes soup
5 Royal round dishes flat
4 Royal round dishes soup
5 Grafs edge round dishes flat
3 Round dishes Trophy shape
3 Round dishes Octagon shape
13 Octagon dishes flat shape
10 Trophy dishes
12 Royal dishes
3 Closet pans used 6 years as working moulds
11 Round bakers
8 Concave oval bakers
8 Oval Trophy bakers, 8 Turtle dishes
8 Grafs edge bakers
4 Trophy gravy dishes, 5 Concave gravy dishes
4 Octagon gravy dishes
3 Grafs edge gravy dishes
3 Gravy dish pans Octagon
3 Gravy dish pans Trophy
6 Covers to gravy dishes
31 Plain drainers different shapes
6 Grafs edge drainers

Tureens, Vegetable dishes etc.

4 Octagonal Soup Tureens, St^{ds}, Knobs & Ears, 10,11,12,13
3 Octagonal Sauce Tureens & St^{ds}, 1 Ear and Knob.
3 Octagonal Root dishes
4 Sizes of Cov^d. dishes square to fit in a Niche, 9,10,11,12
3 Sizes of Cov^d. dishes square hollow brims
1 Fiddlestick Knob
1 Lions head Knob
4 Broadend Tureens 9 10 11 12
3 Covers to Broadend Tureens Octagon
3 Lions head Knobs & 3 Ears
4 Sizes of stands to above Soup Tureens
4 Sizes of stands to Octagon Soup Tureens
1 Sauce tureen & stand round end
1 Cover to Sauce tureen Octagon round end
1 Lions head Knob & Ear
5 Soup tureens & stands Elevated high feet
    8 9 10 11 12
    Long handles and Knobs to above
5 Soup tureens round high feet
    Ears & Knobs to above
4 Soup tureens high footed for concave
2 Stands to above
1 10 In Square Cov^d dish
1 Knob for above
1 Sauce tureen
1 Sauce tureen stand
3 Sizes of square Cov^d dishes strong wetted
    Rose Knobs for each.
1 Soup tureen & stand
1 Rose Knob & Ear to above
1 Sauce tureen & stand
1 Rose Knob & Ear to above
4 Trophy shape Tureens 9 10 11 12
4 Stands to above
3 Trophy shape sauce tureens
3 Stands to above
3 Root dishes
3 Ears to above
8 Sizes of Lions head Knobs
4 Soup tureens grafs edge
3 Sauce tureens & stands grafs edge
3 Long square Cov^d dishes
2 Square Cov^d dishes hollow brims
2 Root dishes
5 Broad end Soup Tureens 8 9 10 11 12
    Ears & Knobs to each size
3 Sauce tureens & stands
3 Long square Cov^d dishes 9 10 11 12
1 Octagon Beef Steak dish Cover & Water pan
1 Soup ladle
1 Sauce ladle

Gravy Boats

6 Oval boats Trophy shape
7 Octagon boats
6 Concave boats
1 Octagon boat grafs edge
6 Sizes of boats grafs edge

Salads

4 Sizes of Square Salads grafs edge 9 10 11 12
4 Sizes of Oval fluted Salads grafs edge
4 Sizes of Oval fluted Salads plain
4 Square Salads
4 Round Salads fluted
3 Round Salads plain
5 Canoe Salads

Supper Sets

1 Plain handle for Supper set Centre
1 Square Supper set which consists of 2 dishes & covers & 1 centre
1 Oval large Supper set which consists of 2 dishes & covers & 1 centre
1 Oval small Supper set which consists of 2 dishes & covers & 1 centre
1 Large round Supper set which consists of 1 dish & cover & 1 centre
1 Small round Supper set which consists of 1 dish & cover & no centre
2 Long Square Cov^d dishes for Supper sets
2 Pickles to above

Pickles & Miscellaneous Tablewares

2 Canoe pickles
1 Diamond small pickle
1 Pickle stand
3 Sizes of pickle leaves
1 Radish tray
1 Artichoke Cup
1 Asparagus tray
9 Sizes of Oval Patties
3 Stands to broth bowls turned
1 Cream cheese stand
1 Cheese Toaster Cover & Water pan
1 Bottom to Water plate
1 Shallow Oyster tub
1 Knife rest
1 Toy table set

Dessert wares

1 Defsert plain Centre
7 Sizes of Melon Pudding cups
4 Sizes of Scollop'd shells
19 Blamonges different patterns
4 Sizes of Oval fruit baskets & stands & bows
5 Sizes of Square comports
5 Sizes of Melon comports
4 Sizes of Royal comports
1 Shell comport
1 Cream bowl & stand
6 Sizes of Trifle dishes round Scallop'd

Jugs, Toilet wares etc.

1 Ice pail handle & bow
3 Sizes of foot pan Ears
1 Wash pot handle
1 6^s Grafs edge Ewer & basin
1 4^s Grafs edge chamber
1 Foot bath
6 Hand basins 2 3 4 6 9 12 turned
3 Coach pots
1 Set Jugs & Mugs single handles 13 Moulds
1 Set Mug handles 5 Moulds
1 Ewer cream handle

18 Snips to Jugs etc
2 Oval hand basins
2 Ewers to above
2 Brush boxes & covers
1 Brush tray no cover
1 Eye cup
1 Square Sope box
1 Small Sope box
1 Bed pan & handle
3 Shaving basins
3 Foot pans used 6 months as working moulds

Teawares

3 Teapots oval fluted 12 18 24
1 Sugar box to above
1 Cream to above
    Spouts & handles to above
3 Teapots Square shape 12 18 24
1 Sugar box to above
1 Cream to above
    Spouts & handles to above
1 Oval Teapot 12
1 Sugar box
2 Creams
    Spouts & handles to above
1 9^s Oval Teapot complete
7 Oval milks & 1 round milk
4 Bute Saucers & shells
4 Sizes of common Saucers & shells
1 Set of Common Cup handles 4 moulds
1 Set of Square Rounded Cup handles 4 moulds
1 Toy Saucer
2 B&B plates turned
3 Sizes of Oval butter tubs & stands
2 Stands to butter tubs turned
1 Toast Rack
2 Cover'd Muffins
3 Teapots 1 Sugar box & Cream for egyptian black complete

Miscellaneous

1 Label
1 Dog trough
1 Card Candlestick
24 Bows Knobs etc
12 Molds of figures
4 Heads to sides of Ornaments

products included many unusual and interesting items beyond the standard and more familiar table, tea and toilet wares.

Perhaps the most useful inventory entry with respect to identifying the Minton products is the list of Block Moulds included in 1817. The list continues for several pages and includes some specific details, such as the design of knobs, handles and tureens. The full Block Mould entry is given in Table 9.2. Note that the original order has been rearranged and grouped into appropriate categories with headings inserted. Of course not included in the listing were the plain round items which could be thrown on a potters wheel and not moulded, such as 'common' teapots and coffee pots, spill vases and bowls. As with the copper plate entry for 1817, it is possible that the inventory only included the moulds actually in use at that time. The moulds were given an overall valuation of £149 1s. 0d. by a Thomas Heath, but valuations for individual moulds were not included. The section on Block Moulds was followed in the inventory by a listing of Working Moulds, but this gives no further clarification of the type of wares, except for entries for 'supper set egg', 'butter boats' and 'spoon trays'.

The listing given in Table 9.2 no doubt includes not only moulds used for blue printed wares, but also those for the other types of products. As indicated in Table 2.2, during this period the factory was producing significant quantities of 'Painted', 'Cream Colour', 'Blue Edge' and 'Brown Line', the inventories listing a wide range of wares for these categories, especially for Cream Colour. There is no indication which of the moulds relate to these non-printed wares, although the Blue Edge was probably applied to the 'grafs' or grass-edged wares and 'Royal' and 'Paris' were established creamware shapes.[4]

It is clear from evidence contained within the early factory sales accounts and inventories that, very soon after the start of production in 1796, a wide and varied range of blue printed earthenwares was being made. The same basic shapes were being produced by other manufactories and distinguishing between the products of the various factories requires close attention to detail of both the shape and potting characteristics, such as the design of foot rings and the placing of stilt marks. The attribution of many of the early Minton patterns has enabled various examples of these early products to be identified. These are illustrated here with emphasis being placed on the early pearlwares, which were produced up to c.1820 and which lacked any formal factory marks. The dinner wares are considered first, followed by dessert wares, jugs, mugs and toilet wares and finally tea wares.

Plates

The most commonly produced components of a dinner service were the plates, with a typical service of c.1800 containing six dozen nine-inch table plates, two dozen eight-inch twifler plates, two dozen seven-inch muffin plates and two dozen soup plates. The earliest plate shapes used by Minton would appear to have been the plain 'Octagon' shape and the plain circular 'Trophy' shape, as shown in Plates 9.1 and 9.2 respectively. These were both close copies of shapes used for Chinese export porcelain, which the early products were looking to imitate. The circular 'Concave' shape, as shown in Plate 9.3, was possibly also produced from an early date, initially for the cream coloured wares, but then also for several printed patterns, notably Chinese Sports. At some time before 1810 the 'Concave-Octagon' shape, as shown in Plate 9.4, was introduced, mainly for the Bird pattern but also occasionally with the Roman pattern. Shortly after this an indented variant of the Concave-Octagon shape was introduced for the Bewick Stag and Camel and Giraffe patterns and the standard dinner plate size became slightly larger. By about 1815 a double foot ring had been added to both types of Concave-

Plate 9.1. Minton Octagon shape pearlware plate. A plain octagonal shape with flat rim and no foot ring. One of the earliest plate shapes, introduced with patterns such as standard Willow, Dagger Border with Temple and Fisherman. It continued in production into the 1830s, mainly with the Willow pattern, with the later examples being more rounded than this earlier and typically more angular Roman pattern example of c.1810. Width 212 mm.

Plate 9.2. Minton Trophy shape pearlware plate. A plain circular shape with flat rim and a single recessed foot ring. One of the earliest plate shapes to be introduced with patterns such as Hermit, Lily, Trophy and Basket, and maintained in production at least until the 1820s. It was used for both dinner and tea wares. This example in the Dahlia pattern is probably from a tea set, c.1810. Diameter 187 mm.

Plate 9.3. Minton Concave shape pearlware plate. A plain circular shape with a concave rim and no foot ring. Probably first used for printed wares around 1810 with several patterns including Chinese Sports, Japan Vase and Star. Perhaps used earlier for painted creamwares. It was maintained in production at least until the 1860s. This example in the Chinese Sports pattern, c.1815, is gilded. Diameter 208 mm. Mark P5.

Plate 9.4. Minton Concave-Octagon shape pearlware plate. The first of several versions of the shape, with an octagonal plan, a concave rim and no foot ring. It was used for several years around 1810, mainly with the Bird pattern. Subsequent versions were slightly larger, one variant had slight indentations and later plates had a double foot ring. By c.1820 a more rounded plan was used. This example of c.1812 is unusual in having a Bewick Stag print which was engraved for use with the slightly indented version. Width 162 mm. Mark P1.

Plate 9.5. Minton Octagon shape dinner plate (Roman pattern as shown in Plate 6.14). Note the rim is flat, there is no foot ring and one of the three single stilt marks beneath the rim is visible. The standard nine-inch plate typically has a width of about 235 mm and was used into the 1830s, though the later examples are less angular.

Plate 9.6. Early Minton Concave-Octagon shape dinner plate (Bird pattern as shown in Plate 6.20). Note the rim is concave to the front and there is no foot ring. This standard nine-inch plate typically has a width of about 235mm and an angular plan matching the Octagon shape in Plate 9.5. The concave rim produces a relatively deep well to the plate with a rounded edge. This shape was used for several years around 1810.

Plate 9.7. Minton Trophy shape dinner plate (Hermit pattern as shown in Plate 4.5). Note the plain circular plan, the rim is flat and there is a single recessed foot ring. The standard nine-inch plate typically has a diameter of about 240 mm. The shape was used at least into the 1820s.

Plate 9.8. Minton Concave shape dinner plate (Star pattern as shown in Plate 5.11). Note the plain circular plan, the rim is concave and there is no foot ring. The standard nine-inch plate diameter is about 250 mm. The shape started to be used for printed wares probably around 1810 and was still being used in the 1860s.

Plate 9.9. Minton Indented Concave-Octagon shape dinner plate (Camel and Giraffe pattern as shown in Plate 6.35). Note the rim is concave, each side is slightly indented and there is no foot ring. This standard nine-inch plate typically has a width of about 247 mm. It was probably only used for a few years, around 1812, before being replaced by the version with the double foot ring shown in Plate 9.10.

Plate 9.10. Minton Indented Concave-Octagon shape dinner plate (Bewick Stag pattern as shown in Plate 6.33). Apart from the addition of a double recessed foot ring the shape and size is the same as the design shown in Plate 9.9, and it was probably introduced as a modified version of that shape in around 1815.

Plate 9.11. Minton Concave-Octagon shape dinner plate (Monk's Rock series as shown in Plate 6.40). Compared to the early version of this shape shown in Plate 9.6, this design has a double recessed foot ring and is slightly larger, the standard nine-inch plate typically having a width of about 247 mm. It has a very angular octagonal plan and was used for patterns introduced between about 1815 and 1820, such as the Monk's Rock series and Dove.

Plate 9.12. Minton Concave-Octagon shape dinner plate (English Scenery pattern as shown in Plate 7.17). Compared to the version of this shape shown in Plate 9.11, this design has a much more rounded octagonal plan, giving a diameter of about 250 mm for the standard nine-inch plate. It is the normal shape used with the patterns introduced during the early and mid-1820s, on the Semi-China body, and was maintained in production for several decades.

Octagon plate. By about 1820 the plain Octagon shape had become less angular, and was being used primarily for the Willow pattern. When the Semi-China patterns discussed in Chapter Seven were being introduced in the early 1820s the main plate was the Concave-Octagon design, which by then had a much more rounded plan. Details of the rims and foot rings of the various Minton plate shapes produced up to about 1825 are shown in Plates 9.5 to 9.12. Very similar plates were produced by other factories, so the correspondence of a plate shape to one of those illustrated cannot be taken as direct evidence of Minton manufacture. It can, however, be assumed that any plates found of the basic shapes described, but which do not conform in detail to the examples illustrated, are unlikely to be Minton products.

Another important feature is the marks left on the plates by the stilts used to support the wares during firing. Throughout this early period, Minton appears to have supported plates using three thimble type stilts beneath the plate, resulting in three single stilt marks beneath the plate rim, as can be noted on several of the pieces shown in Plates 9.5 to 9.12. Except for the very occasional example found with three single stilt marks beneath the central well of the plate, all plates so far attributed to Minton, and which were produced before c.1830, have had three stilt marks beneath the rim. Thus any plates found with stilt marks on the front of the rim, or with triple or quadruple stilt marks beneath the rim, were almost certainly not produced by Minton. The converse argument is, unfortunately, not true, as a small number of other factories also supported at least some of their plates using thimbles which produced three single stilt marks beneath the rim. This potting characteristic is, however, still only found on a relatively small minority of plates produced during this period.

The Minton plate shapes used from about 1825 with the Opaque and Stone Chinas are illustrated in Chapter Eight and are seen to have had more elaborate shapes, typically with moulded rims. These later Minton plates all had double indented foot rings and, up to the introduction of Improved Stone China probably in the early 1830s, are all found with three single stilt marks beneath the rim. The Minton Improved Stone China plates are, however, normally found with three single stilt marks on the front of the rim.

In addition to the early plate shapes discussed above, the 1817 inventory includes block moulds for Bath, Royal and Paris shaped plates. These designs were probably used exclusively for the non-printed products, such as cream colour and brown line wares. 'Paris' and 'Royal' were established creamware tableware shapes at this period, both being illustrated in contemporary shape books such as that of St Anthony's Pottery.[4] Paris was a plain circular shape, as confirmed by the note that the moulds had been turned, possibly with a deep foot ring as used with some early bone china. The Royal shape was a lobed plate design, perhaps originally introduced by Wedgwood. Both Paris and Royal were clearly being used by Minton for dinner wares as moulds for various dishes were included in the inventory and the entry for Royal comports indicates additional use for dessert wares. Apart from plates, no other Bath shape moulds are listed, so this design was probably not used for dinner or dessert wares. Bath Embossed is listed as teaware design C in the shape book of c.1830, but this is an elaborate design which would not have been in use as early as 1817.

Soup plates, such as the examples shown in Plates 9.13 and 9.14, had essentially the same shape and potting characteristics as the corresponding dinner plate, but with a much deeper well. They were similar in size to the standard dinner plate and were sometimes decorated from apparently the same engraving.

Plate 9.13. Minton Concave-Octagon shape pearlware soup plate. A relatively early angular example of the shape with no foot ring and a deep rim. Bird pattern, c.1810. Width 242 mm. Mark P2.

Plate 9.14. Minton Indented Concave-Octagon shape pearlware soup plate. This indented shape was probably first introduced c.1812, but this is a relatively late example. It seems to be in a Semi-China body and has a double recessed foot ring. Camel and Giraffe pattern, c.1820. Width 247 mm. Impressed '7', 5 mm high.

Plate 9.15. Minton Hermit pattern pearlware water plate, c.1810. The main print is taken from the same engraving as used for the plate in Plate 4.5. A moulded base with two handles and a spout has been added to a standard dinner plate. Hot water is poured inside the base to keep the plate hot. Note the block mould for 'bottom to water plate' included in Table 9.2. The inventories also mention 'water pans' which may have been equivalent forms of meat dish. Diameter of top plate 240 mm.

Plate 9.16. Dagger Border with Temple pattern pearlware 18-inch plain Octagon shape meat dish, probably Minton c.1798. Note the angular and relatively long and thin plan on this early dish form. The glaze has crazed and the underglaze blue can be seen to have run or 'flown' slightly in places. Three single stilt marks beneath the rim. Plan 464 mm wide by 326 mm high.

Meat Dishes, Gravy Dishes, Bakers etc.

Meat dishes were a major component of the dinner service and were produced in a range of sizes and shapes. As indicated in the factory price list, for printed wares the standard sizes supplied were 9, 10, 11, 12, 14, 16, 18 and 20-inch, with the intermediate sizes being available for non-printed wares and larger sizes available as special order. The earliest printed dishes produced by Minton were the plain Octagon shape, the oval Trophy shape and the oval Concave shape, and block moulds for each of these are included in the 1817 inventory.

The plain Octagon shape dish was actually produced in several different forms. The relatively long and thin shape used with the Dagger Border with Temple pattern dish in Plate 9.16 was probably the earliest form. A more standard shape was soon adopted for the slightly later patterns such as Fisherman (Plate 3.13) and Pinwheels (Plate 5.13). The dishes for the Monk's Rock series show a further variation with a slightly more flattened rim (Plate 3.37). A further plain octagonal design was introduced for the Bamboo and Flowers pattern (Plate 3.66). The engravings for each of these patterns would be designed specifically to fit their particular form of dish. Probably only for the popular standard Willow pattern would fresh engravings have been produced to fit new dish designs. The Willow dish in Plate 9.18 is of a relatively early long thin shape compared to the more normal later example shown in Plate 9.17. A further flat rimmed octagonal dish form with indented sides was introduced, probably around 1812, for the Bewick Stag and Camel and Giraffe patterns. Given this variety of flat rimmed Octagon dish forms it is surprising that only one entry of 13 block moulds for this shape is listed in 1817.

Plate 9.17. Minton Improved Stone China 22-inch Willow pattern octagonal meat dish, c.1835. Such a large dish would possibly have been purchased as a special item, as the largest dish size supplied as standard in a dinner service was 20 inch. Three single stilt marks beneath the base and three on top within the dish. Width 563 mm. Impressed mark M31 and '22'.

Plate 9.18. Minton Willow pattern pearlware nine-inch octagonal meat dish, c.1805. This early dish is seen to have a relatively long and thin plan compared to the more standard form shown in Plate 9.17, although this may in part be due to the smallness of this dish size. Width 242 mm. Mark P1.

Plate 9.19. Minton Chinese Marine pattern 18-inch Opaque China gravy dish, c.1830. Sometimes referred to as 'Well & Tree' dishes with the gravy well at one side being fed by a 'tree' of shallow drainage channels. Made in the larger dish sizes, with a basic shape which corresponds to the standard meat dish form. The detailed design of the channels varies with the basic design of the dish. Foot ring sections are applied at the opposite end to the well to level the dish. Width 457 mm. Mark M15.

The flat rimmed oval Trophy shape dishes remained fairly standard throughout the early period, although the earliest examples, such as the Hermit pattern dish in Plate 3.1, may be slightly more rounded than later examples, such as the Basket pattern dish in Plate 3.26. The Concave shape dishes were also oval but with a concave rim, an example being the fine Chinese Sports pattern dish in Plate 4.76. Note that the block moulds also include a range of sizes of Trophy and Octagon shape covered dishes.

Meat dishes for several of the popular Semi-China patterns introduced in the early 1820s, such as Italian Ruins (Plate 3.54), English Scenery (Plate 3.57) and Filigree (Plate 3.65) were all of a standard Concave-Octagon form, matching the basic Concave-Octagon plate shape. Dishes for the later patterns introduced on Opaque, Stone and Improved Stone China bodies tended to be of more elaborate shapes, again matching the basic plate shapes, examples being shown in Chapter Eight.

All of the Minton meat dish shapes introduced up to 1830 have no foot ring and have three single stilt marks, either beneath the rim or on the base. Dishes produced before c.1820 do not have any size marks. After this date the dish size (e.g. 16) is normally impressed on the base using numbers about six or seven millimetres high, such as on the base of the drainer shown in Plate 9.20.

Each of the basic dish shapes had a corresponding 'Well & Tree' or gravy dish produced in the larger sizes. Essentially this followed the shape of the dish but had a gravy well on one side fed by a 'tree' of shallow drainage channels. Deep

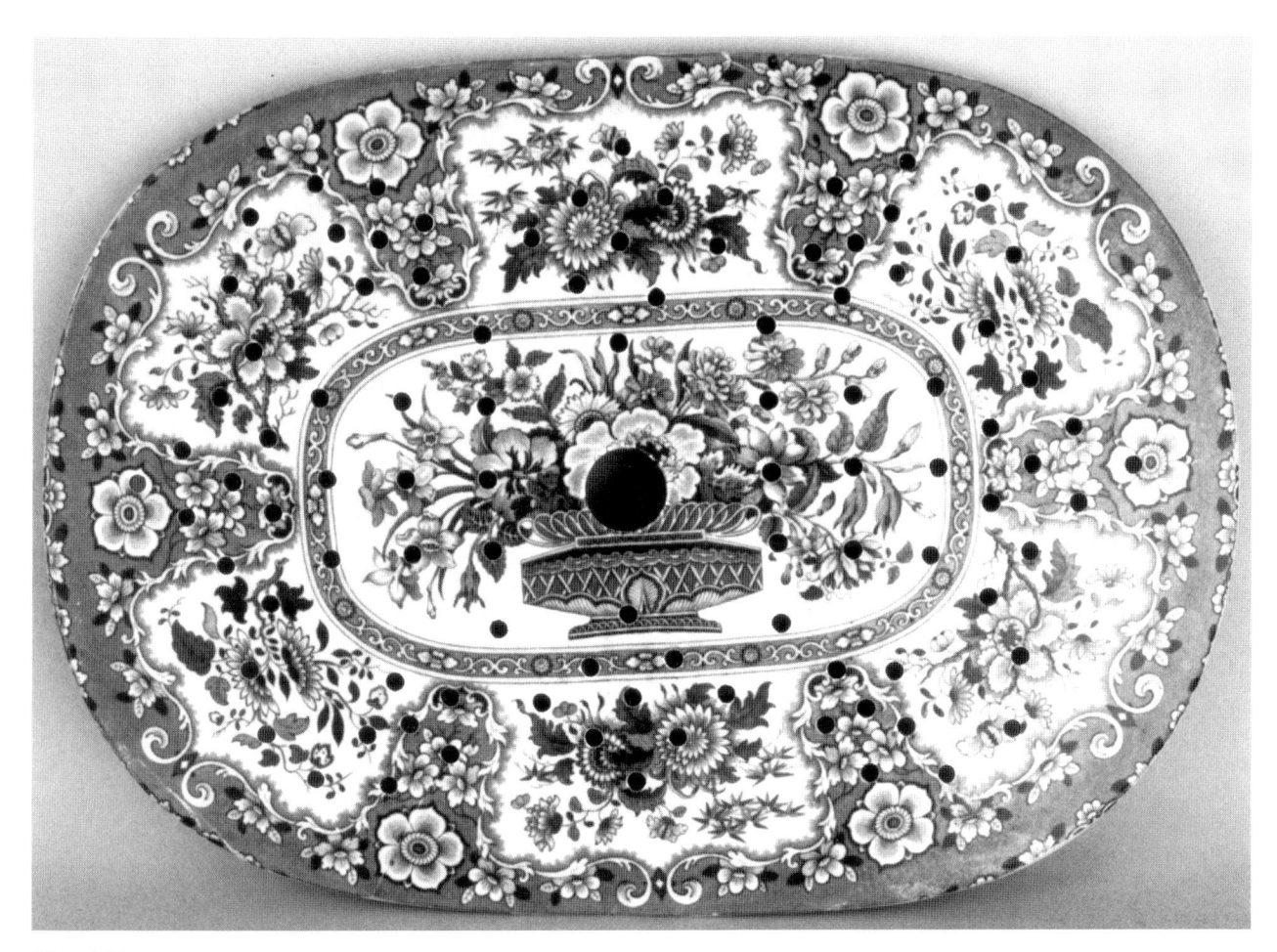

Plate 9.20. *Minton Filigree pattern Semi-China drainer designed to fit the 16-inch meat dish, c.1825. Such drainers were inserted into the standard meat dish, using the central hole to ease handling, so that wet foods such as boiled fish could be served. The exact pattern of the holes may be significant, but insufficient Minton examples have been recorded to determine if they can be used as an aid to attribution. Three single stilt marks on the top. Width 337 mm. Mark M4 and impressed size mark '16'.*

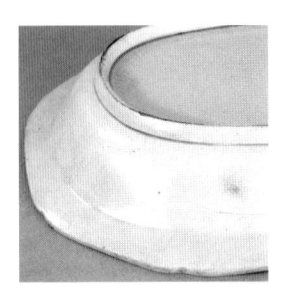

Plate 9.21. Minton Willow pattern pearlware 12-inch baking dish, c.1815. Such relatively deep dishes were probably intended for cooking items such as pies. They were produced in a range of sizes. Note the deep moulded foot ring. Three single stilt marks beneath the rim. Width 320 mm. Mark P14.

foot ring sections were applied at the opposite end to the well to level the dish. An example is shown in Plate 9.19, with further shapes shown in Plates 3.90, 7.25 and 7.29. Interestingly the block moulds also include Trophy and Octagon shape gravy pan dishes and covers. The wares in the inventories detailed in Table 9.1 include a 14-inch gravy dish, cover and pan, as well as a gravy tureen.

To enable the meat dishes to be used for wet foods such as boiled fish, drainers were provided which fitted within the dish. An example is shown in Plate 9.20, which fits the 16-inch dish shown in Plate 3.65. Drainers were available for different shapes and sizes of dish, as indicated by the block mould entry for '31 plain drainers different shapes'. The inventories include 14, 16, 18 and 20-inch drainers.

'Bakers' were relatively deep dishes, presumably intended for cooking items such as pies. The block moulds indicate that these were produced in a range of sizes and shapes. Sizes between seven and 13 inches are mentioned in the inventories. Early Bakers, such as the Willow pattern examples in Plates 9.21 and 3.9 had deep moulded foot rings, whereas the later ones such as the Filigree example in Plate 9.22, and those in Plates 3.86 and 8.88, had no foot ring.

Plate 9.22. Minton Filigree pattern Semi-China 10-inch baking dish, c.1825. Note how the later examples have no foot ring. Three single stilt marks beneath the rim. Width 266 mm. Mark M4 and impressed size mark '10'.

Plate 9.23. Tableware shapes from the earliest extant Minton shape book. This is one of 50 designs, probably entered between c.1830 and c.1845, though some of the shapes, such as this example, were probably introduced much earlier. Note the 'fiddlestick' knobs and plain handles or 'ears', which are referred to in the 1817 list of block moulds. Many of the designs detailed in the shape book have been illustrated in earlier chapters together with examples of corresponding wares. The first 30 designs are reproduced in the Appendix.

Tureens, Vegetable Dishes etc.

Examples of hollow dinnerware items from the early years of production are now relatively rare so it is difficult to build up a comprehensive knowledge of the range of shapes from this period. Examples of plain Octagon shape soup and sauce tureens are shown in Plates 9.24 to 9.26 and Plate 6.16. This shape is still listed in the block moulds of 1817, including reference to the 'ears' used as handles and 'fiddlestick' knobs. This basic shape was used by many factories at this time, so identifying the Minton examples is difficult. The design of the knobs and handles, as detailed in the illustrations, seems to have remained much the same throughout the early period and can be useful as a guide to attribution. Although details of some of the early dinner wares are included in the earliest remaining factory shape book of c.1830, the early Octagon shape is not illustrated. Shape R, as shown in Plate 9.23, appears to be relatively early with fiddlestick knobs and simple ear handles. This may have been produced with certain patterns using the round Trophy shape plates, such as Lily or Hermit, but to date no examples in this shape have been found.

Another early Minton shape was the plain oval design with lion head knobs and handles, illustrated in c.1830 as Shape G (Plate 5.21). This was used both with certain patterns using the Trophy shape plates, such as Basket (Plates 5.20 and 5.21), and with patterns used on Concave shape plates, such as the Chinese Sports example in Plate 9.28. Because this shape was also used by many other factories, as with the octagonal tureens, it is difficult to be certain in identifying Minton pieces. Again the details of the lion head knobs and handles are useful in this respect. Note the difference in handle found between the tureens in Plates 9.28 and 5.21, with the flatter profile of the latter perhaps being a later variant.

For both the Camel and Giraffe and the Bewick Stag patterns, Minton used a variant of the plain oval tureen shape, as shown in Plate 9.29. The same base and lion head handles and knobs are combined with an indented octagonal lid, reflecting the plate and dish shape used for these patterns.

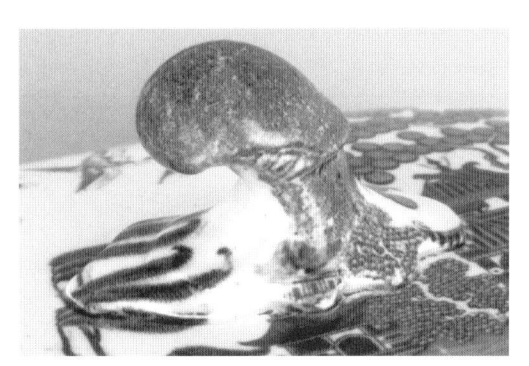

Plate 9.24. Minton Willow pattern pearlware octagonal soup tureen, c.1805. This relatively early tureen shape is in imitation of Chinese export porcelain and was used by many factories. It is included in the 1817 list of block moulds but is not illustrated in the factory shape book of c.1830. Identification of Minton examples is difficult and requires close attention to detail of features such as the 'fiddlestick' knobs and handles. The print used on the lid of this tureen appears to have been taken from the same engraving as used for the baking dish shown in Plate 3.8. The print inside the tureen corresponds to that on the dessert dish in Plate 9.74. The base and lid closely match those used for the Dove pattern tureen shown in Plate 9.27. Four thin 'breather' slots have been cut inside the foot, presumably to allow gas to escape during firing. Length 325 mm.

Plate 9.25. Minton Willow pattern pearlware octagonal sauce tureen, c.1805. The shape closely matches the Pinwheels pattern tureen shown in Plate 9.26. Length 184 mm.

Plate 9.26. Minton Pinwheels pattern pearlware sauce tureen, c.1810. The moulded knob and handles closely match those used on the Willow pattern tureen shown in Plate 9.25. The Roman pattern tureen shown in Plate 6.16, although of the same basic shape and with the same moulded handles, uses a smaller size of fiddlestick knob. Note the deep foot. Length 182 mm. Mark P1.

Plate 9.27. Minton Dove pattern pearlware octagonal soup tureen, c.1815. The lid and base of this example closely correspond to the Minton Willow pattern tureen shown in Plate 9.24. The knob and handles, however, correspond to the distinctive design used by Minton on the Monk's Rock pattern dinner wares, such as the sauce tureen shown in Plates 6.47 and 6.55. Four 'breather' slots cut inside the foot. Length 330 mm. Mark P4.

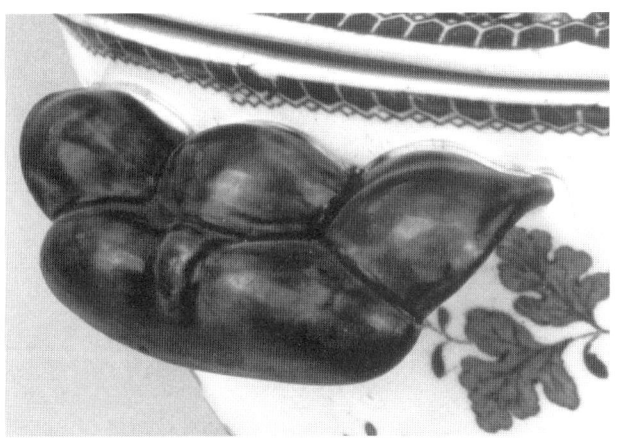

275

Plate 9.28. Minton Chinese Sports pattern pearlware sauce tureen and stand, c.1815. This plain oval shape with lion head handles and knob was standard to many factories during this period. It was included in the shape book as design G. The details of the lion heads can be used as a guide to attribution, although note that this shape was used by Minton for at least 20 years, so it is likely that several moulds were used. Note the difference in handle profile of this example compared to the slightly later Basket pattern tureen shown in Plate 5.21. The sauce tureen has been overpainted in coloured enamels. Tureen length 195 mm and mark P6. Stand width 192 mm, with moulded foot ring.

Plate 9.29. Minton Camel and Giraffe pattern pearlware soup tureen, c.1815. The plain oval base and lion head knob and handles have been combined with an indented octagonal lid. The same combination was used by Minton for the Bewick Stag pattern. The lid shape reflects the indented octagonal plate and dish designs used with these two patterns. The base measures 277 mm across its top, so may correspond to the 11-inch tureen size. The knobs and handles are close copies but of a larger size than those used on the 10-inch size (255 mm across the top) Basket pattern tureen in Plate 5.20. Four breathing slots cut inside the foot and one inside each lion handle mouth. Circular breathing hole beneath the knob and in each handle. Length 360 mm. Mark P4.

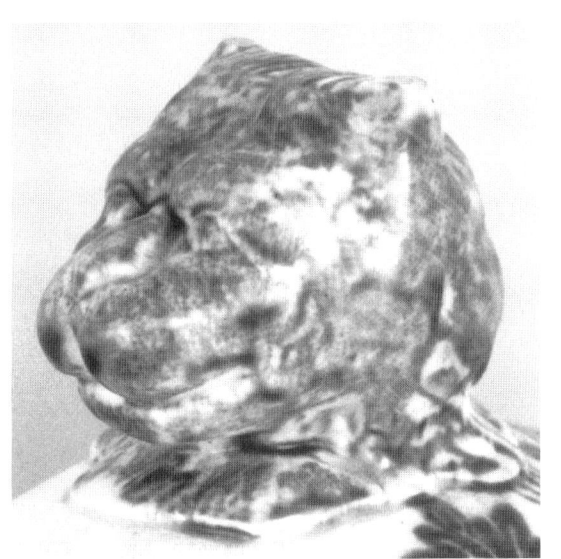

It is unclear which of the block moulds listed in 1817 correspond to these plain oval shapes. They may be the 'Broadend' tureens with lion head knobs, for which there are two entries, one having octagonal lids. Also listed, however, are Trophy shape tureens, again with lion head knobs.

A further tureen shape was used by Minton for the Monk's Rock series, as detailed in Plates 6.47 and 6.55. This unusual shape seems to be unique to Minton but is not illustrated in the c.1830 shape book. It may correspond to the 'strong wetted' shape with rose knobs listed in the block moulds. The same distinctive knobs and handles were used by Minton in combination with the basic octagonal shape for the Dove pattern, as shown in Plate 9.27.

The later tureen shapes used by Minton during the 1820s and 1830s are discussed and illustrated in Chapters Seven and Eight. These are generally all included in the factory shape book of c.1830 (see Appendix), a notable

Plate 9.30. Minton Italian Ruins pattern Opaque China soup tureen stand, c.1830. This basic shape of stand was used by several factories, including Spode. It corresponds to design K in the factory shape book, and Minton appears to have only used it with the Italian Ruins pattern, such as the tureen in Plate 7.15. Moulded foot ring. Width 434 mm. Impressed size mark '11'.

Plate 9.31. Minton Italian Ruins pattern Semi-China circular tureen stand, c.1820. A rare shape of which this is the only example recorded to date (see Plate 7.16 for accompanying tureen). Moulded foot ring. Diameter 332 mm. Mark M1.

Plate 9.32. Minton Monk's Rock series pearlware soup tureen stand, c.1815. Note the distinctive moulded handles, matching the basic handle design used on the tureen. Tureen stands for earlier shapes, such as the plain octagonal examples shown in Plates 3.30 and 3.38, had no handles and can be mistaken for baking dishes. Width 376 mm.

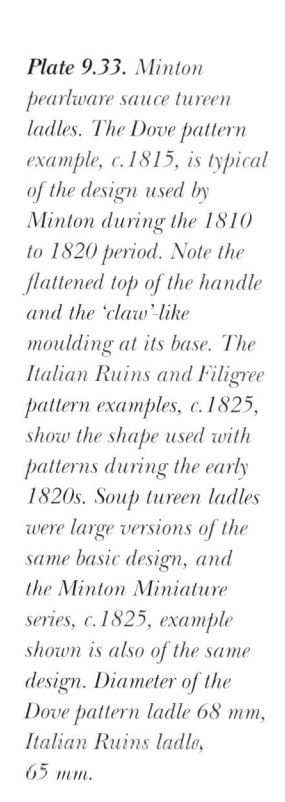

Plate 9.33. Minton pearlware sauce tureen ladles. The Dove pattern example, c.1815, is typical of the design used by Minton during the 1810 to 1820 period. Note the flattened top of the handle and the 'claw'-like moulding at its base. The Italian Ruins and Filigree pattern examples, c.1825, show the shape used with patterns during the early 1820s. Soup tureen ladles were large versions of the same basic design, and the Minton Miniature series, c.1825, example shown is also of the same design. Diameter of the Dove pattern ladle 68 mm, Italian Ruins ladle, 65 mm.

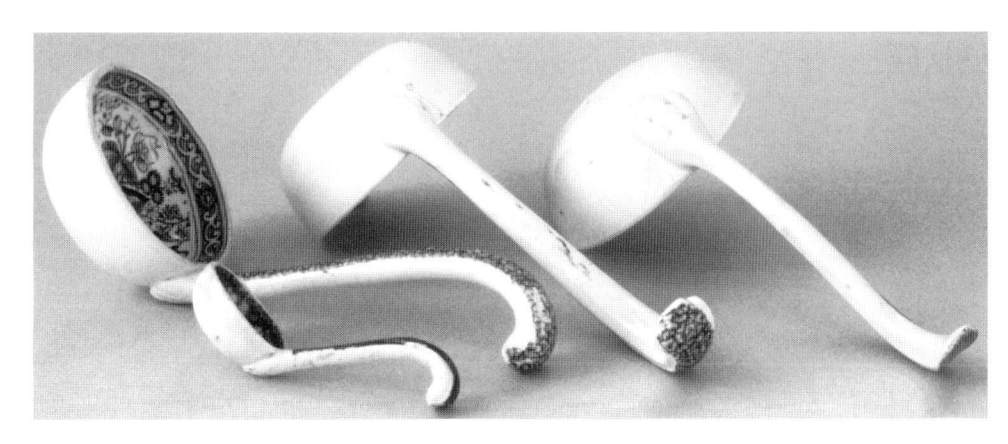

exception being the early round tureen form used for the Italian Ruins pattern, and illustrated in Plate 7.16.

Soup and sauce tureens were originally normally supplied with ladles and stands, but it is unusual to find complete sets today. Some of the delicate ladles have survived, but are normally found as separate items. The moulded ladle

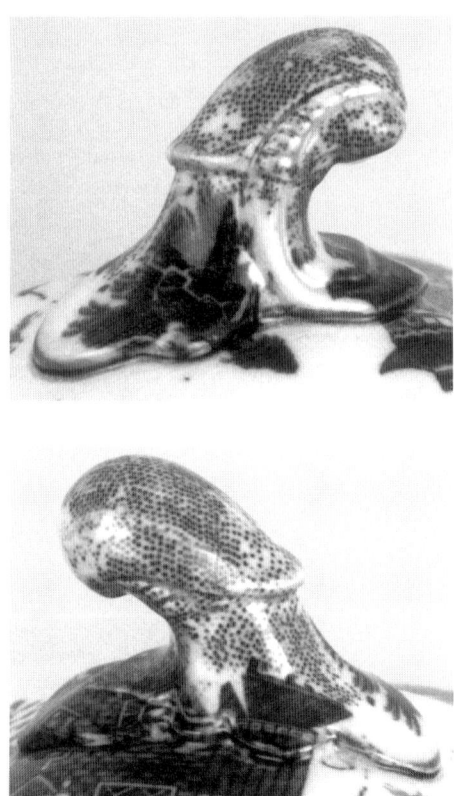

Plate 9.34. Dagger Border with Temple pattern pearlware covered vegetable dish, probably Minton, c.1800. As indicated in the 1817 block moulds, square dishes of this type were a standard item in dinner services and are included in the factory shape book of c.1830 (see Plate 9.23). Note the moulded fiddlestick knob which closely matches that used on the Minton Roman pattern vegetable dish in Plate 6.17, indeed both the knob and the lid of the two dishes could have come from the same moulds, providing further strong evidence for attribution of this Dagger Border with Temple pattern to Minton. Minimum width of dish 225 mm.

Plate 9.35. Minton Basket pattern pearlware covered vegetable dish, c.1830. As detailed in Plate 5.30, the print used inside the base is included in a Minton pattern book of c.1886. Note how the square shape dish was being used with the oval shape tureens corresponding to factory Shape G. An oval shape dish has, however, been noted in a Chinese Sports pattern service. Width of base 226 mm.

handles can be a useful guide for attribution, with the same shape being used with several tureen designs. Details of Minton sauce ladle designs are given in Plate 9.33.

The shape of the stands tends to follow the plan of the tureen. Examples are shown in Plates 9.30 to 9.32, with further examples in Plates 5.22, 6.48 and numerous illustrations in Chapters Three, Seven and Eight. The early examples are relatively plain with deep moulded foot rings, and so are quite similar to 'Bakers'. Later examples again have foot rings, but often have well-defined handles.

Covered vegetable dishes were included as standard items in the dinner service. These were often of a basic square shape, such as the early Dagger Border with Temple pattern dish shown in Plate 9.34 and the Basket pattern dish in Plates 9.35 and 5.30. An oval form has been noted with the Chinese Sports pattern. During the 1820s and 1830s the dish shapes became more elaborate, as indicated by the shape book entries and the examples illustrated in Chapters Seven and Eight.

The 1817 block moulds refer to various interesting vegetable dish forms, including 'dishes square to fit in a niche', 'dishes square hollow brims', 'long square covered dishes' and 'octagon beef steak dish, cover & water pan'. Also listed are 'Root Dishes', which typically constituted a base, a lid and an inner vegetable container sometimes partitioned into either two or four sections. An early example in the Roman pattern is shown in Plate 6.15.

Salads

Early inventories list blue printed square and oval salads in sizes ranging from nine to 12 inches. These were of a relatively plain design, such as the examples in Plates 9.36 and 9.37. Block moulds were also available for round and canoe salads, although these were not necessarily produced with printed decoration. Later salads were produced in a variety of more elaborate shapes, as detailed in the shape book of c.1830, with examples being shown in Plates 7.40, 8.21, 8.73 and 8.83.

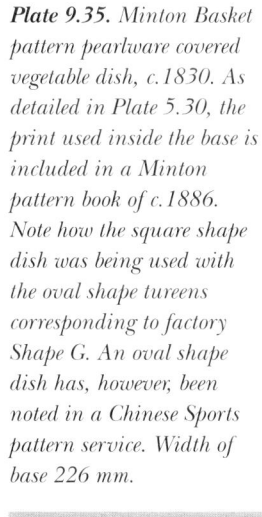

Plate 9.36. Minton Monk's Rock series pearlware square salad bowl, c.1815. Inner print as used on the dessert dish in Plate 6.45. Width 229 mm. Mark P4.

Plate 9.37. Minton Lily pattern pearlware oval salad bowls, c.1805. Canoe shape salads are mentioned in the block moulds. The same inner print is used for each bowl. Ten-inch size with full decoration to outside, length 266 mm. Eleven-inch size, length 289 mm.

Plate 9.38. Minton Roman pattern pearlware octagonal gravy boat, c.1810. Note the distinctive handle form. The pattern matches the design used on the side of the root dish in Plate 6.15. Length 183 mm. Indistinct inscribed size mark, possibly '3'.

Plate 9.39. Pair of Minton octagonal gravy boats, of the same design but slightly smaller than that in Plate 9.38. Willow pattern pearlware, c.1810 with mark P7, and Semi-China Bamboo and Flowers pattern c.1820 with mark M1. Both 155 mm long with an indistinct inscribed mark.

Plate 9.40. Minton octagonal gravy boats, c.1825, of a slightly later form than those in Plates 9.38 and 9.39. Italian Ruins pattern length 165 mm, mark M1. Willow pattern length 131 mm, decorated with a print from a copper plate still remaining at the factory.

Gravy Boats

'Boats' for gravy or sauce were produced from the earliest years and in 1817 the block moulds include Octagon, Concave and oval Trophy shapes, although these were not necessarily all used for printed wares. Plates 9.38 and 9.39 show examples of early Minton Octagon shape boats. Examples of a slightly later Octagon shape, which was probably introduced in the early 1820s, are shown in Plates 9.40 and 7.37. The inventories mention different Gravy Boat sizes ranging from 2nd to 7th. Also included are stands, although an example has yet to be identified.

283

Plate 9.41. Minton pearlware supper set dishes, c.1812, grouped to illustrate how they would normally have been arranged surrounding a central container and within a wooden tray. Note the slightly domed shape of the lid and the characteristic radial alignment of the knobs. The dishes have very similar dimensions, the Bewick Stag and Star pattern dishes each being 307 mm long and the Lily pattern dishes each 304 mm.

Supper Sets

It is clear from the early inventories that supper sets were produced by Minton in significant quantities. They included round and oval sets, both in a small and a large size, with covers and centres. The block moulds also include square and long square covered dishes, with pickle dishes for the latter. The working moulds include reference to a 'Supper Set Egg', indicating that at least one of the designs had a centre designed to hold eggs. Various examples of Minton supper set dishes are shown in Plates 9.41 to 9.45. Note how the knobs are aligned radially which, although not unique to Minton, is unusual, with other factories normally using knobs aligned circumferentially.

Plate 9.42. Detail of the Bewick Stag pattern supper set section base. Note the sharp corners. The moulded foot ring with angular section is typical of Minton supper sets. Mark P2.

Plate 9.43. Minton Monk's Rock series pearlware supper set section, c.1815. See also Plate 6.49 for details of the print used and the shape of the base. Whereas the dishes shown in Plate 9.41 formed a round supper set, this dish is from an oval set, which may have had a large central covered container for holding eggs. Moulded foot ring. Length of dish 375 mm.

Plate 9.44. Minton China Pattern supper set section, c.1805. This dish may originally have been from the end of a large oval supper set. Moulded foot ring. Width 290 mm. Mark P1.

Plate 9.45. Minton pearlware Willow pattern supper set dish, c.1810. Note that compared to the slightly domed lid and angular shape (see Plate 9.42) of the other dishes illustrated, this dish has a relatively flat lid and a more rounded profile. The knob is probably from the same mould as used with those on the Lily pattern dishes in Plate 9.41. The print used on the lid was also used on a diamond-shaped pickle stand of the same shape as the examples shown in Plates 9.46 and 9.47. Moulded foot ring. Length 295 mm. Mark P1 to lid and base.

Plate 9.46. Minton Pinwheels pattern pearlware diamond pickle dish set, c.1810. Note the main print used on the stand is the same as that used on the dessert dish shown in Plate 3.25. Block moulds for diamond pickles and stands are listed in 1817, and included in early factory inventories, which mention both footed and flat stands. This was a standard design for the period being produced by several factories. Details of the pickle dish profile, and of the moulded foot shown below, may help attribution. This basic shape was probably used up to the early 1820s. Later patterns tend to be found on the design shown in Plate 9.48. Width of stand 299 mm. Stand and two dishes mark P1, one dish mark P11.

Plate 9.47. Minton Bird pattern footed diamond pickle stand, c.1810, showing detail of moulded design (see also Plate 6.26). Width 298 mm. Mark P4.

Plate 9.48. Minton Lace Border pattern pickle dish set, c.1830. This design of footed pickle set is found with several Minton patterns including examples on Semi-China, and so was probably introduced in the early 1820s. Note the detail of the central handle shown above, the square base of which helps to locate the four pickle dishes. Minimum width of stand 182 mm. Marks M25 and P15.

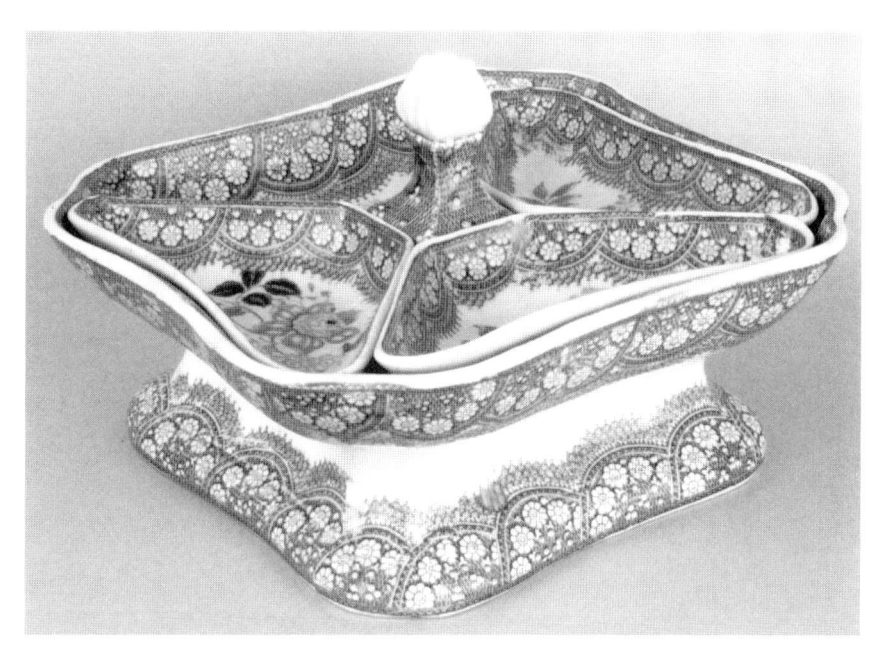

Pickles and Miscellaneous Tablewares

In addition to the more standard plates, dishes and tureens, factories in the early nineteenth century also produced a wide and varied range of interesting dinner and kitchenware items. The early Minton inventories include many such wares, some of which are more familiar than others. Pickle dishes were produced in diamond, leaf and oval shapes, some divided and some with stands. Typical examples are shown in Plates 9.46 to 9.55. Very similar items were, of course, produced by other factories, so attribution can be difficult. For example with the leaf pickles shown in Plate 9.54, non-Minton examples have been noted with essentially the same shape and moulded detail on the underside, suggesting a common supplier of moulds to several factories.

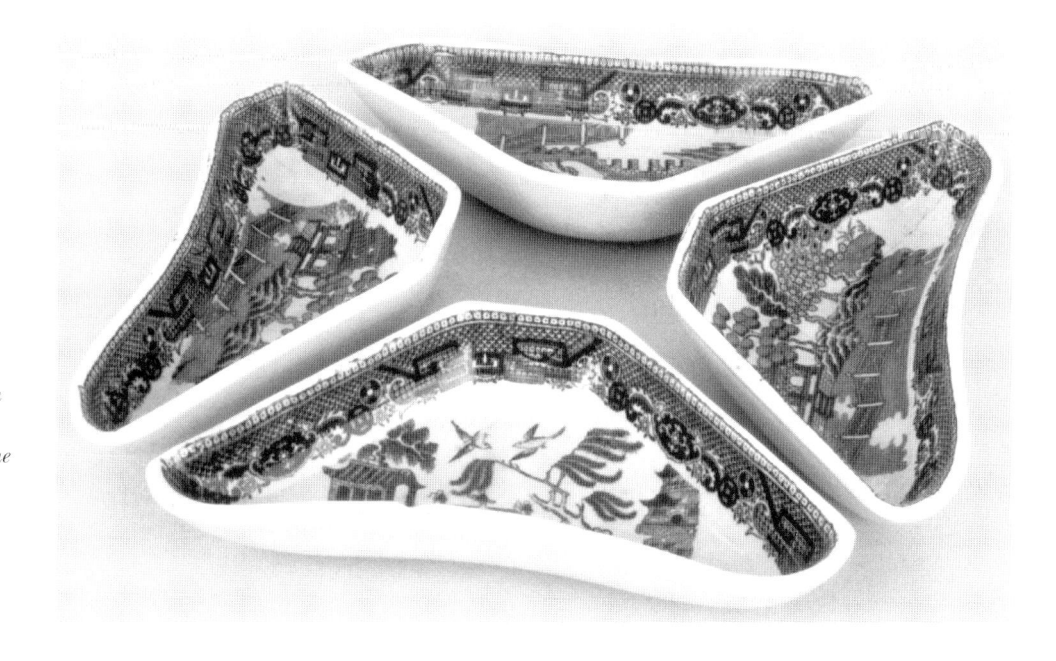

Plate 9.49. Set of four Minton Willow pattern pickle dishes to fit the square footed stand design shown in Plate 9.48. The dishes are all essentially the same shape and size, with lengths of 145, 146, 146 and 147 mm respectively. Two dishes mark P1 and two mark P17.

Plate 9.50. Minton Lily pattern pearlware radish tray, c.1805. Other factories produced a very similar shape. Only one mould is recorded in 1817. The inventories also list 'Radish Tray with butter tubs'. Length 284 mm.

Plate 9.51. Minton Hermit pattern pearlware oval divided pickle, c.1805. These were listed in early inventories. Very similar pickles were made by other factories including Spode. The main print matches that used on the shell pickle in Plate 9.55, and the print used on the divider matches that used around the outside of the 'Pattie' in Plate 9.58. Deep moulded foot ring. Length 140 mm.

Plate 9.52. Minton Willow pattern pearlware asparagus tray, c.1810. These were produced in sets perhaps with a stand. They were supplied by many factories. The Minton examples seem to be characterised by the very rounded corners joining the base and sides. Length 80 mm. Mark P1.

Plate 9.53. Minton Filigree pattern Semi-China shaped dish, c.1825. This slightly later design found in Semi-China may be a pickle dish or could perhaps be from a dessert service. Moulded foot ring. Length 173 mm.

Plate 9.54. Minton leaf pickles. The early inventories include leaf pickles in three sizes, and three moulds are listed in 1817. Of the examples illustrated the Filigree pattern, c.1825, is the largest with a length of 147 mm. The other two are pearlware, c.1810, with the Queen of Sheba pattern example, length 131 mm and mark P4, being larger than the Hermit pattern example, length 121 mm. Note the crisp moulding and well-defined leaf 'veins' on the underside. Attribution of these leaf pickle dishes is difficult as other factories produced almost identical shapes. An example in a Ridgeway pattern has been noted, as well as one decorated with the Chinese Flag Bearers pattern, traditionally attributed to Davenport, both of which had essentially the same design of veins, suggesting that moulds could have been supplied from a common source.

Plate 9.55. Minton Hermit pattern pearlware shell pickle, c.1805. Note the three moulded feet with slight grooving. The print matches that used on the divided pickle shown in Plate 9.51. Width 138 mm. Mark P1.

POTTING POT, OVAL OR ROUND.

Plate 9.56. Minton Monk's Rock series pearlware potting pot, c.1815. Round potting pots are listed in the early inventories and the factory shape book of 1884 includes the illustration shown above. They were used for potting and preserving cooked meats, with the grove enabling a cover to be tied in place. The example illustrated has a rim but no groove. It is decorated with the same print as used on the sauce tureen shown in Plate 6.47. Length 103 mm.

Plate 9.57. Minton pearlware oval pots, c.1810. These items have no groove or rim, so may have been originally supplied with lids. Pinwheels pattern example, length 136 mm, mark P1. Willow pattern example length 112 mm, mark P1.

With some of the smaller kitchenware items their original use is not always immediately obvious. The oval dish in Plate 9.56 has a lip and is probably a 'Potting Pot' intended for potting and preserving cooked meats or fish. The similar items in Plate 9.57 have no lip, so originally may have had lids. The small round and oval dishes with tapered sides and rims shown in Plates 9.58 and 9.59 are probably 'Patty Pans' or 'Patties', used for baking patty (pâté).

In common with other factories, Minton produced a range of custard cup designs, some with lids, examples being shown in Plate 9.66. Typically these would have been supplied in sets with a stand. The small pots with serrated edges shown in Plate 9.67 are particularly unusual and may have been produced as custard cups. The 'comma' shape pots can be found in groups, suggesting that they were originally supplied in sets. Note that a 'straight tailed' example was also produced.

The stands shown in Plates 9.60 to 9.65 may have been intended as cheese stands, though the plain circular examples may have been stands for smaller items such as custard cups. The early inventories include cheese stands in 9, 10, 11 and 12-inch sizes and also mention a square cheese stand.

Plate 9.58. Minton Hermit pattern round 'Pattie' dish, c.1810. These small dishes with slightly tapered sides and flat rims were used for baking pâté. Note that the print used inside the dish has the same distinctive angular treatment of trees on the island found on the copper plate shown in Plate 4.3. The print on the outside is the same as that used on the divider in the pickle dish shown in Plate 9.51. Shallow recessed foot ring. Diameter 119 mm. Mark P7.

Plate 9.59. Minton pearlware Chinese Sports pattern oval 'Pattie' dish, c.1815. Moulds for nine sizes of oval patties are listed in 1817. Flat base. Length 119 mm. Mark P5.

Plate 9.60. Minton Lily pattern pearlware circular stand, c.1805. Circular stands are normally found with a round foot, such as those in Plates 9.61 and 9.62, but this example has a completely flat base. It may have originally been supplied as a stand for some smaller items, such as custard cups or asparagus trays. Diameter 303 mm. Mark P3.

Plate 9.61. Minton Queen of Sheba pattern high footed circular stand, c.1810. A large example which could have originally had a range of uses. The circular foot is quite deep at 56 mm, with a diameter of 233 mm across its base. Interestingly the bottom of the foot is not glazed. Diameter 332 mm.

Plate 9.62. Minton Willow pattern pearlware low footed stand, c.1800. The main print is taken from the same engraving as that used to decorate the dinner plate shown in Plate 4.28. Compared to the example shown above, this stand has a relatively shallow foot, 22 mm high, with a base diameter of 204 mm. Again the base of the foot is not glazed. Stand diameter 272 mm. Marked with two crossed painted underglaze blue lines (see Plate 10.2).

Opposite page:

Plate 9.63. Minton Chinese Marine pattern Opaque China low footed stand, c.1827 (see also Plate 8.47). Length 366 mm. Mark M15.

Plate 9.64. Minton Verona pattern low footed circular stand, c.1835 (see also Plate 8.87). Diameter 280 mm. Marks M28 with no cursive M and P22.

Plate 9.65. Minton Berlin Roses pattern Stone China low footed stand, c.1830 (see also Plate 8.59). Diameter 312 mm. Mark M18.

293

Plate 9.66. Minton pearlware custards, c.1810. The bell-shaped custards are listed in early inventories, but were also supplied by other factories. Hermit pattern height 57 mm. Chinese Family pattern height 54mm, mark P9. Covered handled custard cups. Hermit pattern height 94 mm with typical Minton cup handle. Roman pattern height 82 mm (see also Plate 6.25).

Plate 9.67. Minton Hermit pattern pearlware shaped serrated-edge pots, c.1810. Unusual items found in sets, so perhaps custard cups. The 'straight tailed' example is less common. Height 51 mm.

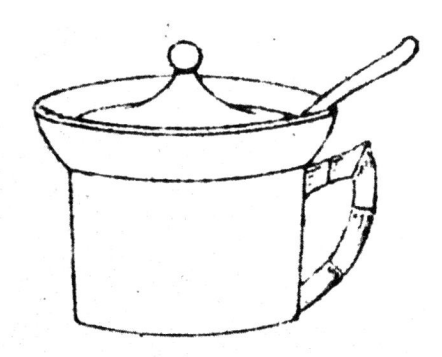

MUSTARD & SPOON.

Plate 9.68. *Minton Verona pattern mustard pot, c.1835. As indicated in the drawing from the 1884 shape book shown above, it would have originally have been supplied with a lid and spoon. Earlier mustard pots would have been similar but of a plainer design. Shown right are early designs for pepper and salt, also taken from the 1884 shape book. Diameter of mustard 84 mm.*

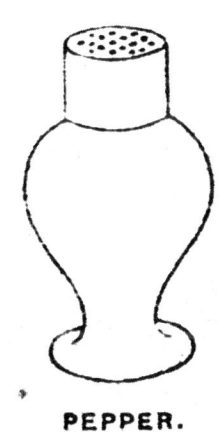

PEPPER.

SALT.

Plate 9.69. *Minton Hermit pattern pearlware covered broth bowl and stand, c.1810. The print used on the lid seems to be from the same engraving as that used for the wicker plate shown in Plate 9.87. Inventories include three sizes of broth bowl and stands, and moulds for circular stands are listed in 1817. Another design of early Minton broth bowl and stand is shown in Plates 5.29 and 5.32. Very similar shapes were produced by other factories. Width of bowl 182 mm, diameter of stand 171 mm.*

Plate 9.70. Minton Hermit pattern pearlware footed dessert comport, c.1810. The inventories include comports or 'Comportiers' in four sizes between eight and 11 inches. Several shapes are mentioned in the block moulds, but these also include creamware products. Although the design illustrated is typical of the period, this particular piece matches the Basket pattern comport shown in Plate 5.23, which is attributed to Minton based on the copper plate engraving. Interestingly the main print used inside the comport appears to have been taken from the same engraving as used for the dessert dishes shown in Plates 9.72 and 9.79. Three single stilt marks inside the rim of the comport. Base length 166 mm, overall length 286 mm.

Plate 9.71. Minton Monk's Rock series pearlware dessert dish, c.1815. The moulded shape and foot ring exactly match the Fruit pattern dish in Plate 3.49. Width 262 mm.

Dessert Wares

Dessert services to accompany dinner wares were available from the earliest years of production, typically in matching patterns. At this period a comport containing fruits may have been served after dinner and individual dishes then used to carry a selection away from the table. Indeed the Fruit pattern appears only to have been used for dessert wares. Some of the shapes produced by Minton up to about 1820, such as those in Plates 9.70 to 9.76 and Plate 3.49, were typical of products from many contemporary factories, so attribution can be difficult. The shell dish shown in Plate 9.72, for example, was probably produced in essentially the same form, with the same handle moulding, by several other factories. The closely

Plate 9.72. *Minton Hermit pattern pearlware shell dish, c.1810. Almost identical dishes were made by other factories, such as that shown in Plate 9.73. The print on this dish matches that used on the wares in Plates 9.70 and 9.79, the latter being a distinctive Minton form. The Dagger Border with Temple pattern dish in Plate 4.50 exactly matches this example, including the blue painted handle moulding. Moulded foot ring. Three single stilt marks inside the dish rim. Width 186 mm.*

Plate 9.73. *Greek pattern pearlware shell dish with ochre painted rim, maker unknown, c.1810. Although a smaller size, note the strong similarity of this dish to the Minton example in Plate 9.72. This version of the Greek pattern is possibly attributable to Herculaneum. Another dish seemingly matching this one is decorated with a version of the Group pattern. Three single stilt marks centrally placed within the dish. Width 175 mm. Impressed heart-shaped workman's mark 5 mm wide.*

Plate 9.74. *Minton Willow pattern pearlware dessert dish, c.1810. The same basic shape was used by other factories and by Minton for bone china.[6] Matching pieces from a service of this design, such as the dish in Plate 9.71, have a similar profile. Three stilt marks inside the rim and on the moulded foot ring. Minimum width 142 mm. Mark P11.*

Plate 9.75. *Minton Lily pattern pearlware dessert dish, c.1810. This example matches the Basket pattern dish in Plate 5.28 and the Water Lily pattern dish in Plate 6.86. Three stilt marks on the moulded foot ring. Minimum width 157 mm.*

Plate 9.76. Minton Willow pattern pearlware dessert dish, c.1810. This dish shape matches those shown in Plates 3.21 and 3.25. The print appears to have been taken from the same engraving as used for the dishes shown in Plates 9.77 and 9.78. The same basic shape was used by several factories. Moulded foot ring following the dish shape. Three single stilt marks on the foot ring and three inside the dish rim. Width 249 mm.

matching example decorated in the Greek pattern shown in Plate 9.73 is possibly attributable to Herculaneum. Minton did, however, also produce a distinctive variant of the shell dish, with a much more angular plan.[5]

Further examples of distinctive Minton dessertware shapes are shown in Plates 9.77 to 9.79. The dish in Plate 9.78 is particularly interesting in that an example has been noted in painted creamware. Furthermore, Minton also produced pearlware dessert wares in some of the unusual shapes used for first period bone china and illustrated by Godden.[7]

Plate 9.77. Minton Willow pattern pearlware dessert dish, c.1810. A distinctive moulded dish shape, exactly matching the Hermit pattern example shown in Plate 9.79. The print on this piece matches that used on the dishes in Plates 9.76 and 9.78. Moulded foot ring following the dish shape. No obvious stilt marks. Width 247 mm. Mark P1.

Plate 9.78. *Minton Willow pattern pearlware dessert dish, c.1810. The print is the same as that used on the dishes in Plates 9.76 and 9.77. The lower rounded lip is raised so as to function as a handle. Relatively deep moulded foot ring following the dish shape. Three single stilt marks on the foot ring and inside the rim of the dish. Width 248 mm.*

With the introduction of Semi-China in the early 1820s, Minton adopted a new dessertware design, as illustrated by the Italian Ruins pattern service shown in Plates 9.80 to 9.84. These distinctive shapes appear to be unique to Minton and were used with a range of patterns, including Fruit, Filigree, English Scenery, Dresden, Florentine and the Monk's Rock series, examples being shown in Plates 6.44, 6.45, 7.38, 7.80, 7.81, 7.83 and 8.10.

Delicate wicker baskets with stands and accompanying plates were another major product of the Minton factory. The block moulds include four sizes of oval

Plate 9.79. *Minton Hermit pattern pearlware dessert dish, c.1810. The distinctive shape matches the Willow pattern dish shown in Plate 9.77. The print matches that used on the comport in Plate 9.70 and the shell dish in Plate 9.72. Moulded foot ring following the shape of the dish. Three stilt marks on the foot ring and inside the dish rim. Width 246 mm.*

299

Plate 9.80. Minton Italian Ruins pattern Semi-China footed dessert comport, c.1825. Minton probably introduced this distinctive dessertware design in the early 1820s for Semi-China. It was used for a range of patterns, including Italian Ruins as shown on the pieces in Plates 9.80 to 9.84. Three single stilt marks inside the comport rim. Overall length 308 mm, length of base 176 mm. Mark M1.

basket and stand with 'bow' handles, and seven and eight-inch size plates. Significant numbers of baskets are listed in the inventories including seven, eight, nine and ten-inch sizes. Examples of Minton wicker ware are shown in Plates 9.85 to 9.90.

Similar items were produced by many factories, but fortunately Minton apparently used the same twig or 'bow' handle moulds over many years. Although other factories also used twig handles, such as on the Spode example shown in Plate 1.6, close examination normally enables differences of detail to be found. Note that between about 1815 and 1820 Minton seems to have changed the way in which the handles were attached, with the ends following the sides, as shown in Plate 9.90, as compared to the earlier arrangement with the ends bent outwards,

Plate 9.81. Minton Italian Ruins pattern Semi-China oval dessert dish, c.1825. Moulded foot ring. Three single stilt marks inside the dish rim. Width 265 mm. Mark M1.

Plate 9.82. Minton Italian Ruins pattern Semi-China square dessert dish, c.1825. Moulded foot ring. Three single stilt marks inside the dish rim. Width 217 mm. Mark M1.

Plate 9.83. Minton Italian Ruins pattern Semi-China dessert plate, c.1825. The shape reflects that of the dish in Plate 9.84. Note the moulded rounded foot ring. Three single stilt marks inside the foot ring. Diameter 212 mm. Mark M1.

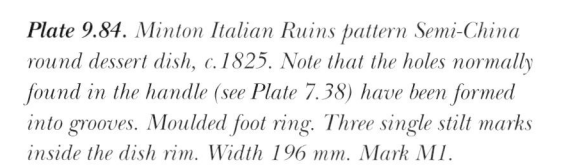

Plate 9.84. Minton Italian Ruins pattern Semi-China round dessert dish, c.1825. Note that the holes normally found in the handle (see Plate 7.38) have been formed into grooves. Moulded foot ring. Three single stilt marks inside the dish rim. Width 196 mm. Mark M1.

Plate 9.85. *Minton Roman pattern pearlware wicker basket stand, c.1810. Blue painted rim. Flat base. Three single stilt marks beneath the wicker work rim. Width 251 mm.*

Plate 9.86. *Minton Lily pattern pearlware wicker basket stand, c.1810. Blue painted rim. Flat base. This example, width 229 mm, has three single stilt marks on the front of the wicker work rim. An accompanying larger Lily pattern stand, width 249 mm, and the larger Plant pattern stand shown in Plate 5.48, both have the stilt marks beneath the rim.*

Plate 9.87. *Minton Hermit pattern pearlware seven-inch wicker plate, c.1810. Blue painted rim. The print matches that used on the broth bowl in Plate 9.69. Note the moulded foot ring design which is relatively thin with a triangular section. This is typical of early Minton wicker plates. From about 1820, a wider double recessed foot ring was adopted, as shown below in Plate 9.88. Three single stilt marks beneath the wicker work rim. Diameter 180 mm. Mark P2.*

Plate 9.88. *Minton Dove pattern pearlware seven-inch wicker plate, c.1820. Blue painted wicker work. Note the double recessed foot ring used on this relatively late example. Three stilt marks beneath the wicker work rim. Diameter 180 mm.*

Plate 9.89. *Minton Willow pattern pearlware wicker basket, c.1810. The detail of the moulded twig or 'bow' handles can help to distinguish between the very similar designs produced by many factories. The inventories include four sizes of basket, seven, eight, nine and 10-inch, and the handle moulding varies with size. This example corresponds to one of the larger sizes, and exactly matches the Plant pattern example in Plate 5.45 and the Dove pattern basket in Plate 9.90. Note however how the handle ends are blended into the basket on the latter. Details of the handles used on the next smaller size basket are shown in Plate 6.19. Three single stilt marks under a flat base. Overall width 265 mm. Mark P4. An accompanying smaller Willow pattern basket is 218 mm wide with mark P1.*

Plate 9.90. Minton Dove pattern pearlware wicker basket, c.1820. Blue painted edges and wicker work. The moulded body and handles match those of the earlier Willow pattern basket shown in Plate 9.89. Note, however, that on this later example the ends of the handle have been blended into the basket sides whereas on the earlier Minton baskets the handles are attached with the ends bent outwards. Three single stilt marks under a flat base. Width 263 mm.

Plate 9.91. Minton English Scenery pattern basket stand, c.1830. Probably a Stone China body, with the same print as used on the 12-inch meat dish (Plate 7.27). Details of the corresponding basket shape are shown in Plates 8.92 and 8.94. Three triple stilt marks underneath a flat base and three single stilt marks on top of the perforated rim. Width 320 mm. Mark M2.

Plate 9.92. Minton Royal Persian pattern Improved Stone China gadroon-edged dessert bowl, c.1835. The later dessertware shapes introduced with the Opaque and Stone China bodies match the more elaborate dinnerware designs. Double recessed foot ring. Three single stilt marks on top of the rim in the moulding. Diameter 227 mm. Marks M16 and M31.

as shown in Plate 9.89. As expected, the moulded detail of the handles changes slightly with size. Plate 6.19 details handles on a smaller basket size. Further examples of wicker items are shown in Plates 3.19, 3.29, 3.33, 5.34, 5.45 and 5.48.

In the late 1820s new dessertware shapes were introduced to accompany the more elaborate dinner wares being produced. These included gadroon-edged wares in patterns such as Chinese Marine and Royal Persian. Embossed dessert wares were also produced, such as the dishes in Plates 7.84 and 7.85. A new design of basket is shown in Plates 8.92 and 8.94, with Plate 9.91 illustrating the design of the accompanying stand.

Jugs and Mugs

It is apparent from the early copper plate lists (Plates 2.2 and 2.3, Table 2.3) that Minton distinguished between the engravings for jugs and those for ewers and bowls. Although several patterns such as Lily were used for both types of wares, some patterns such as Maypole were listed only for jugs, with others such as Castle only for ewers, basins and chambers. In practice the groups of ware seem to be divided more broadly between patterns for jugs, mugs, loving cups and vases, and those for toilet wares.

The factory inventories include numerous entries for jugs and mugs, some with covers. The main bodies of these items would be turned on the potter's wheel, but block moulds for jug and mug handles and jug 'snips' are listed in 1817. Minton seems to have used the same handle moulds for many years and this can be a considerable aid to attribution, particularly for mugs. Examples of early Minton mugs are shown in Plates 9.94 to 9.96. The angular handle on the large Hermit and Boat pattern mug in Plate 9.94 and the plain loop handle on the Bamboo and Flowers pattern example in Plate 9.96 are both much less commonly found than the characteristic handle on the Maypole mug in Plate 9.95. This distinctive moulded shape was used from the earliest years of production until at least the 1820s, further examples being shown in Plates 4.14 and 7.55, and the Hermit and Boat pattern example in Plate 9.96. A later handle form is shown in Plates 8.8 and 8.71.

Plate 9.93. Match pots were produced in many forms throughout the nineteenth century. This standard spill vase design was made in several sizes and can show some variation of shape. They are often decorated with patterns normally used for jugs and mugs, such as the Maypole pattern example shown in Plates 6.56 and 6.57. Pearlware Bird Chinoiserie pattern, c.1805, height 105 mm. Pearlware Bridge pattern with a print matching that used on the opposite side of the teapot in Plate 4.70, c.1810, height 130 mm, mark P9.

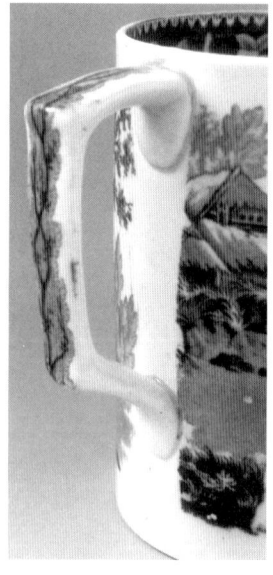

Plate 9.94. *Minton Hermit and Boat pattern pearlware mug, c.1800. The print corresponds to that used on the jugs in Plates 9.97 and 9.98. Note the angular handle design which is unusual for Minton mugs, but is perhaps related to the relatively large size of this piece. Height 140 mm. Mark P8.*

Plate 9.95. *Minton Maypole pattern pearlware mug, c.1815. Note the characteristic handle form which is commonly found on Minton mugs of this period and was used into the 1820s. Height 125 mm.*

Plate 9.96. *Minton pearlware mugs. The Hermit and Boat pattern example with characteristic handle form, c.1800, height 85 mm, mark P4. Bamboo and Flowers pattern with simple loop handle, height 76 mm, marks M1 and P9.*

Plate 9.97. Minton Hermit and Boat pattern pearlware jug, c.1800. The print corresponds to that used on the jug below and the mug in Plate 9.94. Note the characteristic shape and handle form, matching the jugs in Plates 4.19 and 4.53. Height 212 mm. Mark P8.

Plate 9.98. Minton Hermit and Boat pattern pearlware barrel-shaped jug, c.1800. It has a 19-hole perforated strainer across the lip, to retain any skin formed on the surface of hot liquids such as milk, and originally would have had a lid. Note that although the handle form is very similar to that shown above, the inner spur is not joined to the jug. Height 225 mm.

Plate 9.99. Minton footed jugs with plain loop handle. The Hermit and Boat pattern example is early pearlware, c.1805, and is seen to have a turned lip around the upper body. Height 171 mm. The Italian Ruins pattern jug is c.1830, with an Opaque China body. Height 173 mm. Mark M1.

Plate 9.100. Minton Italian Ruins pattern Semi-China jugs, c.1825. The larger jug, height 140 mm, corresponds to the standard 'Dutch' shape, as detailed in the 1884 factory shape book and reproduced in Plate 9.102. A larger size example is shown in Plate 6.54. The smaller jug, height 87 mm, is seen to have the same basic body shape but with a simple loop handle, perhaps because of its relatively small size. Mark M1 to both jugs.

Plate 9.101. *Minton Bamboo and Flowers pattern Semi-China jug, c.1820. This corresponds to the standard 'Roman' shape as detailed in Plate 9.102 and produced by many factories. As with the other jug designs, Minton produced this shape in a range of sizes, other examples being shown in Plates 7.12, 7.54 and 7.56. Height 161 mm. Mark M1.*

Plates 9.97 to 9.101 illustrate various Minton jugs, with the Hermit and Boat pattern examples in Plates 9.97 to 9.99, probably representing the earliest jug forms. The distinctive handle in Plate 9.97, which is similar to the mug handle design, is also used on the jugs in Plates 4.19 and 4.53. Details of 'Roman' and 'Dutch' jugs from the 1884 shape book are shown in Plate 9.102, with corresponding wares in the typical range of sizes being shown in Plates 6.54, 7.12, 7.54, 7.56, 9.100 and 9.101. Very similar jugs were produced by many factories, so attribution is difficult. More elaborate jug shapes were introduced from the late 1820s, such as those shown in Plates 8.6, 8.36, 8.39 and 8.51. Lidded jugs for hot liquids such as milk are shown in Plates 6.50, 8.7 and 9.98. These have a perforated strainer across the lip, intended to hold back any skin that had formed on the liquid surface.

Plate 9.102. *Minton jug designs reproduced from the factory shape book of 1884. These standard jug forms were produced by many factories during the early nineteenth century, so attribution is difficult based on shape alone. The Spode Roman shape was particularly close to Minton's shape. Note that because the body was not moulded, some variation in dimensions occurs.*

JUG, ROMAN SHAPE.   JUG, DUTCH SHAPE

Plate 9.103. Minton English Scenery Semi-China ewer, c.1825 (see also Plate 7.24). This plain design with simple strap handle was probably introduced in the early 1820s to replace the earlier shape illustrated below. Very similar shapes were produced by many factories. The broad lip of ewers enables water to be easily decanted into the accompanying wash basin. Height 240 mm. Mark M2.

Plate 9.104. Minton Bewick Stag pattern pearlware ewer, c.1815 (see also Plate 6.31). This ewer shape was probably made between about 1810 and 1820. It is characterised by the flared base to the strap handle, which is further detailed in Plate 6.52. Height 208 mm.

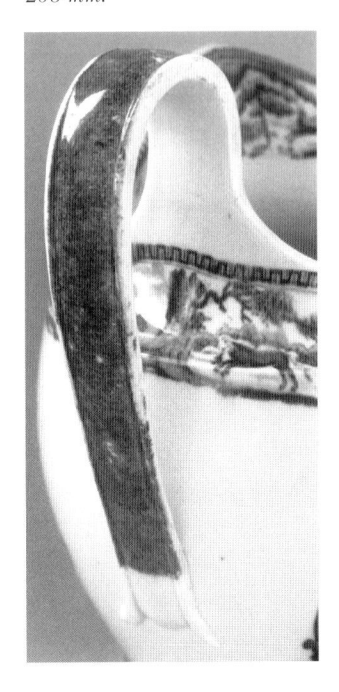

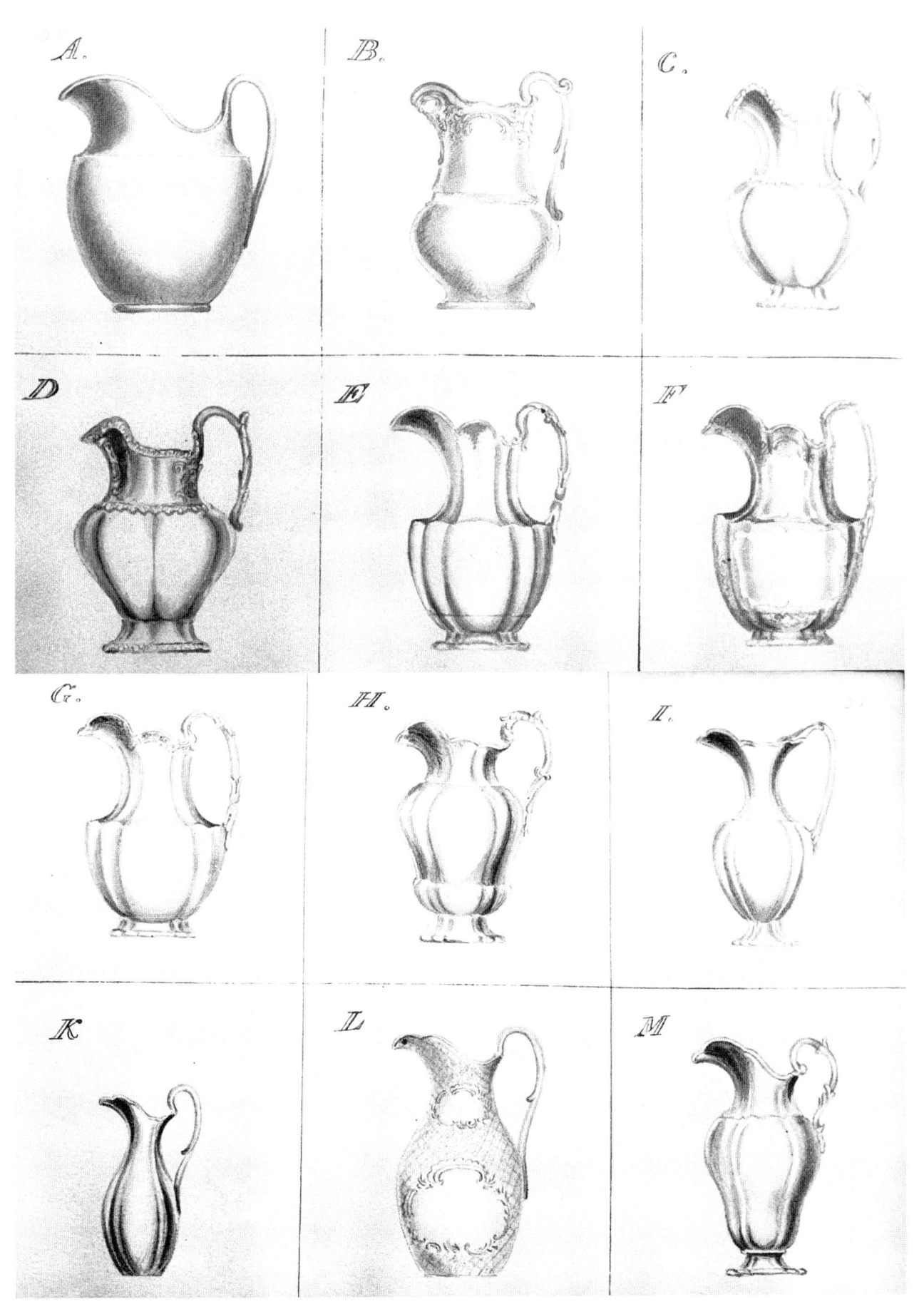

Plate 9.105. Ewer designs reproduced from the earliest remaining Minton factory shape book (MS 1584) which is drawn on paper watermarked 1827. Note the more elaborate and embossed designs typical of the late 1820s and 1830s.

Plate 9.106. Minton Fig Tree Chinoiserie pattern pearlware bowl, c.1800 (see also Plates 4.20 and 4.21). This basic plain circular bowl shape with deep foot was produced in a range of sizes for many years. Diameter 233 mm.

Plate 9.107. Minton Hermit and Boat and Bird Chinoiserie pattern pearlware footed bowl, c.1805 (see also Plate 4.17). Diameter 190 mm. Mark P10.

Toilet Wares

The range of toilet wares produced in the early nineteenth century can be gauged from the inventory entries, which include ewers and bowls, chamber pots, shaving boxes, toothbrush boxes and trays, toilet boxes and round and square soap boxes. Although plain round bowls would not be moulded, the block moulds include six sizes of round hand basins, two oval hand basins and three shaving basins. Also included are moulds for three coach-pots.

Ewers were supplied with a bowl of matching size, and can generally be distinguished from jugs by their wider lip, facilitating rapid decanting of the water. Examples of early Minton ewers are shown in Plates 9.103 and 9.104. The Bewick Stag pattern ewer in Plate 9.104 is the slightly earlier design and has a distinctive

Plate 9.108. Minton Ruined Abbey pattern pearlware flared bowl, c.1820. Although probably introduced before 1820, this shape continued to be used for Semi-China and Opaque China wares. Diameter 311 mm.

Plate 9.109. Minton Italian Ruins pattern Semi-China shallow fluted bowl or dish, c.1825. Moulded foot ring following the bowl shape. Diameter 270 mm. Mark M1.

flared base to its strap handle, as detailed in Plate 6.52. The design of the English Scenery pattern ewer shown in Plate 9.103 was probably introduced in the early 1820s. It has a plain handle design and is very similar to the ewers being produced at other factories. A further example is shown in Plate 7.52. More elaborate ewer shapes were produced from the late 1820s, such as the Florentine Embossed pattern example in Plate 8.12. Details of these later shapes are included in the factory shape book of c.1830, examples being reproduced in Plate 9.105.

The earliest Minton bowl shape is probably the simple round design with deep foot ring shown in Plate 9.106. It was produced until at least 1825, and further examples are shown in Plates 4.13 and 6.60. The Hermit and Boat pattern footed bowl shown in Plate 9.107 is also an early shape, and the Bamboo and Flowers pattern example shown in Plate 7.6 confirms that this shape was also

315

Plate 9.110. Minton Star pattern pearlware unusual footed bowl, c.1815. Diameter 301 mm.

Plate 9.111. Minton Floral Groups pattern toilet wares, c.1825 (see also Plate 7.53). Toilet boxes and toothbrush boxes and trays are included in early inventories. Tray length 173 mm.

produced for many years. The flared bowl design shown in Plates 9.108, 6.53 and 8.38 was probably introduced just before 1820. As indicated in the inventories, the various bowl shapes were all produced in a range of sizes.

Bowls did, of course, have a range of uses and were not just intended as water basins, the fluted Italian Ruins pattern bowl shown in Plate 9.109, the unusual footed bowl in Plate 9.110 and the Chinese Marine bowl shown in Plate 8.50 being examples of more decorative shapes. Further bowl designs were introduced from the late 1820s to accompany the various new ewer shapes such as those shown in Plate 9.105.

The Minton toiletware shapes shown in Plates 9.111 and 9.112 were probably introduced in c.1820 to accompany the standard ewer shape shown in

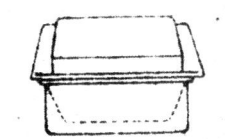

SQUARE SOAP BOX.

Plate 9.112. *Minton Ruined Abbey pattern Opaque China covered soap box, c.1830 (see also Plates 6.61 and 8.35). Above is shown the same basic design reproduced from the 1884 shape book. Early inventories include small and large size square soap boxes and round soap boxes with and without covers. Note that the number and arrangement of the perforations can vary. Box length 105 mm.*

Plate 9.113. *Minton Opaque China covered sponge dish, c.1830 (see also Plate 7.65). The perforated lid is decorated on both sides and has a central 'finger-hole' to aid handling. Width 218 mm. Mark P10.*

Plate 9.103. These relatively plain designs were used over several decades. Very similar items were produced by other factories, so attribution based on shape alone is difficult. The earlier ewer shape shown in Plate 9.104 was accompanied by wares with a slightly indented side, an example being the 'coach-pot' or bordaloue illustrated by Coysh.[8] Some more elaborate and moulded toiletware designs were used after c.1825 with the Opaque and Stone China bodies, examples being shown in Plates 3.77, 7.86, 8.53 and 8.54. The attractive Botanical Vase pattern sponge dish shown below is interesting in that the perforated top is decorated on both sides so that it could act both as a drainer and a lid.

317

Plate 9.114. Minton Bridge pattern pearlware tea wares, c.1805. Oval teapots and square handled cups are recorded in early sales invoices. Details of moulded handles and knobs help in attribution as very similar shaped wares were being produced by many factories during the 1795 to 1810 period.

Plate 9.115. Nankin pattern pearlware toy tea wares, c.1800, probably Minton. The covered sucrier (diameter 65 mm, mark P1) and the teabowl and saucer (mark P1) have gilded rims. The same basic shapes were probably also used for standard size wares.

Tea Wares

The sales accounts discussed in Chapter Two clearly indicated that from the earliest years Minton was producing an extensive range of blue printed earthenware tea wares. The accounts included round cap^t., oval, upright, parapet and egg-shaped teapots, vase-shaped coffee pots and fluted and plain cups with square, bell or round handles. The 1810 factory inventories confirm significant production of printed tea wares, including toast racks, covered butter tubs with stands and toy tea wares. Details of the 1817 inventory entry are given in Plate 2.1, and are seen to include over 57 dozen round teapots. The 1817 block moulds give more detail of teaware shapes, including oval fluted and square-shaped teapots, each in three sizes, and two sizes of oval teapot.

Despite the large output of such blue printed tea sets, relatively few pieces seem to have survived, no doubt a consequence of a high breakage rate. This scarcity of examples combined with the fact that most factories of the time produced tea wares of essentially the same basic design, often decorated with the same chinoiserie-type patterns, makes attribution particularly difficult. Fortunately Minton seems to have used the same teaware moulds over many years, enabling characteristic shapes of handles, spouts, etc., to be established. Also, there is some commonality of design between the earthenware and the more readily identifiable bone china tea wares.

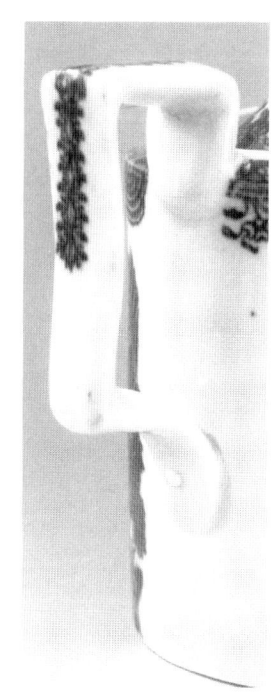

Plate 9.116. Details of Minton Chinaman with Rocket pattern old oval shape pearlware teapot. Apart from differences in the handle design, this shape is very similar to that used by Minton for bone china (Plate 4.84). This basic teapot shape was produced by many factories during the 1795 to 1810 period, in both earthenware and china. It is normally relatively easy to distinguish between the various factory versions by comparison of design details such as handle, knob, spout etc. In some cases however, such as with the teapot shown in Plate 5.9, the designs can be very similar and attribution becomes more problematical. Length 245 mm. Mark P1.

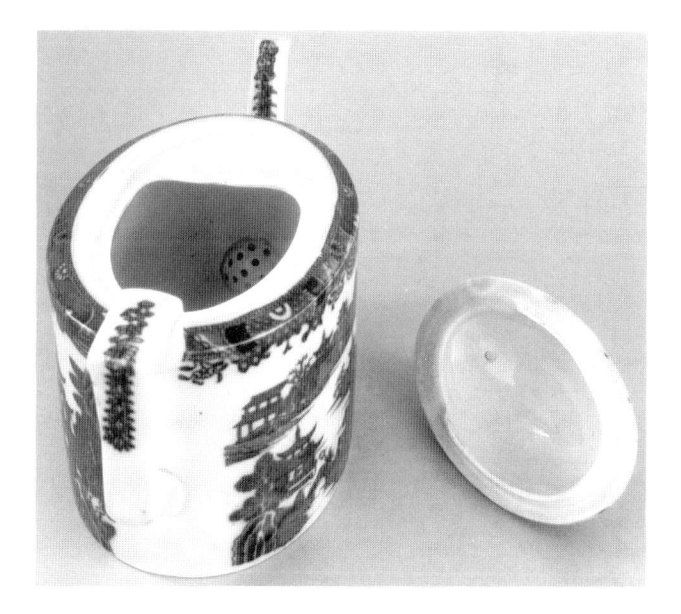

The shape of the Minton old oval shape teapot, although superficially similar to designs from other factories, can normally be distinguished based on the detail shown in Plate 9.116. In addition to moulded oval tea wares, also widely produced at this time were the 'common' round tea wares with plain globular teapots such as the toy tea set shown in Plate 9.115. Attribution of such items is difficult as the body size and shape can vary, although spouts and handles were often moulded.

Minton tea wares of this period were often embellished with gilding, a practice also used by other major factories such as Spode and Ridgeway. Occasionally items are also found with blue painted edge decoration, probably corresponding to the 'blue top't' teawares listed in the early inventories (Table 2.2). It is useful to note, however, that to date no examples of Minton tea wares have been confirmed with ochre painted edges or rims.

Around 1808 Minton introduced a 'new oval' shape teapot for its bone china tea wares. The pearlware teapot shown in Plate 6.68 confirms that the same

Plate 9.117. Details of Minton Farmyard pattern pearlware London shape teapot. Probably corresponding to the square teapot moulds listed in the 1817 inventory and produced between about 1815 and 1825. The distinctive moulded knob, handle and spout distinguish this Minton design from the many similar teapots produced by other factories. This shape was possibly superseded c.1825 by the new 'Cottage' design shown in Plate 9.119. Length 265 mm. Mark P2.

Plate 9.118. Minton pearlware bowls from tea sets. The larger Farmyard pattern Bute shape slop bowl, c.1815, with recessed foot ring, diameter 130 mm and mark P9. Chinese Garden pattern bowl, c.1810, with blue painted rim and raised foot ring, diameter 106 mm and mark P12.

Plate 9.119. Details of the Cottage shape teawares from the Minton shape book of c.1830. This design was probably introduced in the early 1820s. It was used for both bone china and earthenwares. The same distinctive knob design is retained from the earlier shape shown in Plate 9.117.

Plate 9.120. Cottage and Cart pattern toy tea wares, c.1820, probably Minton (see also Plates 6.74 and 6.75). Examples have been noted in pearlware, Semi-China and Opaque China so these attractive toy tea sets were probably still being produced in the late 1820s. Note the characteristic cup handle shape and the correspondence of the basic teapot shape to that shown in Plate 6.73. See also Plate 7.59 for a similar cream jug in the Floral Vases pattern. Interestingly the lid from the covered sucrier (diameter 72 mm), acts well as a stand when removed.

basic shape was used for blue printed earthenwares. This Minton form can normally be distinguished from the very similar designs of other factories by its distinctive moulded spout. The same spout was used by Minton on the round pearlware teapot with a 'cape' around the lid shown in Plate 4.36. The unusual handle form on this teapot was retained for the later 'caped' or 'cap^t' design shown in Plate 6.73. Both basic 'caped' teapot shapes were also produced in the smaller 'toy' size, examples being shown in Plate 3.45 and below in Plate 9.120.

The square shape teapot moulds listed in 1817 probably correspond to the London shape design detailed in Plate 9.117. The distinctive knob, handle and spout normally distinguish this from the numerous other London shape designs, although some non-Minton examples closely copy this shape. Interestingly this earthenware London shape differs significantly from that introduced by Minton for bone china in about 1812, although it is possible that a more closely corresponding earthenware shape remains to be identified.

By c.1825 Minton had introduced new London shape tea wares, termed 'Cottage', as detailed in the shape book of c.1830 and shown above in Plate 9.119. This design was used for both bone china (Plate 4.43) and earthenwares (Plate 11.2).

Plate 9.121. *Minton pearlware Bute shape cups with square rounded cup handles, 1810 to 1820 (see Plates 4.77 and 4.79). Small Farmyard pattern cup diameter 75 mm, mark P1. Earlier Bute shape cups (Plate 5.7) had more angular square handles as detailed on the coffee can in Plate 9.126.*

Plate 9.122. *Farmyard pattern Bute shape cup, c.1815, detailing the square rounded handle, diameter 84 mm. Bamboo and Flowers pattern London shape cup, c.1820 (Plate 7.5).*

Plate 9.123. *Water Lily pattern cup (Plate 6.82) with a weak double-kick loop handle, similar to those used on china by several factories, including Minton.*[10]

Plate 9.124. *Minton China Pattern bone china cup, c.1800. Note the typical early ring handle with thick cross section. Diameter 82 mm.*

Minton produced a typical range of plain and fluted tea bowls, cups and cans with a variety of moulded handles. The early Minton square handle shape is quite distinctive in having a sharp-angled rectangular cross section. It is detailed on the coffee cans in Plates 9.125 and 9.126, but is also found on teacups (Plate 5.7) and custard cups (Plate 9.66). By about 1810 Minton had introduced a different square handle with a rounded, almost circular cross section, as detailed in Plates 9.121 and 9.122. The 1817 block moulds include a set of 'square rounded cup handles'. Interestingly a similar change to a more rounded ring handle occurred with china teacups. It seems that the square rounded handle was only used on cups, with the coffee cans changing to the distinctive loop handle detailed in Plates 9.125 and 9.126. Further Minton cup handle shapes are detailed in Plates 9.122, 9.123, 9.127 and 4.69. The rounded handle with an inner spur shown in Plate 9.127 is also found on the corresponding cream jug.[9]

Minton seems to have mainly used two saucer shapes for early tea wares: the straight sided 'Bute' shape with a recessed foot ring shown in Plate 9.128, and the

Plate 9.125. Minton pearlware coffee cans, c.1800 to 1815. The fluted Chinese Family pattern can (Plate 4.55) and the Bridge pattern can (Plate 4.71) both have the characteristic early square handle form with a sharp-angled rectangular cross section. The Chinese Sports pattern can (height 65 mm, mark P7), which has been overpainted in enamels, has the later rounded loop handle with a single kick.

Plate 9.126. Details of the most commonly found Minton coffee can handles. The distinctive moulded square handle with a sharp-angled rectangular cross section was probably superseded c.1810 by the single kick loop handle on the Floral Vases pattern can.

Plate 9.127. Coffee cups, c.1800 to 1810, probably Minton (see also Plates 4.55 and 4.58). Both cups have distinctive handle forms. The handle with an inner spur on the Chinese Family pattern coffee cup was also used for the corresponding milk jug, and very similar handles were used by several factories on porcelain cups.[11]

323

Plate 9.128. Minton Bute shape saucer with almost straight sides and recessed foot ring. This shape was used on both early pearlware and bone china. It was probably superseded c.1810 by the slightly modified version with rounded sides shown below in Plate 9.130. Similar shapes were used by other factories. Stylised Floral pattern saucer from Plate 5.7.

Plate 9.129. Minton 'Common' shape saucer with rounded sides and raised foot ring. This basic saucer shape was produced by most factories. Minton used it for both normal and toy-size pearlwares and also for bone china. Bridge pattern saucer from Plate 4.74.

Plate 9.130. Minton Bute shape saucer. This shape with rounded sides was probably introduced c.1810 to accompany cups with the new square rounded handles. It may have replaced the straight sided design shown in Plate 9.128. The same basic shape was used by other factories. Chinese Sports pattern saucer from Plate 4.77.

Plate 9.131. Minton London shape Semi-China saucer. Note the distinctive rounded profile and foot ring. This example is decorated in the Bamboo and Flowers pattern (Plate 7.5) and accompanies the cup detailed in Plate 9.122. Ridgeway produced a very similar shape.[12] Note that the bone china Floral Vases pattern London shape saucer in Plate 7.61 differs in having straight sides.

Plate 9.132. Minton Floral Vases pattern Semi-China round sucrier with ring handles, c.1825. Diameter across open top 101 mm. Mark M1.

Plate 9.133. Minton Fallow Deer pattern pearlware stand with gilded rim, c.1815. The creamer in this pattern shown in Plate 6.66 is of a round porringer shape, so this may be a stand for a matching round teapot. Alternatively it may be a Butter tub stand. Recessed foot ring. Diameter 155 mm. Mark P10.

standard or 'common' round sided shape with a raised foot ring shown in Plate 9.129. The same basic shapes were used with early bone china. By c.1810 the round sided 'Bute' shape with recessed foot ring shown in Plate 9.130 had been introduced, probably with the new square rounded cup handles. Both Common and Bute saucer moulds are listed in 1817. By c.1820 the London shape saucer with distinctive profile shown in Plate 9.131 was in use. Opaque and Stone China tea wares were produced with a range of more elaborate and embossed shapes, such as shown in Plates 8.13, 8.14 and 8.24.

Plate 9.134. Minton Bridge pattern pearlware old oval teapot stand, c.1805. Details of the Minton version of this pattern are clearly illustrated on this stand. As shown in Plate 9.114, it fits the teapot in Plate 4.70. Flat base. Width 187 mm. Mark P1.

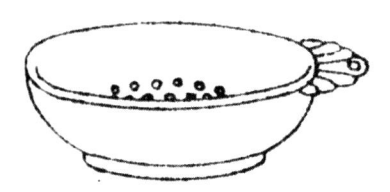

EGG DRAINER.

Plate 9.135. Minton China Pattern pearlware egg drainer, c.1805. The same design with distinctive moulded handle is illustrated in the 1884 shape book, as reproduced above. The precise use of these wares is subject to some doubt, as the perforations are normally too small to allow egg white to drain from its yolk. They may have simply been used to drain water from boiled eggs and some may have been used to strain lemon juice or boiled milk being added to tea. Diameter 95 mm.

Plate 9.136. Minton egg cups. The design of the simple footed Willow pattern egg cup, c.1815, is seen to be still included in the 1884 shape book, as shown below. Height 59 mm. The Semi-China 'frame' shape Floral Vases pattern example, c.1825, is for use with egg cup stands. The turned outer ring, which rested on the stand frame, is clearly visible. The rim diameter of this example is 47 mm.

The early Minton inventories include egg cups, stands with between three and six cups and egg drainers. Such wares are often found decorated with teaware patterns, but given that some supper sets contained egg cups, these would presumably be decorated in dinnerware patterns. The early egg cup stands were of a simple circular footed design with varying numbers of holes, as produced by other factories. The rectangular stand design shown in Plates 9.137 and 9.138 is more distinctive and was probably introduced in the early 1820s. The stands held special 'frame' egg cups which rested in the stand holes on an outer turned ring. It is apparent from Plate 9.137 that there was significant variation in the size of these egg cups, perhaps so that they could accommodate the inevitable differences in egg size.

EGG CUP.

Plate 9.137. Minton Floral Vases pattern Semi-China egg cup stand, c.1825. This rectangular frame design was probably introduced in the early 1820s. It was used with a range of patterns and is also found in smaller four and five-cup sizes, such as the example shown below. The cups vary in both height and diameter, which ranges from 45 to 48 mm. Length of stand 229 mm, marks M1 and P14.

Plate 9.138. Minton Floral Vases pattern Semi-China egg cup stand, c.1825. The cups are Opaque China, c.1830, and may have been bought as replacements. They have smooth bases, compared to the stepped bases of the earlier Semi-China cups shown above. Length of stand 201 mm, marks M1 and P13.

Plate 9.139. Minton Verona pattern perforated 'shaker', c.1835. An unusual item perhaps intended for dispensing sugar. It is refilled through a hole in the base. Note the typical jug handle shape. A clear glazed earthenware body, perhaps Improved Stone China. Height 125 mm. Mark P15.

Plate 9.140. Minton Farmyard pattern pearlware covered box, c.1815. Perhaps intended for butter. Diameter across open top 98 mm. Mark P12.

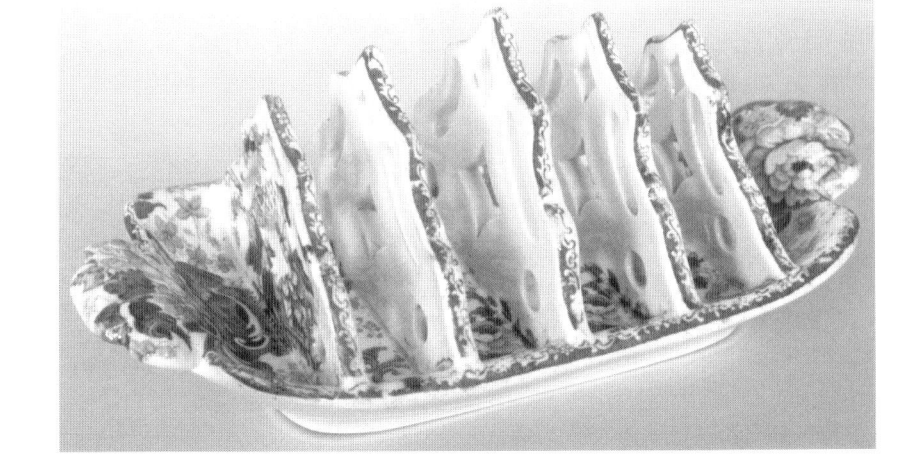

Plate 9.141. Minton Claremont pattern Stone China toast rack, c.1830. Length 203 mm. Mark M20 and an impressed heart 7 mm wide.

Plate 9.142. Minton sick feeders. Flora pattern Opaque China, c.1828, length 148 mm. Verona pattern Stone China, c.1835, length 146 mm. Both examples have a plain four-hole diamond-shaped strainer.

Medical Wares

Minton produced a variety of medical wares including eye cups, pap boats, spitting pots and sick feeders. These were probably mainly supplied in plain creamwares, but some blue printed examples were also made, such as the sick feeders shown in Plate 9.142 and the pap boat in Plate 9.143.

Plate 9.143. Minton Genevese pattern Opaque China pap boat, c.1828. Used for feeding invalids or children. Note the design below from the 1884 shape book. Length 122 mm. Mark M14. Also shown below from the shape book is an eye cup design. These were also included in the 1817 inventory.

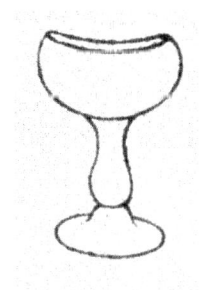

EYE CUP.

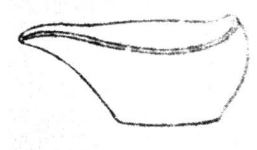

PAP BOAT.

References

1. Minton MS 2759, 3052, Price List (Minton Archives).
2. D. Drakard and P. Holdway, *Spode Printed Ware* (Longman, 1983), p. 39.
3. D. Edwards and R. Hampson, *English Dry Bodied Stoneware* (Antique Collector's Club, 1998), p. 212.
4. C. Blakey and H. Blakey (eds.), *Joseph Sewell's Book of Designs* (St Anthony's Pottery, Newcastle Upon Tyne, republished Tyne & Wear Museum, 1993), p. 8.
5. J. Heywood, *NCS Newsletter*, No. 82, 1991, p. 23.
6. G.A. Godden, *Minton Pottery & Porcelain of the First Period* (Barrie & Jenkins, 1968), plate 29.
7. Godden, *Minton Pottery & Porcelain*, plate 31.
8. A.W. Coysh, *Blue Printed Earthenware 1800-1850* (David & Charles, 1972), p. 104.
9. Godden, *Minton Pottery & Porcelain*, plate 2.
10. M. Berthoud, *An Anthology of British Cups* (Micawber Publications, 1982), p. 34.
11. Berthoud, *British Cups*, p. 36.
12. G.A. Godden, *Staffordshire Porcelain* (Granada Publishing, 1983), p. 229.

Chapter Ten

Early Minton Factory Marks

Although Minton used distinctive marks on much of its first period bone china (see Plate 10.1), no formal factory marks were used on Minton earthenwares for about the first 25 years of production. Some informal marking of many of the early printed earthenwares was done, however, with the application of small workman's marks. From about 1820 onwards more formal marking was introduced as an indication of the type of body, initially Semi-China, followed by Opaque China, Stone China and Improved Stone China. The marks for these later bodies often also included a cursive capital initial M to indicate Minton manufacture, but this was by no means always the case. Later printed marks also normally included the pattern name. Details of these various categories of marks are given below.

Workman's Marks

Throughout Thomas Minton's time at Stoke, it was common practice for workmen in the potteries to be paid on a piecework basis. Payment was dependent on wares being produced 'good from the oven', following successful firing. It was therefore necessary for the larger factories to operate a system whereby the output of the many various craftsmen or teams of transfer printers could be identified. A typical example of such practice was that used at the Spode factory,[1,2] were it is likely that each transferring team had its own individual mark. These Spode marks initially were simple painted lines and symbols, followed by the use of small printed marks.

The earliest Minton printed wares typically have no obvious workman's marks. This was perhaps because the limited scale of production in the early years meant that the workman could be identified from the type of ware or from its pattern. Only as output increased such that more than one team was needed to produce a given pattern would marking strictly become necessary. As with Spode, there is evidence that the earliest of these were simple painted marks. Some early Minton Willow pattern wares have a simple pair of painted crossed lines, as shown in Plate 10.2. The popularity of this pattern makes it a logical candidate for early distinguishing workman's marks. Similar marks, also shown in Plate 10.2, are found on Trophy and Dagger Border with Temple pattern wares. These marks are clearly of limited significance with respect to attribution.

It is apparent that as the Minton factory output grew, the use of workman's marks became much more common, with the adoption of a range of small but distinctive printed marks. A majority of the Minton pearlwares identified to date bear these simple marks, enabling a list to be compiled, as detailed in Table 10.1. This includes each mark reproduced at normal size and, for clarity, magnified approximately fourfold. Although very similar printed marks were also used at other factories, many of the Minton marks are sufficiently distinctive and consistent to be very useful as a tool in attribution, especially when several different marks can be linked to the same pattern. Attribution should, however, always be done with consideration also of the shape, potting characteristics and the type of body and glaze of the ware.

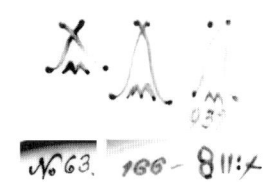

Plate 10.1. Painted marks used on Minton first period bone china. The earliest products have only the pattern number. The crossed swords mark alone seems to have been used for patterns without a formal pattern number, including some printed patterns such as Broseley. The early second period bone china is not normally marked, though some printed patterns had specific marks associated with them, such as shown in Plates 8.104 and 11.5.

Plate 10.2. Examples of early painted workman's marks probably used at the Minton factory, c.1800. Similar marks were used at several factories, including Spode, so attribution based solely on such marks is unreliable.

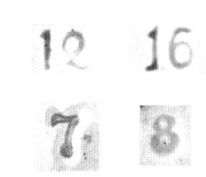

Plate 10.3. Examples of typical impressed marks occasionally found on Minton wares. The 12 and 16 are examples of size marks which started to be used on meat dishes from the early 1820s. The single numerals are workman's marks found on some later pearlwares and Semi-China wares. Very similar marks were used at other factories.

Table 10.2 gives details of the occurrence of workman's marks on the various Minton patterns. To some extent the range of marks depends on the number of examples of each pattern found, with less marks reported for the rarer designs. Following the introduction of the more formal printed marks in about 1820, the number and range of printed workman's marks is seen to be reduced.

Compared to the printed marks, impressed workman's marks are much less common on the earliest Minton earthenwares. Small impressed numerals in the range 1 to 9 and about 3 to 5 mm high are found on some of the later pearlwares. Similar impressed numbers, sometimes slightly larger up to 6 mm high, are also found on some Semi-China wares. Asterisk type marks were also used. From the early 1820s impressed numbers approximately 7 mm high were used as size marks on meat dishes and similar items. Typical examples of these marks are shown in Plate 10.3. In isolation they are not particularly helpful as a guide to attribution as very similar impressed marks were used at other factories.

Formal Marks

The use of more formal marks on Minton earthenwares seems to date from around 1820. Such marks were not intended to indicate the factory name, but rather the type of body used. This was possibly done as an aid to sales as invariably the mark implies some variation of the more exclusive bone china body. This was despite the fact that the body was still earthenware and not translucent. The earliest of these was Semi-China, followed by Opaque China and Stone China and then Improved Stone China. Minton was not alone in using such marks, with the same body names being common to many contemporary factories. Thus care must be taken when trying to use these marks as an aid to attribution. Fortunately the marks used by Minton, once identified, can normally be distinguished from the similar marks of other factories, although in some cases the differences are slight. There is also the possibility that because the marks were normally engraved with the pattern on the copper plate engravings, they would pass to and could be used by another factory if the plates were sold on.

Details of various formal printed marks found on Minton wares up to the end of the Thomas Minton period in 1836 are given in Table 10.3, with Table 10.4 showing similar or associated marks by other makers. Many of the Minton marks include the pattern name and, from the late 1820s, often a cursive M to represent Minton. At the end of Table 10.3 is the distinctive Minton Improved Stone China impressed mark, with the very similar mark used by Meigh given in Table 10.4. For clarity details of these marks as transcribed by Mumford are also given.[3]

It is important to note that the association of the printed marks with the original pattern engravings means that the mark is not necessarily a true indication of the actual body used. For example patterns introduced during the Semi-China period, which was probably between about 1820 and 1825, would incorporate a Semi-China type mark. If the pattern was used in say 1830 on Stone China, the original Semi-China mark would still be used. Likewise when the earlier pearlware patterns were used on the later bodies, no formal printed mark is normally found as none would have been included on the original engraving.

References

1. D. Drakard and P. Holdway, *Spode Printed Ware* (Longman, 1983), p. 212
2. R. Copeland, *Spode's Willow Pattern and other Designs after the Chinese*, 3rd ed. (Studio Vista, 1999), p. 189.
3. H. Mumford, *Friends of Blue Bulletin*, No. 71, 1991.

Table 10.1. Characteristic Early Minton Printed Workman's Marks

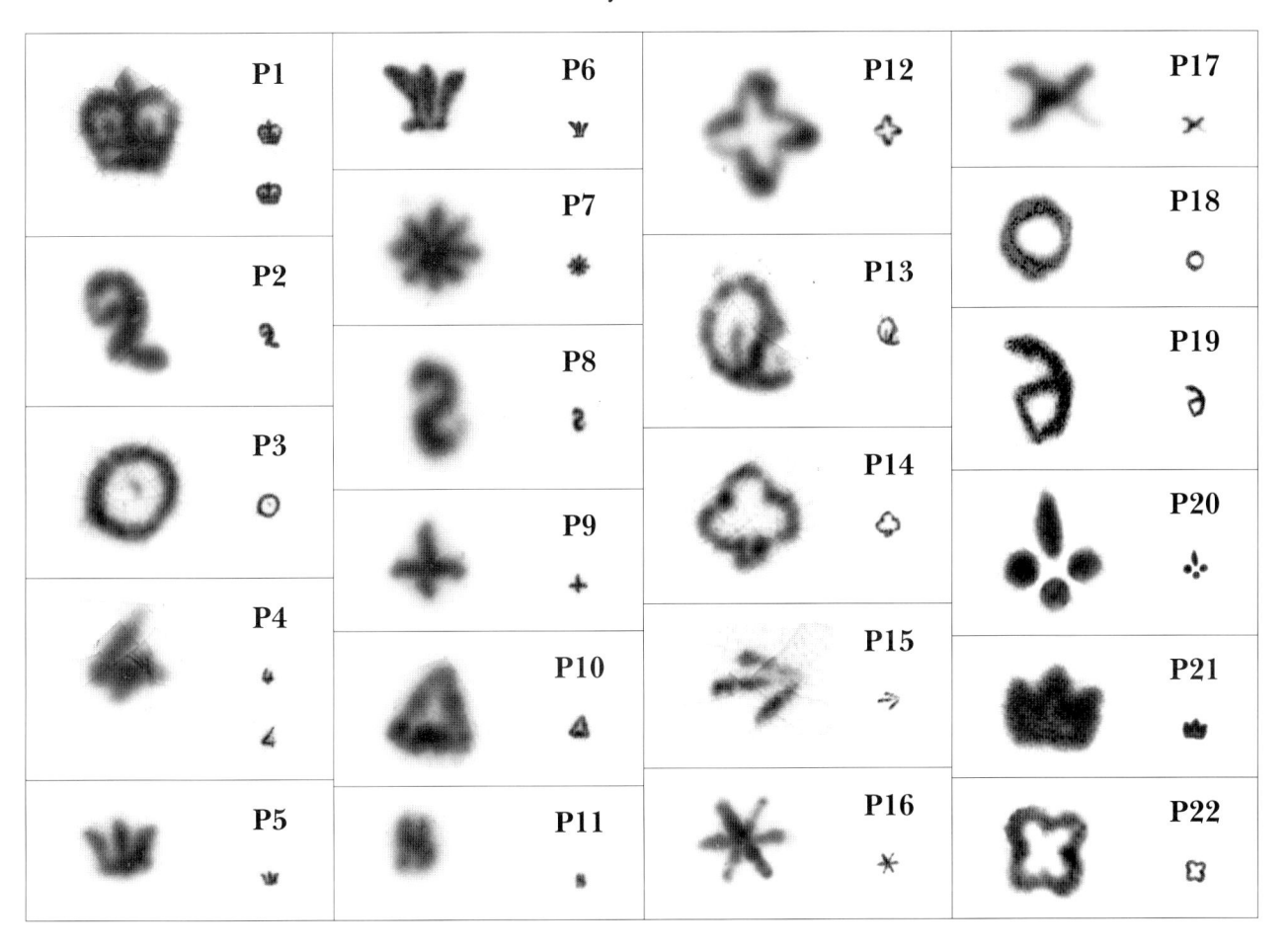

Table 10.2. Recorded Usage of Characteristic Early Minton Printed Workman's Marks

Hermit, *P1, P2, P7*
Hermit and Boat, *P4, P8, P10, P12*
Bird Chinoiserie, *P10*
One Man Chinoiserie, *P5*
Willow, *P1, P11, P14, P17*
Chaplin, *P9*
Broseley, *P14*
Fisherman, *P6, P10*
Chinese Family, *P1, P9, P10*
Pearl River House, *P3, P10*
Chinese Garden, *P3, P12*
Nankin, *P1*
Bridge, *P1, P3, P4, P9, P18*
Chinese Sports, *P1, P5, P6, P7*
Oriental Family, *P9*
Chinaman with Rocket, *P1*
China Pattern, *P1*
Lily, *P1, P2, P3, P9*
Stylised Floral, *P4, P7*
Pinwheels, *P1, P11*
Basket, *P5, P7, P14, P17*
Dahlia, *P7*
Plant, *P4*
Shepherd, *P2*

Queen of Sheba, *P1, P11*
Roman, *P5, P6, P7*
Bird, *P2, P4*
Bewick Stag, *P1, P2*
Camel and Giraffe, *P4*
Monk's Rock, *P4, P5, P6, P14*
Castle Gateway, *P12, P14*
Maypole, *P13, P14*
Dove, *P4*
Ruined Abbey, *P13*
Fallow Deer, *P1, P10, P11*
Cottage and Cows, *P2*
Domed Building, *P12*
Farmyard, *P1, P2, P9, P12*
Forbes Castle, *P15*
Cottage and Cart, *P2, P13, P16*
Apple Tree, *P12*
Benevolent Cottagers, *P4, P6*
Water Lily, *P1, P6*
Bamboo and Flowers, *P2, P9, P13, P15*
Dying Tree, *P15*
Italian Ruins, *P18*
English Scenery, *P16*
Miniature Series, *P17*

Girl with Puppies, *P13*
Floral Cottage, *P2*
Botanical, *P16*
Floral Vases, *P13, P14, P16*
Leaf, *P2*
Botanical Vase, *P10*
Filigree, *P4, P14*
Dresden, *P18*
Florentine, *P13, P14, P20*
Florentine Embossed, *P4*
Dresden Flowers, *P2*
Flora, *P2*
Corinthian, *P15, P16*
Genevese, *P10, P16, P19*
Chinese Marine, *P10, P15, P16, P19, P21, P22*
Royal Persian, *P18*
Berlin Chaplet, *P14*
Claremont, *P21*
Trellis and Plants, *P16*
Arabesque, *P16, P22*
Lace Border, *P15*
Verona, *P22*
Sicilian, *P4, P15, P22*

Table 10.3. Early Minton Formal Printed and Impressed Marks

M1. *Used on several patterns (pp. 153–59 and 176–82) and found on some Broseley pattern copper plates (p.68). Imitation marks include U2a and U2b.*

M2. *Used on the English Scenery series (p. 160).*

M3. *Used on the Minton Miniature series (p. 172). Each mark names the view featured in the print. Found on several copper plates.*

M4. *Used on the Minton Filigree pattern (p. 184). Found on a copper plate engraving (Plate 7.75). An imitation mark includes the initials 'JC & S' (mark U3).*

M5. *Used on the Dresden pattern (p. 190). Note the related mark M6.*

M6. *Used on a version of the Dresden pattern found on embossed wares probably made by Minton (p. 191). A similar mark was used by the Don pottery.*

M6a. *Used on the Japan-type Pattern No. 53 (Plate 8.71). The same mark was presumably used with other pattern numbers.*

M7. *Used on the Florentine pattern (p. 195).*

M8. *Used on a version of the Florentine pattern found on embossed wares (p. 199).*

M9. *Used on the Dresden Flowers pattern (p. 200). Found on several copper plates.*

M10. *Used on the Flora pattern (p. 200–1).*

M11. *Used on the Swiss Cottage pattern (p. 201).*

M12. *Used on the Corinthian pattern (p. 203). Note the related mark M13.*

M13. *Used on a version of the Corinthian pattern found on embossed wares (p. 203).*

M14. *Used on the Genevese pattern (p. 206). Found on several copper plates. Imitation marks have different maker's initials.*

M15. *Used on the Chinese Marine pattern (p. 212). Imitation marks either have different maker's initials, such as mark U5, or no initial.*

M16. *Used on the Royal Persian pattern (p. 218). Note the related mark M16a.*

M16a. *Used on the Royal Persian pattern (p. 218). Note the related mark M16.*

M17. *Used on the Wreath pattern (p. 220).*

M18. *Used on the Berlin Roses pattern (p. 220). A copper plate has the cartouche mark without the heraldic lion, suggesting that this may have been applied separately.*

M19. *Used on the Berlin Chaplet pattern (p. 220). An imitation mark was used by another factory, mark U6.*

M20. *Used on the Claremont pattern (p. 224). Found on several copper plates.*

M21. *Used on a series featuring landscape views (p. 225). It includes a typical cursive M and the heraldic lion closely matches those in M18 and M19. The mark has yet to be found on wares attributable to Minton, so either it is an imitation or the copper plates with mark were sold on.*

M22. *Used on the Amhurst Japan pattern (p. 226). The number indicates the style of additional painted decoration, with 62 probably the earliest. Other versions include 824, 3768, 3769 and 9437.*

M23. *Used on the Trellis and Plants pattern (p. 228).*

M24. *Used on the Arabesque pattern (p. 230).*

M25. *Used on the Lace Border pattern (p. 232).*

M26. *Used on the Rose and Violet Wreath pattern (p. 234). Found on a copper plate.*

M27. *Used on the Rose and Violet Star pattern (p. 235).*

M28. *Used on the Verona pattern (p. 236). Found on several copper plates. Cursive M not always present.*

M29. *Used on the Sicilian pattern (p. 240). An imitation mark was used by Pountney and Allies, mark U7.*

M30. *Used on the Floweret pattern (p. 246). Found on a copper plate.*

M31. *An impressed mark probably introduced in the early 1830s and used on wares decorated with a range of patterns (transcribed below for clarity). Note the apparently meaningless border symbols. Mark widths between 15 and 30 mm have been noted. A very similar mark was used by Charles Meigh, mark U8.*

335

Table 10.4 Some associated marks by other makers

U1. *Characteristic printed mark from the Passion Flower border series used on a meat dish (Plate 7.23) imitating the view of Ripon in the Minton English Scenery series.*

U2a. *Printed seal mark by an unknown maker imitating the Minton Semi-China mark M1 and used on a version of the Floral Vases pattern (Plate 7.63).*

U2b. *Printed seal mark by an unknown maker imitating the Minton Semi-China mark M1 and used on a jug decorated with a floral print painted over in coloured enamels (see Plate 7.88).*

U3. *Printed mark imitating the Minton mark M4 and used on a black printed Filigree pattern dish (Plate 7.76). Neither the initials nor the accompanying impressed mark have been linked to any factory.*

U4. *Printed mark used on a version of the Floral Vases pattern (Plate 7.57). A similar type of mark was used by the Swillington Bridge pottery in Yorkshire.*

U5. *Printed mark imitating the Minton mark M15 and used on a version of the Chinese Marine pattern (Plate 8.42). Numerous copies of this mark are found with different initial letters, including B, B&S, B&G, F, G, L.W. and O, some of which have been linked to specific factories (see p. 212).*

U6. *Printed mark by an unknown maker imitating the Minton mark M18 and used on a version of the Berlin Chaplet pattern (Plate 8.63).*

U7. *Printed mark imitating the Minton mark M29 and used on a version of the Sicilian pattern (Plate 8.93). Also visible is the impressed name mark for Pountney and Allies.*

U8. *Impressed seal mark by Charles Meigh imitating the Minton Improved Stone China mark M31 (also transcribed below for clarity). Note the use of non italicised letters and, with some use of greek symbols, MEIGH and HANLEY in the border, which distinguish this mark from the Minton one.*

Chapter Eleven

Black Printed Wares and Bat Prints

Black printing on pottery was introduced during the eighteenth century and by 1810 factories such as New Hall, Miles Mason and Spode were using prints of landscapes, flowers and shells to decorate porcelain or bone china tea sets. A technique for applying such decoration was bat printing, in which a small 'bat' or sheet of jelly-like glue was used to transfer the pattern from the engraving onto the glaze of the article being decorated. A full and interesting account of the process is given by Drakard and Holdway.[1] An advantage of bat printing was that the glue could stretch to accommodate the shape of the piece being printed. The resultant slight distortion of the print can sometimes be detected. The degree to which the bat prints fused with the glaze depended on the colour being used and the temperature of firing. With some examples it is difficult to be sure if a print has been applied on or under the glaze.

Minton seems to have made only limited use of bat printing to decorate its first period bone china. A recent review of patterns[2] identified only pattern numbers 534, 619, 634 and 723, all featuring shell prints as shown in Plate 11.1. More extensive use of bat printing is indicated by the 1810 inventory copper plate list (Plate 2.2), which includes 33 'plates for black printing & printing on the glaze'. Although some of these engravings may have been for 'pluck and dust decoration'[1] on bone china, such as with pattern numbers[2] 204, 236, 242 and 409, it is likely that they were also used to print on earthenwares. There are specific entries for black printed wares in the inventories between 1818 and 1825 (Table 2.2). The 1821 entry includes reference to cups, saucers and cans, oval teapots and creamers, 'capped' teapots, plain toy teas, embossed four, five and six-inch plates, beakers, jugs, mugs

Plate 11.1. *Minton first period bone china cup and saucer printed in black with shells and gilded, pattern number 619 c.1811. The decoration has been 'bat printed' onto the glaze. Thirty-three copper plates for black and on-glaze printing are included in the 1810 inventory. Diameter of saucer 135 mm. Both pieces with blue painted Sevres-type mark including 'M' and '619'.*

Plate 11.2a (see also Plate 11.2b opposite). Minton black bat printed earthenware teapot with black painted rim and knob, c.1825. This teapot corresponds to the Cottage shape included in the factory shape book of c.1830, and it matches the bone china Broseley pattern example shown in Plate 4.43. The print is not in the Bat Print book. It is based on an engraving of Beeston Castle (see Plate 6.36) and the same view was used by Minton on the 20-inch meat dish in the Monk's Rock series. Flat triangular 15-hole strainer. Length 275 mm.

and egg cups. A more substantial output of black printed china tea wares is apparent from about 1825, when bone china was re-introduced at the factory.

First period Minton china can normally be identified from the painted pattern number and Sevres-type mark. The earthenwares and second period china are not normally marked, so attribution must depend more upon shape and the details of prints. Fortunately a record of some early prints is provided by a book remaining at the factory titled 'Bat Prints'.[3] It is undated but was still in use at the end of the nineteenth century as some of the prints are quite late and one (B39) is dated 1882. Many of the prints seem to be relatively early and some probably date from before 1836. They seem to be mainly intended for tea wares and are roughly grouped into subjects including landscapes, flowers and shells. Many of the landscape designs are reproduced, approximately to scale, at the end of this chapter and numbered B1 to B59. Although normally printed in black, the prints are also sometimes found in other colours including blue, brown and green.

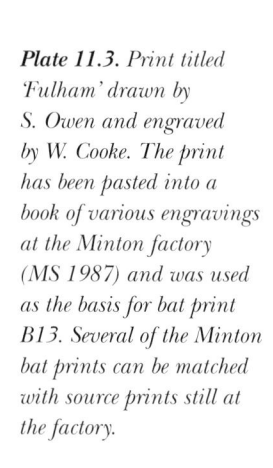

Plate 11.3. Print titled 'Fulham' drawn by S. Owen and engraved by W. Cooke. The print has been pasted into a book of various engravings at the Minton factory (MS 1987) and was used as the basis for bat print B13. Several of the Minton bat prints can be matched with source prints still at the factory.

Plate 11.2b. Details of the opposite side of the teapot shown in Plate 11.2a. The print of Southend is included in the Bat Print book (B2) as are the small prints used on the lid (B3).

Examples of tea wares which can be linked directly to these Minton prints are shown in Plates 11.2 to 11.9. Some have clearly been 'Bat printed' on the glaze, such as the teapot in Plate 11.2, whereas some others appear to be underglaze printed. Interestingly some of the prints included in the Bat Print book correspond to designs used for underglaze blue printing, including Italian Ruins (B11), Forbes Castle (B10), the Minton miniature series (B4 to B6), and the Monk's Rock series (B7 and Plate 11.2a). Source prints for some of the engravings were found at the factory, such as the view of Fulham Bridge in Plate 11.3 and used as a basis for print B13. Other source prints are shown in Plate 2.7 and Plates 7.47 to 7.49.

References

1. D. Drakard and P. Holdway, *Spode Printed Ware* (Longman, 1983), p. 40.
2. R. Cumming and M. Berthoud, *Minton Patterns of the First Period* (Micawber Publications, 1997).
3. Minton MS 3580, Bat Print Book (Minton Archives).

Plate 11.4. Minton underglaze black printed pearlware teapot with black painted rims and knob, c.1820. Decorated on each side with print B1, which is based on an original source print featuring Mr Keene's residence on the Thames (see Plate 7.47). The lid is decorated with prints B3, as used on the teapot shown in Plate 11.2. Length 233 mm.

Plate 11.5. *Minton Felspar Porcelain Berlin Embossed shape teacup decorated underglaze in blue with prints of fruit, with gilding, c.1830. A piece of excellent quality with additional printing inside the cup. Diameter 79 mm. Printed mark as shown above.*

Plate 11.6. *Minton bone china tea plate with black bat printed decoration, c.1830. Decorated with prints from the factory Bat Print book, including B23, B25 and B35. An accompanying cup and saucer are shown in Plate 11.7 below. Diameter 197 mm.*

Plate 11.7. *Minton bone china French shape coffee cup and tea saucer with black bat printed decoration, c.1830. Decorated with prints from the factory Bat Print book, including B23, B25 and B34. Saucer diameter 154 mm, cup diameter 83 mm.*

Plate 11.8a (above left) & 11.8b (above right). Pair of Minton bone china saucers printed underglaze in blue, c.1830. Both prints are included in the factory Bat Print book (B4 and B5), and the same views were used for designs in the Minton Miniature series. The print titled 'St Mary's Church, Dover' is based on a source print of that name published in 1814 and still at the factory (Plate 7.49). Diameters 143 and 145 mm.

Plate 11.9. Minton bone china toy cup and saucer with brown bat printed decoration, c.1835. The decoration includes print B24 from the factory Bat Print book. Saucer diameter 116 mm, cup diameter 65 mm.

Plate 11.10. Minton bone china teacup and saucer with brown bat printed decoration and gilding, c.1840. Saucer diameter 143 mm, cup diameter 84 mm. Painted pattern number 3748.

B1

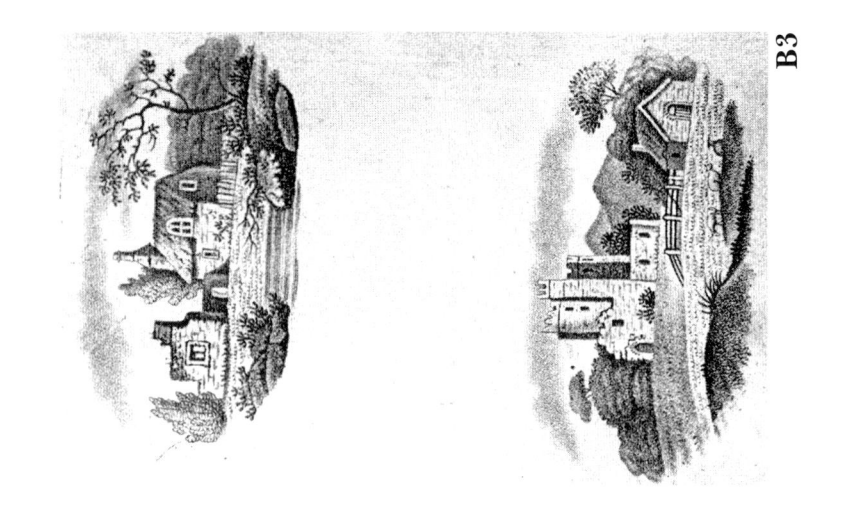

B2

B3

B5

B7

B4

B6

B8

B10

B9

B11

B12

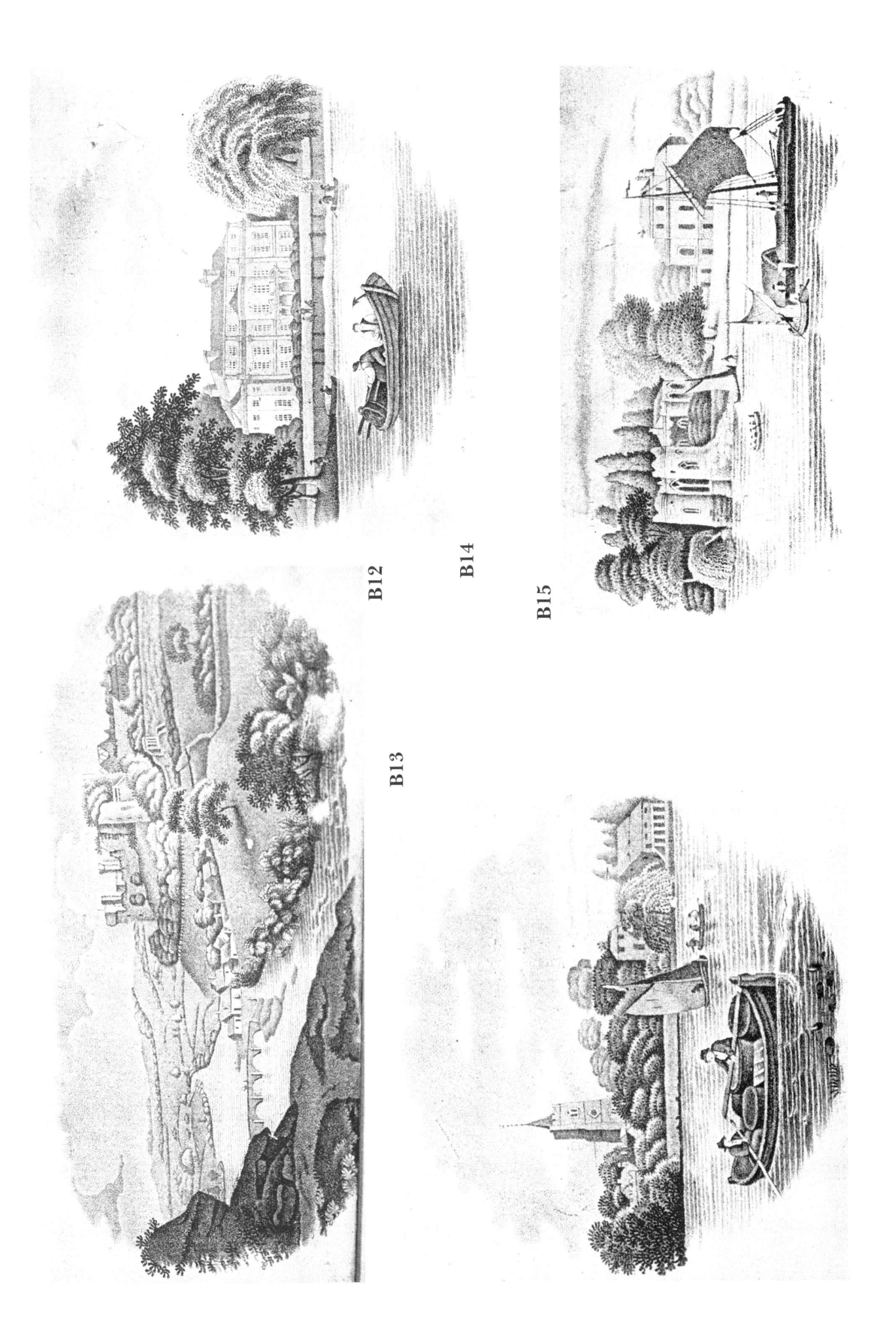

B13

B14

B15

B16

B17

B18

B19

B20

B21

B22

B24

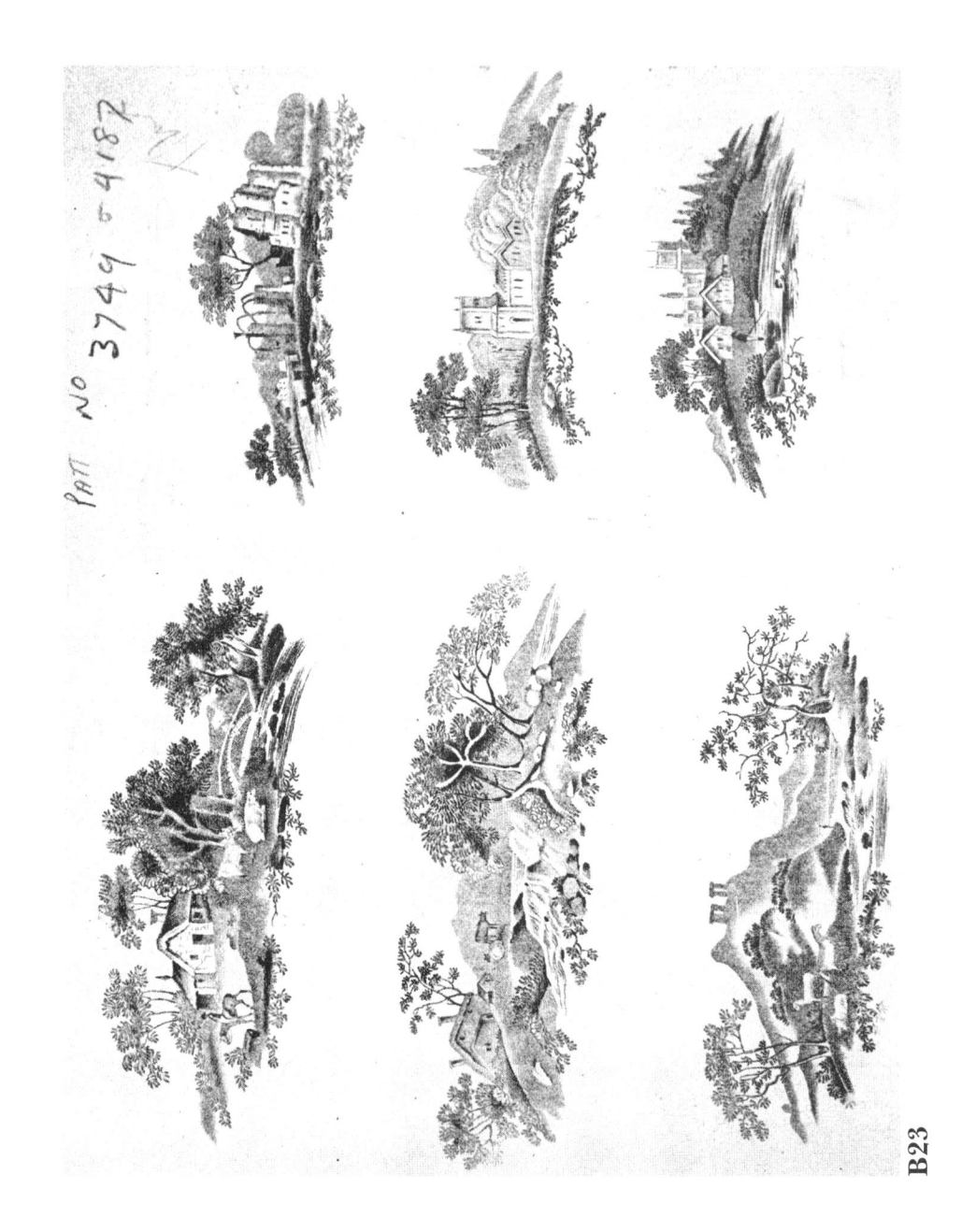

B25

B23

348

B26

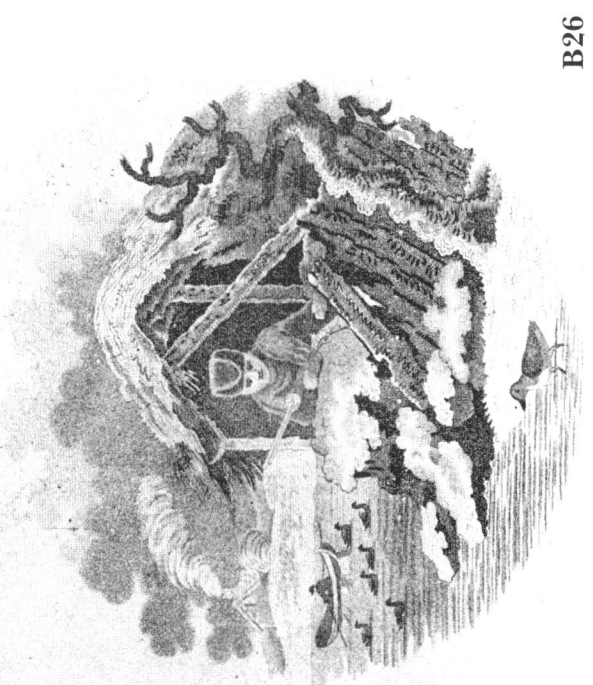

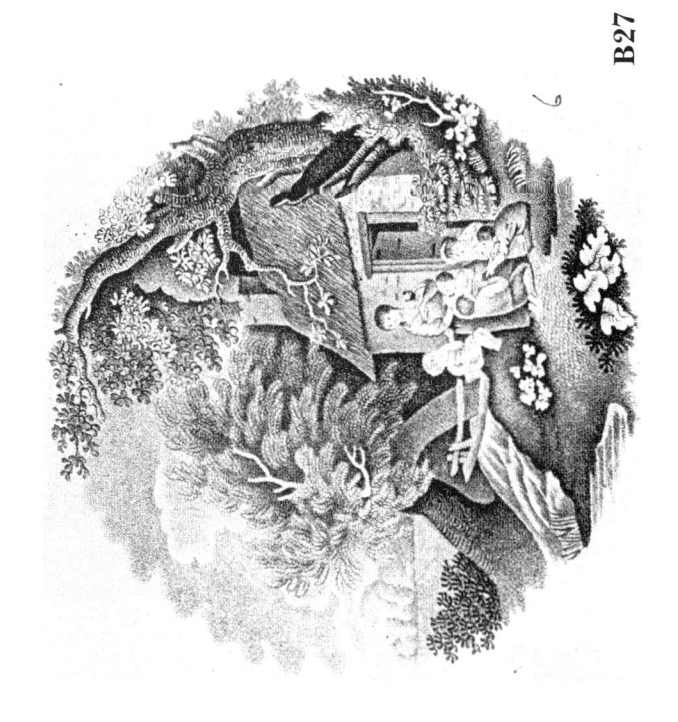

B27

B28

B29

B30

B31

B32 WILTON ABBEY.

B33

B35

B37

B34

B36

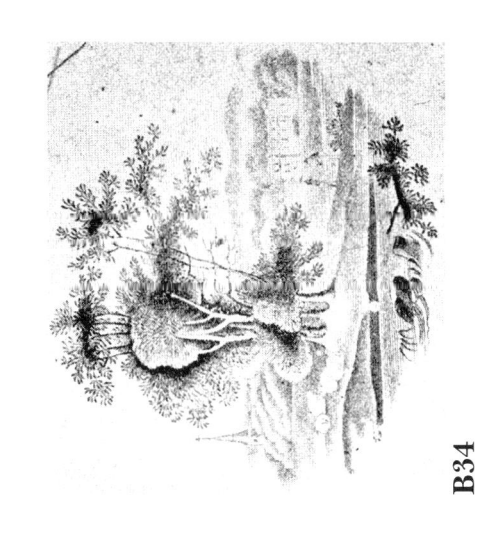

B40

LAKE HOUSE, WILTS.
Seat of Rev.d E. DUKE.

B41

CROM CASTLE.

B38

CLARENDON HOUSE.

B39

BUSBRIDGE HALL 1882.

B42

B44

B43

B45

B46 — The Cloister Front of the New Building, St John's College.

B47 — Easterton Chapel.

B48 — The Fitzwilliam Museum.

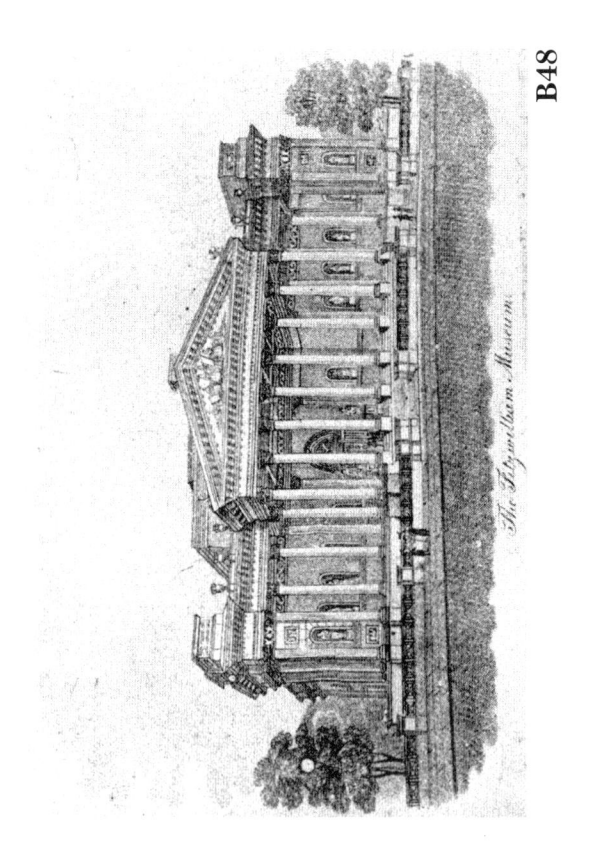

B49 — Library & New Buildings, Trinity College.

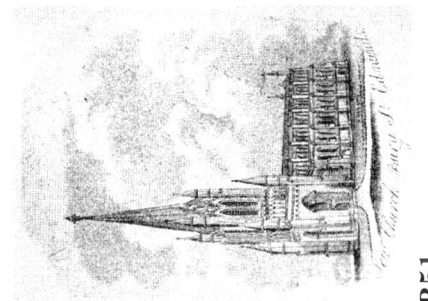

B52

B53

B51

B55

B50

B54

355

B56

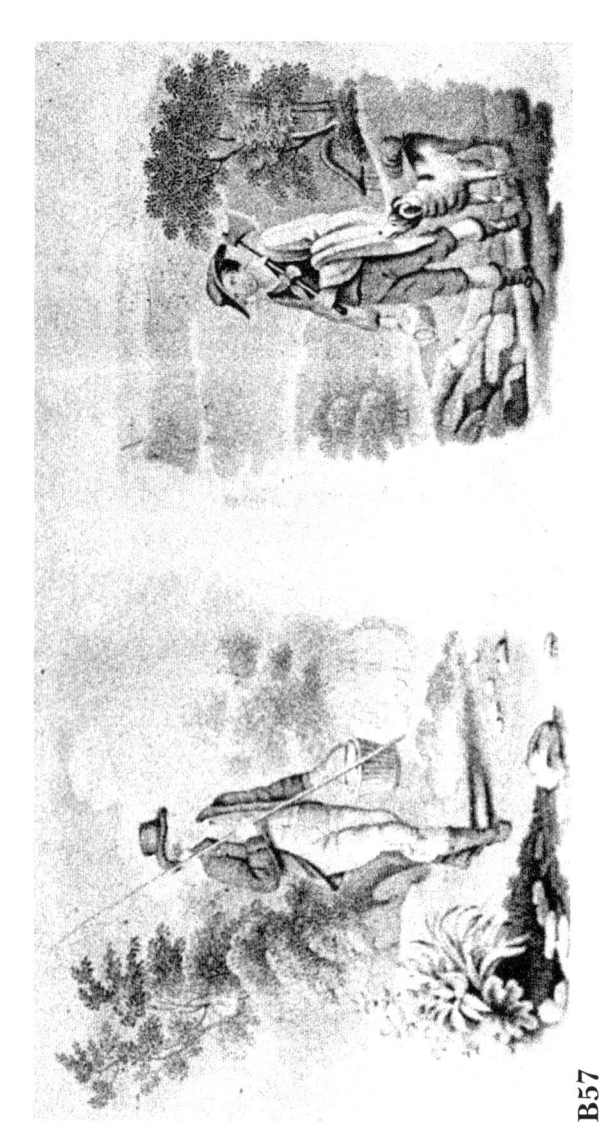

B57

B58

B59

356

Appendix

Dinnerware Designs from an early Minton Factory Shape Book

The earliest remaining shape book (Minton MS 1584) is drawn on paper watermarked for 1827. It starts with details of 50 tableware designs, followed by separate sections for tea wares and then jugs. Each design is lettered, A to Z then AA to ZZ, although some letters were not used. The first 31 dinnerware entries are by the same hand and most may have been entered when the book was started to represent the designs available at that time. This initial set of entries is not in chronological order and some of the shapes would appear to have been introduced much earlier than 1827. The later designs entered in the book are in a different style, probably by other draughtsmen. The first 30 dinnerware designs are reproduced in this Appendix. The typical layout for each design can be seen to include details of the soup and sauce tureens, the covered dish, the salad bowl and a plan of the basic profile. It has been reported that the thirty-seventh entry, NN, was used during the Minton & Boyle period (1836 to 1841) and that a shape registered in 1846 was not included in the book.[1]

1. G.A. Godden, *Minton Pottery & Porcelain of the First Period* (Barrie & Jenkins, 1968), p. 40.

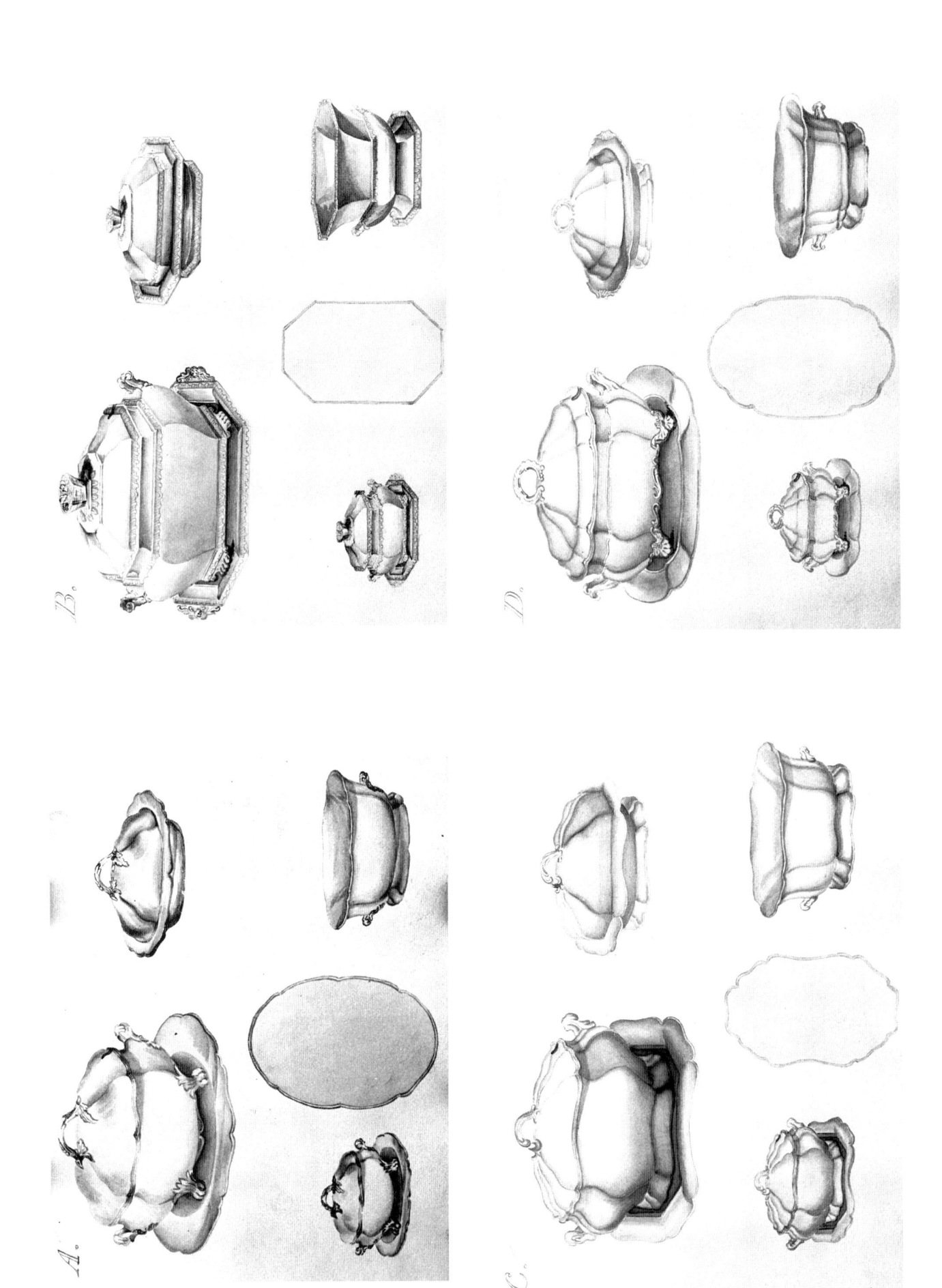

A.

B.

C.

D.

359

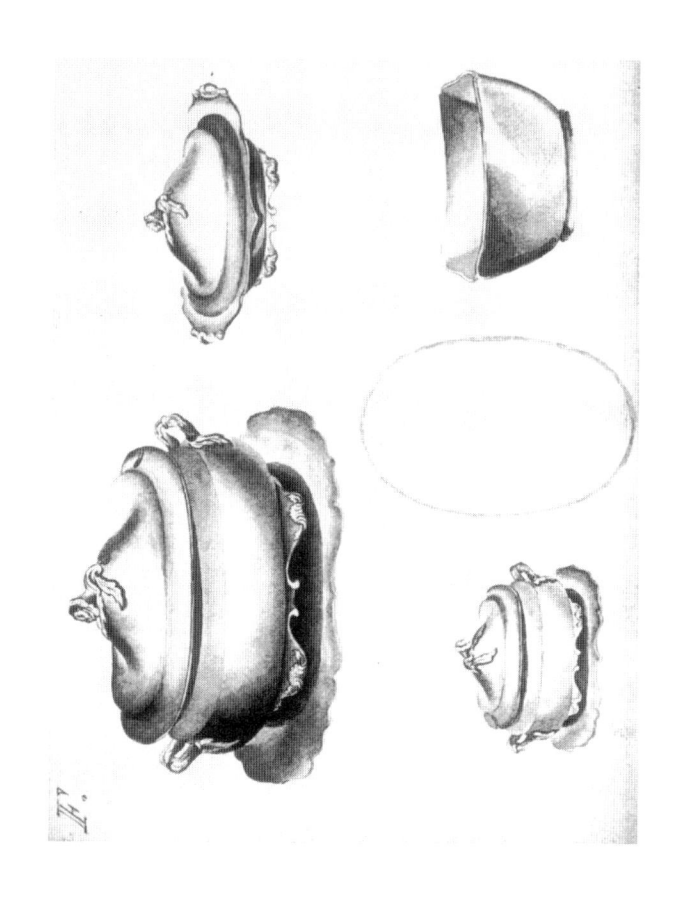

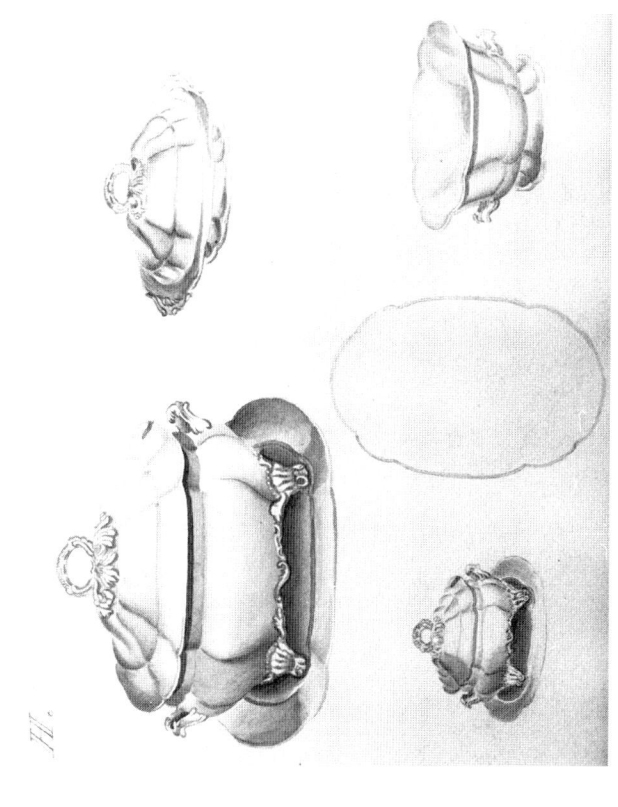

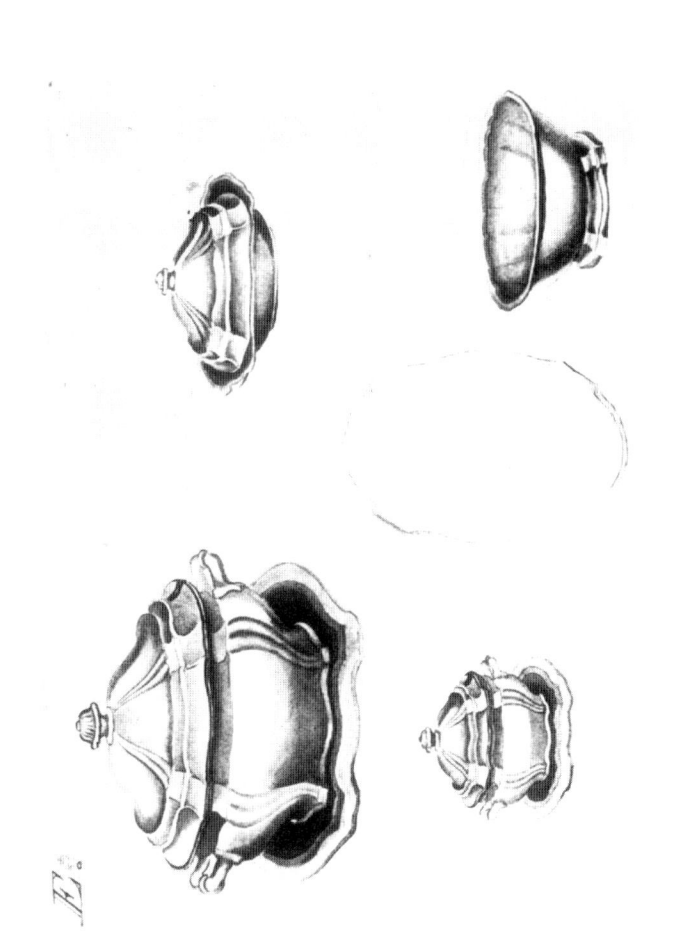

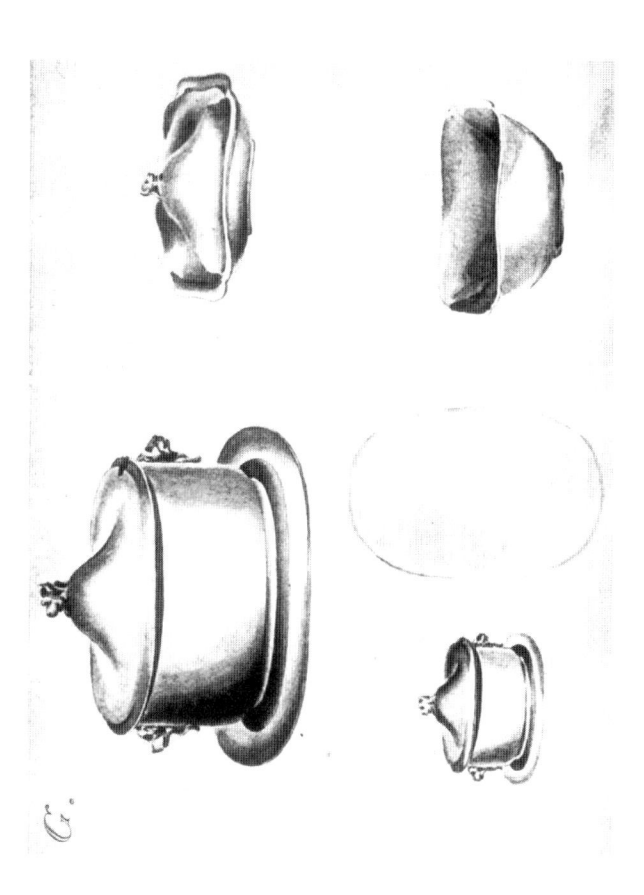

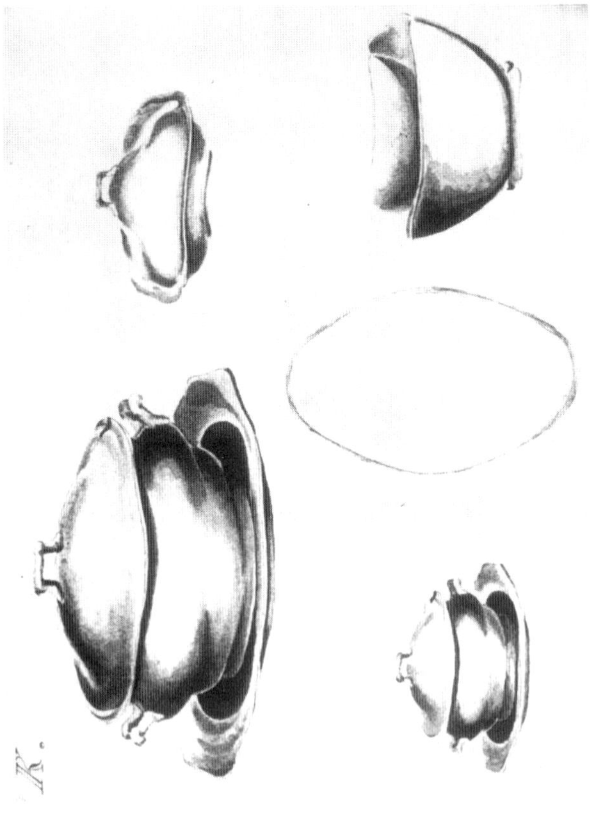
K.

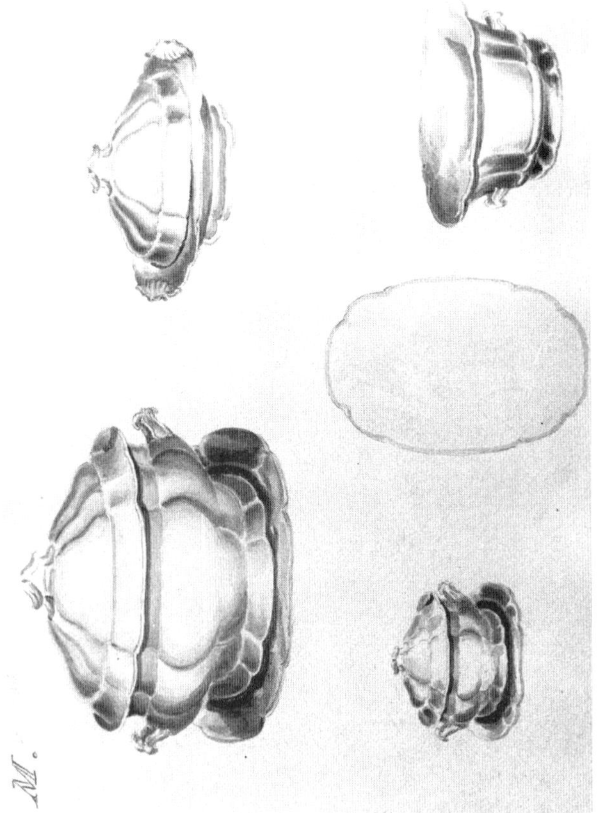
M.

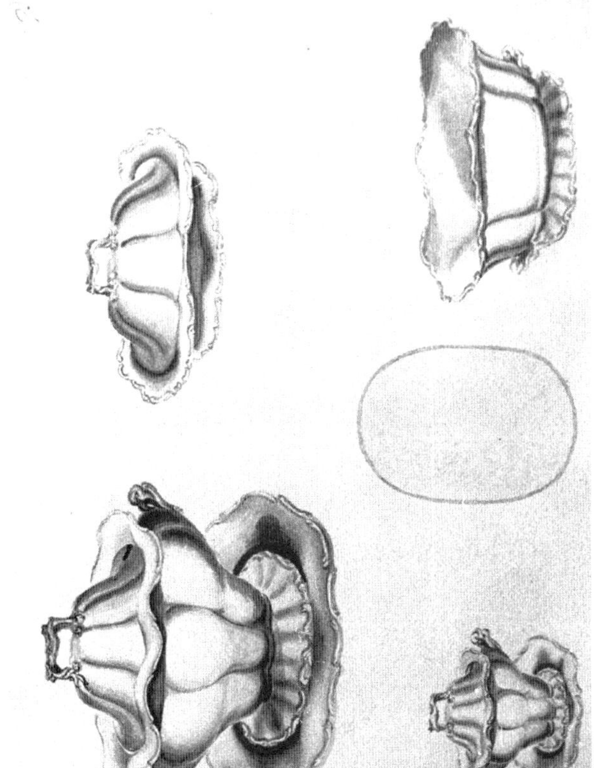
I.

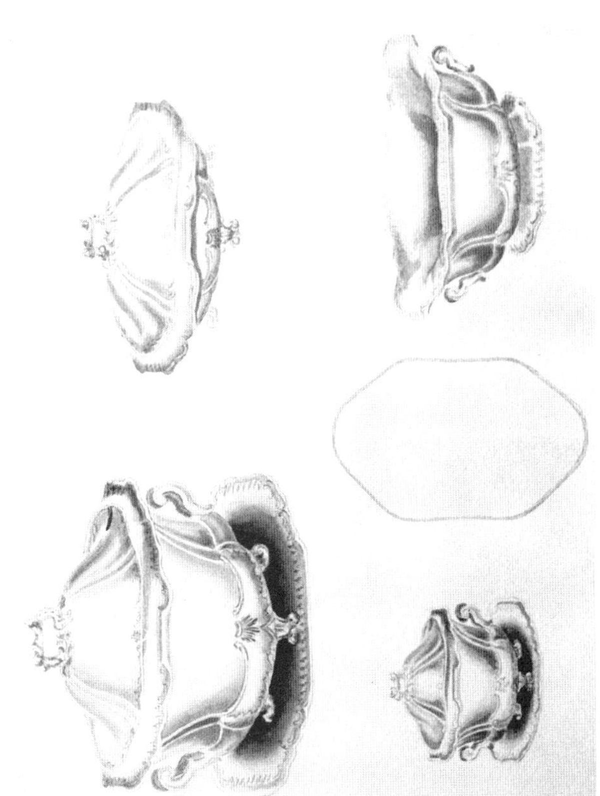
L.

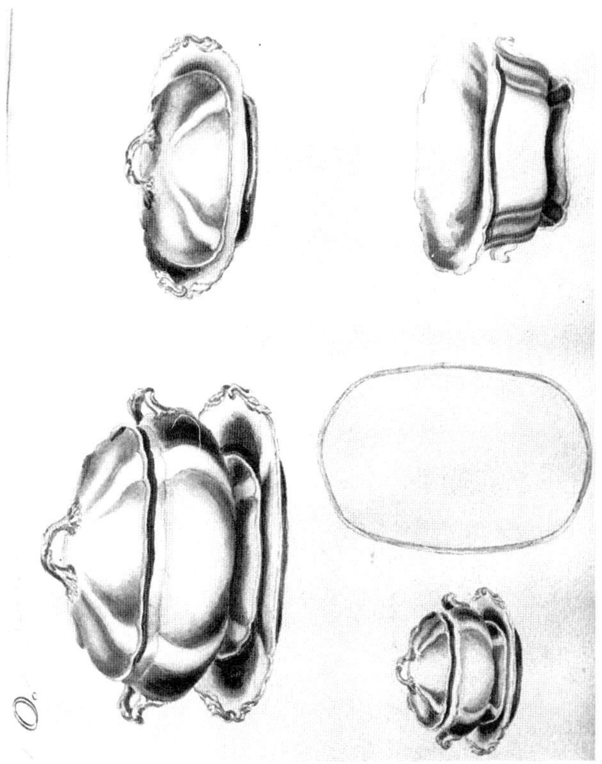
O.

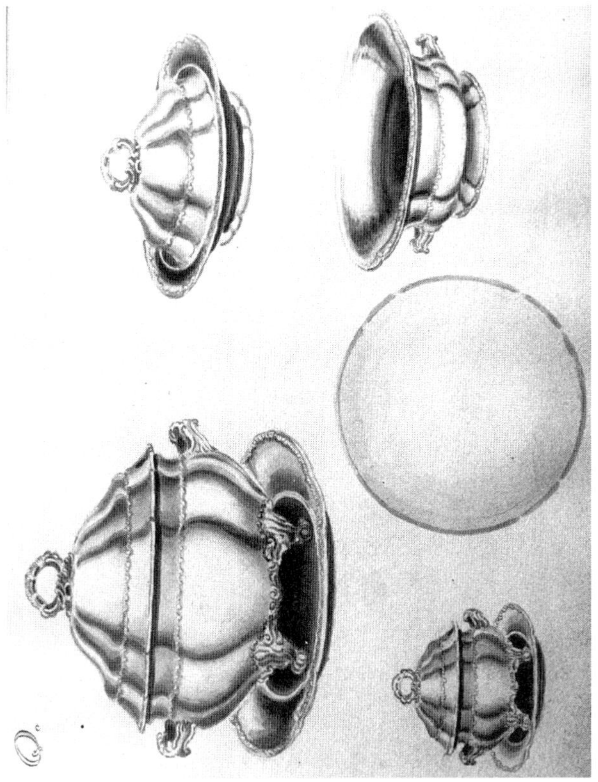
Q.

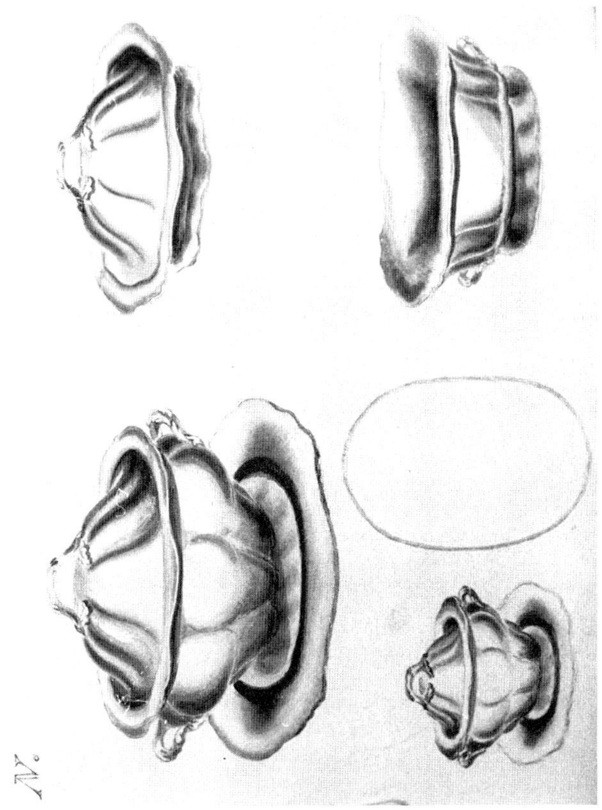
N.

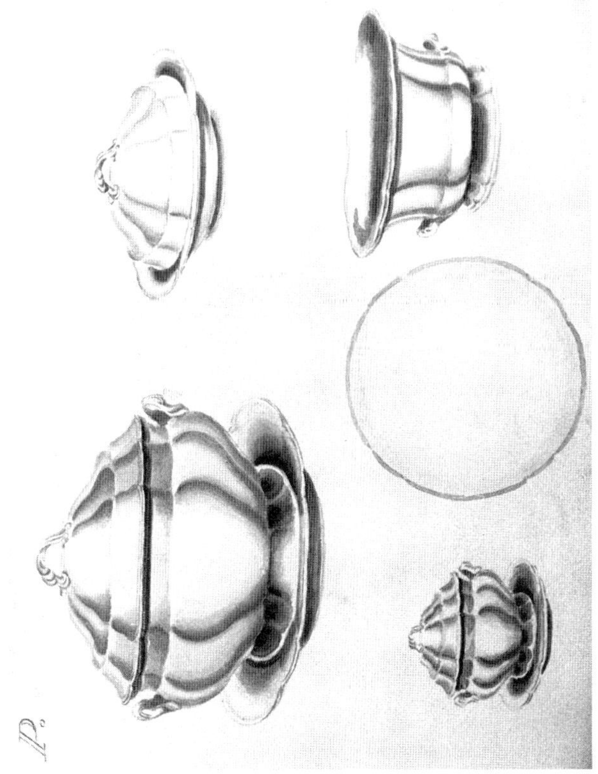
P.

362

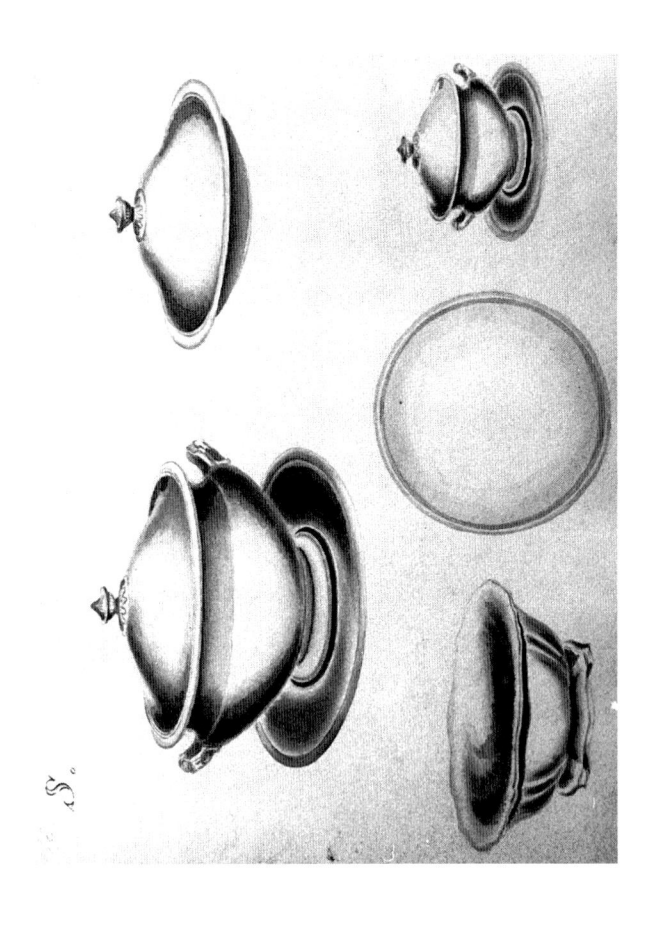

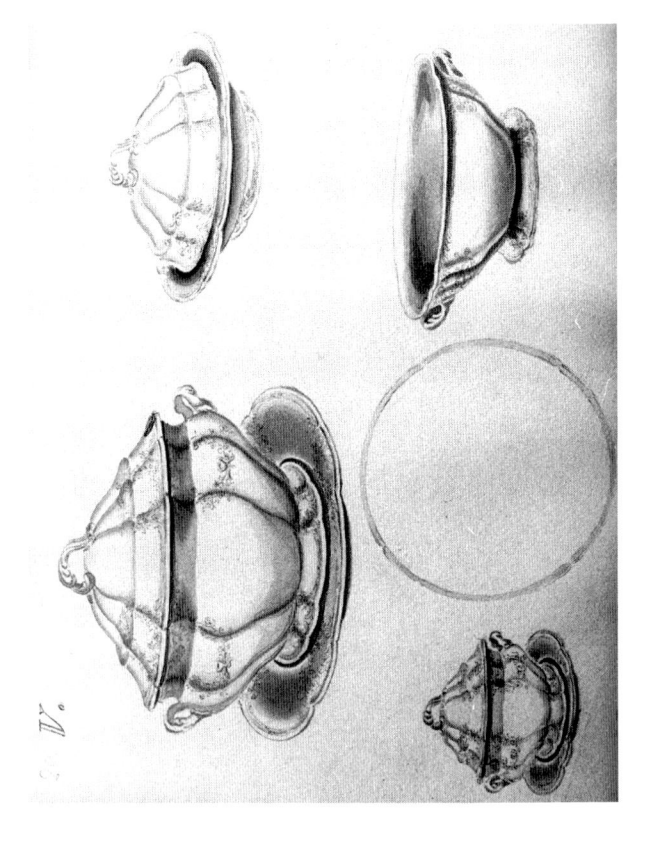

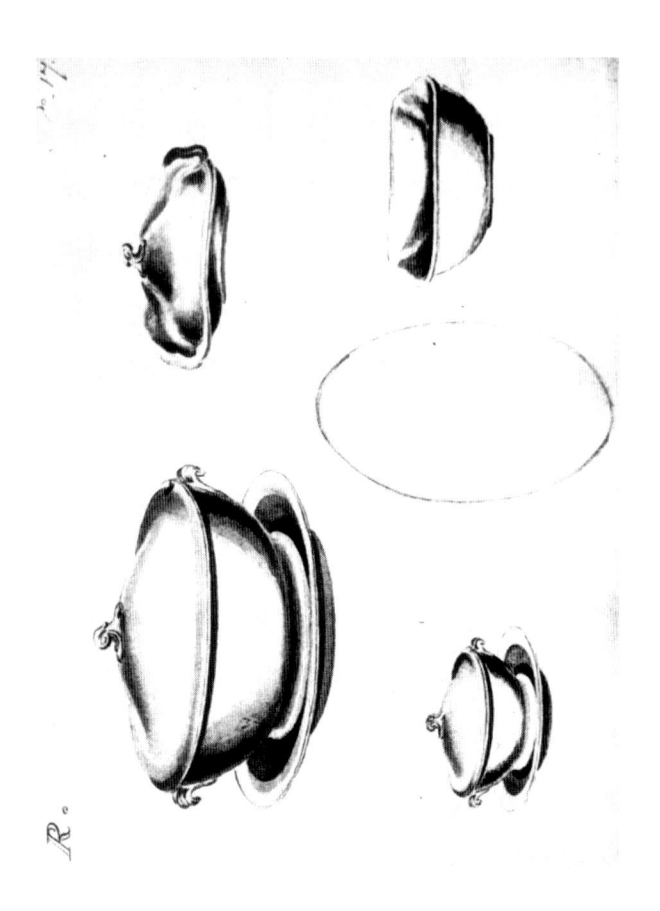

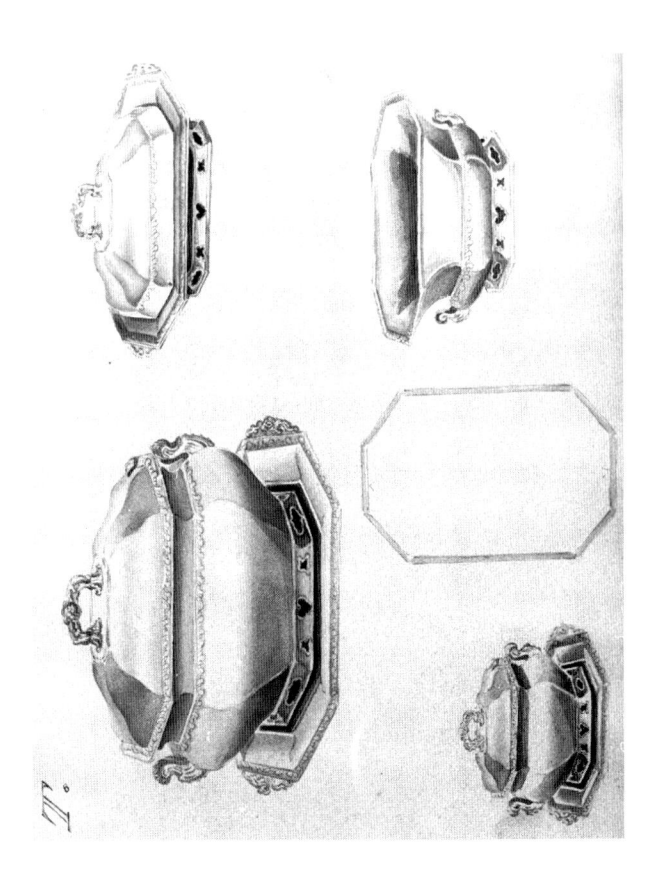

363

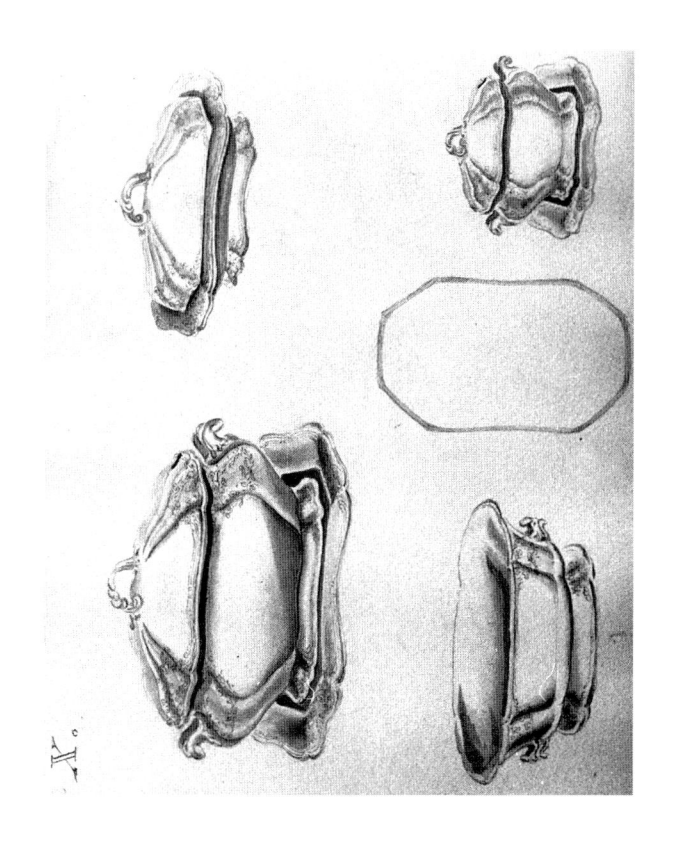

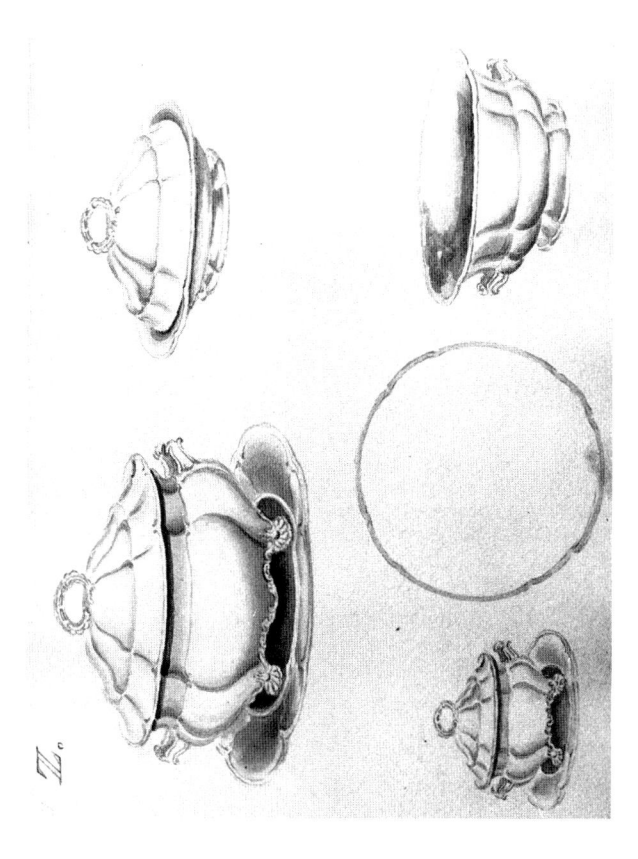

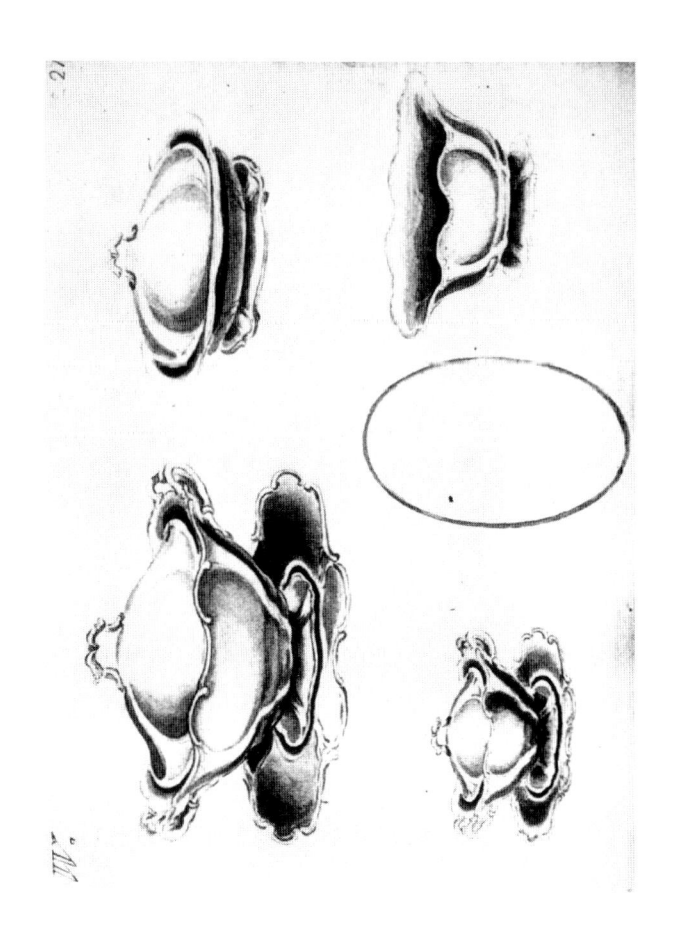

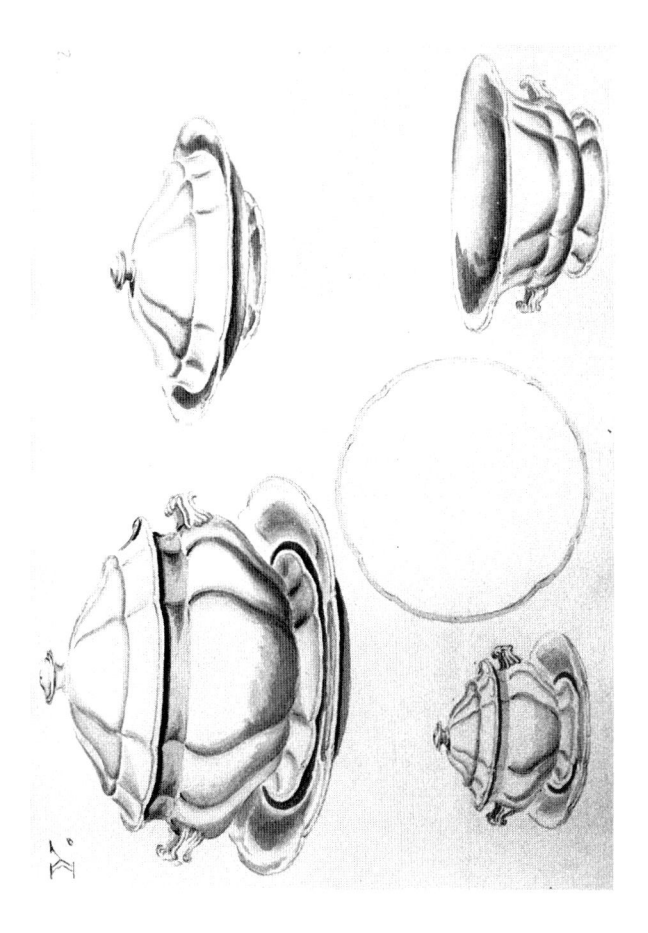

AA.

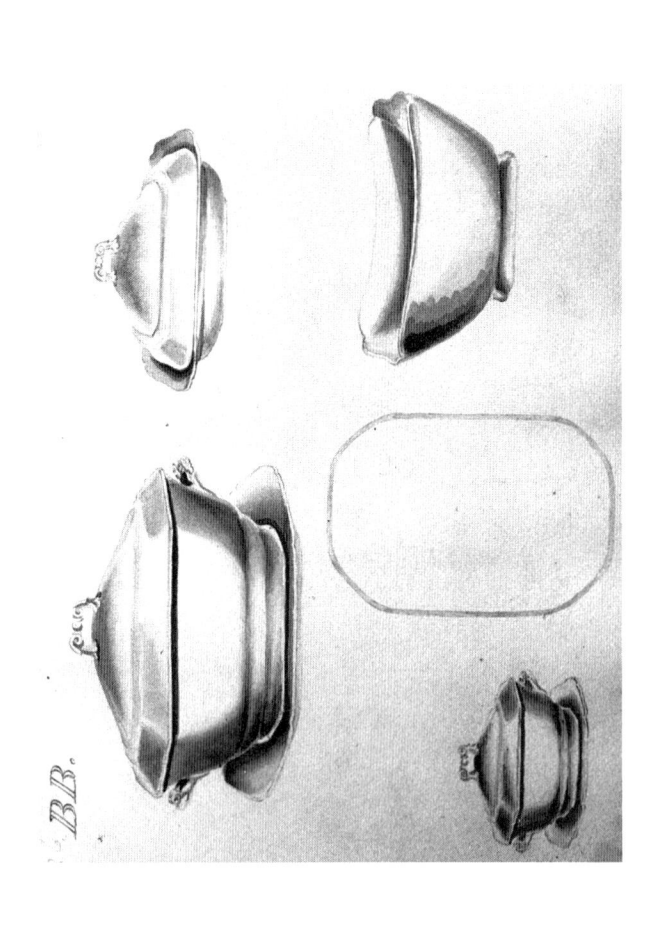

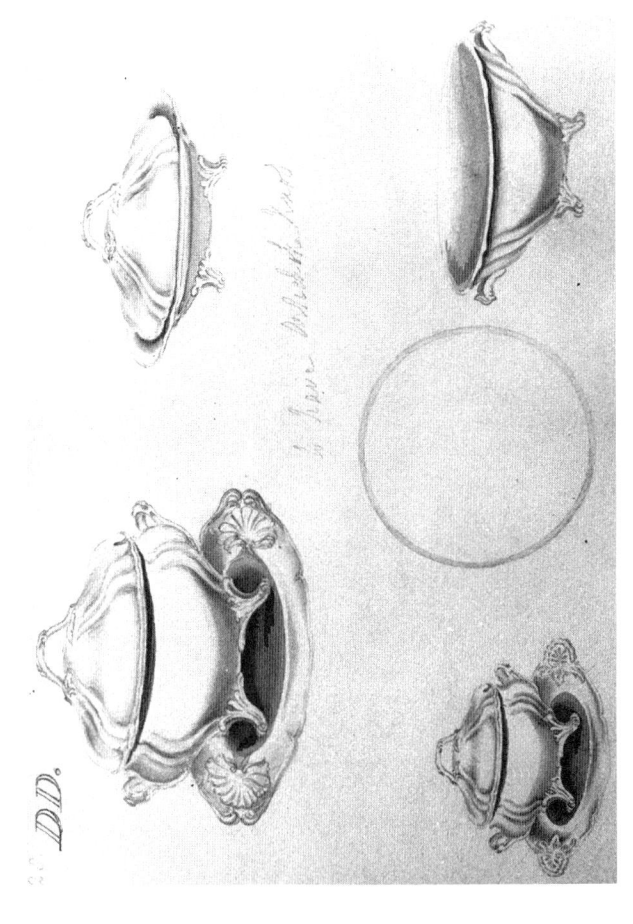

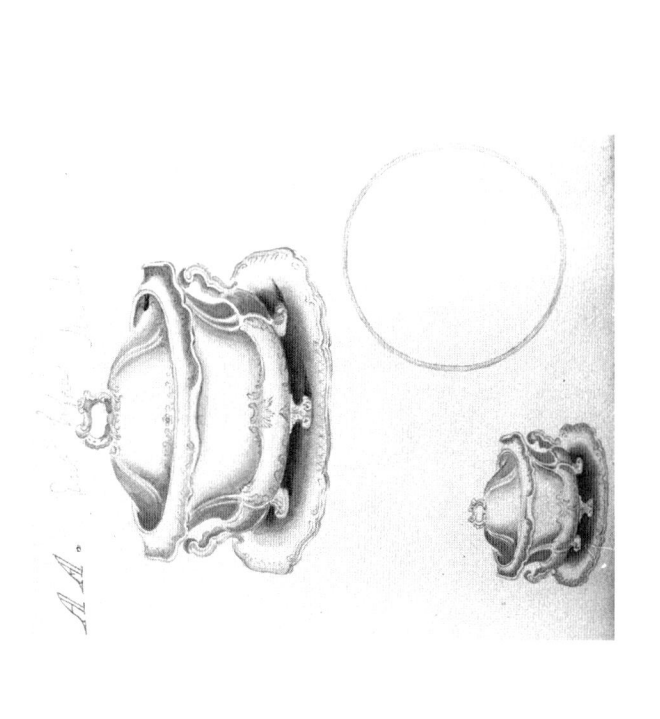

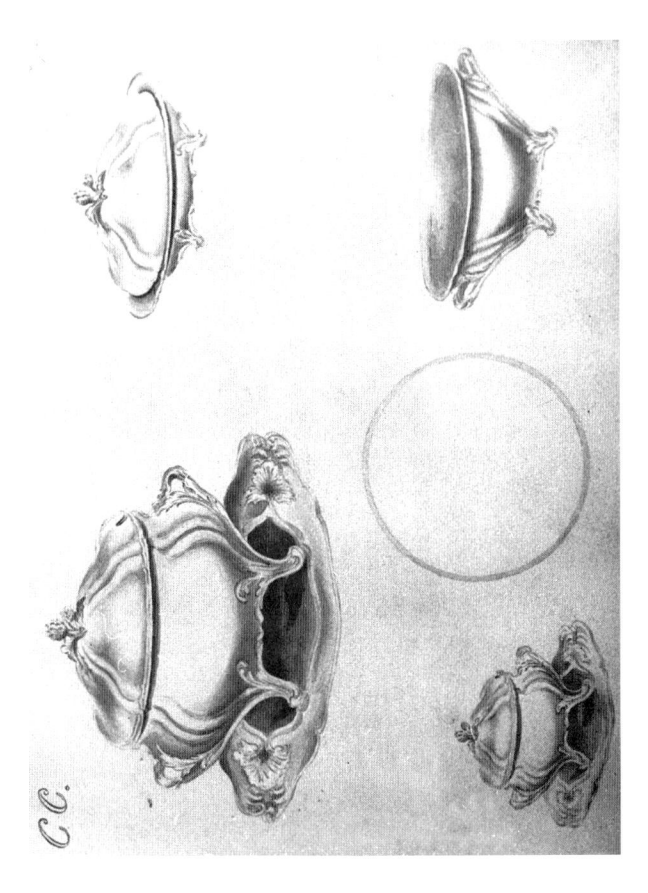

BB.

CC.

DD.

365

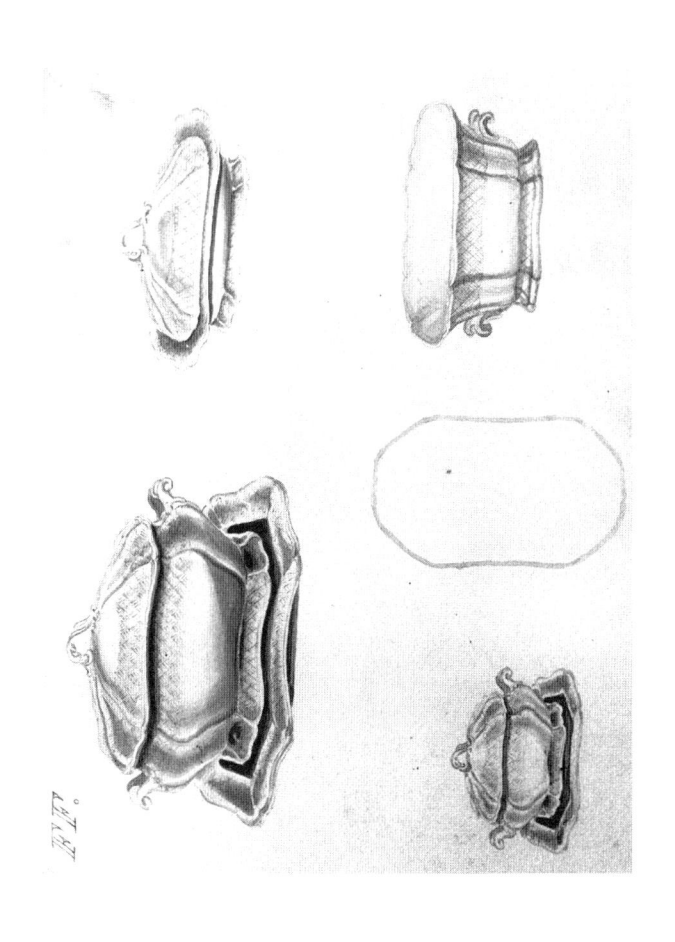

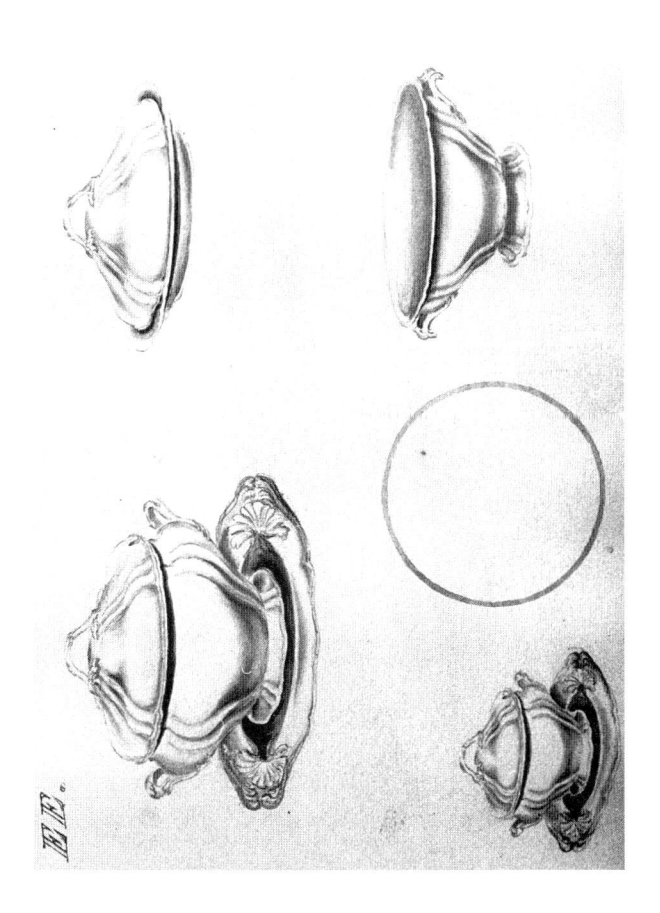

General Index

Pages denoted by italicised numerals include illustrations.

A

Allsup, 64
Argyll, 58
Armorial wares, 213, 218
Asgill House, *174*
Asparagus tray, *288*, 261, *291*

B

Baerne, Mr, 20
Baker & Son, 224
Baking dish, *27*, *46*, *113*, 183, *238*, 258–60, *272*, 274, 279
Barker, 27, 70, 71
Barker & Son, 212
Bat Print book, 22, 48, 136, 145, 157, 158, 172–75, 338–56
Bat printing, 10, 18, 48, 337
Bath shape, 260, 266
Bathwell and Goodfellow, 104
Beardmore and Edwards, 224
Beckford, Thomas, 169
Beeston Castle, 127, *128*, *338*
Bell Vue Pottery, 212
Bengrove, *134*
Berlin Embossed shape, *340*
Berlin patterns, 220
Bewick, Thomas, 120–27
Birch Sunday School, 68
Black printed, 14, 128, 174, 337–40
Black printing, 17, 337
Block moulds, 14, 132, 260–62, 266, 268, 270–74, 277, 280–84, 296, 299, 307, 314, 318, 322
Blue edge, 14
Blue top't, 14, 17, 143, 320
Booth, 4, 9
Bowl, *25*–27, *34*, *37*, *54*–*58*, *137*, *140*, *141*, *155*, *211*, *216*, 259, 261, *314*–*16*
Boxes, 192, 259, 261, 314, 316, 317
Boyle, 7, 23, 357
Brandenburg House, *173*
Bridge Houses, 2, 8
Broth bowl, 43, 102, *103*, 201, 259, 261, *295*, 303
Brown line, 14
Burnell, 60

Bute shape, 261, *322*, *324*
Buxton, Geo., 20
Buxton, Saml, 20
Bysham Monastery, 172

C

Callcott, Sir Augustus Wall, 148
Canterbury Cathedral, 168
Carter, Thomas, 10
Carisbrooke Castle, 141
Cartlidge, Mary, 9, 20, 21
Castle Forbes, 145, 344
Caughley, 1–3, 5, 11, 28, 29, 64, 66, 69, 71, 72, 89
Charenton, 160
China printed fluted, 65
China Works, 9
Clews, 193, 206
Coalport, 32, 51, 54, 58, 66, 89, 107, 108, 110
Coffee pot, 11, 15, *36*, *112*, 113, *147*, 259, 262, 318
Coffee can, 15, 57, *58*, *65*, *66*, *72*–*74*, *77*, *78*, *89*, *90*, 103, *110*, *155*, *180*, 259, *322*, *323*
Coffee cup, 66, 67, *73*, *74*, *323*, 340
Comport, footed, 99, *100*, 259, 261, *296*, *299*, *300*
Concave shape, 80, *92*, *109*, 260, *263*, *264*, 268, 270, 273
Concave-Octagon shape, 153, 260, *262*–*67*
Copper plate room, 20, 21, 88, 94
Copper plates, 6, 7, 11, 14–21, 23, 25, 29–31, 38, 42, 49, *50*, 56, 60, 62, 64, 66, *68*, 69, *72*, 76, 78, 87–89, 92, *94*–*96*, 106, 107, 111, 127, 133, 153, 172, 192, 206, 218, 224, 236, 246, 247, 337
Corf Castle, 173, 175
Cork & Edge, 236
Cottage shape, 65, *67*, *321*, 338, *339*
Covered vegetable dish, 70, *102*, *119*, *158*, *171*, 175, *197*, 222, 223, *243*, *245*, 259, 260, *280*, *281*
Cream colour, 14
Cup handles, 261, *322*, *323*, 325
Custard, *122*, 259, 290, 291, *294*, 322

D

Davenport, 51, 52, 144, 257, 289
Day, Joseph, 19–21

Dessert dish, *30*, *31*, 92, *102*, *134*, 150, *151*, *157*, 160, 161, *170*, *189–92*, *198*, *254*, 259, 261, 274, 282, 286, *296–301*
Diamond pickle, 259, 261, *286*
Dixon, Austin and Co., 194
Don Pottery, 53, 194
Doncaster, Henry, 2
Donovan, 110, 151
Drainers, 259, 261, *271*, 272, 326

E

Edge Malkin & Co., 206
Egan, Richard, 11
Egg cups, 259, *326*, 338
Egg cup stand, 259, 326, *327*
Egg drainer, *326*
Embossed wares, 14, *42*, 43, *191–93*, *199*, *203–05*
Ewer, *40*, 120, *125*, *137*, 161, *163*, 171, *177*, 182, *199*, 211, 259, 261, *312–17*
Exeter, 81

F

Faulkbourn Hall, 167, 171
Fell & Co, 212
Ferrybridge, 212
Fiddlestick knob, 70, *118*, 260, 273, *275*, *280*
Fonthill Abbey, 169
Footed stand, *215*, *221*, *292*, *293*
Foot ring, double recessed 153, *265*, 267
Foot ring, single recessed, 49–53, 105–07, 121, 142, 176, 263, *264*
Ford, Joseph, 20
French shape, *340*
Fulham, 48, *338*, 339, 345

G

Gloucester, 167, 170, 171
Godwin, Thomas & Benjamin, 206
Goodfellow, Thomas, 218
Grantully Castle, 160, *166*
Gravy boat, 62, *170*, *216*, *233*, 257, 259, 261, *283*
Gravy dish, *47*, 259, 261, *270*, 272
Greatbach, 2
Griffiths, Beardmore & Birks, 225

H

Hammersely, 19
Hancock, 1
Harley, 79, 92
Harlow, J., 64
Harrison, 106
Harvey, 167
Hassels, 4, 20, 21, 114, 148
Heath, 4, 70, 106, 262
Hemmings, Geo., 20
Herculaneum, 32, 114, 115, 165, 297, 298

Hicks, 1
Hillcock and Walton, 148
Hollins, 7
Hollinshead, 10

I

Ibbertson, 21
Indented Concave-Octagon shape, *126*, *127*, *265*, 267

J

J.C. & S., *187*, *336*
Japan wares, 14, 149, 226–28
Jewitt, Llewellynn, 1–8
Jug, 14, 19, 25, 26, *40*, 56, *57*, 58, 63, 72, 76, 77, *83*, 90, *114*, 133, *136–38*, *157*, *178–180*, *182*, 192, *194*, *198*, 206, *210–212*, 216, 226, *227*, *256*, 257, 259, 261, *307–311*, *321–23*, 328, 337

K

Keeling, Samuel, 19
Kirk, 32, 114–19
Knottingly Pottery, 114

L

Ladle, 96, 99, *139*, *159*, *173*, 259, 261, *279*, 281
Lanercost Priory, 174
Laurie & Whittle, 104
Leaf pickles, 287, *289*
Lechlade, 174, *175*, 343
Lewis Woolf, 212
Lion head handles and knobs, *98*, *99*, 104, 260, 273, *276*, *277*, *281*, *284*
Lockhart & Arthur, 236
London shape teapot, 66, 144, *320*
Lucas, Thomas, 2
Ludlow Castle, 21, *22*

M

Marks
    Formal printed marks, 153, 332, *334–36*
    Impressed workman's marks, 23, 151, 184, *332*
    Painted marks, *331*
    Printed workman's marks, 332, *333*
Mason, Miles, 66, 69, 110, 337
Medical wares, 329
Meigh, 1, 218, 332, 336
Methven, David & Sons, 236
Middiman, 21, 127–29, 133
Minton and Sons, 7, 13
Minton, Arthur, 1, 2, 5, 9, 12, 20
Minton, Herbert, 2, 5, 7–10, 19, 20
Minton, Thomas, 1, 2, 4, 6–10, 13, 20, 39, 59, 160, 187, *249*, 257, 331, 332

Minton, Thomas Webb, 7–9
Mintons, 7, 62, 87, 174, 227
Mug, 14, 19, *26, 35, 45, 54, 63*, 90, 133, 138, *178*, 179, 195, *198*, 225, *228, 256*, 257, 259, 261, 307–09, 311, 337
Mustard pot, 259, *295*

N

New Hall, 74, 75, 337
Norfolk Hotel, 68

O

Octagonal shape, 3, 51, *60, 70, 71*, 260, *263, 264*, 266, 268, 273, 277, 283
Octagon shape dish, 132, 154, 260, *268*

P

Parkes, Samual, 8
Paris shape, 260, 262, 266
Pattern book, 11, 20, 21, 23, 43, 46, 59, 66, 67, 87, 89, 94, 95, 97, 98, 99, 101, 102, 103, 108, 206, 207–11, 217, 224, 226, 227, 232, 281
Pattern names, 11, 12, 15, 19, 23, 332
Peace Rejoicing, 9
Phillips, George, 236
Pickle dish, *123*, 259, 261, 284, *286–89*, 291
Pluck and dust, 337
Pot Works, 5
Potting pot, 290
Poulson, 5–10, 12
Pountney & Allies, 240, 241
Pountney & Goldney, 241
Pownall, 5, 10, 12
Price list, 13, 14, 257, 258, 268
Printed ware best, 13, 14

R

Radish tray, *101*, 259, 261, *288*
Rathbone, Thomas, 142
Reed Taylor & Co., 206
Richards, James, 2
Ridgway, 181
Ripon, 160–64
Rogers, 60, 61, 142, 212
Root dish, *118*, 259, 260, 281
Royal shape, 65, 260, 262, 266

S

Salad bowl, 23, 96, 102, *134*, 170, *171*, 174, 175, *204*, 222, 228, *229*, 230, *235*, 259, 260, 281, *282*, 357
Sauce tureen, 23, 96, *99*, 101, *118, 135, 138, 139*, 148, *154, 159, 167*, 170, 171, *173, 196, 202, 208*, 209, 219, *226, 242, 255, 256*, 259, 260, 273, *274–76*, 279, 290, 357

Sauce tureen stand, *32, 34, 38, 45, 46, 100, 135, 139, 159, 167, 172, 197, 203, 215, 219*, 259, 260, *276*
Semi-China seal mark, 68, 153
Shaw, Simeon, 1–3, 6, 8
Shaw, Jesse, 20
Shell dish, 70, *71*, 127, 148, 261, 296, *297*–99
Shell pickle, 288, *289*
Shoe Lane, 95, 236
Shorthouse, 57
Sizing methods, 257
Slop bowl, 15, *39*, 65, *73*, 90, 156, *200*, 259, *320*
Smith, Thomas, 9, 19, 160
Soap box, *140, 210*, 259, 261, 314, *317*
Soup tureen, *48*, 96, *98*, 99, 101, 125, 158, *159, 168, 169, 172*, 182, *188, 214, 219*, 230, *231*, 234, *244*, 246, *247, 252, 253*, 259, 260, *274, 275*, 277
Soup tureen stand, *42, 159*, 189, 259, 260, *278, 279*
Southend, 339, 342
Spill vase, *48*, 55, *138, 139*, 262, *307*
Spode, 1–6, 9, 11, 27, 29, 32, 41, 59, 60, 62, 63, 69, 70, 74, 75, 78, 79, 89, 106, 110, 113–115, 139, 158, 176, 184, 212, 218, 257, 278, 288, 300, 311, 319, 331, 337
Sponge dish, *182, 317*
St Anthony's Pottery, 266
St Mary's Church, Dover, *175*, 341
Staffordshire knot, 181
Steel, Samual, 9
Stevenson, 26, 28, 33, 51, 52, 56, 82, 83, 106, 120, 124, 125, 163, 164, 171, 232
Stilt marks, 23, 51, 106, 120, 125, 176, 225, 230, 262, *264–66*, 270
Stock valuation, 13, 14
Stone Works, 5–7, 9
Stringer, 4, 8, 9, 19
Sucrier, 15, 21, 22, 65, 146, *150*, 173, *200, 201*, 259, 260, *318, 321, 325*
Supper set, 92, 123, *135*, 136, 261, 262, *284, 285*, 326
Swansea, 4, 52, 92
Swillington Bridge Pottery, 179, 212

T

Teapots, 11, 14, 15, 21, 22, *28, 29, 33*, 35–37, *40*, 58, *64*, 65, *67*, 72, *76–79, 82–84*, 90, *91, 111–13*, 135, *143–47, 155*, 173, 174, 179, *180–82*, 201, *239*, 257, 259, 261, 262, 307, *318–21*, 325, *337–39*, 357
Teapot stand, *29*, 89, *325*
Tenby, 127, 128, 129
Toast rack, 261, 318, *328*
Toy tea wares, 15, 17, 18, *27, 42, 76–78, 143, 146, 180, 200*, 201, *318*, 319, *321*, 324, 337, *341*
Trays, 291, 314, 316

Trophy shape, 51, 88, 92, 96, 98, 99, 106, 107, 109, 149, 260, 262–*64*, 268, 270, 272, 273, 277, 283
Turner, 1, 3, 6, 28, 82, 83, 89

W

Walker, William, 9
Wayte, 8, 64, 87
Webb, Mrs, 8
Webb, Sarah, 8
Wedgwood, 2, 11, 32, 36, 55, 64, 107, 109, 113, 142, 225, 266
Wedgwood, Ralph, 75

Wedgwood & Co., 114
Whieldon, 2
Whittow & Harris, 94, 95
Wicker basket, *6*, 14, *32*, *33*, *104*, 107, *108*, *109*, *120*, 148, 259, 261, 299, *304*, *305*
Wicker basket stand, *110*, 259, 261, *302*
Wicker plate, *30*, *84*, 109, 259, 260, 295, *303*
Wildblood, 2
Windsor Castle, 18, 114, 164
Wood, Enoch & Sons, 145, 160, 168
Worcester, 11, 28, 71, 72, 89, 165
Working Moulds, 262
Wyllie, 11, 12, 79, 140, 144, 147, 157

Index to Patterns

Pages denoted by italicised numerals include illustrations.

A

Acorn and Oak Leaf Border series, 163, 164
Amhurst Japan, *45, 226, 227*
Apple Tree, 12, 17, 18, *36, 147*
Arabesque, *46, 230, 231*, 234
Arabian, *217*

B

Bamboo, 16, 18, 154
Bamboo and Flowers, *41*, 148, *153–56*, 268, *307, 308, 311*, 315, *322, 324*
Basket, 16, 18, 20, 21, *31, 94–105, 120*, 125, 228, 229, *253, 254*, 263, 270, 273, 276, 277, *281*, 296, 297
Benevolent Cottagers, *35, 148*
Berlin Chaplet, *45, 220–24*
Berlin Roses, *45, 220–22, 293*
Bewick Stag, *33*, 120, *125–27*, 137, 262, *263, 265*, 268, 273, 277, *284, 312*, 314
Bird, 16, 18, *33*, 117, *120–25, 262–64, 267, 286*
Bird Chinoiserie, *26, 55, 307, 314*
Blue Dragon, 3
Blue Rose Border series, 225
Botanical, *40, 178, 256.*
Botanical (Wedgwood), *109*
Botanical Groups, *40, 176, 177*
Botanical Vase, *41*, 140, *182, 183, 317*
Brick, 13, 16, 18
Bridge, 12, 20, *29, 78, 79*, 111, 157, *307, 318, 323–25*
Bridgeless Chinoiserie (see Hermit), 25, 49
British Views, *44*, 225
Broseley, 1, 2, *3*, 12, 17, 18, 21, *29*, 49, *64–69*, 84, 111, 143, 145, 153, 338
Buffalo, 2, 3

C

Camel and Giraffe, *33*, 125, *127*, 262, *265, 267*, 268, 273, 277
Carisbrooke Castle, *37, 141*
Castle, 17, 18
Castle Gateway, *34, 137*
Chaplin, *26, 63*

Cherub Medallion Border series, 165
Chinaman with Rocket, *28*, 56, *82, 83, 319*
China Pattern, 16, 18, *30, 84, 249, 285, 322*
Chinese Family, *28, 72, 73*, 81, *294, 323*
Chinese Fence, *46, 232*
Chinese Figure, 16, 17, 76, 77
Chinese Garden, *28, 76, 77, 320*
Chinese Marine, *42, 45*, 198, *212–19*, 228, *270, 293*, 307, 316
Chinese Sports, *29, 80*, 81, 127, 149, *250, 256*, 262, *263*, 270, 273, 276, 281, *291, 323, 324*
Chinese Temple, 17, 18, 64, 69, 84
Cities and Towns series, 167
Claremont, *44, 224, 328*
Corinthian, 19, *44*, 193, *202–05*
Corinthian Embossed, 44, 203, *205*
Cottage, 12, 18, 19, 133, 143, 148
Cottage and Cart, *35, 146, 321*
Cottage and Cows, *35, 143*
Covered Wagon, *141*

D

Dagger Border, 11, 70
Dagger Border with Temple, *27, 70, 71, 263, 268, 280*, 281, 297, 331
Dahlia, *32*, 107, *108*, 111, 112, *263*
Domed Building, *36, 143*
Dove, 17, 18, *34*, 135, *139*, 144, 153, *255*, 265, 274, 275, 277, 279, *303–05*
Dragon, 17, 18, *31, 110*, 151
Dresden, 14, *42*, 168, *190–93*, 198, 299
Dresden Embossed, *42*, 191, *192*, 199
Dresden Flowers, *42*, 64, *200, 201*
Dying Tree, *39, 156*

E

English Scenery, 19, 20, *39*, 114, 156, *160–71*, 175, 188, *251, 252*, 265, 270, 299, *306, 312*, 315
Exotic Birds, *38*, 149

F

Fallow Deer, *36, 142, 325*
Farm, 12, 144
Farmyard, 17, 18, 20, *36*, 144, 145, *320, 322*, 328
Fig Tree Chinoiserie, *26, 56–58*, 256, *314*

Filigree, *41*, 168, 182, *184–90*, *251*, *253*, *255*, *270–72*, *279*, *288*, *289*, 299
Fisherman, *28*, *71*, *72*, 263, 268
Flora, *43*, 200, 201, *329*
Floral Cottage, *41*, *176*
Floral Vases, *40*, *179–81*, 321, *323–27*
Florentine, *43*, 193, *195–99*, 216, 228, 299
Florentine Embossed, *199*, 315
Floweret, *48*, *246*, *247*
Forbes Castle, *37*, *145–47*, *339*
French series, 160
Fruit, *37*, *148*, 149, 296, 299
Full Nankin, *3*

G

Genevese, *43*, 201, *206–11*, 226, *329*
Girl with Puppies, *39*, *176*
Grapevine Border Series, 145
Greek, 114, *115*, *297*, 298
Grotto, 12, 17, 18
Group pattern, 297

H

Hermit, 11, 16–18, *25*, *49–54*, 106, *249*, *263*, *264*, *267*, 270, 273, *288*, *289*, *291*, *294–99*, *303*
Hermit and Boat, *25*, *54*, 55, *256*, *307–11*, *314*, 315

I

Image, 11, 12, 15–18, 72
Image Landscape, 17, 18
India, 11, 12, 16, 18
Indian Procession, 113
Italian Ruins, *38*, 79, 153, *157–59*, 254, 255, 270, *278*, *279*, *283*, *299–301*, *310*, *315*, *316*, 339

J

Japan patterns, 149
Japan Rose, 14
Japan Vase, *37*, *149*, 263
Jasmine, 15, 17, 18, 212

K

Key, 16, 18
Kirk series (see Roman) 114

L

Lace Border, *46*, *232–33*, *287*
Landscape, 17, 18, 133
Leaf, 16, 18, *40*, *182*
Light Blue Rose Border series, 225
Lily, 11, 13, 14, 16–18, 20, 21, *30*, *38*, *87–89*, *263*, 273, *282*, *284*, *285*, *288*, *291*, *297*, *302*, 307
Lizard Armorial, 213, 218
Lyre, 111, 112

M

Mandarin, 4, 5, 62
Maypole, 17, 18, *35*, *138*, *139*, *256*, 307, *308*
Miniature series, *38*, *173–75*, *279*, 341
Monk's Rock series, *34*, *127–39*, *250*, *254*, *255*, *265*, 268, 275, 277, *279*, *282*, *285*, *290*, *296*, 299, 338, 339

N

Nankeen Temple, 11, 70
Nankin, 1, 3, 16, 18, *27*, *76–78*, *318*
Nelson, 16, 18
New Flowers, 19
No. 53, 14, *45*, *228*
No. 59, *45*, 212
No. 89, *45*, *228*
No. 252, *48*, *246*, *247*

O

Old Basket, 21, 94
Old Brickhouse, 20
Old Corinthian, 19
Old English Scenery, 19, 20, 160
Old Groups, 20
Old Japan, 14
Old Pattern, 17, 18
One Man Chinoiserie, *27*, 57, *58*, 82
Oriental Family, *29*, *81*
Ornithological Series (see Bird) 33, 63, 120

P

Pagoda, 15, 16, 18, 64, 77
Passion Flower Border series, 160, 161, *163*, 169
Pearl River House, *26*, *74*, *75*, *323*
Peony, 16, 18
Pine, 11, 15, 17, 18
Pineapple Border series, 160
Pinwheels, *31*, *91–93*, 268, 274, *275*, *286*, *290*
Plant, 16, 18, *32*, *109*, *110*, 302, 304

Q

Queen Charlotte, 79
Queen of Sheba, *32*, *113*, 114, *289*, *292*

R

Red House, 15, 16, 18
Riverside Cottage, *39*, *156*, 161
Roman, 16, 18, 21, *32*, *114–20*, 139, *262–64*, 275, 280, 281, *283*, *294*, 302
Rose and Violet Star, *47*, *235*, *236*
Rose and Violet Wreath, *47*, 48, 231, *234–36*, 239, 247
Rose Border series, 171
Rose Bud, 12, 140
Rose Flower, 16, 18
Royal Lily, 87

Royal Persian, *45*, 214, *218*, *219*, *306*, 307
Ruined Abbey, *34*, *140*, 210, *315*, *317*

S

Shepherd, 17, 18, *33*, *111–13*
Sicilian, *47*, *240–46*
Star, 16, 18, *30*, *92*, 149, 263, *264*, *284*, *316*
Steed, 17, 18
Stylised Floral, *30*, *90*, *91*, *324*
Swiss Cottage, *43*, *201*

T

Temple, *69*
Trellis and Plants, *46*, *228–30*
Trophy, 13, 15, 16, 18, *31*, *106*, *107*, 331
Tulip, 11, 13, 16, 18

Turkish Figure, 16, 18
Two Figures, 3, *4*

V

Verona, *47*, 231, *236–40*, *293*, *295*, *328*, *329*
Village, 17, 18
Violin, *91*

W

Water Lily, *38*, *150*, *151*, 297, *322*
Willow, 2–6, 11, 13–18, *20*, 21, *27*, *59–63*, 109, 113, *252*, 257, 263, 266, 268, *269*, *272*, *274*, 275, *283*, *285*, *287*, *288*, *290*, *292*, *297–99*, *304*, 305, *326*, 331
Windsor Castle, 16, 18, 114
Wreath, *44*, 45, *220*, 221